THE
UNSETTLED
RELATIONSHIP

Recent Titles in
Contributions in Labor Studies

Social Workers and Labor Unions
Howard Jacob Karger

Capitalist Development and Class Capacities: Marxist Theory and Union Organization
Jerry Lembcke

Occupation and Class Consciousness in America
Douglas M. Eichar

Our Own Time: A History of American Labor and the Working Day
David R. Roediger and Philip S. Foner

Women, Minorities, and Unions in the Public Sector
Norma M. Riccucci

Labor Relations in Europe: A History of Issues and Developments
Hans Slomp

The Fictitious Commodity: A Study of the U.S. Labor Market, 1880–1940
Ton Korver

The Re-education of the American Working Class
Steven H. London, Elvira R. Tarr, and Joseph F. Wilson, editors

New Trends in Employment Practices
Walter Galenson

Order Against Chaos: Business Culture and Labor Ideology in America, 1880–1915
Sarah Lyons Watts

The Emancipation of Labor: A History of the First International
Kenryk Katz

The Unsettled Relationship

Labor Migration and Economic Development

EDITED BY
Demetrios G. Papademetriou

AND
Philip L. Martin

FOREWORD BY
Diego C. Asencio

CONTRIBUTIONS IN LABOR STUDIES, NUMBER 33

GREENWOOD PRESS
New York · Westport, Connecticut · London

Library of Congress Cataloging-in-Publication Data

The Unsettled relationship : labor migration and economic development
/ edited by Demetrios G. Papademetriou and Philip L. Martin ;
foreword by Diego C. Asencio.
     p.   cm. — (Contributions in labor studies, ISSN 0886–8239 ;
no. 33)
  Includes bibliographical references and index.
  ISBN 0–313–25463–X (alk. paper)
  1. Alien labor—Developing countries. 2. Developing countries—
Economic conditions. 3. Economic development. I. Papademetriou,
Demetrios G. II. Martin, Philip L., 1949–   . III. Series.
HD8943.U57 1991
338.9′009172′4—dc20   90–45603

British Library Cataloguing in Publication Data is available.

Library of Congress Catalog Card Number: 90–45603
ISBN: 0–313–25463–X
ISSN: 0886–8239

First published in 1991

Greenwood Press, 88 Post Road West, Westport, CT   06881
An imprint of Greenwood Publishing Group, Inc.

Printed in the United States of America

The paper used in this book complies with the
Permanent Paper Standard issued by the National
Information Standards Organization (Z39.48-1984).

10 9 8 7 6 5 4 3 2 1

Contents

FOREWORD BY *Diego C. Asencio*   vii

INTRODUCTION   ix

PART I. CONCEPTUAL AND THEORETICAL ISSUES IN INTERNATIONAL LABOR MIGRATION   1

1. Labor Migration and Development: Research and Policy Issues
Demetrios G. Papademetriou and Philip L. Martin   3

2. Labor Migration: Theory and Reality
Philip L. Martin   27

PART II. LABOR MIGRATION AND DEVELOPMENT IN AFRICA   43

3. Binational Communities and Labor Circulation in Sub-Saharan Africa   *Aderanti Adepoju*   45

4. International Labor Migration in Southern Africa   *Timothy T. Thahane*   65

PART III. LABOR MIGRATION AND DEVELOPMENT IN GREECE AND TURKEY   89

5. Migration and Development in Greece: The Unfinished Story
Demetrios G. Papademetriou and Ira Emke-Poulopoulos   91

6. Migration without Development: The Case of Turkey   *Ali S. Gitmez*   115

PART IV. LABOR MIGRATION AND DEVELOPMENT
IN ASIAN EMIGRATION COUNTRIES   135

  7. Migration from Pakistan to the Middle
      East   *Shahid Javed Burki*   139

  8. Emigration and Development in South and
      Southeast Asia   *Charles Stahl and Ansanul Habib*   163

PART V. LABOR MIGRATION AND DEVELOPMENT
IN LATIN AMERICA, MEXICO, AND THE CARIBBEAN   181

  9. The Effects of International Migration on Latin
      America   *Sergio Diaz-Briquets*   183

 10. Caribbean Emigration and Development
      Patricia R. Pessar   201

PART VI. THE UNSETTLED RELATIONSHIP
BETWEEN MIGRATION AND DEVELOPMENT   211

 11. Migration and Development: The Unsettled
      Relationship   *Demetrios G. Papademetriou*   213

 12. Immigration and Economic Development
      *Commission for the Study of International
      Migration and Cooperative Economic Development*   221

      APPENDIX: Social Indicators of Development   243

      REFERENCES   285

      INDEX   307

      CONTRIBUTORS   311

Foreword

International migration is one of the most complex and contentious issues facing the international community today. After a lengthy debate, the United States enacted in 1986 the Immigration Reform and Control Act (IRCA) to reduce unauthorized (illegal) immigration. The act instituted a system that went beyond emphasizing such standard responses as enhanced border enforcement to offer legal status to more than 3 million unauthorized aliens and institute a system of penalties against employers who continue to hire aliens without U.S. work authorization. The legislation also established the Commission for the Study of International Migration and Cooperative Economic Development and charged it with searching for mutually beneficial policies that promote stay-at-home development.

The authors of this valuable and timely book have set out to investigate the linkages between international migration and the development of sending societies. In almost all cases, they paint a rather somber picture: international migration has not led, or at least cannot be linked directly, to significant development in African, Southern European, Asian, and Latin American emigration countries. The clearest lesson to emerge from the case studies in this book is that international migration for employment, whether officially organized or self-motivated but facilitated by ethnic networks, is not a short-cut to effective development—notwithstanding often substantial remittances. Instead, such migration often distorts a country's development in ways that guarantee continued migration pressures.

The Commission for the Study of International Migration also learned that emigration is not a shortcut to development. The commission's work made clear that patterns of immigration to the United States, even from countries with extensive histories of U.S. immigration, have not produced the type of development that keeps migrants at home. Instead, several decades of migration have made Mexico and nations in the Caribbean Basin and Latin America ever more dependent on the U.S. labor market. The executive summary of the commission's report to the U.S. Congress appears as Chapter 12 of this volume.

The commission recognized that only broadly based development can break this cycle of dependence. It also recognized, however, that this is primarily a long-term solution. In the short to medium term, development is in fact more likely to increase migration pressures. As a result, the commission recommended a series of initiatives that would substantially increase access to the U.S. market by migrant sending societies. In the commission's view, if the less-developed countries are to be induced to stop exporting people, industrial countries must be much more receptive to the products of migration countries. The commission's primary recommendation for accomplishing this goal of stay-at-home development is the negotiation of a free trade area between the United States and its neighbors. In addition, the commission believes that a federal Agency for Migration Affairs could better predict the impact of U.S. policies on immigration and give migration a higher priority in trade, development, and finance issues.

In the course of their deliberations, the commissioners became convinced that simply promoting market-led growth is not enough to deter migration. Indeed, there is likely to be a J-curve effect, as the disruptions of development first increase migration pressures before enough jobs with secure futures are created to keep migrants at home. However, knowing that migration pressures will increase before they decrease is no reason to delay promoting stay-at-home development in migration countries.

The commission's extensive research has confirmed another of this book's major findings, namely, that there are few examples of truly cooperative development policies that reduce migration pressures. The literature is replete with examples of what has not worked; it contains few references to successful policies that can serve as policy paradigms.

Industrial country efforts to promote stay-at-home development will receive increased attention in the decades ahead. *The Unsettled Relationship* complements the commission's work by showing how past inattention to migration issues has often aggravated, rather than reduced, migration pressures. Like the work of the commission, toward which the editors of this volume made a significant contribution, the authors in this volume make a valuable contribution to the study of international migration by recounting the negative lessons of the past in order to avoid making the same mistakes in the future.

Diego C. Asencio, Chairman
Commission for the Study of International Migration
and Cooperative Economic Development

Introduction

What is the most effective use to make of existing labor, to employ it
abroad or to leave it unemployed at home?

Charles Kindleberger

Large-scale emigration is an irrational and very costly means of getting rid
of surplus population.

Gunnar Myrdal[1]

International labor migration is one of the most unsettled sociopolitical issues of
our time. If one country has high levels of unemployment, and another faces
labor shortages, should workers migrate across national borders? Most analysts,
governments, employers, and migrant workers answer yes; a country with unemployed labor should export its unemployed workers if it can. The harvest of
remittances and returning workers who were trained abroad is expected to accelerate economic growth enough to reduce unemployment and pressures to
emigrate. Labor-importing countries expect to soon be over the labor-shortage
phase of their development, limiting their need for migrant workers to a decade
or less.

The realities of international labor migration are different. Instead of temporary migrant workers who stay abroad for only a short time, migrant workers
have become a structural feature of economies in Western Europe, the Middle
East, South Africa, and the United States. Instead of emigration promoting
catch-up development, emigration countries complain that they got the glittering coins of remittances but little development.

This book explores the unsettled relationship between emigration and development. During the 1950s, uneven economic growth in a world which had embraced free trade and the creation of new nation-states saw international labor
migration as a beneficial feature of the new world economy. The six Western Eu-

ropean nations that formed the European Economic Community (EEC) in 1957 made the free circulation of labor among member nations a pillar of the EEC, along side the abolition of barriers to trade in goods. During the mid-1950s, the U.S. employment of temporary Mexican farmworkers or braceros exceeded 500,000 annually, helping to establish migration links between United States and Mexican labor markets that subsequently expanded.

One hallmark of labor migration since World War II has been the assumption that stays abroad would be temporary. Nineteenth and early twentieth century migration was viewed as settler migration; the migrants left with their families and possessions to seek a new life abroad. Although many planned to return, and many in fact did, a relatively expensive and cumbersome transportation and communication system, as well as success abroad, encouraged most of the young immigrants to settle in countries such as the United States, Canada, Australia, or Argentina.

Postwar labor migration, by contrast, was assumed to be temporary by both emigration and immigration countries. The need for migrant workers was assumed to be temporary, so that in the United States, employers of braceros could offer them contracts of six weeks to eleven months, and in Europe, initial contracts were typically for one year. If migrants were needed again the following year, they would be readmitted to the United States or their contracts would be renewed in Europe. This system of short-term contracts and renewals emphasizes the temporary nature of labor migration; it made it easier for labor importing countries to send migrants home when they were no longer needed.

THE THREE R'S OF LABOR MIGRATION

Emigration countries similarly assumed that individual migrants would return after one or two years abroad and that the need and opportunity to export labor would persist for only one or two decades. In most emigration countries, there was initially little thought given to how workers who wanted to go abroad should be selected and what programs should be developed to encourage their return. As migration streams matured, sending governments tried to intervene, but there was no theory or little experience to help them develop effective policies to influence recruitment, remittances, and returns.

The effects of emigration on labor exporters summarized by these three "R's" occur on different levels. Recruitment affects who emigrates, and thus impacts on employment and production. Remittances affect the living standards of migrant households, and thus the growth of communities and regions. Finally, returning migrants affect the quantity and quality of the work force.

Individual migrants benefit from international labor markets, but benefits to emigration countries are much less clear. The central conclusion of the migration and development literature is that there is no iron law which automatically translates remittances and returning migrant skills into economic development. Recruitment often selects the employed and skilled workers needed for development at home; remittances are usually spent in ways that benefit individuals but do not necessarily lead to job creation; and returning migrants frequently retire rather than become agents of socioeconomic change.

Emigration nations have not followed consistent policies to deal with labor migration, and the empirical studies in this volume are replete with what-might-have-been speculation on how countries could have used the window of opportunity opened by migration to hasten development. A recurring theme is that emigration countries should have done more to assist returning migrants, but this recommendation illustrates a major migration policy dilemma. Should sending countries subsidize returning migrants and their remittances to maximize the development payoffs from emigration, which might increase inequalities and spur more migration, or should they assume that migrants and emigration regions are already taken care of by emigration and focus their development efforts elsewhere? The absence of an automatic emigration, remittance, and development link thus yields disappointment in many emigration areas that were neglected because sending country governments assumed that migration would take care of their development.

The studies in this volume conclude that labor migration does not resolve development dilemmas. A common suggestion is that labor-receiving states should do more to help translate remittances and returning worker skills into development so that emigration becomes unnecessary. This is a formidable and complex task: sending and receiving countries may not agree on what, where, and how much should be done. The development programs which have been funded by receiving nations have not been notable successes from either sending or receiving country perspectives. Labor sending and receiving nations should cooperate to manage worker migration and development in order to reduce emigration pressures, but there are few examples or models of such cooperation which have been successful.

THE PLAN OF THE BOOK

This book helps to sort out the relationships between emigration and development. In addition to comprehensive introductory and concluding essays, the book focuses on the relationship between migration and development in Africa, between Mediterranean countries and Europe, between Asian labor exporters and Middle Eastern importers, and on the effects of emigration on development in Latin America and the Caribbean.

Part I reviews international labor migration theories and concepts. Chapter 1 notes that international migration surged during the first and third quarters of the twentieth century. However, the sources and destinations of migrants changed between the first and third quarters, as have the issues raised by migration. First quarter migrants were encouraged to be settlers by host nations, although many returned to their countries of origin; third quarter migrants were expected to be temporary residents, although many settled abroad. First quarter migration streams were halted by restrictive legislation and the worldwide depression; attempts to halt third quarter migration have been uneven and not notably successful.

People migrate for survival and mobility. Survival migrants are persons pushed abroad by the lack of alternatives at home; mobility migrants are pulled abroad to better themselves. There are many groupings of migrants, and several theories of why individuals migrate. Economic theories ask whether it is rational for an individual or household to go abroad, usually by comparing a low but certain local income against a higher but uncertain income abroad. Theorists who have historical or structural perspectives focus on the economic and other factors that keep a reserve army of unemployed persons willing and ready to emigrate.

The causes and consequences of international labor migration remain in dispute, but certain features of labor migration are well-recognized. Recruitment tends to select the best and brightest from the emigration nation manual work force; remittances do not automatically get converted into job-creating investments; and returning migrants are not often the missing spark plugs needed for development. Migration does not solve development problems; instead, it sometimes aggravates them. A better understanding of migration and development linkages would help make the window of opportunity opened by migration a more effective development tool.

Chapter 2 asks why there is often a gap between theory and reality in international labor migration. The balanced growth theory of labor migration argues that the migration of 5 to 10 percent of a country's work force should reduce profits, raise wages, and reduce unemployment. Adding 5 to 10 percent foreign workers to a host country work force should raise profits and reduce wages. The net effect of labor migration should be to increase the economic output of the two countries and to reduce wage and income differences between emigration and immigration nations.

Instead of the balanced growth expected by theory, the reality is often asymmetric development which increases inequalities between emigration and immigration countries. Labor migration forges new links between nations, but rarely reduces the economic gaps which encouraged workers to emigrate. Instead, the three R's of recruitment, remittances, and returns usually serve to increase the dependence of emigration countries on immigration countries. Experience has yielded mostly negative lessons: how rational immigration country-directed recruitment creams an emigration country's work force of its best and brightest manual workers; how difficult it is for emigration countries to regulate or channel remittances into sustainable job-creating development; and how hard it is to use the skills acquired by returning migrants to promote development.

Part II reviews the effects of labor migration in Africa. Chapter 3 summarizes labor migration patterns in sub-Saharan Africa, where the distinction between internal and international migration is blurred. Ineffective border controls and arbitrary national boundaries push some traditional migrations into the international sphere, as when Kenyans cross the Tanzanian border daily to work on their farms. African labor migration is distinguished by its undocumented character, its cyclical and seasonal patterns, and the dominance of migrants from neighboring countries. The reasons for migrating vary, but uneven development generates large and fluctuating wage differences that encourage migration. Ghana, which imported labor until the 1960s, had 25 percent of its work force abroad by the early 1980s, reflecting deteriorating economic conditions in Ghana. There have also been expulsions of migrant workers. Ghana expelled Nigerians in 1969, and Nigeria expelled Ghanians in 1983.

Some African migration is survival migration. For example, half of Lesotho's males are employed in South Africa, and their remittances are the major source of government revenue. Adepoju argues that even if emigration is the only way to secure employment in such countries, sending communities do not experience accelerated development because the ambitious workers are abroad. Remittances are substantial, but it appears that a high fraction are spent to maintain migrant households. Returned migrants have been agents of socioeconomic change in a few countries, but the migrants that earn the most (as miners) are also those most likely to retire at age 35 or 40, after 15 years in the mines. Labor-importing countries have gradually tightened restrictions on migrant workers, so that borders have become more important barriers to migration in Africa.

In Chapter 4, Thahane explores labor migration in the 11-nation Southern Africa region (Angola, Botswana, Lesotho, Malawi, Mozambique, Namibia, South Africa, Swaziland, Tanzania, Zambia, and Zimbabwe). South Africa, with one-third of the region's population, has a history of reliance on "foreign" workers. Thahane recounts how native Africans lost their land to white settlers, and then found that working for wages in white-owned mines or on white-owned farms was the only employment option. The countries that continue to rely heavily on South African mines for employment—Botswana, Lesotho, Malawi, Mozambique, and Swaziland—are dissatisfied with the effects of migration on their own development, but seem to be unable to break the cycle of migration and stagnation.

Thahane concludes that South Africa has been the major beneficiary of the labor migration patterns that its mines and farms established and continue to control. Numerous advisors have attempted to assist the major labor exporters to reduce their dependence on the South African labor market, but with limited success. The pessimistic picture painted by Thahane suggests that the development patterns shaped by migration in Southern Africa will be very difficult to alter without massive external assistance.

Part III examines the effects of emigration on Greece and Turkey. In Chapter 5, Papademetriou and Emke-Poulopoulos explain how rural-to-urban Greek migration was transformed into migration to Europe in the 1960s. Greeks debated the benefits and costs of this migration, with the government defending emigration as a blessing, but this chapter concludes that migration may have aggravated as many problems as it resolved. For example, returning migrants preferred to settle in urban areas, leaving the rural areas that they left behind with a work force unattractive to industry, and aggravating congestion in Athens and Salonica. Returning migrants become investors or retire; they are not usually innovative agents of change. Remittances were often expended for housing, fueling real estate and building materials inflation.

Greece did not reap the expected dividends of migration for two reasons: too much was expected of migration, and Greek policies often hurt rather than helped migration-induced development. The authors argue that Greece should work with immigration countries such as Germany to get venture capital and technical assistance for Greek businesses started by remittances, to secure other forms of assistance from Germany and other European countries, and to develop better economic and labor market policies in Greece.

Chapter 6 reviews the reasons why emigration has not promoted development in Turkey. Gitmez emphasizes the unrealistic hopes that Turkish leaders placed on emigration and remittances; returning workers were to be the agents of socioeconomic development in Turkey during the 1960s, while their remittances would make viable Turkey's import substitution development strategy.

Turkish emigration began with the small-scale recruitment of mostly skilled urban workers in the 1960s, but Turkish and German policies soon converted Turkish labor migration into a mass flow of unskilled workers from both rural and urban areas. After the 1973–74 European bans on the further recruitment of migrant workers, Turkish migrants began to settle abroad. The Turkish population in Germany, for example, rose after 1973 despite the recruitment ban because family unification and Turkish births in Germany more than offset exits. However, the composition of the Turkish population in Germany changed from mostly workers to mostly nonworking spouses and children. Gitmez explores differences between migrants who settled abroad and those who returned, concluding that unskilled migrants from rural areas who left their families in Turkey were most likely to return.

Gitmez concludes that emigration did not lead to development in Turkey. Despite the emigration of 1.5 to 2 million workers, the return of at least 1 million, and remittances of more than $25 billion, Gitmez concludes that Turkey has not jumped up the development ladder, that is, Turkey grew, but not faster than nonmigrant countries. Migrants and their families benefitted from migration, but Turkey as a country can benefit only if it adopts economic policies which encourage and assist returning migrants to make full use of their remittance savings and skills.

Part IV reviews the effects of emigration on the development of countries which sent workers to oil-exporting Middle Eastern nations, especially after the 1973 oil price hikes. Chapter 7 examines the effects of temporary worker migration on Pakistani development. Pakistan sent a larger fraction of its work force abroad in a shorter period of time than did Turkey, but the 2 to 3 million Pakistani migrants went primarily to Middle Eastern oil exporters after 1974, while most of Turkey's 1.5 to 2 million migrants went to European nations before 1974.

Burki notes that Saudi Arabia's second five-year development plan in 1975 launched a Middle Eastern labor migration which involved 2 to 3 million workers, 10 to 15 times more than Saudi Arabia planned to import. Of an estimated 2 million foreign workers in Saudi Arabia in 1978, Burki reports that two-thirds were Arabic speaking workers from places such as Yemen and that 20 percent or 400,000 were from Asian countries, including 100,000 Pakistanis. Burki asserts that these estimates of Pakistani and other migrants are low; by 1979, Burki estimates that there were 750,000 to 1 million Pakistani migrants in Middle Eastern countries.

Most Pakistani migrants came from the northwest, a relatively poor area which was sending one-third of its annual work force growth, or 150,000 migrants, out of the area. Burki explains that construction projects during the 1960s led to a system in which crews of young male and often unmarried workers were recruited from various villages, and these workers became familiar with migration to do construction work for multinational firms. Labor migration to the Middle East continued this pattern; Pakistani migrants from North West Frontier province were not hard to recruit because they had a history of leaving the area and living in labor camps to work for three to five years on construction projects within Pakistan. Up to half of Pakistan's migrants were from the northwest.

Burki describes how the changing demand for labor in the Middle Eastern countries affected the characteristics of Pakistani migrants. As construction jobs gave way to maintenance and service sector jobs, Pakistan responded with training centers that taught the skills needed abroad.

By the mid-1980s, Burki estimates that 2.5 to 3 million Pakistanis were employed abroad and that these migrants remitted $3 billion annually through official channels and an additional $1.5 to $2 billion unofficially. Burki notes that Pakistani migrants to Middle Eastern countries appear to save and remit more than did Turkish migrants to Europe. Poor migrant households, which devote two-thirds of their incomes to food, spent over half of their remittances to improve day-to-day living, but Pakistani migrants also invested in land, doubling land prices in some areas. Similarly, investments in housing helped to triple brick and cement prices during a period when the overall price rise was 40 percent. Burki recounts the benefits of emigration to migrant households: incomes doubled in the one-fourth of all households which included migrants, and young household members got more food, health care, and education. The households without migrants, which were one notch above these migrant households in income, became relatively worse off.

What of the future? Burki does not believe that Middle Eastern oil exporters can quickly or significantly reduce their need for foreign labor. There may be a change in composition, for example, from construction to maintenance, and such a change will likely lead to the settlement of migrant families abroad. Burki argues that Pakistani migrants are not likely to flood home, but neither is another foreign labor market likely to offer Pakistan a safety valve for its rapid work force growth.

Chapter 8 shifts the focus to the Philippines, Thailand, Sri Lanka, Bangladesh, India, and Pakistan. Stahl and Habib review first the effects of emigration on unemployment and conclude that, for instance, the emigration of 2.5 percent of the Filipino work force has relieved unemployment pressures and has not generally caused skill shortages that were severe enough to limit production and thus lead to second-round layoffs in the Philippines. This generally optimistic conclusion rests on the observation that the massive surpluses of even skilled labor in most Asian countries make complaints of emigration-induced production disruptions rare.

Stahl and Habib present evidence that suggests that migrants often use the skills they already have while abroad. The relatively few migrants who acquire new skills abroad prefer self-employment upon their return, so that emigration and return have not generally increased human capital stocks in labor-exporting countries.

The authors argue that the magnitude and effects of remittances on development are the litmus test of the benefits of labor migration. Remittances increase the incomes of migrant households, increase national income and savings, and generate foreign exchange. In the early 1980s, an estimated 2.5 million Asian migrants remitted $8 billion, or over $3,100 each. Generally, migrants use remittances to buy necessities and luxuries, to pay off debts, and to purchase (or construct) housing and buy land. The remittances that are saved can be invested to expand the emigration country's capacity to produce and to export. Stahl and Habib briefly discuss attempts to estimate the overall effects of remittances on a sending country's economy and note that, by one estimate, each Bangladeshi migrant in 1983 created about three jobs at home with his remittances.

Stahl and Habib conclude that labor migration is neither a panacea nor a Pandora's box for development. Emigration does not automatically translate into development because migrants do not acquire new skills. Remittances, while useful, do not launch investment by themselves. However, neither has emigration from Asian countries led to skilled worker shortages causing production bottlenecks, nor did emigration keep poor labor exporters poor. Exporting labor is, in Stahl and Habib's conclusion, a useful tool to promote development that works best if an economy is primed for development.

Part V summarizes studies of the effects of emigration on countries in Latin America, the Caribbean region, and Mexico. In Chapter 9, Diaz-Briquets examines the effects of emigration from Latin America at national, regional, and individual levels. He notes that several countries have experienced substantial emigration flows, including Paraguay, Colombia, and Mexico, and that emigration from some of the smaller countries has been sufficient to slow or stop population growth.

The effects of emigration and remittances on national labor markets and economies are harder to disentangle, but Diaz-Briquets concludes that the emigration of unskilled workers is not a serious problem for the larger emigration countries, while remittances contribute substantial foreign exchange to sending countries. He also notes the negative macro consequences of emigration: stagnation if internal markets become too small to achieve economies of scale, the draining off of protest which permits entrenched leaders to stay in power, and the often permanent loss of young, vigorous, and better educated workers.

Diaz-Briquets turns next to the regional consequences of migration, noting that border cities are especially sensitive to changes in migration flows. However, the most important negative effect of a recession in a destination country, such as Venezuela for Colombian migrants, is the decreased trade which affects a variety of industries and cities. The border city pain of recession-reduced migration is real, but macroeconomic effects in the emigration country are much larger.

Diaz-Briquets reviews studies of the effects of emigration on the villages migrants depart from and concludes that remittances in Latin America are spent to improve living standards, to build housing, and to buy land and livestock. Most investments generate rents for their owners; only the minority of investments in services such as restaurants or stores generate jobs, and most of these remittance-created jobs go to local family members or relatives of the migrant. Remittances alter the structure of rural communities, creating a new class of rich residents, and the resulting tension between the traditional and migrant elite can inspire development or resentment. Migrant households clearly benefit from remittances, but their effect on villages is more complex.

Diaz-Briquets concludes that emigration can reduce unemployment pressures in small countries or those with high emigration rates, that migration and remittances can have limited effects in rigid societies with unequal incomes that are not primed for development, and that the major losses associated with emigration are of the brain-drain type. He does not believe that this generally pessimistic picture of emigration's failure to generate development will be altered until labor importers work cooperatively with labor exporters.

Chapter 10 examines emigration and development in the Caribbean. Pessar traces contemporary migration patterns to the adaptation patterns of ex-slaves after emancipation: ex-slave owners continued to own the land, and ex-slaves responded by migrating. Migration from island to island was a way to escape discrimination and inferior status at home, to earn higher wages, and eventually it became a rite of passage for youth.

Pessar traces middle-class emigration to development policies which favored low-wage export industries and did not leave a place for the middle class. The middle class consequently migrated to the United States, Canada, and the United Kingdom. There has been enough emigration from some Caribbean islands to reduce population growth despite high fertility and longer lives. Pessar argues that middle class emigration is deleterious; it leads to production bottlenecks, provokes rapid turnover in managerial and professional jobs, and requires local educational institutions to train more people than will be employed locally.

Emigration has also feminized agriculture and promoted more land speculation than investments which increased food and fiber output. Pessar notes that, in many cases, migrants let land lie fallow because there is a shortage of farmworkers. Pessar concludes that Caribbean nations should turn away from low-wage export industries and emigration because these policies do not promise to effectuate development. Instead, education and training systems should be reoriented to satisfy domestic labor needs, small-scale agriculture should be strengthened, and the return intentions of emigrants should be reinforced.

Part VI reviews the unsettled relationship between migration and development. Chapter 11 notes that migrant families clearly benefit from remittances, but it is less clear whether their communities and societies benefit as well. Labor importers hold the key to future labor flows, and a recognition by them that labor migration cannot be simply a temporary borrowing of another country's unneeded workers would be a first step toward developing bilateral and multilateral policies which promote development as well as migration.

Chapter 12 is a lagniappe for readers. The Immigration Reform and Control Act of 1986 created a commission to "examine the conditions in Mexico and such other sending countries which contribute to unauthorized migration to the United States." In the language of this book, why didn't several decades of recruitment, remittances, and returns promote stay-at-home development in the countries sending migrant workers to the United States?

After three years of studies and hearings, the commission concluded that migrants come to the United States illegally for economic reasons and that, although more development is the long-run solution to emigration pressures, in the short and medium terms development is more likely to increase migratory pressures. Nonetheless, the commission called for expanded trade and more development assistance to promote the economic growth which will eventually reduce emigration pressures.

Despite this J-curve effect of first more and later less emigration, the commission called for expanded trade and more development assistance to promote the economic growth which eventually reduces emigration pressures, asserting that "expanded trade between the sending countries and the United States is the single most important long term remedy" for such pressures.

The commission report emphasized that promoting stay-at-home development is a formidable task. Since 1950, the populations of Mexico and the Central American nations have tripled, so that Mexico alone adds almost 1 million job seekers to its labor force each year. These job seekers find few jobs in modernizing agriculture, so they flock to urban areas and strain infrastructures and labor markets. The commission recognized that an integrated and long-run oriented program which includes programs for family planning, rural job creation, and export-led manufacturing growth will be needed to create economies and labor markets which keep potential migrants at home. To coordinate U.S. policies to-

ward migration areas, and to assess the migration impacts of proposed U.S. policies, the commission recommends the creation of an independent Agency for
Migration Affairs.

NOTE

1. Cited in Straubhaar, 1988:13, 232.

THE
UNSETTLED
RELATIONSHIP

Part I

Conceptual and Theoretical Issues in International Labor Migration

Today there are 20 to 30 million migrant workers in the United States, Europe, Africa, the Middle East, and Latin America. These guest or migrant workers are living and working outside their country of origin and citizenship. Many are in an irregular or undocumented status in the country in which they work. They remit $40 to $50 billion annually to their home countries, and many eventually return home with savings and skills acquired in another country's labor market.

The practice of one nation, usually richer, borrowing a poorer nation's workers or tolerating their illegal entry is controversial in both sending and receiving nations. Controversy erupts because the mutual benefits expected to flow from migrant workers have, in practice, often turned into mutual dependence: sending nations become dependent on another country's labor market for the employment of some of their workers, while labor-importing nations get addicted to an ample supply of foreign workers. Emigration or labor-sending states often become frustrated when the migrant worker patterns which evolve are changed unilaterally by labor-receiving nations, especially if workers are expelled or encouraged to depart just when remittances are most needed, as when migrants are sent home during a recession.

Why has international labor migration been a disappointment to labor exporting and importing countries? Labor importers learned that the migrant labor tap could not be turned on and off at will, and labor exporters learned that there is no automatic process which turns remittances and returning migrants into development. The frustration is especially evident among intellectuals in emigration countries, some of whom argue that temporary labor migration is just another scheme foisted on poor countries by rich ones to keep them poor.

Part I reviews international labor migration theories and concepts. Chapter 1 notes that international migration surged during the first and third quarters of the twentieth century. However, the sources and destinations of migrants changed between the first and third quarters, as have the issues raised by migration. First quarter migrants were encouraged to be settlers by host nations, although many returned to their countries of origin, while third quarter migrants were expected to be temporary residents, although many settled abroad. First quarter migration streams were halted by restrictive legislation and the world-wide depression; attempts to halt third quarter migration have been uneven and not notably successful.

People migrate for survival and mobility. Survival migrants are persons pushed abroad by the lack of alternatives at home; mobility migrants are pulled abroad to better themselves. There are many groupings of migrants, and several theories of why migrants migrate. Economic theories ask whether it is rational for an individual or household to go abroad by weighing the more certain local income against the uncertain income abroad. Theorists who have historical or structural perspectives focus on why economic and other factors keep a reserve army of unemployed persons willing and ready to emigrate.

The causes and consequences of international labor migration remain in dispute, but certain features of labor migration are well-recognized. Recruitment tends to select the best and brightest from the emigration nation manual work force; remittances do not automatically get converted into job-creating investments; and returning migrants are not often the missing spark plugs needed for development. Migration does not solve development problems; instead, it sometimes aggravates them. A better understanding of migration and development linkages would help to make the window of opportunity opened by migration a more effective development tool.

Chapter 2 asks why there is often a gap between theory and reality in international labor migration. The balanced growth theory of labor migration argues that the migration of 5 to 10 percent of a country's work force should reduce profits, raise wages, and reduce unemployment. Adding 5 to 10 percent foreign workers to a host country work force should raise profits and reduce wages. The net effect of labor migration should be to increase the economic output of the two countries and to reduce wage and income differences between emigration and immigration nations.

Instead of the balanced growth expected by theory, the reality is often asymmetric development which increases inequalities between emigration and immigration countries. Labor migration forges new links between nations, but rarely reduces the economic gaps which encouraged workers to emigrate. Instead, the three R's of recruitment, remittances, and returns usually serve to increase the dependence of emigration countries on immigration countries. Experience has yielded mostly negative lessons: how rational immigration country-directed recruitment creams an emigration country's work force of its best and brightest manual workers; how difficult it is for emigration countries to regulate or channel remittances into sustainable job-creating development; and how hard it is to use the skills acquired by returning migrants to promote development.

1

Labor Migration and Development: Research and Policy Issues

Demetrios G. Papademetriou and Philip L. Martin

Few socioeconomic phenomena in the post–World War II period have proven as controversial or as difficult to regulate as international migration for employment. Within this migration process, few components have been as resistant to analysis and appraisal as the relationship between emigration, return migration, and development.

Except for forced population movements and exchanges, international migration in the twentieth century has occurred with particular vigor during two periods: the century's first and third quarters. At the turn of the century, the principal destination countries were the United States, several Latin American countries, and Western European countries such as France and Germany, which had been emigration nations during the 1800s.[1]

Since World War II, there has been a widening and a deepening of the migration process. Significant countries of emigration have come to include: (a) virtually all Mediterranean countries, which sent labor first to Western European countries and, since the early 1970s, to the oil-rich Arab countries;[2] (b) Southeast Asian countries, whose nationals are employed in both Middle Eastern labor markets and those of Malaysia, Singapore, and Australia, as well as North America;[3] and (c) many Latin American and English-speaking Caribbean countries, whose emigrants are now found in the United States and Canada[4] as well as such South American destinations as Venezuela, Argentina, and Brazil.

One must take special note of Mexico as a major source country. Mexico's northern states have a complex historical symbiosis with the United States, and developments since World War II have created an almost binational social and economic community with the U.S. Southwest. Africa is another special case which exhibits attributes of migration relationships spanning all types identified elsewhere in the world. In Africa, the standard distinction between internal and international migration loses much of its meaning because borders are often arbitrary and population movements often occur among family members who live in adjacent state jurisdictions. Many people in Africa follow patterns of movement for economic survival and mobility that predate the formation of current state entities and were encouraged—directly and indirectly—by colonial administrations (Thahane, Chapter 4; Mlay, 1985; Adepoju, 1983 and Chapter 3). The African situation has deep historical roots and is defined as an "*international* migration problem" primarily because of the relatively recent creation of African states.

The source countries have changed, the character and volume of migration have changed, and the debate over newcomers in receiving countries has changed. International migration requires destination countries to balance the natural fear and distrust of foreigners against the economic need for migrant labor. Migration is further complicated because many host and sending governments find that the rules and dynamics of international migration interfere with their ability to formulate and implement domestic policies.[5] Given global economic difficulties and the sociopolitical problems which economic problems accentuate, the massive movement of people across national borders promises to continue to be one of the most challenging policy dilemmas facing the international community in the 1990s.

International migration claims a place on the political agenda of many societies. This status has been attained despite efforts by many political and economic elites to depoliticize the migration issue and treat it as if it had only an economic dimension. The failure to confine migration to economics can be observed in many countries. The Federal Republic of Germany (FRG) and France are experiencing anti-immigrant activities fueled by high unemployment, economic uncertainty, and the increasingly xenophobic comments of some politicians. In these countries, migration was to have been a temporary and circular flow of workers, but has developed into a settlement immigration. This settlement process has not been reversed by measures such as the halting of labor recruitment in 1973–74 and the programs designed to facilitate the "voluntary" return of foreign nationals. In Great Britain, the number of those who have an unchallenged right to domicile and citizenship has been reduced several times, despite such efforts violating the letter and spirit of Britain's commitments to other Commonwealth countries.

The United States in 1986 enacted amendments to its Immigration and Nationality Act to control illegal immigration—the dominant issue in U.S. immigration debates at the time. Continuing concerns about the U.S. agricultural sector's reliance on temporary foreign contract labor and an ongoing discussion about the legal immigration system promise that immigration policy will retain its place at the forefront of the U.S. political agenda. Canada, Australia, Switzerland, South Africa, Nigeria, Argentina, Venezuela, Malaysia, and most oil-producing Gulf states are pursuing immigration-control policies with considerable vigor, although their ability and commitment to implementing them vary significantly.

While destination countries seek to limit immigration, labor senders are frustrated by both their inability to derive the full complement of economic benefits thought to inhere in the temporary or circular emigration process, and to contain the socioeconomic and political costs which are a byproduct of migration. Why did emigration not automatically lead to development? Development does not mean simply economic growth, such as the increased GDP brought about by remittance income. In some cases, emigration, which increases GDP, may in fact impede development. Nadir Fergany makes this point in its extreme form for the Arab region when he points out that true development requires structural social, economic, and political changes, which together allow the productive forces in a society to grow and diversify "in the direction of the satisfaction of the basic needs of all its people as a first step toward higher levels of welfare" (1983:4).

Development is a multidimensional process that depends on a number of attributes—such as a country's human and material resources, social and physical infrastructure, skills, capital, political stability, governmental efficacy, and *immigration and emigration*. Analyses often focus on the effects of only one component in this entire process of development—emigration, and even more narrowly, migrant remittances—and proclaim the entire institution of emigration a failure because it did not bring about development. In some instances, emigration may contribute to the sending country's stagnation. Analyses must remember that the goals of private individuals (the migrants) will not necessarily be compatible with those of their state or, for that matter, with the expectations of public and private sector managers and planners.

TYPES OF MIGRATION

Why do migrants migrate? At the most general level, it might suffice to use a simple dichotomy that distinguishes between what Urzua (1981) calls "survival" and "mobility" migrants. The former are found principally in Asia, Africa, and the Latin American/Caribbean region and comprise the rural abjectly poor who may or may not be proletarianized prior to going abroad. Pessar (Chapter 10) notes that survival migrants dominate inter-Caribbean migrants and concludes that survival migrants are "legacies of the plantation economy." Survival migrants are pushed into the migrant stream by structural poverty and they reflect household decisions about survival. Survival migrants tend to be young single males with few skills and little education and often lack necessary work and residence permits. They often hold marginal jobs abroad (in agriculture, mining, and the informal sector) and they often experience spells of unemployment while earning relatively low wages. Survival migrant earnings are typically meager, their savings and remittances are modest, and remittances are often spent on consumption for the survival of the household.

"Mobility" migrants are usually recruited from abroad. They range from technical and managerial personnel to proletarianized internal migrants who often use cities as staging areas for international migration. Some are peasants recruited directly by private industry in advanced industrial societies. Recruitment takes place usually through the intervention of either private labor contractors (the prevalent mode in the Middle East and South Asia) or through licensed representatives of receiving countries (the dominant European and Southern African models). Mobility migrants are pulled away from home by better economic and social opportunities. The decision to emigrate, however, rests with households which make some members movers and others stayers. These household decisions are made on the basis of family goals, which are in turn shaped by such factors as internal household dynamics, gender-based role divisions, and birth rank. Migration decisions are also shaped by the social and economic organization of the community, so that, for example, social reproduction and inheritance patterns which determine how land is going to be allocated can influence decisions about migration (Mlay, 1985; Urzua, 1981; Adepoju, Chapter 3; and Caldwell, 1969).

Structural social and economic conditions also set the stage for mobility. Briquets (1985) argues that the development strategies pursued by political and economic elites strongly influence emigration patterns, and Pessar (Chapter 10) shows how export-oriented industrialization in a number of Caribbean islands encouraged the emigration of the middle classes because foreign investors brought in expatriate managers, and the lower-middle classes frequently emigrated to escape the roller coaster of the international economy.

Professional and highly skilled technicians and managers may be recruited for overseas assignments (the Gulf states' model), or they may be attracted abroad when the structural impoverishment of their country and paucity of professional opportunities there combine with the hard-to-resist enticements of professional rewards abroad to fuel the process known as brain drain.[6]

Mobility migrants are better educated and more skilled than survival migrants. Mobility migrants hold better jobs, earn better wages, adjust abroad more readily, and are better able to reconstitute their families there if they so wish. While the reasons for the emigration of this group may lead one to expect a certain degree of economic rationality in their savings and return decisions, experience shows that events surrounding their ability to unite their families in the host country often militate against both their return and their capacity to act as agents of social and economic change upon return.

POLICY RESPONSES

International migration is the product of a complex interplay of economic, social, political, cultural, linguistic, and religious forces. The precise mix of these forces varies widely with each historical period and with each specific migration flow and influences the type and intensity of the reaction by the receiving country's population. It is precisely because of this complexity, however, that laissez-faire policies and unilateral actions—the dominant pattern of past responses—are now increasingly inadequate in bringing about desired policy outcomes.

A partial explanation for policy failures lies in the fact that the magnitude and character of recent international population movements have undergone substantial changes. International migration, including refugee flows, is now probably larger than at any other time during the last two centuries—although migration to the United States of America at the turn of the twentieth century probably was at its highest level in history, and the population shifts occurring after the redrawing of the political map at the end of World War II, especially in Eastern Europe and South Asia, were for a short period of time more significant than the current estimates of about 14 million refugees (U.S. Committee on Refugees, 1989). Persistent underdevelopment, political polarization within states, regional conflicts, ethnically and religiously motivated persecution, and the consequences of the continuing global economic difficulties for less-developed countries suggest that, if anything, the pressures for international migration will remain at very high levels.

Some of this international migration will continue to be the classic types of permanent family immigration and the migration of highly skilled and professionally trained manpower. To a certain degree, both of these types of migration can be controlled at the destination point.[7] *Temporary* and *irregular*[8] labor migration, however, have become the most significant recent types of international migration. The many forms of temporary migrants, such as "guestworkers," "seasonal workers," "circular workers," and "contract workers,"[9] as well as types of irregular workers, such as those who enter a country clandestinely or who violate the terms of their legal entry (as when students fail to return home upon completing their studies or tourists enter the labor market) have increased in number. One reason for the increase has been that industrial democracies thought such workers would provide a flexible way to deal with labor bottlenecks. Although the precise point when destination countries learned that there is nothing more permanent than a temporary worker cannot be pinpointed, it is clear that:

- many temporary and irregular workers have become de facto permanent immigrants;

- their presence poses severe social, cultural, linguistic, and political challenges for the receiving countries;

- the legal ambivalence toward their presence abroad, and the administrative discretion to which they are subject, have given rise to severe social and economic adjustment problems among such workers; and

- the sending societies have not yet realized many of the benefits which the "temporary" emigration of their citizens had been expected to provide.

THEORIES OF MIGRATION

International migration is clearly a process structurally central to both sending and receiving societies, and it signifies a sending country's penetration by and incorporation into the world economy. This conflict view (Papademetriou,

1983b; also, see Portes and Walton, 1981; and Wood, 1982) perceives development and underdevelopment as parts of a single integral totality which simultaneously depends on and recreates conditions for economic inequality worldwide. There are several major theories of migration.

Classical Economics Models

The classical economics tradition focuses on equilibrium models that treat migration as a voluntary and rational decision made by individuals who seek to enhance their economic position by responding to the higher wages offered away from home (Lewis, 1954). Their mobility ensures their optimal distribution and hence their efficient allocation.

Such migration models are highly reductionist and mechanistic (Sjaastad 1962; Lee, 1966; Todaro, 1976). They predict that individuals, acting as *homo economicus*, will have adequate information; will use such information in a rational, cost/benefit fashion; and will invest in their future by moving to areas where capital and most other resources are abundant but labor is scarce. Such mobility serves to restore the balance between unequally distributed resources across space in a manner that presumably benefits all—destination places, sending places (principally through remittances), and the migrants themselves. (For critiques of these models, see Papademetriou and Hopple, 1982; Wood, 1982; Portes and Walton, 1981: ch. 2; Arizpe, 1981; and Kearney, 1986).

The intrinsic appeal of classical economic models lies in their articulation of a formal theory of individual behavior and their generation of testable hypotheses, that is, in their empirical order and methodological orthodoxy. However, such order and consistency often occurs at the expense of a better understanding of the structural factors which shape migrations. Classical economics models ignore the international politicoeconomic environment, the internal and international distribution of production factors and natural resources, and the state-level economic and political decisions that directly affect individual decisions to migrate. Furthermore, these models often confuse detail with social structure, and frequently commit the fallacy of composition by assuming that since individuals benefit, the society must necessarily benefit. Classical models are often ahistorical, and they presume movement toward an equilibrium (Papademetriou, 1983b).

The classical school includes human capital, expected income, and intersectoral linkage economic models. The first two encompass the many variants of the Sjaastad (1962) and Todaro (1976) models, but include several nonpecuniary costs and benefits. Among them are the opportunity costs for foregone earnings due to migration, the disutility of leaving one's familiar environments for unfamiliar ones, and the perceptions of and uncertainties about expected income—rather than actual wage rates—at destination (Rivera-Batiz, 1980).

The intersectoral linkage model is grounded in the idea that changes in the social and economic structure of one region have an impact on other regions of a

country, as well as on relevant regions of other countries. Such linkages can be of
a backward, forward, or final demand nature. For instance, effective rural development programs which substantially raise the standard of living of a given rural
area can lead to increased demand for such items as fertilizers, farm implements,
machinery, and credit—thus increasing economic activity in urban areas. Forward
linkages benefit urban areas through increased demand for transport and storage
facilities for agricultural commodities, agriprocessing facilities, and wholesaling
for internal or international distribution. Finally, the increased disposable income
of rural residents can generate an increased demand for goods and services produced regionally and/or abroad, which will result in additional employment generation there—the so-called final demand linkages (Hirschman, 1957).

There have been substantial modifications of these theories. Todaro (1981)
recognizes migration as a force contributing to both unemployment and structural imbalances between urban and rural areas. Harris (1978) has come to view
migration as a response to underlying inequalities in development (see Kearney,
1986).

Even these classical models are criticized by conflict theorists. Conflict theorists object to the classical models' portrayal of migration as the calculated result
of *individual* actions motivated by self-interest. Conflict theorists see migration
in the context of class structure and conflict. Both Marx (1853) and neo-
Marxists (Nikolinakos, 1973; Castles and Kosack, 1973; Castells, 1975) view
emigration as the result of the incorporation of less-developed sectors (such as
traditional rural economies and periphery countries) into more economically advanced sectors (such as cities or center countries). This process of incorporating
developing areas becomes cumulatively unequal and leads to the weakening of
the position of the developing sectors vis-à-vis the advanced ones. Human and
capital resource flows thus reflect a process whereby excess labor from subsistence sectors and economies migrates to the modern sectors and economies.
Low wages assure that the workers will generate a surplus which allows the accumulation of more capital. Hence, contact between unequally developed states
becomes a means of additional surplus extraction by the advanced state and migration should not be expected to lead to equilibrium among regions but rather
to the "progressive subordination" of the weaker regions to the stronger ones
(Portes and Walton, 1981: 28).

Historical-Structural Models

Historical-structural models of migration shift the focus from individual actions to national and international political and economic forces, from the study
of microbehavior to macrosocial processes.

Historical-structural models are often grounded in Marxist-Leninism. They
treat migration as a necessary (albeit insufficient) component in capitalism's
constant struggle to arrest and reverse its propensity toward both long-term
and cyclical crises. Capital, in its historical search to respond to the continuous

rise in the cost of labor, has often relied on the periphery to temporarily alleviate the problem. For example, imperialism initially provided the necessary conditions by opening new markets and offering abundant cheap raw materials for the imperial nation. In addition, it created new investment opportunities for capital and brought in cheap commodities through foreign trade. The excellent returns on such imperialistic investments were made possible by a system of economic exploitation that was buttressed by direct political and military domination that assured the supply of cheap raw materials, cheap labor, and labor-intensive production (Lenin, 1939; Hobson, 1971; Portes and Walton, 1981).

These arguments recur in the *dependencia* and world-system literature.[10] These off-shoots of Marxism have generated a substantial following and an equally substantial critical evaluation. Most of the criticism centers on the historical structural literature's lack of conceptual clarity and its theoretical confusion, and the fact that its basic tenets do not lend themselves to conventional empirical investigation, so that their central assumptions thus are offered as articles of faith. These problems are further exacerbated by the frequent casual and inexact use of concepts. Caporaso (1978a, 1978b) points out that dependency denotes the "process of integration" of peripheral states into the international capitalist system and seeks to assess the "developmental implications" of such incorporation for the periphery. Dependency studies the effects of international capital on the class structure of peripheral actors and the role of the state "in shaping and managing the national, foreign, and class forces that propel development within states" (Caporaso, 1978a:2). The historical and structural nature of this process, however, and the internal disarticulation of peripheral actors, make it very difficult to apply this sort of analysis to anything less than the global level because only parts of the peripheral nation are integrated within the world capitalist system. When one adds the historical nature of this incorporation and the internal disarticulation of the peripheral states, one appreciates the almost insurmountable problems of empirical measurement (see Caporaso, 1978a, 1978b; Skocpol, 1977; Cardoso, 1979; Duvall, 1978; Portes and Walton, 1981; de Janvry and Garramon, 1977).

Historical-structuralists analyze international migration by tracing the roots of migration to financial and trade contacts among politically and economically unequal units. Such contacts usually result in the stagnation of the weaker unit. Whether surplus is siphoned off by the national metropolis or by international capital, the effect on pressures for emigration is similar. Emigration is fueled by the penetration of capitalist modes of production in traditional agriculture. For example, the plantation system which stimulates emigration in Latin America, the Caribbean, and parts of Africa displaces agricultural labor directly through mechanization and the introduction of international market prices for agricultural commodities.

Migration can often be traced to the institutional and sectoral imbalances brought about by a state's incorporation into the world capitalist system. Once this process has commenced, key structures of less developed states become "remolded" to fit external demand, and the resulting structural imbalances promote emigration (see Portes and Walton, 1981; Sassen-Koob, 1984). As the essays on Africa, Europe, and South Asia make clear, the state has historically played a critical role at both ends of the migration stream as the often active and deliberate promoter of emigration.

Foreign labor occupies a distinct position in advanced industrial societies as an expedient with which to overcome labor-demand pressure. This function, however, is only one side of capital's use of foreign labor. It is applicable most explicitly to the situation in South Africa but also to the European labor bottlenecks which resulted from the economic upsurge of the 1950s and 1960s and to the more recent Gulf states' conditions of absolute labor shortages.

Another function of foreign labor is considerably more complex. This function views the already proletarianized (that is, introduced to modern [wage] modes of production) labor in the periphery as a labor reserve army placed at the disposal of core capital under conditions of the core's choosing (Castells, 1975; Nikolinakos, 1973). The various types of contract labor systems and irregular migration are classic examples of this explanation. By implication, this labor reserve is utilized under exploitative terms. Entry wages are frozen by contracts for the contract period, usually one year, but routinely renewable; migrant social-welfare rights are frequently constricted and at times suspended; geographic and industrial mobility is often legally restricted; and, finally, foreign workers are typically granted only a special or inferior legal status. These features are common both to *de jure* and *de facto* foreign labor programs. Industries use contract labor to moderate wage increases and sometimes to reverse the wage and labor standard gains which indigenous labor has made.

Evaluation

The historical/structural perspective places migration within the context of the gradual absorption of less-developed states and regions into the world economic system. This process is thought to release a number of expulsive forces; the new division of labor results in class conflicts which imbalance the system and compel workers to view migration as a viable alternative. But the most important insight which the historical structural perspective has contributed to the understanding of the dynamics of international migration is to highlight the shortcomings of economic theories of migration. Both schools are burdened by their theoretical formulations.

Historical-structural models that explain migration on the basis of disruption and conflict focus on the world capitalist system. However, such a global perspective often loses sight of the many historical and contextual variations in international migration. With their unitary view of the global economic system, historical-structuralists often underestimate the economic dynamism of some peripheral states, such as how migration brings peasant communities and households into direct contact with international capital, and how such linkages become vital to the reproduction of the peasant domestic unit by simultaneously preserving and exploiting village-based agricultural economies (see Meillassoux, 1981, for a discussion of this linkage in Africa; see also Kearney, 1986: 341–45).

A second consideration involves the complex role which women play in international migration. Rural women play important roles in migration. Women are preferred workers in the export production zones of developing countries made attractive by tax and other concessions (see Sassen-Koob, 1984) and as producers of food and goods to be sold cheaply in the informal sector, but also as "nonsalaried producers of value which sustains households . . . and from which migrant workers are delivered to capital" (Kearney, 1986:345).

There should be more case studies of international migration. Case studies can shed light on the unique aspects of specific migration flows while specifying (and thus making more accurate) extant theoretical models. George (1979) advocates a dialogue between "systematic" case studies and what he labels the "statistical-correlative" approach, or moving between quantitative and case studies. George recommends employing qualitative procedures by using the "historian's methodology of explanation," where the investigator "subjects a single case in which that correlation appears to more intensive scrutiny, . . . in order to establish whether there exists an intervening process, that is, a causal nexus, between the independent and the dependent variable" (1979:46; see also Papademetriou and Hopple, 1982; for a typology of case studies and a strong statement on the usefulness of "theoretical" case studies, see Lijphart, 1971).

Historically informed and contextually rich theoretical case studies can explain phenomena as diverse as the famine-induced Irish emigration to the United States of America in the 1840s, the migrations which have resulted from political and religious persecution in the past several centuries, and the forced migrations of Africans to North America. Exclusive adoption of the view of international migration as part of the international process of capital accumulation thus risks reducing a multifaceted process to one which serves only the needs and strategies of capital. Such a view deflects attention from the role which political relationships and struggles, social institutions, cultural forces, and the allocation of power on the basis of class/race/ethnicity/religion have had on specific migration processes. What is needed is better attention to the often idiosyncratic forces that reflect how private and public interests interact and affect migration.

Where do the positions of the classical and conflict schools converge? Their convergence rests on the recognition that, although recourse to migration is usually the result of a household survival strategy, the household's choices have been defined by structural factors relating to the position and degree of a state's integration into the global economic system. Students of international migration should thus remain aware of the interdependence between the international politicoeconomic system and migration, and of the economic and sociopolitical implications of such interdependence.

Neither classical economists, who view migration and return as a rational calculus, nor Marxists and neo-Marxists, who emphasize the structural forces which shape and constrain individuals' actions, have explained migration completely. Migration takes place in neither an economic nor a sociopolitical vacuum, and individual and household decisions about migration are indeed shaped by macrostructural variables. These macrostructural variables are influenced by decisions in labor-sending countries, a result of the political process which determines the type of, and the manner in which, resources will be mobilized to resolve the basic conflicts between capital and labor within each state's cultural and historical context (Berger and Piore, 1980).

THE RECEIVING COUNTRY–SENDING COUNTRY MIGRATION NEXUS

Receiving Countries

Advanced industrial societies frequently report labor shortages in some labor markets. The structural nature of these labor shortages arises from a combination of social, demographic, economic, and political factors that include the following:

- Demographic trends of below-replacement-level birth rates and increasing dependency ratios due to the aging of the population, as in Europe. Some analysts predict a similar condition for the United States, which already reports labor shortages in undesirable labor market sectors.

- The restructuring of labor markets into primary and secondary sectors, each with distinct human capital requirements (see Papademetriou, 1983b; Piore, 1979). While most advanced industrial societies are capable of filling the primary sector's labor demand (the Gulf states, Canada, and Australia have often been major exceptions), secondary sector employers often ask for low wage alien labor, either because of actual shortages (Europe in the 1960s, South Africa) or because indigenous labor refuses to perform socially undesirable jobs at the (low) wages that are offered.

- Growth in secondary sector economies and labor markets because of variable demand patterns for industrial products; important but marginally profitable industries; a growing market for private and public services which are labor-intensive; a persistent demand for temporary and seasonal work; and a proliferation of jobs which native workers are reluctant to take because of low wages, poor working conditions, and undesirable social status.

- The manpower needs of natural-resource-based economies which could not be sufficiently abated either through labor-force rationalization policies or through aggressive capital intensive industrial strategies. Most major oil-exporting economies fit this description, as do on occasion such South Asian countries as Malaysia and Singapore.

- Realigning political forces which have enabled minorities, ethnics, and labor in general to score marked political and eventually economic gains. These gains have forced capital to look elsewhere for its profits since producing labor intensive goods in advanced industrial societies makes their price uncompetitive in the world market. The flight of capital and industrial jobs for developing nations is becoming a structural feature of the United States and many European economies.

In response to these trends, some labor-thirsty countries negotiated bilateral agreements with the labor-surplus countries in their region for importing workers on a temporary basis. This has been the prevalent model for Europe, South Africa, and the Gulf states, as well as for various U.S. and Canadian agricultural worker programs. Other labor-short states simply formulated and implemented immigration policies which, although restrictive in their legal requirements, tolerated and thus encouraged the inflow of a largely spontaneous and clandestine immigrant force. This has been the dominant U.S., intra-African, intra-Latin American, and European situation in recent years.

Formal and informal labor migration gradually evolved into a condition in which the labor importers became dependent on a continued supply of foreign labor. At the same time, this labor supply became more and more independent of the actual labor needs of the host economies. The assumption that foreign worker recruitment could be started and stopped as desired proved unrealistic. Instead, as migration flows matured and labor-demand pressure persisted, the temporary and revocable nature of the arrangement began to recede and give way to expanding opportunities for family reunification, some occupational mobility, and the all but formal establishment of settlement immigration. Only South Africa and, to a lesser degree the Gulf states, have been able to resist this gradual evolution from temporary to permanent migrants. However, Burki (Chapter 7) argues that as the labor requirements of the Gulf states shift from infrastructure construction to infrastructure maintenance, settler immigration will also occur in this region.

Sending Countries

The impacts of labor migration on advanced industrial societies have been studied extensively. However, there has been less analysis of the impacts of emigration on less-developed countries despite growing evidence that emigration has been unable to deliver most of the expected benefits.

Many labor-surplus countries had great expectations for labor migration. Mired in economic stagnation, they saw the opportunity for the emigration of their unemployed and underemployed workers as an unqualified blessing. Their hopes overlooked such negative developmental consequences of migration as the depletion of their already meager supplies of skilled manpower, the age and sex selectivity of emigration, and the possibility that the socioeconomic gains from the skills and remittances of returning emigrants might be only marginal.

Migration Selectivity. Most people in developing nations do not migrate. Migrants are not only young, healthy, and dynamic; their very selection by the household for emigration suggests that they will accept risk and are more likely to have the human capital characteristics that will serve them well abroad. These individual attributes of migrants are further reinforced by the selectivity and screening criteria employed both by private labor contractors and official recruiters, and by the additional mechanism of periodic contract reviews following the initial contract period. Employers and authorities often deny contract and/or residence permit extensions to those foreign workers who have shown themselves to be less than ideal workers, or who simply have not made the expected progress in adapting to the new social environment. Whether the setting is Europe in the 1960s, the Gulf states in the 1970s, segments of U.S. agriculture since the early 1940s, or South Africa for the past 100 years,[11] this cumulative selectivity, while assuring foreign labor users a supply of whichever foreign workers they prefer, at the same time drains the sending countries' reservoir of many of the young workers who are most likely to contribute to their own countries' development.

Most migrants participating in organized labor migrations have human capital characteristics that are superior to the population at large, and most are employed prior to emigration. Labor emigration countries are often involved simultaneously in more than one type or system of migration, and these countries with relatively meager supplies of qualified people are rarely able to provide the right mix of incentives that might entice such people to stay home.

Some of the countries involved in the international migration system experience monumental losses in manpower and skills. This is especially true in Africa. Lesotho had more than 50 percent of its adult males working in South Africa in the early 1980s; Botswana's formal sector routinely employs fewer Botswanans than are employed in South Africa; Malawi had more than 20 percent of its adult males abroad in 1966; in 1975, 17 percent of the population of Burkina Faso (then Upper Volta) lived abroad; in 1983, more than 10 percent of Ghanaians (and nearly a quarter of that country's workers) were emigrants (Adepoju, Chapter 3). Similarly, Jamaica and the Barbados had, respectively, 21 and 25 percent of their population living in the United States in the mid-1980s (Pastor, 1985b). And in 1973, 15 percent of Paraguayans lived abroad, while between 1963 and 1975 almost 8 percent of Uruguayans emigrated. On the basis of such data, some analysts decry emigration for "robbing" the sending countries of valuable human capital.

The cause-effect relationship is not really as unequivocal as it appears. The examples above are the exceptions and involve either small nations (Latin American and Caribbean examples), or nations with immense resource voids and population pressures (Southern African states, Egypt, and North Yemen) and a combination of economic mismanagement and ecological deterioration (other African examples) that has created severe emigration pressures. As a rule, emigration involves only 1 or 2 percent of a sending country's labor force. For instance, the Philippines have only about 2.5 percent of their work force abroad, while the comparable rate for Pakistan is 1.7 percent and for most other South Asian countries about 1 percent (Stahl and Habib, Chapter 8). And Greece, a relatively small country of under 9 million people throughout the 1960s, with only replacement-level fertility, continued to register positive population growth despite significant levels of emigration to Europe and other destinations (Papademetriou, Chapter 11).

But what of the *quality* of population lost through emigration? This is a more serious problem, particularly if the skills lost are difficult to replace. Sending countries face two major problems: first, losses in output and capital formation due to interindustry linkages, which may further reduce domestic employment (Stahl and Habib, Chapter 8); and second, disruptions in production and productivity, as emigrating skilled and managerial talent is replaced by less skilled and experienced individuals who might offer lower quality services for higher unit-of-labor costs (Burki, Chapter 7). In some cases this can lead to production bottlenecks and wage inflation.[12] Emigration can be indiscriminate, tapping low- and medium-skilled workers as well as highly trained manpower.

There is also an ethical dimension to this problem which must not go unnoticed. While some speak of opportunity costs, surplus brain power, and the right to emigrate as a basic human right, the emigration of high level manpower from the less-developed to the advanced industrial countries clearly constitutes a drain of scarce and expensive human resources. Brain drain migrants are a subsidy to the rich from the poor, and such a subsidy can only increase the asymmetry between the two types of countries.

The Geography and Political Economy of Return. The age and sex selectivity of emigration often changes the composition of the population in emigration regions. Local and regional demographic profiles can be altered as emigration skews sex and age cohorts and often leads to high dependency ratios. More important, however, is that such changes have significant implications for the social organization and power relationships in the life of villages and small towns. By removing the younger and more progressive members of a community via emigration, antiquated social structures can be preserved and entrenched.

But what of return migration? Evidence from all regions studied in this volume suggests that many migrants opt to return to the rural and small-town communities from whence they originated, regardless of whether they emigrated directly from these or after an intermediate stop in a larger city. Since this is the case, one must study the linkage between returns and changes in the social and political power structures of labor-sending communities. The impact of individual returned migrants on these relationships has been largely discounted in the extensive literature on European migration (see Abadan-Unat, 1976; Böhning, 1976; Cerase, 1974; Entzinger, 1978; Hoepfner and Huber, 1978; Trebous, 1970; Van Gendt, 1977.) However, a significant and regular flow of returned migrants will likely strengthen the cumulative potential for change as it creates an atmosphere initially of confrontation and eventually of change. The evidence for such migration-induced modernization is limited, but the reason may be because there are few studies that focus on the effects of *permanent* return migration on rural and small-town communities.

Many researchers assume that migrants intend to return to major cities and become aggressive entrepreneurs and skilled industrial workers. Since entrepreneurship thrives most often in larger cities, and industry is almost exclusively concentrated in and around the largest cities, returning migrants are assumed to accelerate the patterns of internal migration toward large cities which most emigration countries are experiencing. In many studies, economists focus on aggregate data and expect that returning migrants will go to where the skills gained abroad will be most valuable, the cities. Structural sociologists, on the other hand, do not necessarily expect migrants to return to their points of origin.

Such studies appear to pay too little attention to the motivations of migrants and fail to stay in touch with migrants during their journey abroad so that researchers can anticipate with better accuracy the migrants' intentions upon return. Evidence from African migration, recent surveys on returned migrants to Greece and Turkey, evidence from Pakistan and South Asia, and research in Mexico (Massey et al., 1987), and Columbia (Diaz, 1987), suggest that migrants do return to rural areas and small towns, and their return has at least a modest local development impact.

The negative demographic effects to which migration gave rise are not irreversible, return migration to rural and small-town communities does occur, and returned migrants do have local development effects. A return movement is more likely to become an agency of change for development if it is at the migrant's initiative, to the community or region of origin, and is part of a regular flow. Furthermore, returning migrants should have maintained an active interest in the affairs of the community, reinforced both by regular visits and through the proxy of a family left behind. Once a tradition of return is established, returning migrants might be more successful agents of change if they can show both financial success abroad and financial responsibility upon return. However, few return movements exhibit more than a few of these attributes. Massey et al., (1987), report on one such case in a study of four communities in Mexico. One of the reasons why there are so few such cases, however, might reflect the difficulty researchers have had in discerning the developmental impacts associated with migration flows which have not yet reached full maturity.

The Skills and Remittances of Return Migrants. The third area in which labor-sending countries may have been too optimistic is in overestimating the development promises of skills and remittances. Migrant workers receive exposure to the discipline and rhythm of industrial life, but such qualifications are only a passive byproduct of industrial life and, in many cases, migrants have received such exposure prior to emigration.[13] Relatively few migrants add to existing skills or acquire new technical skills. Most receiving countries do not need significant numbers of skilled foreign workers; instead, they need workers able to fill mundane services jobs, do agricultural work, and do repetitive tasks. It is not usually in the employers' interest to offer foreign workers either skill-enhancement opportunities or formal technical training, and both practice and laws (in the South African system) reinforce this.

When technical skills are acquired by migrants, one of three things is most likely to occur (see Papademetriou, 1978, 1985a). First, the worker will often be reluctant to return home because of his or her economic integration into the host society. Migrants who acquire skills usually achieve occupational advancement, increased economic rewards, and social acceptance.

Second, if an industrial migrant worker returns, he or she is usually reluctant to engage in industrial work. The evidence on this point is incontrovertible in Europe and the Gulf states, although evidence from the Caribbean and Latin America is mixed because industrial jobs are not the dominant jobs for which these nationals are recruited. Evidence from Africa is even more complicated because overt racism and ethnic discrimination play a much larger role in determining an immigrant group's place in the host labor market. If a worker has acquired substantial new skills and holds a responsible position abroad, he or she might be unwilling to work in the home country at lower wages and inferior work conditions. Furthermore, migrants who return may no longer be interested in the vigors of industrial work, or may feel that they have paid their dues and prefer the independence of owning their own businesses, or may simply opt for semiretirement upon return.

Third, even if the migrant worker is neither reluctant to leave the host society nor to engage in industrial work at home, the skills that returning workers bring home are often irrelevant in the country of origin, which is not likely to have the type of technologically advanced industry that could use newly acquired technical skills. To this, one must add the possible reluctance of the home country's industrial management to offer responsible positions to returnees for fear that they may have been contaminated with syndicalist ideas while abroad (Papademetriou, 1982; 1985b).

The question of the utilization of remittances and transferred savings arouses even more controversy. Remittances do relieve some of the sending countries' balance of payments difficulties, and they do contribute to capital formation and to a country's per capita national income, but their role in promoting development is less clear. The significance of remittances can be demonstrated in several ways. Some authors have juxtaposed annual remittances for major labor exporters against such yardsticks as total invisible receipts, exports and imports, and foreign aid received (see Papademetriou, Chapter 11; Burki, Chapter 7; Thahane, Chapter 4; and Stahl and Habib, Chapter 8). Worker remittances from the Federal Republic of Germany alone, since the late 1950s, approach DM 150 billion (Papademetriou, 1985a). Pakistanis are thought to remit approximately $3 billion per year (Burki, Chapter 7). And the flow of irregular migrants to the United States involves the annual transfer of several billion dollars to Caribbean islands (Pastor, 1985b; Papademetriou and DiMarzio, 1986; Papademetriou, 1985c).

Such studies paint only a one-dimensional picture of remittances. To appreciate how remittances affect the overall structure of the remittance-assisted country, one must observe whether such funds are used productively, how such uses may be linked to other processes and larger social and economic activities, and what effect they might have on improving the living standards of the migrant household and the community's income distribution. (See Adler, 1980; 1985; Arizpe, 1981; Fergany, 1982; Hönekopp and Ullman, 1982; Penninx, 1982; Stahl, 1982; Fong and Lim, 1982; Galbraith, 1979; Gilani, 1983; Weiner, 1982.)

Remittances are spent in three major ways. First, remittances are used to invest in housing and land purchases, often accounting for as much as three-quarters of total remittances.[14] Remittances are also used to purchase consumer goods, retire debts, and carry out family-centered activities. Only a small fraction of the total goes into financial instruments and toward investment in such productive activities as the purchase of agricultural equipment and the financing of service-sector activities, such as opening small stores and service stations, or purchasing buses, trucks, and taxis.

Migrants use their earnings in a manner consistent with their reasons for migrating, but such spending behavior has unintended economic and social consequences. For example, investments in housing may distort the real estate market and be responsible for serious inflationary pressures in wages and building materials in the entire building sector. In a fairly typical situation, Burki (Chapter 7) reports that recent Pakistani inflation in building supplies is several times that of the country's commodity price index. Furthermore, housing construction has complex multiplier effects: it leads to high demand for building materials, but many of these items may have to be imported. Kirwan (1981) points out that construction has high multiplier effects, but only while it lasts. Hyperactive construction sectors in what are otherwise sputtering economies can cause severe distortions in labor and material costs in that sector, and often exacerbate social and economic inequalities as an inflated real estate market places the building or purchasing of a house beyond the reach of many citizens.[15] Together with similarly increasing costs for farmland, it is clear that one of the most important consequences of migration may be the creation of a new system of social stratification along the lines of migrant and nonmigrant households (see Balan, 1985; Diaz-Briquets, Chapter 9).

Second, migrant households often purchase consumer goods with relative abandon in a limited market, causing broad demand-pull and sometimes cost-push inflation. In some countries, migrant remittances are not substantial enough to affect internal markets (see Diaz-Briquets' discussion of Latin America, Chapter 9), but in most countries, inflation is clearly fueled by remittances.

Third, the increasing demand for luxury imports to satisfy substantial consumption appetites of migrant families often leads to similar behavior by nonmigrant households, as the latter have their consumption aspirations raised by the former. A corollary to these changing consumption patterns is the increased economic and psychological value of foreign products, so that foreign currency reserves must be used to import such products.

Migrant households spend their remittances in ways that are consistent with their reasons for migrating: to improve their living condition and enhance their overall social and economic status. Migrant spending may also eventually have cumulative impacts which increase farm productivity, create employment for members of nonmigrant households, and in the long run transform agrarian societies. While Massey and his associates found different traces of such migrant behavior in four communities in Mexico (1987), one should be cautious not to overgeneralize from these cases because these communities had been thoroughly immersed in the Mexico/U.S. migration stream for more than a generation in a manner which had created thriving binational communities in both countries. Migrants from these Mexican communities were imbedded socially and economically in Mexico, and treated work in the United States in a manner similar to that of some U.S. long-distance commuters who view their several-hour-long daily trek from rural counties to large metropolitan areas as a necessary evil for improving their economic life in their home areas.

The initial coincidence of interests between labor-scarce and labor-surplus societies gave rise to an enthusiasm for both organized and spontaneous labor migration, but hindsight shows that from the perspective of both sending and receiving societies, migration has had unexpected consequences. Migration is neither capable of correcting the underlying weaknesses of the socioeconomic structure of receiving societies nor can it provide a *substantial* and *sustained* impetus for the socioeconomic transformation of emigration countries. The major contribution of the migration process may thus be the progressive disappearance of national boundaries for labor and the transformation of labor into a structural component of the international political economy.

An Overview of the Issues

For most labor importers, the experiment with labor migration has been largely an economic success, though increasingly a social and political liability. Foreign workers provided the labor necessary to maintain economic growth during times of labor scarcities. As migration streams matured, however, the role of foreign labor in the host country's economy changes (Mehrlaender et al., 1981; Papademetriou et al., 1983). The labor supply becomes increasingly independent of demand, and foreign labor becomes entrenched in positions natives avoid, thus creating a structural dependence on foreign labor. With the liberalization of restrictions in such areas as family reunification and residence and work permits, receiving countries become de facto immigration nations, while paying lip service to the alleged temporariness of the foreign worker presence.

Permanence generates new problems. Second-generation migrants may have only a tenuous social and economic place in their country of residence. The social and cultural issues resulting from increasing racial, ethnic, and linguistic heterogeneity result in the politicization of migration. Migrants become more assertive of their social and economic rights, and natives react to rising infrastructure and social costs and to the perception that there is economic competition between migrant and native workers.

Labor-sending countries have also become aware that the return on their investment in migration has been limited. There have been dividends, such as relief from unemployment and remittances, but emigration has failed to provide a discernible and measurable development impetus. When large-scale emigration coincided with development, as in Italy (King et al., 1984; Calvaruso, 1984; Kubat, 1984), the basic ingredients for development predated the temporary emigration of labor. These ingredients include a large and diverse economy, a large and relatively modern agricultural sector which would not be starved for labor as a result of emigration, an already socially and politically mobilized population, a relatively effective system of private and public administration, a large and relatively modern infrastructure, and a financial system capable of channeling remittances to the private sector efficiently.

This is not to say that other emigration countries of worker origin have been unaffected. The economic progress of many sending countries has been influenced by remittances, but remittance transfers have not played a major role in the overall development of these countries. Remittances have played a role in agricultural mechanization, the housing boom, the proliferation of small service establishments, and the growth of tourist-related infrastructure. Migration has also accomplished at least one important goal: it has significantly improved the economic fortunes of many of the families of those who emigrated, and in some instances, of their communities.

Individuals benefitted from migration, but a look at the entire migration picture points to many missed opportunities. How can sending societies increase the benefits from migration? One way is by gaining better access to the markets of the receiving countries. Diaz-Briquets (Chapter 9) points out that the worst consequence of a severe recession in the receiving country is not the return flow of migrants,[16] but the loss of economic contacts between the two countries due to the economic contraction. The problem is felt most acutely in border areas throughout the Americas, where mutually dependent binational communities have flourished, but this problem has also appeared in the Gulf states (Seccombe, 1985).

Migrant-sending countries have won improved access to the markets of receiving societies. But can these closer links be traced directly to the migration relationship? Trade data from Europe show that the structure of trade between sending and receiving countries, although changing significantly over the course of the migration process, does not vary systematically with the proportion of migrants in a receiver's labor market. Furthermore, investment in sending countries also does not appear to be significantly affected by migration patterns. The Federal Republic of Germany had invested about $1 billion in Turkey by 1976, but this level of investment is roughly equal to that of France, which has few Turkish workers. Between 1952 and 1972, only about 12 percent of the entire Western European direct investment abroad went to countries of emigration.

The fact that investments in sending nations have not been particularly profitable is certainly one reason why they were not expanded. Finally the foreign investment patterns of countries that are primary receivers of another state's workers, such as the FRG and Greece or Turkey, have not changed significantly over the last two decades (Hiemenz and Schatz, 1979; Papademetriou, 1985a).

Even if they did not increase their investment in sending nations, some immigration nations have assisted migrants to pool their savings in order to invest in their home countries. The Federal Republic of Germany, for instance, has had such programs with Turkey, Yugoslavia, and Greece; France has attempted several variations of such training programs with Algerians, Spaniards, and Portuguese; and the Netherlands offers similar programs to workers from all of the sending countries (see Collaros and Moussourou, 1978; Gregory, 1978; Haberl, 1978; Kirwan, 1981; Mendez and Moro, 1976; Pennisi, 1981). The funds committed for these projects have been significant, but the total number of workers involved has been modest. Management failures and difficulties in obtaining sustained financing have made for few successful projects. One additional reason for the limited success of such programs is that sending countries have made only a few concerted efforts to assist migrant-led investments (see Martin, Chapter 2 for a discussion of the dilemmas associated with such assistance). The literature reports many isolated instances of such assistance programs for migrants, but most are not integral parts of a comprehensive development strategy.

Two other areas where public intervention might allow sending societies to capture some of the promised fruits of migration are use of remittances and return migration. As pointed out earlier, remittances stimulate aggregate demand, which may result both in cost-push and demand-pull inflationary pressures and, if returned migrants prefer imported goods, in a deteriorating balance-of-payments picture. Domestic capital markets rarely offer the necessary incentives to direct remittances toward productive activities, and the public sector often fails to provide the necessary direction for investment. Lesotho, for instance, is one of many labor exporters which denies its nationals the same preferential treatment it offers foreign investors (see Thahane, Chapter 4). Failures in public and private management militate against the optimal utilization of remittances. Migrants invest in construction because it remains the sector most actively supported by sending-country governments, which for reasons of social peace have offered incentives and concessions in building which are not provided to the rest of the economy.

As sending countries gain a better understanding of the forces impacting the development process, initiatives to integrate remittances and returnees into their economy and society will increase. What is also needed, however, is a better understanding of the place of each country in an increasingly interdependent world and the challenges and responsibilities which migration poses for governments at both ends of the flow. For example, receivers can manipulate the migrant inflow with some success, but they have been quite unsuccessful to influence the return flow. If receivers understood that return migration is often a noneconomic decision in which social and family factors dominate, then they might better achieve the objective of inducing returns—if and when that is indeed an objective—by improving the conditions in sending nations through special education programs, investments in infrastructure improvements, and employment-generating activities in cooperation with sending governments. Such initiatives recognize that the home community remains a primary reference point and a principal determinant of migrant behavior and that improvements there will have the important long-term effect of reducing emigration pressures. Cooperating with countries of worker origin can have the additional benefit of encouraging the departure of longer-term migrant workers: those most likely to have gained residence rights, those to be perceived as being in occupational competition with native workers, and, because of family reunification, those thought to place a burden both on infrastructure and on social services.[17]

The analytical complexity of migration stems from difficulties such as the failure to understand the social and political context of each flow; the paucity of reliable longitudinal data; the failure to anticipate the frequent incompatibility between individual and societal goals; the confusion between short-term and long-term benefits and liabilities; and the juxtaposition of economic benefits, which are usually tangible and immediate, and social and political costs which are much less discernible and appear in the future. These difficulties make causal ordering hard to specify, thus confusing source analysis with process analysis and leading to subjective and biased conclusions. The outcome is that our ability to predict migration flows and their impacts on receiving societies is still quite limited, as is our understanding of the linkages between emigration, return, and development.

NOTES

1. Germany fits this description most precisely, but France and Switzerland also employed large foreign populations during that time (see Papademetriou, 1983a).

2. Countries in Southern Europe, however, have not contributed substantial numbers of workers to the Arab countries. For religious, cultural, and political reasons, the Arabs have relied mostly on intraregional sources of labor from East and South Asia.

3. Asians have comprised the largest block of legal immigrants to the United States for about a decade. In the 1980s, that dominance reached absolute majority levels repeatedly.

4. One must note here that, traditionally, most English-speaking Caribbean emigration has been directed toward Great Britain. Economic uncertainty there, however, coupled with an increasingly hostile reception and an increasingly restrictive immigration policy (along with reforms in U.S. immigration policy) redirected that flow toward the United States in the last 20 years.

5. For example, how does immigration affect unemployment? To understand how immigrants affect unemployment, one must first disaggregate "unemployment" and "immigrants." In the United States, for example, some workers employed in what some economists call the "secondary labor market" may be likely to be adversely affected by

the competition of immigrants for low-pay, low-status, uncertain, or seasonal-duration work because most immigrants and refugees enter the U.S. labor market at that level. In such labor markets, there may be labor shortages because native workers avoid such jobs. Should destination countries require employers who offer jobs that natives shun to change or perhaps even eliminate some of these jobs, or should these countries admit immigrants and try to deal with the problems of native workers separately? Similarly, for some sending societies, the selectivity of emigration and the society's dependence on remittances may interfere with the ability to engage in sustained developmental initiatives and to exercise their full sovereign prerogatives which include the protection of their nationals that work abroad. The situation in Southern Africa demonstrates this point (see Thahane, Chapter 4).

6. A number of countries have repeatedly decried such losses. Among them one finds Jordan, Pakistan, North Yemen, Egypt, Ghana, and virtually all Caribbean island nations. Two recent surveys of Grenadan university graduates indicate that more than four out of five had emigrated, while less than one in twenty medical doctors stay on their island. The loss of managers, senior civil servants, and technical persons throughout the Caribbean is extremely severe (see Pessar, Chapter 10).

7. Opportunities for permanent legal immigration, however, have gradually shrunk throughout the world as traditional immigration countries seek to balance demands for family reunion by their newest residents and citizens with their own best judgments about current and future labor market needs and their international responsibilities to offer refuge to the displaced.

8. A term preferred by international agencies. Other terms denoting the same class of migrant are "illegal" and "undocumented."

9. The term *guestworkers* is most frequently used to refer to Europe's "temporary" labor system. *Seasonal workers* are found throughout the world and are employed in such activities as agricultural work, the tourist industry, etc.; Switzerland, Venezuela, France, and the United States are among the largest users of such labor. *Contract workers* denote labor arrangements which are usually for a finite duration and which occur within legal parameters involving both the country of origin and the country of destination. Migration to the oil-producing Gulf states and the South African labor migration system are the largest examples of this type of labor arrangement. The United States has also repeatedly relied on this type of labor through arrangements with Mexico and several Caribbean nations. Europe's experiment with foreign workers can also be said to fit under this rubric, as are arrangements involving intra-Eastern European labor exchanges. Finally, *circular workers* refer to the usually self-initiating journey in search of work in neighboring states undertaken by many African and Latin American migrants. Much of intra-less-developed country migration is of that last type, as are historical migration movements involving border cities.

10. Portes and Walton (1981) point out the many distinct aspects of both the dependency and the world-system schools. These range from the *dependentistas'* focus on the impact of core capital in peripheral countries, to their view of the internationalization of capital accumulation as a process beneficial to core nations as a whole, and the inhibition or perversion of the national development process by the penetration of international capital. The world-system school, on the other hand, views the international economy in terms of the expansion of core capital; further, it asseses the impact of imperial policies on the internal class structure of core countries; and, finally, it allows for the possibility

of development for semiperipheral countries (which, of course, occurs at the expense of their own working classes as well as of other, less developed actors) and for the theoretically important position that development cannot occur in isolation—although the ranking of states in the world-system can shift without altering the basic mechanisms of accumulation on a world scale. In any event, both schools focus on the distribution of power between states and classes, and both downplay the utility of the classical modernization approach, while stressing the process of state formation and the role of state policy in furthering imperialism and dependency (see Wallerstein, 1974; Cardoso, 1979; Frank, 1969).

11. Nowhere is this collusion of capital and the state apparatus starker than in South Africa. Thahane (Chapter 4) recounts a remarkable tale of thorough coordination between that country's extraction industry and the government designed to guarantee the former an adequate and pliant labor force and keep wages low while the government engaged in a policy of rapid transformation of the economy from an agricultural one to one of diversified industry and services. The initiatives created a monopsony system for labor from the region reinforced by "poll-taxes" and "pass laws," prohibitions against blacks purchasing land individually or communally or sharecropping, a "color bar" against the advancement and training of blacks in mine occupations, and a "whites only" policy for most nonmining occupations. In the 1960s, South Africa reinforced these controls by limiting recruitment through "Government Labor Bureaus," declaring South African blacks "foreign workers" needing special permission to work outside of mining, and weeding out those blacks from the surrounding areas who had gained permanent residence privileges.

12. Fergany (1983) reports that skill losses in North Yemen are so severe that in certain job categories wages are as high as in Saudi Arabia. Farraq (1987) reports similar, if isolated, examples for Egypt.

13. This is not to deny that this gain might not be more relevant for migrants originating in countries considerably less developed than most of those in the Mediterranean littoral and where, presumably, industrialization and the resulting proletarianization of the work force might be more marginal. In view of the discussion by Sassen-Koob (1984), however, and with the major exception of the African case, one might expect that the proletarianization of the work force usually precedes emigration.

14. This refers to the proportion of funds still available after the migrant households' basic needs, such as improved nourishment, health, and education costs for children, are met. How much is left will be determined by the size and economic condition of the household. In most cases involving African migrants (but also in many cases of Latin American, Caribbean and South Asian migrants), where the poorer households are involved in the migration stream, consumption can basically deplete remittances. As we have discussed elsewhere in this essay, this is as expected for survival migration.

15. In addition, it becomes much costlier for the public sector to finance the development of public housing and other infrastructure.

16. Return flows, whether voluntary or "encouraged," have been almost always far less severe than analysts had routinely predicted when economic or political conditions in the host country change significantly. With the exception of the very few recent outright expulsions (such as those of Nigerians by Ghana in the late 1960s, of Ghanaians and others by Nigeria twice in the 1980s, and of Salvadorans by Honduras in 1969), both migrants and hosts seem to be, in fact, willing to wait out the downturns. As a result,

when measures to entice and "assist" migrants with repatriation are taken, they have only the most modest of impacts.

17. This statement reflects the reality that in some instances, the economic benefits to the receivers associated with migration are overshadowed by perceptions of severe social and cultural costs.

2

Labor Migration: Theory and Reality

Philip L. Martin

Can labor migration accelerate development and thus make emigration self-stopping? There are two broad approaches to answer this question. The question could be interpreted to ask why any development process might cause disruptions which spur emigration, or it could be interpreted to ask how a history or tradition of migration from an area has affected development patterns and what kind of trade and investment programs might convert migrant remittances and worker returns into the kind of economic development which makes emigration unnecessary. An example of the development-migration linkage is to ask whether the expansion of the export-oriented fresh vegetable industry in northern Mexico which depends on migrant farmworkers from southern Mexico reduces or increases undocumented migration to the United States. An example of the migration-development linkage is to ask why four decades of migration from and remittances to Mexico's central highlands have not led to the kind of economic development which makes emigration from this region unnecessary.

Three quotes illustrate the spectrum of opinions about the benefits of worker migration to emigration countries:

> Migrants want to come; employers are eager to have them. The economic development to which they contribute is desirable. But instead there is the perversity of the present attitudes: the governments of the receiving countries seek to prevent the influx, those of the supplying countries deplore the exodus. Fortunately, the power of government in this matter is small so the movement continues. (Galbraith, 1979:222-23)

> The main economic benefits of emigration are far less certain than has been maintained hitherto. They may possibly be negative in the aggregate. (International Labor Organization [ILO], 1974:96)

I should also like to propose the establishment of an International Labor Compensatory facility ... [that] would draw its resources principally from labor-importing countries ... to [assist] developing labor exporting countries in proportions relative to the estimated cost incurred due to the loss of labor. (ILO, 1977:283)

Galbraith argues that laissez-faire is the best policy toward labor migration while the ILO notes that the benefits of exporting labor may be so chimerical that emigration countries should be compensated by the countries that import their workers.

This chapter focuses on the migration-development linkage. It reviews the theory of how recruitment, returns, and remittances are expected to generate economic development which makes emigration unnecessary, and why these three migration "R's" have usually been a case of good intentions gone awry in practice. The chapter focuses on practical programs and policies which can promote development without encouraging emigration, and concludes with a migration and development research agenda.

Most labor migration has its genesis in recruitment by employers or their agents from receiving nations. This recruitment creates information networks and economic dependencies that soon become institutionalized, a process which yields the aphorism that migration streams are much easier to start than to stop. For example, much of the illegal Mexican migration to the United States in the 1970s and 1980s can be traced to the recruitment of bracero farmworkers in Mexico's central highlands from the 1940s to the 1960s. Village families prospered from the external pipeline of remittances, but this private prosperity did not often produce economic multipliers which made it rational to stay at home. Indeed, the central lesson of the recruitment-network-development studies is that recruitment gets the migration network started; the network supplies the border crossing and job information to keep it going (without regard to the legal status of migrants abroad); and the private affluence but uneven and uncertain pace of skill and remittance-induced local development maintains the continuing economic rationale for emigration (Mines, 1982).

Major unresolved migration-development questions are why remittances have not accelerated development in emigration areas to reduce emigration pressures, and what kinds of mutually beneficial economic programs could reduce emigration. The conclusions of this chapter are mostly negative: that is, there is a long list of development patterns in emigration areas that did not reduce emigration pressures, and very few that did. The central policy conclusion is that there is no automatic process which converts skills and remittances into the kind of development which discourages emigration or, in other words, laissez-faire policies toward emigration regions usually guarantee continuing emigration pressures (Richards and Martin, 1983).

WORKER MIGRATION: AN OVERVIEW

Economic theory suggests that the international migration of labor is beneficial to sending and receiving nations because scarce resources (labor) are reallocated to a more efficient or higher wage use. For example, the Organization for Economic Cooperation and Development (OECD) noted that "Post-war European growth has been distinguished by the useful role played by migration" (OECD, 1978a:i). This "balanced growth" perspective sees migration for employment as a rational way to improve area or worldwide economic efficiency and output by transferring labor from surplus to shortage areas both within and across national borders. Rapid economic growth in Western Europe was threatened in the 1960s by labor shortages or an excess demand for labor, while Southern European nations had an excess labor supply. South-to-north labor migration permitted job vacancies in Western Europe to be filled without inflationary pressures or costly adjustments such as automation at home or investment abroad,[1] and labor migration eased the pressures and costs of Southern European unemployment and generated remittances to spur development.[2]

Balanced Growth

The notion that exporting labor can reduce economic differences between areas is termed balanced growth because the transfer of labor helps the emigration area to catch up economically to the immigration area. Economic theory promises a narrowing of income differences between emigration and immigration areas on several grounds; for example, the export of unemployed workers and the import of their remittance savings gives the labor-emigration area an extra boost which accelerates its development. Emigration should be self-stopping because wages rise as migrants leave and jobs are created with migrant remittances.

The balanced growth theory views labor as an exportable resource: unemployed labor can be exported directly via emigration, or exported indirectly in the form of goods and services if production facilities or tourism centers are established in the areas with unemployed labor. In either case, the remittances or revenues derived from exporting labor from the area improve living standards, hasten economic development, and eventually make emigration unnecessary. Emigration is usually a much faster and surer way to provide employment and wages to unemployed workers in lagging areas than top-down foreign aid, and emigration was embraced as a mutually beneficial process by most of the labor surplus and labor deficient European nations during the 1960s.

The standard textbook treatment of migration asserts that migration is controversial because, even though both sending and receiving countries gain, there are winners and losers in each country. In receiving countries, employers (owners of capital) and skilled (complementary) workers gain, while unskilled (competing) workers see their wages depressed.[3] In sending nations, employers lose and unskilled workers gain. Thus, economic theory suggests that free(er) migration is akin to free trade: it is economically desirable, and opponents of free migration are really trying to protect their narrow economic interests.

Economists have contributed little to the debate over international worker migration because the theory is so clearcut. For example, Greenwood (1983:177) asserts that "economists have generally taken the position that migration is beneficial to countries of emigration," although he concedes that two issues need further study: "the effects of remitted earnings on countries of emigration . . . [and] the effects of skills learned abroad by migrants who later return to a poor country." A recently published international economics textbook notes that opposition to labor migration mostly involves protecting economic self-interests (in labor-receiving countries), and then says that "cultural opposition" to immigrants in host nations is often used to cloak this economic protectionism. This text goes on to note that there may be legitimate concerns about admitting poor immigrants if host governments guarantee minimum levels of housing, education, and other social services to migrant workers whose skills may not enable them to earn enough to make work an attractive alternative to welfare in the host nation (Yarbrough and Yarbrough, 1988).

Economists prescribed free labor migration as a natural analogue to free trade, and this anticipation of a world with barriers at borders was reflected in the statements of international organizations. For example, the 1949 Migration for Employment Recommendation of the International Labor Organization stated: "It should be the general policy of Members [countries] . . . to facilitate the international distribution of manpower and in particular the movement of manpower from countries which have a surplus to those that have a deficiency" (para. 4(1)).

The concept that economic growth should not be slowed in one (rich) country for lack of labor, if labor could be "borrowed" from another (poor) country, was soon adopted by other international organizations, such as the Organization for European Economic Cooperation (OEEC) in 1953 (now the Organization for Economic Cooperation and Development), and the European Economic Community in 1957. Abadan-Unat notes that "the assumption was widespread that the largely government-promoted exodus of workers from the Mediterranean basin was beneficial, and totally so, to these countries" (1976:2).

Mutual benefits was the theme of most 1960s assessments of migration for employment in Europe.[4] However, during the early 1970s, recession and stagflation, combined with the perception that the sociopolitical costs of absorbing the increased number of settled foreigners were rising in Western Europe, prompted a general stop to labor recruitment and a reassessment of the benefits and costs of labor migration. The economic turnaround was sudden: in the Federal Republic of Germany in 1973, there were three job vacancies for each unemployed person. By 1975, there were almost five unemployed persons for each job vacancy. Labor-importing nations worried about foreigners working while natives were unemployed and about the costs of integrating the foreign 5 to 10 percent of their work forces and populations. Labor-exporting nations were upset by unilateral decisions to stop recruitment in the middle of ambitious development plans which assumed that emigration and remittances would continue.

These mutual worries led to reassessments that were often critical of immigration countries. Immigration nations made decisions to stop recruitment unilaterally, and even though the recruitment bans were accompanied by measures which relaxed family unification rules and otherwise promoted the integration of foreigners who wanted to remain in Western Europe indefinitely, labor-sending countries complained that they were not consulted. An OECD report issued in 1978, for example, was quite critical of these unilateral Western European decisions to stop recruiting foreign workers:

> Restrictions on international labour flows are simply an obvious form of protection. The policy is intended to protect domestic jobs, wages, and the "integrity" of social transfer systems, in the face of cutbacks in demand for labour, public budgets, and medium-term growth prospects. The costs of these decisions— potential inflationary pressures due to continued lack of responsiveness of domestic wages to international competitive pressures, growing job vacancies in certain sectors or occupations, illegal or "black" markets, the failure of new labour and capital markets to develop within the OECD area, for example—may not have been given adequate consideration. (OECD, 1978a:2)

The OECD report argued that restricting labor migration to Western Europe has or will reduce overall economic efficiency or output. Stopping labor migration, in this balanced growth view, thus makes it more difficult for emigration nations to assist themselves and generates less wealth in immigration nations to share with them.

Even though immigration restrictions reduce economic growth, the OECD report concluded that there would not be a revival of large-scale migration between the OECD nations. The report instead outlined a number of measures to promote job-creating growth in labor surplus areas, such as having host nations invest in emigration countries and provide reinsertion funds for returning migrants, but its major recommendation was that OECD nations seek to maximize employment and to reduce economic differences within the entire OECD area, so that there would not be large-scale migration from poor to rich nations. The report also called for more consultation between receiving and sending country governments, so that one country would not stop labor migration without creating employment in an emigration area.

Asymmetric Development

An alternative to this balanced growth theory that labor migration reduces inequalities between sending and receiving areas is a theory of asymmetries. Balanced growth studies tend to be macro focused, emphasizing the importance of remittances in a nation's balance of payments or the savings to the emigration country implicit in not having to invest $50,000 or more to create each job at home that is held by a migrant abroad. Asymmetric studies, on the other hand, usually examine village or area economies in order to determine how emigration affected the area's economic trajectory.

Most village and area studies support the asymmetric hypothesis that migration for employment increases inequalities or differences between sending and receiving areas rather than diminishing them, as the balanced growth vision suggests. This means that, instead of emigration and remittances priming an area for an economic takeoff, the remittances are a "fortune in small change" which widen rather than reduce differences between emigration and immigration areas (Penninx, 1982). The asymmetric studies argue that the existing economic structure did not generate sufficient jobs and development before emigration began, and that remittances and returning migrants reinforce the trends which prevent a take-off. The reasons why emigration does not produce an economic take-off are many. Returned workers do not return to the sending area or they do return but use remittances nonproductively, for example, to speculate on real estate or to imitate a successful service such as a delivery service, a taxi, or a shop. Many returned migrants retire upon their return, asserting that they are too exhausted from hard work abroad to work at home. The skills learned abroad may not be useful back home because the emigration area's economy or technology is different. Emigration in the extreme may distort development. Young children, for example, may not stay in school if the wage for unskilled work abroad is several times the wage for skilled work at home. Asymmetric studies criticize emigration because it allegedly distorts and perhaps slows development in the migrants' areas of origin (Abadan-Unat, 1976; Penninx, 1982; Schiller, 1976).

There are many reasons why asymmetries which increase inequalities between sending and receiving areas seem to dominate the factors encouraging balanced growth. Labor recruitment tends to attract skilled, ambitious, and often employed workers so that, instead of recruiting persons whose economic contributions will not be missed, recruitment attracts the workers needed to make an area take off economically. The vacancies created by emigrants are not always filled by the unemployed who remain behind, so economic development may slow down.

Second, many researchers find that remittances tend to have minimal long-term development multipliers because they are more apt to be spent on housing, land, or imported consumer durables than invested in enterprises which use local inputs or otherwise foster the backward or forward production linkages which would increase local employment. The empirical literature is replete with references to the "nonproductive" use of remittances for land purchases, for gold, for dowries, or for taxis and other service sector enterprises. Finally, the settlement abroad of the best and brightest from an emigration area can make migration "cumulative and self-perpetuating" (Abadan-Unat, 1976:384), in the sense that people leave an area because it is less developed and then remittances and returns reinforce the dependence of the area on an external labor market. The pessimistic conclusion of most empirical studies is that "without vigorous measures many potentially favorable effects of migration on the home country will not materialize, while many adverse ones will" (Abadan-Unat,1976:386).

The balanced growth theory argues that because emigration provides some of the strategic factors needed for an economic take-off, such as capital from outside the area, then remittances will in fact ensure an economic takeoff (Penninx, 1982:782-83). However, empirical researchers find that there is no law which automatically converts emigration, remittances, and returns into economic development, so that studies which stop with the identification of apparent contributors to development—the relief of unemployment or an influx of remittances and returned workers—overlook the tendency of the emigrants to be "needed" at home, for remittances to be "squandered," or for the training that was received abroad to be useless upon return (Penninx, 1982:783-84).

Roger Böhning's review (1984) of European labor migration patterns and policies in the 1950s and 1960s led him to conclude that actual worker migration policies and patterns evolved in ways that maximized the benefits of worker migration to receiving nations. According to Böhning, it was not until the 1973–74 "recruitment stops" throughout Northern Europe that labor emigration nations such as Italy, Greece, and Yugoslavia asked the ILO and OECD to reassess the benefits of worker emigration to sending nations. The major conclusion of the reassessment studies was that the remittance and returning skills benefits of temporary labor migration were far less likely to be realized in sending nations than had been assumed, and that temporary worker migration in Europe had widened, rather than decreased, inequalities between sending and receiving nations (OECD, 1975; 1978a).

The mid-1970s reassessment of emigration's "real" benefits to labor-exporting nations prompted calls for government-to-government agreements that would make emigration and remittances part of the sending country's development plan. For example, the 1976 ILO World Employment Conference adopted a nonbinding Program of Action which recommended that recruitment be organized by bilateral and multilateral government-to-government agreements which are "based upon the economic and social needs of the countries of origin and the countries of employment." Paragraph 42 states that migrant worker agreements should "even out fluctuations in migration movements, remittances, and returns in order to make worker migration a predictable and continuous part of sending country development programs" (Böhning, 1984:9). This ILO recommendation was a response to the experiences of some labor exporters such as Turkey, whose 1972–77 Five Year Plan anticipated the "export" of 350,000 workers. However, the 1973–74 European-wide halt to labor recruitment meant that Turkey exported just 250,000 workers during this period (Kubat, 1979:249).

International worker migration is thus, in many instances, a case of good intentions gone awry. Emigration generates important benefits in labor-exporting nations, such as relieving domestic unemployment, remittances, and obtaining a more-skilled work force. But there are also costs to labor exporters, such as in-opportune recruitment stops, inflationary remittances in good times and re-duced remittances when they are needed most, and workers returning with skills for which there is no market in the sending nation. Disappointment may have been less pronounced if labor migration had not been trumpeted as a pana-cea for development dilemmas (Papademetriou, 1978). A central conclusion of the migration and development literature is that it is very easy to overestimate the benefits of exporting workers (Martin, 1980).

Opponents of immigration controls in labor-importing countries have sug-gested that generous and interventionist foreign assistance policies might steer sending-country development in directions which reduce emigration pressures (National Council on Employment Policy, 1976; Cornelius, 1978). However, few labor-importing nations have contributed enough foreign assistance or in-tervened enough abroad to reduce emigration pressures. Morrison (1982) reviewed assistance, trade, and investment policies to reduce emigration pres-sures and concluded that the linkages between such policies and migration are small, indirect, and only felt in the long run.

MIGRATION AND DEVELOPMENT: THEORY

What does economic theory have to say about how development processes af-fect migration pressures? There are several distinct types of theory which might illuminate migration-development linkages. The international trade literature emphasizes the rapid growth in world trade and the resulting interdependence of industrial economies, that is, the worldwide character of economic cycles.

The basic international trade model suggests that countries should specialize in the production of goods for which they have a comparative advantage. Comparative advantage is usually linked to abundant supplies of capital, labor, or land, so that Hong Kong should specialize in labor-intensive manufacturing and Canada in wheat production. Comparative advantage may also result from a combination of factor supplies and climate (California fruits and vegetables), a reputation for quality or reliability (French wine and German machine tools), or technological sophistication (U.S. aviation products). The factor-price-equaliza-tion-theorem suggests that free trade will eventually equalize factor prices (e.g., wages) even if there is no labor migration between countries. However, wages will equalize only if there are no trade barriers such as tariffs and there are no nontraded goods, such as haircuts or hotel room cleaning.

In the basic trade model, endowments or quantities of capital, labor, and land are fixed for each country, and there is no technological progress in how goods are produced. The classic economic model of intercountry labor migration can be illustrated simply: labor moves from lower to higher wage countries, total economic output rises, but the lower wage country experiences higher wages and lower output. In Figure 2.1, if all workers are paid the value of their marginal product, and there are initially 10 million Turks employed in Turkey at a wage

Figure 2.1
Gainers and Losers from Labor Migration

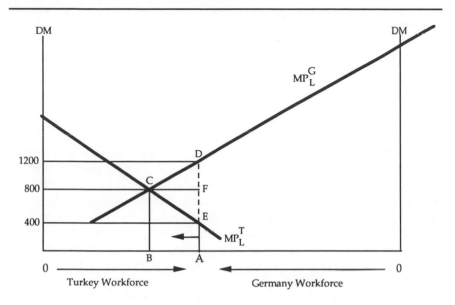

Labor is assumed to be more productive in Germany than in Turkey, as
illustrated by the marginal productivity curves (MP). At A, 10 million Turks are
employed in Turkey at a wage of 400 DM per month (E) and 20 million Germans
are employed in the FRG at a wage of 1200 DM per month (D). The migration of
2 million Turks to the FRG, the movement from A to B decreases employment in
Turkey to 8 million, raises Turkish wages and reduces German wages to 800 DM
at C, and increases employment in the FRG to 22 million. What is the effect of
this migration? German (world) output increases by CDE, of which CFE goes to
the migrants. The 2 million migrants who used to earn 80 million DM monthly
in Turkey now earn 160 million DM in the FRG. The total Turkish wage bill
increases from 400 million DM to 640 million DM; the total German wage bill
falls from 24 billion DM to 17.6 billion DM. The migrants gain, and so do
German capital owners and stay-at-home Turkish workers. German workers
and Turkish capital owners lose.

equivalent to DM 400 per month, the Turkish wage bill is DM 400 million per
month. In Germany, assume there are initially 20 million German workers each
paid DM 1200 per month, and the German wage bill is DM 24 billion monthly. In
Figure 2.1, Turkey's labor market is at E and Germany's is at D when there is a
three-to-one wage gap.

What happens if 2 million Turkish workers migrate to Germany? If productivity is unchanged in both countries, there may be a new equilibrium at C, so that
22 million workers (20+2) in Germany earn DM 800 monthly and 8 million

workers (10−2) in Turkey also earn DM 800 monthly. In this example of labor migration equalizing wages in the two countries, the Turkish wage bill increases 60 percent and the German wage bill falls 27 percent. Clearly, if Germany was the economy which could absorb additional labor, and Turkey had surplus labor, labor migration increased German and decreased Turkish output.

The total output of the two countries increases by the triangle CDE because the labor which moves from Turkey to Germany is more productive in Germany. However, Germany gains and Turkey loses: profits in Germany increase as wages decrease, and profits in Turkey decrease as wages increase. German workers lose, and Turkish workers who stay at home gain.

Economic analysis of migration from low- to high-wage areas emphasizes the net gain to total output ("the world") because workers shift from low- to high-wage (productivity) jobs. Most economic analyses attribute opposition to immigration in receiving countries to unions opposed to wage-depressing additional workers and to governments concerned about importing unskilled workers who may be tempted to forsake low-wage and unpleasant jobs for a life of welfare. Sending-country governments sometimes oppose emigration because they fear that brawn and brain drains may lead to bottlenecks that impede their development and because the sending society may lose its investment in the education and training of the migrants.

More sophisticated attempts to model labor migration have yielded few additional insights. Ethier (1985) develops a model of lower-wage migrants who are partial substitutes for native workers, and then shows that an immigration country producing an export good can keep the native work force fully employed by sending migrants home when export demand and prices fall. Alternatively, the goods-exporting country could keep its factories operating at full capacity by substituting cheaper migrants for native workers and thus lower export prices enough to stimulate export demand. Ethier's model rests on two assumptions that European immigration countries try to avoid. In Ethier's model, migrants get lower wages than similar native workers, and migrants are at least partial substitutes for native workers, that is, there is some displacement of natives by migrants.

Most economic analyses stop with this static analysis, which concludes that migration benefits "the world," helps individual migrants and their employers (owners of capital), but may hurt employers in sending countries and competing workers in receiving countries. Such analysis does help to explain why many employers favor and most unions oppose imported labor, but does not explain other arguments against rich countries recruiting labor from poor countries. Additional arguments in receiving countries against importing workers include the possible adverse effects of too much labor on technological progress, the effects of importing low-wage workers on domestic underclass and economic inequalities, and the effects of a large number of resident immigrants on cultural and national identity, such as language differences.

Sending-country opposition to emigration emanates from nationalistic frustration at not creating enough jobs for citizens; from the theory-defying increased inequalities between nations despite the movement of workers from low- to high-wage areas; and from concerns that remittances are "glittering coins" which do not really promote economic development. Sending-country opposition to emigration is usually associated with nationalistic intellectuals who believe that richer countries take advantage of developing nations: most migrants and most finance ministers, by contrast, welcome the opportunity to generate earnings abroad. There is usually enough un- and underemployed labor in developing countries so that the sending-country employers who should complain about emigration-induced wage hikes do not.

MIGRATION AND DEVELOPMENT: REALITY

The major effects of worker emigration on development are linked to the three R's of recruitment, returns, and remittances. The theory is that un- and underemployed workers will be recruited to work abroad; the reality is that recruiting employers both prefer, and are likely to obtain, workers who are employed at home. As might be expected, an employer seeking auto assemblers at prevailing union wages in an industrial country can and probably prefers to attract skilled and employed workers in the sending country. As a result, German autos are often assembled by Turkish mechanics and California builders have Mexican carpenters working as laborers or helpers. Skilled employees are usually in short supply in developing countries;[5] if too many emigrate, developing countries can face spot labor shortages which cause their factories to be even less efficient or which slow down construction projects. Many emigration countries have 20 to 40 percent of their populations engaged in farming; there is sometimes enough recruitment of skilled urban workers, followed by secondary migration from rural to urban areas, to cause farm production to decline. In at least one instance (the Yemen Arab Republic), emigration has meant that maintenance on terrace and irrigation systems has been abandoned, so that restoring previous levels of food production after two decades of emigration would require massive infrastructure investments.

Recruitment

Worker recruitment eventually creates networks which link cities or villages in the sending nation to labor markets in the receiving nation. These networks become valuable assets because they control access to foreign jobs which pay five to ten times local wages. Potential migrant workers are often willing to borrow money to pay for the visas or to go abroad and work at these higher wages. When emigration is organized and legal, such as under the H-2 (now H-2A) program for Jamaicans and other British West Indians in certain segments of U.S. agriculture or the migration between South and Southeast Asia and Saudi Arabia in the late 1970s, migrants sometimes pay bribes to government or private go-betweens in order to be selected to work abroad. If official recruitment is centralized, it spurs internal migration to the recruitment locations and, since there is typically a surplus of migrant job seekers, it generates a local day-labor market offering jobs to workers who are waiting to become migrants.

If recruitment is unofficial, the emigration is private and often illegal and the job network becomes a semipublic asset of the village whose "pioneers" are or have been working abroad. Such private-illegal networks link many U.S. farms and factories with Mexican villages, and recruitment involves an already employed migrant arranging with a U.S. employer for the employment of his family and friends, informing them of the arrangement, often helping to finance the trip, and advising them how to get across the border and to the work site. Once in the United States, the already employed migrant usually helps to arrange housing and transportation, and often trains and is otherwise responsible for the new employee in the work place (Frisbie, 1975; Mines, 1982). Such networks are semipublic in the sense that migration information spreads throughout the village, so that villages in very similar economic circumstances can send very different proportions of their workers abroad because of their differential access to such a network (OECD, 1978b).

There are a variety of recruitment mechanisms which move migrant workers across borders; there is no consensus on the best migrant recruitment mechanism. One reason for the variety of recruitment arrangements is that there is little agreement on the roles of governments, employers, and migrants in recruitment. At one extreme are those who argue that international labor migration should be regulated by government-to-government agreements, and that labor-receiving countries sensitive to the needs of sending countries should permit the sending countries to arrange recruitment so that it minimizes internal disruptions. At the other extreme are the employers who prefer to hire the best migrant workers, even if this means "creaming" the sending country's work force and leaving behind production bottlenecks. Much of the discussion and actual recruitment falls somewhere between these extremes. The issues to be resolved include whether and how to regulate public and private migrant recruitment agencies, whether fees or taxes might be levied on migrants and for what purpose, and what selection mechanism should be used to select migrants. For example, should emigration countries develop formulas that favor unemployed persons from a poor area and disfavor potential migrants with "critically needed" skills?

Sending countries have ambiguous policies toward returns. Their general stance is that they favor the return of their human capital, but not right now. Sending countries are not usually in a position to encourage returns with financial incentives, so incentives to return usually begin in receiving countries. However, return carrots have not induced many returns: French, German, and other European host countries that offered lump-sum social security and other payments to returning migrants appear to have attracted mostly persons who were planning to return in any event.

Remittances

Remittances are the raison d'être for migration. Remittances are immediate, private, and flexible. At the macro level, remittances are a source of hard currency that can be used to purchase needed foreign components and supplies, spent locally to generate jobs, or taxed by the sending country government. The private nature of many remittances makes it hard to calculate their exact magnitude, but remittances worldwide may be as high as $50 billion annually.

Remittances clearly improve the economic welfare of individual migrants and their families. Initially, remittances provide money for daily living and debt repayment, then consumer durables, and finally funds to invest in better housing, land, or a small business. Remittance levels are often maintained over time because the settlement abroad which encourages migrants to remit less is offset partially by their ever-higher earnings which permit migrants to remit more.

A central puzzle is why remittances so rarely promote enough development in an emigration area to make emigration unnecessary. A vast literature notes that many migrants spend remittances on imported consumer durables and cars, minimizing local job multipliers. Money spent on better housing has mostly a one-shot job multiplier, and there is widespread criticism of remittances used to speculate on and inflate land prices, bride prices, and housing prices. Since migrants typically come from relatively few areas within a country, remittance-induced inflation is also concentrated in these areas, making nonmigrant families in these areas worse off because they must pay the higher prices wrought by remittance-induced inflation without remittance assistance. It is in this inflation sense that emigration increases inequalities within sending nations.

How could remittances be converted into migration-reducing development? The major lesson from emigration countries is that dispersed remittances will not automatically create self-sustaining economic activity. If remittances are to be the external pump which primes an area for an economic take-off, they need to be coordinated to provide the infrastructure necessary for development or sending governments must find additional funds to invest in infrastructure. Lack of infrastructure helps to explain why a visitor can drive over dusty roads to villages which have a few very nice houses built with remittances—houses for which their owners must sometimes make arrangements for their own power supply because the rest of the village is without electricity. Without a mechanism to share remittances and construct infrastructure, emigration areas become examples of Galbraith's "private affluence and public squalor," but in this case the lack of infrastructure can squander an opportunity for development (Galbraith, 1957).

Remittances and development are often another example of good intentions gone awry. Remittances do make individual migrants and their families better off, but they are rarely the spark which creates enough economic activity to make emigration unnecessary. The lessons of experience seem to present sending nations with a Hobson's choice: do they assume that remittances will "take care of" emigration areas and focus their development efforts elsewhere, or do they take their limited development funds and try to use them to maximize the development payoff from remittances? The neglect strategy makes emigration areas ever more dependent on an external labor market, as in Mexico's central highlands; the subsidize-the-remittances strategy increases regional inequalities within emigration nations.

Returns

Returns are the third major parameter of worker migrations. Generally, organized legal labor migrations involve employer-migrant contracts which stipulate the duration of stay abroad, while illegal labor migrations have no such announced return policies. Generally, sending and receiving governments organize or tolerate worker migrations expecting "100 percent" returns. However, there is an inevitable leakage into permanent residence in the receiving countries. The rate of leakage depends primarily on a mix of receiving country policies, internal controls and enforcement, and opportunities in the sending country. Saudi Arabia's employment of Korean and other Asian migrants probably stands at the minimal leakage end of the spectrum, and U.S.-Mexican or Venezuelan-Colombian migration probably stands near the other end. The European nations are somewhere in the middle: they initially enforced the rotation of guestworkers, but over time they tolerated the conversion of temporary workers into permanent residents. The European experience is the source of the aphorism that "there is nothing more permanent than temporary workers," a reference to employer addiction to imported workers and the tendency in an industrial democracy to gradually break down the barriers which encouraged migrant returns in order to avoid the development of a class of helots.

MIGRATION AND DEVELOPMENT: THE RESEARCH AGENDA

Migrant recruitment, remittances, and returns have rarely led to a job-creating economic take-off in migration areas which naturally reduced emigration pressures. Instead, most emigration areas have become dependent on an external labor market for jobs and remittances. For example, folk wisdom in Mexican emigration areas advises the young to work in the United States but to "live" or enjoy life in Mexico (Mines, 1982).

The research agenda centers on the three "R's" of recruitment, remittances, and returns. How can the legal recruitment which initiates most subsequent migration minimize the emigration of a developing country's best and brightest? Is it an undue interference with employer and individual rights to restrict initial emigration to unskilled or unemployed workers in certain regions? Should limits on immigration be established so that emigration areas do not become depleted of skilled labor and too dependent on an external labor market and remittances?

A major recruitment question is whether government-to-government recruitment programs are better than private arrangements. That is, if there is to be legal labor emigration, should it be regulated by a government-to-government arrangement in order to maximize migration's developmental contributions? If the answer is yes, should recruitment regulations involve a selection formula to minimize disruptions, so that recruitment is, for example, restricted to certain areas, ages, and skill levels? If such a system is desired, is there sufficient knowledge of how migration is linked to development to write such recruitment regulations and, even if agreed to by receiving-country employers, can they be enforced?

The second major issue is the remittance-development linkage. Once again, the literature suggests that a laissez-faire policy improves the lives of migrants and their families but does not necessarily promote the kind of economic development which makes emigration unnecessary. The literature thus suggests that governments might tax or otherwise marshall a portion of migrant remittances, invest in infrastructure, and provide technical assistance to promote job-creating development.

There are many practical problems with asking labor-sending governments to channel remittances. First, most migrants will resist sharing their remittances with their governments; cynics suggest that one reason labor-sending countries prefer government-to-government recruitment agreements is to expedite the collection of exit and remittances taxes. A few countries understand that efforts to tax remittances (and a failure to maintain a stable currency) wind up keeping migrant savings in the host country. Remittances illustrate the chicken-egg problem inherent in the migration-development dilemma: the same factors which encourage emigration discourage the investments necessary for job-creating development, and government efforts to reinvigorate or redirect investment and development by taxing or channeling remittances are viewed with understandable suspicion by the migrants. Research is needed on better ways to channel remittances privately to promote development, and on how to link international grants and loans with remittances to foster job-creating development.

The third "R" is returns: how can the skills of returning workers best promote job-creating development at home? The literature suggests that many migrants do not acquire skills abroad which are useful at home because they may be employed in factories which use machinery and technologies not available at home. Other skills may have low at-home returns because they are well-paying only abroad, such as domestic household work, landscaping, or janitorial service work. However, there are a substantial number of migrants employed in construction, manufacturing, and service jobs which have the potential to transmit skills useful at home.

The literature suggests that some migrants acquire skills abroad that are used when they return. However, a leitmotiv in the literature is that migrants want to save money while working abroad in order to have a different job back home, so that the U.S. assembly-line migrant wants to buy a taxi or delivery truck in Mexico and not be a factory operative in Mexico City. There has been discussion at the ILO and several initiatives in Europe that provide training for soon-to-depart migrants which would be more useful in their home countries (Gendt, 1977). However, there seems to be little enthusiasm on the part of host nations to provide such training and on the part of migrants to participate.

What is to be done? Most studies of migration-development linkages conclude with a plea for more aid and cooperation to accelerate economic development and to curb emigration pressures. It is hard to argue with such pleas: the problem is that they do not provide models or experience for labor-sending and receiving nations to actually reduce emigration pressures.

NOTES

1. Lutz (1963) emphasized how selective immigration made adjustments in relative wages unnecessary in postwar Europe. As native workers abandoned industries and occupations with low productivity growth and low wages, selective immigration filled the job vacancies with migrants and thus obviated adjustments in relative wages which would have brought labor supply and demand into equilibrium without migration.

2. Kindleberger (1967) distinguished between the static and dynamic advantages of emigration. The static advantages include remittances; the disadvantages include production bottlenecks caused by selective emigration. Kindleberger's dynamic advantages include higher incomes for the families of migrants, the training of migrants abroad, and the transfer of labor with a low or zero productivity in agriculture to relatively high-wage jobs abroad.

3. Some industries which may disappear without immigrant workers preserve jobs for skilled and unskilled workers. If the workers whose jobs are preserved by immigrants become and remain unemployed—a result not anticipated in this economic theory—then the jobs-preserving benefits of immigrant workers may outweigh the depressed wage losses.

4. Böhning (1975:251) notes that the governor of the Bank of Greece expressed doubts about how beneficial labor migration was in the mid-1960s, and that both Finnish and outside authorities concluded that labor emigration to Sweden had negative consequences for Finland.

5. The skilled worker wage premium is often less in developing than in developed nations.

Part II

Labor Migration and Development in Africa

Part II reviews the effects of labor migration in Africa. Chapter 3 summarizes labor migration patterns in sub-Saharan Africa, where the distinction between internal and international migration is blurred. Ineffective border controls and arbitrary national boundaries push some traditional migrations into the international sphere, as when Kenyans cross the Tanzanian border daily to work on their farms. African labor migration is distinguished by its undocumented character, its cyclical and seasonal patterns, and the dominance of migrants from neighboring countries. The reasons for migrating vary, but uneven development generates large and fluctuating wage differences that encourage migration. Ghana, which imported labor until the 1960s, had 25 percent of its work force abroad by the early 1980s, reflecting deteriorating economic conditions in Ghana. There have also been expulsions of migrant workers. Ghana expelled Nigerians in 1969, and Nigeria expelled Ghanians in 1983.

Some African migration is survival migration. For example, half of Lesotho's males are employed in South Africa, and their remittances are the major source of government revenue. Adepoju argues that even if emigration is the only way to secure employment in such countries, sending communities do not experience accelerated development because the ambitious workers are abroad. Remittances are substantial, but it appears that a high fraction are spent to maintain migrant households. Returned migrants have been agents of socioeconomic change in a few countries, but the migrants that earn the most (as miners) are also those most likely to retire at age 35 or 40, after 15 years in the mines. Labor-importing countries have gradually tightened restrictions on migrant workers, so that borders have become more important barriers to migration in Africa.

In Chapter 4, Thahane explores labor migration in the 11-nation Southern Africa region (Angola, Botswana, Lesotho, Malawi, Mozambique, Namibia, South Africa, Swaziland, Tanzania, Zambia, and Zimbabwe). South Africa, with one-third of the region's population, has a history of reliance on "foreign" workers. Thahane recounts how native Africans lost their land to white settlers, and then found that working for wages in white-owned mines or on white-owned farms was the only employment option. The countries that continue to rely heavily on South African mines for employment—Botswana, Lesotho, Malawi, Mozambique, and Swaziland—are dissatisfied with the effects of migration on their own development, but seem to be unable to break the cycle of migration and stagnation.

Thahane concludes that South Africa has been the major beneficiary of the labor migration patterns that its mines and farms established and continue to control. Numerous advisors have attempted to assist the major labor exporters to reduce their dependence on the South African labor market, but with limited success. The pessimistic picture painted by Thahane suggests that the development patterns shaped by migration in Southern Africa will be very difficult to alter without massive external assistance.

3

Binational Communities and Labor Circulation in Sub-Saharan Africa

Aderanti Adepoju

This chapter has five sections. The introduction is followed by an outline of the major migratory flows in Africa and a summary of the unique circumstances in the region. Section three is devoted to the causes of emigration and the strategies that guide migration decision processes in Africa. The effects of emigration on the sending country's development are discussed in section four and focus on three issues: employment, remittances, and return migration. The final section deals with policy challenges and summarizes key findings.

Africa is heterogeneous with respect to its population, land area, ecological features, political processes, resource endowment, and economic development. Resources, employment, and income-earning opportunities are not evenly distributed between and within its countries and subregions. Indeed, there exists a great variation between the relatively prosperous coastal economies and those in the savannah hinterland, especially the Sahel region, whose countries are some of the world's poorest. In fact, sub-Saharan African countries may be grouped into two economic zones: the oil-exporting, relatively richer countries (Nigeria, Gabon, Angola, Congo, Zaire, Ivory Coast); and the non-oil-exporting and lesser-developed countries. The oil exporters are the attraction for migrants within the region (E.C.A., 1981; World Bank, 1981).

Data on international migration within Africa are scarce. Although the literature has grown and improved considerably, most of the research on international migration centers on the Southern African region. What distinguishes international migration in Africa is the blurring of the distinction between internal and international migration and the ineffective policing of the long national frontiers. The absence of natural geographical barriers and the arbitrary setting of borders which cut across homogeneous social and ethnic groups make the distinction between internal and international migration difficult to make. Hence, some migration that elsewhere would be classified as internal in Africa occurs across national frontiers.

MAJOR MIGRATORY FLOWS IN AFRICA: INTERNAL OR INTERNATIONAL MIGRATION

The types, volume, and direction of international migration in Africa are closely related to the continent's complex historical and political experiences as well as to its economic structures. A number of factors have generated both economic migrants and refugees in Africa. Among them are colonial rule, the artificial boundaries demarcating socially homogeneous units into separate states, the complementary economic conditions and strong economic links with colonial countries, the politics of independence and the postindependence struggle for leadership, and the ecological deterioration in most parts of Africa (Adepoju, 1984a).

Migration in the sub-Saharan region was initially associated with trade, slavery, evangelism, nomadism, and internecine warfare. In most of the region, colonial rule altered both the causes and nature of such movements, institutionalized some existing patterns, and stimulated new waves of migration. In particular, the economic development strategy that various colonial governments pursued largely shaped the direction of migration in both the colonial and postcolonial eras (Addo, 1972; E.C.A., 1981).

International migration in Africa thus has its roots in economic, political, religious, and ecological factors. Prominent among economic factors are the wide disparities in economic development and employment opportunities between countries. In addition, new migration streams have emerged in response to the favorable situations created by the formation of economic unions, such as the now defunct East African Community and the Economic Community of West African States which guarantees free movement of labor within member countries (Adepoju, 1985). The arbitrariness of international boundaries which separated many ethnic groups, as well as political disturbances in many parts of the continent, have played major roles in undocumented migration. Finally, considerable southward migration has resulted from the Sahelian drought as well as from movements of pastoralists and nomads, and pilgrims from the Sahelian countries and Nigeria (E.C.A., 1981). These movements show no regard for national boundaries.

Historically, the cultural affinity of communities split by artificial national boundaries has facilitated the free movement of persons across Africa. Often, immigrants belong to the same tribes as the population of the host country, speak the same language, and share common customs. Examples abound: the Ewes in Togo and Ghana; the Yoruba in southwest Nigeria and Benin; the Fulani across the northern belt of virtually all West African countries; the Banyarwanda in Rwanda, Uganda, and Zaire; the Makonde in Mozambique and Tanzania; the Kakwa in Uganda, Sudan, and Zaire; the Mende-speaking people, and the Vasi and Kroos in Liberia and Sierra Leone. In West Africa, for example, the Fulani live in eight countries in the sub-region: Nigeria, Mali, Gambia, Ivory Coast, Liberia, Guinea, and Guinea Bissau. Similarly, the Ashanti live in Ghana and Ivory Coast; the Tuareg are found in Niger and Mali; the Hausa in Nigeria and Niger; and the Wolof in Senegal, Gambia, and Mauritania (see Table 3.1).

As in other African subregions, the "closely interconnected" distribution of ethnic groups within the countries of the Economic Community of West African States (ECOWAS) no doubt facilitates migration (Chukwura, 1984). Historically, these groups cross national boundaries in a manner they regard as movement between localities, not countries. (See Ohadike and Tesfaghiorghis, 1975.) More important, migrants have been readily received and easily assimilated among the same ethnic groups. In fact, along the Nigeria/Benin or Kenya/Tanzania borders, instances exist where members of an extended family live on both sides of the national frontiers and commute daily from their residences to their farms (Adepoju, 1983b). Large, unpoliced, porous borders which lack physical landmarks facilitate the free flow of migrants to neighboring countries that offer better employment. According to Zachariah and Conde (1981), "West Africa is one of the few regions of the world where relatively large-scale free movement of people across international boundaries still takes place."

Nomads and seminomads roam with their livestock over extensive areas without being identifiable with any specific national division. These include the Fulani in West Africa, the Kal Tomacheq of Mali and Niger, the Galla and Masai of Kenya, and the Somali of Somalia, Kenya, and Ethiopia. Nomads usually undertake seasonal transmigration in patterns which ignore international borders. These nomads usually succeed in claiming whatever nationality suits them best at a given point in time (Ware, 1978; E.C.A., 1981). Similarly, herdsmen and fishermen are by the nature of their activities "compelled" to move around. Movement by herdsmen is either seasonal or of a more irregular nature as they search for pastures and/or places to sell their stock (Conde 1979:61). Fishermen behave similarly. Ghanaian fishermen migrate along the coast of West Africa. Whether they cross international boundaries or not is incidental to this movement.

In the Nigerian context, it is evident that the influx of immigrants into the country is difficult to control because Nigerian borders are too vast and porous and hence difficult to police effectively. The enforcement problem is further complicated by the fact that nationals of such neighboring countries as Benin, Niger, Chad, and Cameroon have common features, cultures, and traditions with Nigerians. As a result, identification of aliens is difficult once they enter Nigeria and mix with people of the same ethnic/cultural milieu.

Finally, African immigrants in Central Africa, especially in Gabon, Equatorial Guinea, Zaire and Príncipe, and São Tomé, are mainly temporary migrants who shuttle between their homes and the mines, plantations, and cash-cropping areas in the host countries. Border regulations in the region are not stringent and can be circumvented. As a result, much of migration across Africa is largely undocumented; such undocumented flows probably eclipse legal or documented flows (Adepoju, 1983).

Table 3.1
The Major Ethnic Groups in Countries of ECOWAS

Country	Major Ethnic/Linguistic/Tribal Groups
Benin	Fon, Adma, Bariba, Yoruba
Burkina Faso	Mossi, Bobo
Gambia	Mandingo, Fula, Wolof, Jola, Serahuli
Ghana	Akan, Ashanti, Guan, Ga, Ewe, Moshi-Dagomba
Guinea	Foulah (or Peul), Malinke (or Mandingo), Soussou
Guinea-Bissau	Balante, Fulani, Mandyako, Malinki, Pepel
Ivory Coast	Agnis-Ashanti-Baoule, Kroumen, Mandingo, Senoufo, Dans-Gouros, Koua-Koua
Liberia	Kru, Mandingo, Gola
Mali	Mande (Bambara, Malinke, Sarakolle, etc.) Peul (or Fulani), Songhai, Tuareg, Moor
Mauritania	Moors (Arab and Berber stock); Peul, Molof, Sarakole, Toucouleur
Niger	Hausa, Djerma-Songhai, Peul, (Filani), Toubous
Nigeria	Hausa, Fulani (Fulbe), Ibo, Yoruba, Edo, Efik, Ibidio, Ijaw, Tiv, Nupe
Senegal	Wolof, Peul (Fulani) Toucouleur, Diola, Mandingo
Sierra Leone	Temne, Mende
Togo	Ewes, Mina, Cabrai

Source: Adapted from Chukwurah, 1984.

Cyclical migration is another feature of the African migratory scene. Cyclical migration meets the differing peaks of labor demands in various parts of the continent. Its various types—frontier, seasonal, and short-term migration—are found especially in West and East Africa, where they are simply an extension of long-standing patterns. In most cases, such movements are confined to neighboring countries with similar cultural, socioeconomic, and ethnic characteristics. In East Africa, for example, approximately 80 percent of immigrants in Tanzania in 1978 originated from neighboring countries while Mtwara received 99 percent of its immigrants from Mozambique, and the Tabora and Rukwa regions received, respectively, 97 and 83 percent of their cyclical immigrants from Burundi. In addition, Kagera in the West Lake received 97 percent of its immigrants mainly form Uganda (31 percent), Rwanda (45 percent) and Burundi (21 percent) (Mlay, 1983). As with other types of migration, proximity and cultural links facilitate the immigration process.

Cyclical immigrants in Central Africa are also drawn basically from adjoining countries. In 1975, 60 percent of immigrants in Cameroon were Nigerians, and two-thirds of them lived in the southwest region which adjoins Nigeria. In the Congo Republic, 41 percent of immigrants originated from Zaire. The clustering of immigrants is also obvious in Chad and Zaire. In the mid-1970s, about 84 percent of all immigrants in Chad lived in the south while Angolan immigrants in lower Zaire constituted 98 percent of the total foreign nationals (Adepoju, 1984a). In the early 1970s, immigrants in Equatorial Guinea were drawn from one major source: Nigeria. Before their 1973 forced repatriation, Nigerians comprised 60 percent of the immigrant resident population there and constituted 55 percent proportion of the work force in the coffee and cocoa plantations (Adepoju, 1984a).

The major sending countries in sub-Saharan Africa are Burkina Faso, Togo, and Mali in West Africa; Lesotho, Botswana and—to a lesser extent—Swaziland in Southern Africa; Malawi, Burundi, Rwanda, and Mozambique in East Africa; and Cameroon, Central African Republic, and Angola in Central Africa. With 51 percent of the adult Basotho males in the Republic of South Africa in 1983, Lesotho ranks as the main emigrant country in sub-Saharan Africa. In 1975, 17 percent of the native population of Burkina Faso lived abroad. In 1960, of all immigrants from Togo, 94 percent of Togolese emigrants were enumerated in Ghana. Until the end of the 1960s, Mozambique, Malawi, and Lesotho were the major sources of labor for South Africa's mines. Recruitment from Mozambique ceased with independence in 1972, and Malawi adopted similar measures in 1974 following the airplane crash which killed Malawian migrant laborers travelling to South Africa (Adepoju, 1984a).

International migration in West Africa has been dominated by clandestine or undocumented migration of unskilled persons. Recently, however, professionals from Ghana have also become noticeable in such streams. In Southern Africa, migration is temporary and conditioned largely by South Africa's immigration laws. Refugee migration is a major feature in Central and, especially, Eastern Africa. In all, labor migration is common in the sub-Saharan region. Clandestine migrations are most frequent among nomads, especially between Somalia, Kenya, and Tanzania.

In Central Africa, São Tomé and Príncipe, Equatorial Guinea, Zaire, and Gabon are the principal destinations for immigration. Gabon and Zaire contain rich mineral deposits which attract both skilled and unskilled workers. The cocoa, coffee, and sugar plantations in São Tomé and Príncipe and Equatorial Guinea attract thousands of laborers from Nigeria, Angola, Cameroon, and Niger. In Eastern Africa, rich plantation agriculture in Uganda, Zambia, and Kenya, copper mines in Zambia, and industry and plantations in Zimbabwe have been and continue to be attractive to migrant workers from Malawi, Burundi, and Rwanda.

Laborers from Malawi, Mozambique, and Zambia are recruited for the mines and plantations in South Africa and Zimbabwe, and workers from Rwanda and Burundi work in the rich agricultural areas of Kenya, Uganda, and Zambia under contract arrangements. Permanent migration is not permitted in South Africa. Contracts are for up to two years and migrants cannot move their families to the mines. By restricting family migration, South Africa ensures that migrants can neither settle permanently nor integrate into the host community (Gordon, 1981). Accordingly, migrants leave their families at home, work for the two years stipulated in the contract, and return to their families for as long as is economically feasible. Later, they might sign another contract, giving rise to what has been termed "oscillatory" migration. With the Aliens Control Act of 1963, South Africa reduced considerably the volume of worker immigration (especially from Botswana, Lesotho, and Swaziland [BLS]), altered the sexual composition of the work force in favor of males, and basically confined workers to the mines. A subsequent South African policy favored the employment of migrant workers with previous experience in the mines, while the internalization policy of 1977 has reduced reliance on imported (African) labor to the mines in favor of labor from the homelands (Colclough, 1980; de Vletter, 1982; see also Thahane, Chapter 4).

The characteristics of migrants reflect the types and nature of their migration. Refugees escaping war, famine, and drought are usually old persons, women, and children. Labor migration to South Africa and seasonal migration from the savannah regions of Mali, Burkina Faso, and Niger to the coastal countries of Senegal, Ghana, and Ivory Coast are male dominated. Migrants are typically unskilled, uneducated, and predominantly adults. Emigrants from Africa to Europe and North America, however, include both skilled persons, such as scientists, doctors, and technicians, and some unskilled adult laborers (Gould, 1985; Bennell and Godfrey, 1983). In general, migrants within Africa include a high proportion of young adult males of working age who often have lower levels of schooling than the populations they join.

In West Africa, most labor migration can be more correctly regarded as commercial migration and involves both males and females. The case of Nigerians in Ghana prior to 1969 is a case in point. What began as labor migration to the cocoa-growing and lumber areas of Ghana evolved into commercial migration in diamond mining, trading, and commerce (Addo, 1972; Brydon, 1985; Mabogunje, 1972).

CAUSES OF EMIGRATION

The decision to emigrate can evolve along a continuum which starts from an awareness of the opportunities available at various locations and progresses to the stages of the predisposition to move, inclination to move, intention to move and, finally, the actual movement. This conceptualization requires information and knowledge about the specific attributes of the different possible destinations. The channels of information which facilitate both the decision to move and the relocation process include family members and other persons who had migrated earlier, as well as feedback information on the range of opportunities available to the potential migrants at destination. Due to a myriad of constraints, the intention to migrate does not always lead to actual migration. These constraints may include the inability to generate sufficient funds to finance the journey, and government policies on who can migrate, to where, for how long, and from what countries (Oberai, 1983).

The migration decision can be greatly influenced by past experience which, in certain cases, may be institutionally determined. Facilitating factors and external constraints both affect the direction and timing of out-migration. For instance, household decision makers may selectively allocate their household members into categories of movers and nonmovers based on the strategy which makes sense for specific households in different settings. This decision will routinely reflect collective family goals, the changing internal dynamics of the household structure, the gender division of roles, and the importance of birth rank (Urzua, 1981; Caldwell, 1969).

As is pointed out by Thahane (Chapter 4), the case of Lesotho illustrates vividly how such factors as the incorporation of Lesotho's economy into that of the Republic of South Africa and the systematic creation of a cheap labor reserve have made migration the only viable option for most young Basotho. In the process, the decision about where to go has been institutionally determined. When to go, another critical element in the decision-making process, has been systematically programmed by a series of laws in the Republic of South Africa. One can argue that the decision about who should go has also been decided by factors beyond of the control of the household in Lesotho (Adepoju, 1984a; Burke, 1981). For one thing, females are not allowed to accompany or join male migrants (Izzard, 1984). More important, South Africa's recent stabilization policy, which gives employment preference to experienced migrants, rigidly defines who can be recruited and employed in its mines.

The case of Ghana illustrates the compelling reasons for and changing circumstances of mass emigration. When Zachariah and Conde (1981) argued that the Ghanaians were, and still are, nonmigratory except for family reasons, they did not foresee the impending economic and political crisis in Ghana which led to the massive exodus of both professional and unskilled Ghanaians. Zachariah and Conde found that in 1970 only 1 percent of Ghanaians were living outside of Ghana (1981). Yet, barely half a decade later, Ghana had become a major sending country, perhaps surpassing the record set by Burkina Faso in West Africa. By 1983, close to 10 percent of the Ghanaian population and about 25 percent of its labor force was working in Nigeria, Ivory Coast, Togo, Lesotho, Zimbabwe, other parts of Africa and Europe, and even the satellite homelands of the Republic of South Africa. Yet, until the 1960s, Ghana and the Ivory Coast were the leading labor importing countries in West Africa, indeed, the real "gold coast" of the subregion (Adepoju, 1985).

Although they seem to be supported by the 1960 and 1970 censuses, the myths that Ghanaians do not emigrate (and definitely not to Nigeria!) and that Ghanaian females are short distance migrants no longer hold. Ghana, which in

1969 expelled its Nigerian and other foreign workers, suddenly found her nationals going to Nigeria by the thousands to escape Ghana's poverty (Adepoju, 1985). This flow had a number of interesting characteristics. In a survey of Ghanaian teachers in Nigeria, for instance, 16 percent of them had worked in the private sector in Ghana prior to emigrating to Nigeria, 10 percent had been self-employed, and 40 percent had been employed in the government services. More than one-third of the respondents were unemployed in Ghana before leaving for Nigeria in search of employment (Obasi, 1983).

The exodus of Ghana's skilled and unskilled persons, regardless of sex, reflected the country's serious economic predicament. There were severe shortages of gasoline and spare parts. Public transportation was completely paralyzed and the movement of persons, goods, and foodstuff became prohibitively expensive. Factories operated at 30 percent capacity, inflation increased dramatically, and teaching and research facilities were virtually abandoned. Basic foodstuffs were beyond the reach of most workers; a loaf of bread cost a full day's wages (Anarfi, 1984; Adepoju, 1985). These circumstances were further aggravated by government policies, which included ill-advised farm initiatives and the expulsion of all aliens in 1969. The latter decision hit the cocoa industry particularly hard. Production declined, prices dropped, and smuggling to the neighboring countries intensified.

During the 1960–82 period, Ghana, in fact, experienced an average negative growth rate of 1.3 percent per annum in GNP per capita, while neighboring Nigeria, Togo, and Ivory Coast recorded more than 2 percent annual growth rates. Finally, Ghana's estimated GNP per capita was $400 in 1979, but dropped to $360 in 1982.

At the same time, Nigeria's booming construction industries and service sector were attracting large numbers of migrant workers both from countries of the Economic Community of West African States (ECOWAS) and non-ECOWAS countries. The Nigerian oil boom and its consequent expanding of employment opportunities and huge wage increases of the mid-1970s generated equally huge wage differentials between Nigeria and her neighbors. This coincided with an era of rapidly deteriorating economic conditions in neighboring ECOWAS countries and especially in Ghana.

Throughout most of Africa, real incomes have been on the decline for the past several years, while prices have been rising. The latter has seriously eroded the pay of both professionals and laborers. As the E.C.A. (1986:201) pointed out:

> Salaries and other forms of remuneration have also been affected by the economic downturn. Real incomes have declined in all African countries, against the doubling and, in some cases, the tripling of the cost of living and the shortages of essential commodities which have pushed up prices of these commodities. In 1982, the real value of a Ghanaian doctor's monthly salary had dropped to the equivalent of US $42; in Uganda a permanent secretary earned the equivalent of a mere US $40 every month; whereas in Sierra Leone a university professor receives US

$66 per month today. These are extreme cases of low remuneration to high level manpower in Africa but, in general, the average salary of the African highly skilled professional does not exceed the equivalent of US $400 per month. Yet Lagos is more expensive than London, Freetown than Paris, and Accra than Lisbon.

As a result, the poor and deteriorating working conditions for most professionals, poor morale, and the prevailing social environment became intolerable for those who had options to seek employment in other countries "by virtue of the international character of their skills and qualifications" (E.C.A., 1986:202). The same argument, however, can be advanced for the many unskilled workers who could find employment in the agricultural and related activities of the more prosperous African countries. In addition to emigrating laborers, one also finds thousands of farmers and nomads fleeing drought-affected areas following the many years of severe ecological deterioration in several parts of the region. Finally, political upheavals and general instability also generated additional emigrants although such instability can only be understood within the broader context of the social, economic, and political conditions prevailing in Africa.

EFFECTS OF EMIGRATION ON THE SENDING COUNTRIES' DEVELOPMENT

Tapinos recently argued (1982) that the effects of emigration on the labor-exporting countries can be analyzed at three levels: the impact of the departure of workers on employment, production, and wages; the transfer of funds and its effects on the living standard of family members, the resultant income distribution, and productive accumulation and growth; and the effects of return migration on the stock of human capital.

These impacts, however, are also affected by the nature of the sending economies, the volume and composition of the migration stream, and the extent and disposition of remitted income. Where emigration is on an extensive scale and male dominated, as in Burkina Faso, Lesotho, Malawi and Chad, the dominant economic sector of food production can be adversely affected, especially where innovative approaches are not introduced. At both the micro (family) and macro (societal) levels, social and economic organization is disrupted by mass emigration, which creates additional demands on female-headed households. The question which must be explored, however, is whether remitted incomes help offset these losses (especially in cases such as Lesotho, which derives half of its foreign exchange from migrant remittances).

Employment

The economies of sub-Saharan African countries are largely underdeveloped. Within this general pattern, however, there are sharp contrasts between the relatively prosperous economies of some coastal countries and the few oil and mineral rich countries and those of the poorer countries of the Sahelian region and other land-locked countries. In many of the less fortunate countries, the public sector is small, and the bulk of the working population is employed in agriculture. The existence of tiny states whose boundaries raise serious obstacles to free mobility of factors of production seriously impairs the economic development of these countries (World Bank, 1981).

In Eastern Africa, the major countries of emigration are Rwanda, Burundi, and Malawi, very poor countries with few natural resources and/or acute population pressure on the land, and preindependence Mozambique. For these countries, emigration has been a means of relieving the domestic labor market of the unemployed persons, as well as a source of foreign exchange earnings. In Malawi, for instance, remittances from migrants working in South Africa formed the third most important source of national income in the early seventies (Mlay, 1983; Adepoju, 1984a; Christenson, 1984).

In Southern Africa, Lesotho's dependence on the migrant labor system to generate employment and remittances is no doubt the most acute among the BLS countries (Botswana, Lesotho and Swaziland). About half of Lesotho's males are employed in South Africa and their remittances constitute the most important source of government revenue. Here, a complex combination of factors, such as historical circumstances, geopolitical location, and unfavorable ecology, have turned Lesotho into a major reserve of cheap labor for South Africa's mines. The South African stabilization policy severely curtails the chances of novice workers being recruited and has led to a decline in the number of households in labor-exporting countries which have access to migrant incomes. In Botswana, migrant employment in South Africa is about 10 percent greater than formal employment in the country, and remittances comprise about one-fifth of the household income for the poorest 10 percent of the population. Among the BLS countries, Swaziland is least dependent on South Africa's employment. Its migrant workers are probably no more than one-third of the domestic labor engaged in the formal sector (Colclough, 1980).

The implications of migration must also be viewed from the migrant's perspective. Most Eastern Africa migrants in South Africa and Zimbabwe are unskilled or semiskilled workers, principally in mining and agriculture. They have no organized unions to fight for their interests, and their periods of stay in areas of destination are quite restricted. Migrants from Rwanda and Burundi are usually unskilled workers who are employed during the intensive weeding and harvesting periods on cash crop farms. They are often exploited by the receiving communities while they continue to maintain traditional cultural patterns and do not easily integrate into the indigenous communities. Migrants from Kenya, especially the Luo, have also provided a readily available source of blue collar labor in construction, commerce, and railway services in Uganda. A large number are also employed as farm laborers and night watchmen (Adepoju, 1984a).

Many of these migrants cross the borders clandestinely and normally confront a series of problems: unemployment or insecure employment and lack of adequate shelter and other basic needs (ICEM 1974). Initially, some engage in rural employment close to the border and only later move to the towns in search of jobs initially in the informal and later in the formal sectors. In most cases, they are offered and readily accept wages below the statutory minimum for the country. In general, illegal immigrants work as farm laborers, tailors, shoe-shiners, hotel stewards, auto repairers; they are routinely excluded from participating in most formal sector economic activities because they are without work permits and have limited skills. For instance, this has been the case with most Ghanaian immigrants in Nigeria. They work in hotels, construction, and maintenance services, and in the absence of necessary documentation (residence and work permits), are prepared to accept any pay (Fashoyin, 1985; Adepoju, 1985).

Immigrants in West Africa also tend to concentrate in low status jobs. Agriculture, the principal economic sector in the subregion, attracts a sizeable proportion of immigrants, especially from Burkina Faso, Mali, and Chad. The other major immigrant employing sectors are mining, commerce, and services in which immigrants occupy positions not filled by the natives. In Ivory Coast, some immigrants can be found in professional, technical, and administrative jobs and an estimated 35,000 Ghanaians were employed as teachers in Nigeria in early 1983 (Adepoju, 1984a).

For such very poor countries with few natural resources and increasing population pressure as Rwanda, Burundi, and Malawi, international migration is a source of employment for their nationals and foreign exchange earnings for their governments. The thinking in these countries is that seasonal migration during slack periods in agricultural activity does not adversely affect agricultural production. Rather, it eases the pressure on food and other resources at critical periods. Others, however, seriously question the gains for the sending countries. In the medium and long term, such gains are thought to be marginal because remittances by unskilled laborers are often meager and are likely to be invested in expenditures which may depress the market for local products. Furthermore, skills acquired abroad are often not relevant for tasks at home. For instance, a returning mine worker or farm laborer on a large plantation which uses machinery to pick fruits would not find these skills useful to cope with the more limited resources on his family plot or small enterprises at home (Burke, 1981).

As a result, the traditional labor source areas in East Africa—Burundi and Rwanda in particular—do not appear to have benefitted much from the export of labor over many decades. At the peak of emigration from Malawi in 1966, more than 20 percent (and in some localities up to 75 percent) of the country's adult males were abroad. Such high rates of absence have been associated with social and economic disruptions at home. Although emigration tends to initially relieve unemployment in the sending countries, the relative flow of skills can be so great as to result in critical manpower shortages at home (Tabbarah, 1984). This has been the case of Ghana since the late 1970s. The deteriorating economic situation in Ghana in the 1970s literally pushed a large number of professionals, academics, artisans, and technicians to Nigeria and beyond. The result was a shortage of the type of high level manpower required to manage Ghana's economy and services. On arrival in Nigeria, most Ghanaian immigrants accepted any jobs they could find. Almost invariably, these were jobs scorned by Nigerians with similar skill and background. Even the skilled immigrants accepted lower wages or jobs a step or more lower than Nigerians of comparable education and skill.

Anarfi (1982) has argued that the large influx of Ghanaians to Nigeria adversely affected their employment opportunities there and led to low wages, little or no job security, high turnover and few, if any, job rights. Partly because few employers were entitled to or in fact obtained the required expatriate quota permits, jobs were not registered and contracts of employment were not formalized. As a result, aliens could not press for benefits since most of them were knowingly employed in irregular situations (Adepoju, 1985).

Not all Ghanaians working in Nigeria were illegal immigrants. Many legal Ghanaian immigrants worked as skilled workers and enjoyed job benefits comparable to those of Nigerians. Their contribution has been in satisfying the current needs of the Nigerian economy by providing the much needed skills in key sectors. Viewed in this way, the immigration of skilled persons into Nigeria seems beneficial to both the immigrants and the Nigerian economy, but it represented a tremendous loss to Ghana where the skilled immigrants' services were in equally great demand. The illegal immigrants, on the other hand, concentrated in construction, textiles, dock and harbor work, and similar menial jobs. It is known that many among them worked for wages below the statutory minimum for the country. As a result, many observers feel that they flooded the labor market and dampened the prevailing wages by creating a situation of labor surplus at the unskilled level (Fashoyin, 1985). It is not particularly surprising, however, that some migrants settled for relatively low status occupations in the informal sector. Unskilled internal migrants behave in a similar manner and the informal sector becomes their major sector of absorption in the cities.

Even when unskilled Ghanaian immigrants working in Nigeria were earning low wages, it made rational economic sense from the migrant's perspective. He could smuggle out even a meager salary to Ghana and exchange it at six, seven, even ten times the official rate and thus accumulate as much money as the wages of the highly paid Ghanaian professionals. Alternatively, immigrants could purchase consumer items and household goods that flooded the Nigerian market. Once successfully conveyed to Ghana, these could be sold at twenty times their purchase price in Nigeria, and the "smugglers" could make huge profits even after allowing for the cost of transportation, the customs charges (both official and unofficial), and the unofficial black market exchange rate between the Nigerian cedi and the Ghanaian naira (Adepoju, 1985).

As long as the economy of Nigeria prospered, it seemed to have an almost limitless thirst for all types of labor. Both public and private sectors kept expanding and readily absorbing the cheap labor provided by the influx of immigrants. In fact, some industries actually recruited immigrants, especially

Ghanaian workers, and assisted them to enter Nigeria clandestinely, contrary to the provisions of the 1963 Nigerian Immigration Act that directs such companies to obtain expatriate quotas for foreign workers. This golden era ended abruptly when thousands of aliens were expelled from Nigeria in 1983 and again in 1985. During the 1983 expulsion, about two million persons (mainly Ghanaians) were affected. The large return of Ghanaians to a fragile economy was disastrous initially (Brydon, 1985), although the shock was absorbed over time thanks to massive relief aid, the determination of the Ghana government, and favorable weather (heavy rainfall). It has been widely reported that those among the expellees who did not find their way back to Nigeria returned to their farms and, as a result, there followed an abundance of food production and harvests in Ghana.

The impact of migration on the agriculture and food production system of the sending countries is an important consideration, especially in situations where farming relies heavily on physical input in a predominantly hoe-and-cutlass technology. In cases where full-time farmers migrate to the mines and devote only a small fraction of their time to farming (when on leave), agricultural production is likely to deteriorate significantly, as is the case in Lesotho (Elkan, 1980). The notion that emigration and the resulting shortage of labor can induce technological change, including more rational and intensive use of labor, land, and capital resources, has little empirical support in such cases as Lesotho, Burkina Faso, Mali, and Malawi. The selectivity of migration in favor of young adult males leaves behind older farmers who are more conservative and not responsive to new ideas and innovations. In other words, by syphoning off energetic young persons from rural areas, emigration in fact retards technological advances. The evidence is also mixed regarding whether returnees may acquire new skills which could be useful in organization and production in the home community (Mabogunje, 1972).

There are also many direct social costs to migrants. At the family level, migration to the mines has become a survival strategy with very high social costs. Disruption in marital ties, alternate arrangements for child rearing, occupational hazards in the mines and plantations, and poor living conditions are but a few such costs (Murray, 1980). Because of South African restrictions on family migration, approximately 40 to 60 percent of married women in Lesotho are wives of absent migrants (Gordon, 1981). Since the average miner not only spends approximately fifteen years of his working life away from home but also tends to migrate in his late twenties, thirties, or forties—the critical years of marital life and child-rearing—women are increasingly saddled with additional responsibilities as heads of households (Elkan, 1980). Restricted interaction between family members due to the prolonged absence of the male breadwinner increasingly erodes family bonds and solidarity. As a result, social norms related to child-rearing, decision making and control, sex-differentiated economic roles, and other social obligations have undergone considerable changes (Izzard, 1984).

Remittances

While migrant-sending countries lose a cross section of their manpower, they do derive some benefits in return in the form of remittances. Remittances may come through official channels (deferred pay or special taxes), as consumer and durable goods, or as cash sent or taken home when the migrants visit or return to their home place (Tabbarah, 1984; Adepoju, 1984a). The volume of remittances is a function of several variables, including the size of the migrants' wages, the migrants' propensity to save, and the length of stay and institutional arrangements for deferred pay (Tapinos, 1982).

Most migration surveys in Africa record substantial remittances by migrants to their home place (Knowles and Anker, 1981). The best known examples of the remittance mechanism in West Africa include Nigerians in Ghana prior to their expulsion in 1969, Ghanaians in Nigeria prior to their expulsion in 1983, Burkinabe in Ivory Coast, and Nigerians in Equatorial Guinea (Adepoju, 1984a). The volume of remittances which passes through official channels no doubt severely underestimates the total amount of transfers. In parts of West Africa there are few currency restrictions—in fact, the Francophone countries of the region use a uniform currency. Since migrants move frequently between countries of origin and destination, currency trafficking is common. Hence, private remittances could be much larger than indicated by transfers through official channels (Zachariah and Conde, 1981).

Nowhere in Africa are the effects of migration on employment and remittances as pronounced as in Southern Africa, particularly Lesotho. Well-defined agreements between the governments of South Africa and sending countries require migrants to send home a proportion of their incomes. Total migrant remittances to Lesotho in 1978 and 1979 (including direct remittances, deferred pay, and cash and goods in hand) were estimated to represent about 42 percent of the country's gross national product. At the peak of the "golden age" of emigration from Lesotho (1975–76), net remittances were actually thought to exceed the gross domestic product. The uncertainty of earnings from this source, however, could have grave economic consequences as migrant labor constitutes Lesotho's main source of employment revenue (de Vletter, 1982). As a result, remittances require careful management to enhance their long-term contribution to development.

The disposition of remittances is an area where the sparse empirical evidence is contradictory and based mostly on informed speculation. Our knowledge is constrained further by the research approach; surveys normally focus on intended rather than actual use of remittances by the recipients.

It is generally observed that since remittances constitute private transfers of funds, governments have no direct control over their disposition. As a result, it is very difficult to mobilize remittances for investment purposes. Some authors point to evidence that African migrants are consumption oriented and that by indulging in conspicuous consumption rather than investing earnings in productive activities, they tend to fuel inflation (Böhning, 1977). Others assert that some of the remittances are in fact used to pay laborers on the farm, the school fees and maintenance expenses of migrants' children and other relations at home, and the setting up of small-scale businesses. The remaining is often saved toward the event of return migration (Caldwell, 1969; Adepoju, 1984a).

Although Böhning (1977) noted that the long-run impact of remittances on development depends on their disposition, that is, whether they are spent primarily on consumer goods or are invested in productive ventures, remittances clearly enhance the recipients' current and future living standards—as long as they exceed what the migrants could have earned by remaining at home. Although, clearly, only a small fraction of remittances is channelled into productive investment, and most remitted funds are spent mainly on consumption and the acquisition of such items as livestock and on building or improving houses, one thing is certain: heavy dependence on remittances can pose serious problems. This is particularly troublesome for such states as Lesotho where opportunities for mine work in South Africa are expected to absorb fewer non-South African black workers.

Spending remittances on consumer goods by the migrants' families is to be expected in situations where these often poor households have adopted a survival strategy of sponsoring one or more of their members to enter the migrant labor system. Hence, the disposition of remittances can be expected to be related to the emigration decision-making process. Urzua (1981) distinguishes between mobility and survival strategies and argues that these migrants who move as a result of a survival strategy will come from poorer families and will be less educated than those following a mobility strategy. Survival migrants are pushed by poverty and unemployment, while mobility migrants are pulled by the prospects of better economic and social opportunities.

Thus, while the decision-making process of mobility migrants is expected to approximate the model of economic rationality, survival migrants are desperately in search of whatever work they can get, in any location, and at any wage, usually below the ruling market rate. In the latter situation—a situation typical of virtually all African migration—migrants are compelled to remit, sometimes regularly, part of their earnings to augment the living conditions of the family members left behind. Mobility migrants, on the other hand, are most likely to be better educated, skilled, and to be drawn from middle-class to well-to-do households. The economic effects of emigration, therefore, must be analyzed at three levels: the migrant's, the migrant's family/household/community, and the migrant's country.

Another critical issue is the magnitude and disposition of remittances, as well as the effects of this disposition on income distribution and the development process of the labor-exporting countries. One must also consider the effects of the loss of skilled persons to sending societies through emigration. Where critical labor shortages accompany the emigration of high-level manpower, the replacement effect can be cushioned only where the intermediate cadre is socially mobile (but even then at a cost of low marginal productivity.)

The shifting social and economic roles of the women who remain behind has become critical to rural economic activities. In Lesotho, for instance, where owners lose title to land left fallow for more than two years, women increasingly till the land, partly to retain title but also to supplement meager family incomes, especially when remittances are inadequate, unreliable, and insufficient to maintain the families left behind. It has also been found that internal migration of females in search of subsistence wage income to meet needs not covered by irregular and uncertain remittances has increased.

Return Migration

It is often contended that experienced migrant workers constitute a disciplined labor force accustomed to work norms in large organizations. As a result, their experiences could be valuable to the sending countries if the labor market situation there were conducive to the effective use of their "talents." Routinely, as noted earlier, the skills migrants acquire during their migration career are not relevant for the types of jobs available at home. This is due to the fact that the economies of both sending and receiving countries are likely to be widely different.

This is an especially important observation since many African sending countries are experiencing increased return migration. Yet, the discrepancy between skills learned abroad and skills useful at home should not be overstated. Some migrants do return with useful new skills and working capital. Upon their return, these migrants may serve as agents of socioeconomic change and cultural diffusion and introduce new production and organization techniques—including active participation in cooperative farming, credit associations, and other related activities (Mabogunje, 1972). Adegbola (1976) has shown that return migrants from Ghana to Nigeria in 1969 and 1970 not only introduced new crops, but also contributed to the breaking of social rigidities that hinder economic change. Some returnees were also found to be active in stimulating communal projects. Indeed, several schools, hospitals, and community centers in the villages were constructed by the contributions, supervision, and encouragement of return migrants.

On the other hand, returnees can also pose problems for sending countries. Countries whose nationals were expelled (e.g., Ghana in 1983) were suddenly faced with problems associated with resettling them. Because these countries were often unable to make adequate provisions to receive and reintegrate their nationals, the task was often left to friends and families. In the absence of such a support network, however, some returnees remain unemployed and poor, thus constituting severe social and administrative problems for their governments. Following the expulsion of Ghanaians from Nigeria in 1983, the Ghanaian government, already under stress from a long term economic decline combined with a poor 1982 harvest, confronted the challenge of the influx of roughly 10 percent of its total population with a food-and-commodity-short economy (Brydon, 1985).

In Niger, the estimated 150,000 to 200,000 returnees in 1983 added to the jobless pool, which in turn disrupted the traditional seasonal migration pattern that hitherto relieved unemployment during the slack season of agricultural activities. The decline in foreign exchange could have been even more disruptive because Niger derives substantial foreign exchange from the earnings of emigrants. Migrants from Niger affected by Nigeria's expulsion order included seasonal migrant workers to Nigeria.

The case of migrants to South Africa is also instructive. A substantial proportion of miners contract and suffer from a variety of physical and stress-related illnesses. Some are disabled, assaulted, or even die in mining accidents. In fact, mine accidents account for two-fifths of the mortality among the Basotho mine laborers. Those who escape these hazards generally return home exhausted, often with uncertain futures in a domestic economy unable to absorb them in productive employment (Gordon, 1981; Coclough, 1980; Burke, 1981).

When return migrants have earned high wages in the host countries and have enjoyed better living and working conditions (as is often true for immigrants in the oil-rich countries of Nigeria, Gabon, Libya, or in the agriculture-rich countries of the Ivory Coast), their reinsertion into the conditions of lower wages and poor working conditions in the home country can be a frustrating experience. Some are unable to adjust and compete effectively in the domestic economy. The attendant frustration and resulting loss of motivation may be disastrous for the returnees.

Policy Challenges

Prior to their independence, few African countries had adopted legislative and administrative measures to deal with international migration. Since independence, the regulation of international migration has become an important political issue in Africa, and governments have exercised considerable control over the volume and composition of flows. During the late 1970s and early 1980s, adverse economic conditions led most African governments to implement direct and indirect initiatives relating to immigration laws. These included work permits, registration of aliens, visa and passport requirements, and specification of certain categories of desired or undesired immigrants. The general trend over the last decade has been to discourage both the emigration of skilled labor and the immigration of unskilled and semiskilled labor.

A number of factors have in recent years led governments in Central Africa to adapt or redefine their immigration policies. Predominant among these is the tightening of immigration regulations in times of economic downturns. Gabon, for instance, had been a major importer of contract workers through labor agreements with such supplier countries as Burkina Faso. In 1977, Gabon declared a new policy of maintaining, but not increasing immigration. Since 1979, Gabon's expressed policy has been to conserve available job opportunities for Gabonese. In another instance, Equatorial Guinea has repeatedly appealed to the source countries of illegal immigrants to cooperate in checking these flows.

As a rule, most Central African countries now pursue nationalization policies that increasingly replace foreigners employed in jobs for which local workers are available. In recent years, depressed economic conditions and the attendant rising unemployment have led to policies of mass immigrant expulsions from such countries as Gabon and Zaire. These initiatives have been followed despite continuing commitment to the principles of Pan-Africanism and the formation of regional economic and customs blocks such as the Common Economic and Customs Union (UDEAC).

Restrictions on immigration in West Africa are also a postindependence development. Following attainment of political independence, national governments strove to improve the general welfare of their people. Sluggish economic growth, maldistribution of income, rising unemployment, and galloping inflation, however, forced governments to tighten their immigration laws and invoke laws and regulations relating to the entry, residence, and employment of nonnationals. Aliens became a frequent target as scapegoats, and a wave of expulsions and repatriations swept over several African countries. These expulsions and repatriations may have been particularly shortsighted, since controlling immigration requires cooperation between sending and receiving countries. This is especially true with regard to illegal immigration, because illegal immigrants are not only illegal when they enter the host country, but also when they have left their home countries without the appropriate travel documents and exit visas.

Policies invoked by countries of emigration have generally been liberal. Not only is freedom to emigrate often recognized, and in some cases even enshrined in national constitutions, but some governments permit traditional emigration streams to continue. In the drought-stricken Sahel belt, labor emigration is viewed as a relief from pressing domestic problems, and for Burkina Faso and Mali, remittances constitute a substantial source of foreign exchange. However, Burkina Faso's attempts to divert international migrants to internal destinations have generally been unsuccessful, for the domestic labor market is simply unable to absorb large numbers of migrant workers and local wages cannot compete with those available outside the country.

In East Africa, land-locked, limited-resources countries (Rwanda, Burundi, and Malawi) have from the colonial period depended on income earned by exporting labor to richer neighboring countries. Emigration has been a traditional solution for both population pressure and poverty, and remittances represent a large portion of these countries' foreign exchange earnings. Until recently, most countries have tended to accept emigration where there has been a traditional system of labor migration. Bilateral arrangements between sending and receiving countries have been negotiated, especially with South Africa.[1] However, even where immigration has continued, regulations concerning timing and volume have been tightened. For example, Malawi has introduced regulations governing the numbers of emigrants who may go to South Africa and the length of their contracts. At the other extreme, countries with surplus labor and unemployment problems, notably Kenya, have made arrangements with the oil-rich Arab countries to supply them with labor on a contract basis. Most countries, however, are less liberal toward the emigration of their more educated and better skilled workers. Even though the brain drain problem has been almost negligible, Tanzania and Uganda have instituted regulations to restrict the emigration of professionals and civil servants. These include bonding, restrictions on foreign exchange, and centrally scrutinized applications for travel abroad. Such measures are considered necessary in the face of declining economic growth and the propensity for skilled personnel to emigrate to the richer states in Southern and Eastern Africa (Adepoju, 1984a).

Nationalist reaction against the employment of foreigners, the tightening of labor markets due to worsening economic conditions in the region, and the general suspicion of local people directed at migrants from other countries are likely to lead to further restrictions on international migration. Increasing unemployment in Zimbabwe, for instance, will restrict opportunities for foreign laborers in that country. With a more inward-looking South Africa, it is unlikely that substantial migration to that country will persist in the 1990s. The only positive development in that region in terms of continued mobility of labor is through the creation of the Southern African Development Coordinating Conference (SADCC) and the institution of the Preferential Trade Area (PTA). However, these institutions are still in the embryonic stage and already there are signs that their further development may be difficult and their impact limited (Adepoju, 1984a).

Events in Ghana and Nigeria, in particular, show that foreign migrant laborers are tolerated only at the discretion of the host government. Under such circumstances, immigrants lack a political base and are unable to bargain. Even where they are needed to supplement local labor, few steps are taken to ensure that their departure does not severely affect the economies of both sending and receiving countries.

As the countries of independent Africa impose stricter restrictions on the movement of people across their borders, it is almost certain that voluntary international migration will be considerably curtailed. Furthermore, with increasing pressure on the Asians involved in industrial and commercial activities in Kenya and Tanzania, it is likely that Eastern Africa will experience an exodus of Asians.[2] At the same time, pressures for emigration from such poorer countries of the region as Rwanda, Burundi, Lesotho, Mali, Mauritania, and Burkina Faso are likely to continue.

NOTES

1. Except by Tanzania and Zambia, which prohibit recruitment by South Africa.

2. Uganda has recently invited the Asians it expelled in the early 1970s to return, but few are expected to take advantage of that offer because of their prior treatment and Uganda's continued instability.

4

International Labor Migration in Southern Africa

Timothy T. Thahane _____

This chapter explores the evolution of international labor migration in Southern Africa and highlights some of its unique aspects. Furthermore, it examines the factors that influence demand for labor in South Africa; looks at the organization of labor recruitment and the respective roles of the different states; and reviews the benefits and costs of the labor migration system on the host and home countries and the policy options facing the latter, given expected demand and policy changes now taking place in the former. The analysis follows a historical perspective which places migration within the political economy of the region.

In the case of internal migration, the migrant normally faces no legal constraints on movement, whereas "an international migrant is invariably confronted with a series of sometimes complex regulations relating at first to exit from the country of origin, and later entry into, residence within, and exit from the receiving country." (Adepoju, 1984b:441). In the case of international labor migration, demand for labor originates with employers in one country and triggers a migration response from another country. The process requires the availability of candidates who are prepared to move for various reasons, mostly economic. Noneconomic push or pull factors may predominate in particular situations, such as those involving refugees.

The roles of home and host governments differ from one situation to another. In the precolonial period, the role of the sending government was indirect and limited to provision of travel documents, licensing of private recruiting agencies, and ensuring that recruits underwent some kind of medical checkup. No efforts were made to regulate remittances or provide incentives to increase the flow or to invest remittances productively. However, this passive role of the sending governments has been changing since independence in the 1960s. On the other hand, the role of the host government was always critical in determining the rate of entry, the degree of enforcement of the immigration regulations, the duration of stay of migrants, and their mobility once admitted. As we will see, most African countries which experience in-migration, especially in West Africa, do not have strong administrative systems to carry out all these tasks. South Africa, by contrast, has the administrative capacity and resources to promulgate and rigidly enforce the regulations for entry, stay, and movement inside the country.

THEORETICAL CONSIDERATIONS

A satisfactory explanation of labor migration in Southern Africa requires a choice of a theoretical framework which enables one to appreciate the economic and social forces operating in both labor-sending and labor-receiving countries. It is not sufficient to explain migration movement solely "in terms of the attraction of better pay for work elsewhere" (Marks and Richardson, 1984:5), even though this may be an important cause of migration. There are other push factors that give rise to migration, including the economic relationships and government policies in emigration countries. Equally important are the various forms of social, political, and economic organizations in the host country that may act to pull or repel migrants.

Two theories that have had considerable influence on migration studies are the Lewis two-sector model (Lewis, 1954:139-91) and the Harris-Todaro model (Harris and Todaro, 1970:126-42) both of which use the neoclassical economic analysis to explain migration. These theories view migration as an individually determined process that responds to wage rate differentials between the modern industrial sector or country, and the traditional subsistence agricultural sector or economy in another. Lewis argues that during the process of economic development, labor in the industrial economy will be paid a price equal to its marginal product. This price will be higher than the average product of labor in the subsistence economy, where household members share in the product of those who work regardless of the contribution each makes. As long as this differential exists, labor will move from the agricultural subsistence to the industrial economies. The basic decision to move rests with the individual or household while the major attraction is the improvement of the migrant's welfare and that of his or her family.

Harris and Todaro modified the Lewis hypothesis by introducing the probability of finding a job in the host country in the migrant's decision-making processes. This modification draws attention to the importance of information networks, their reliability and quality. Among the most important information channels, particularly in Africa, are relatives and friends in the host country on their return home after a tour of duty. They provide information on wages, working conditions, social life, guidance, and shelter before the migrant finds a job. They also provide an important cultural and psychological crutch to a newly arrived migrant.

The major weakness of these theories is their disregard of noneconomic factors that influence the migrant's decision to move. The distribution of assets, land tenure systems, population pressures, taxation practices, and other governmental policies in the labor-supplying countries play an important role in the migrant's decision to move. In the Harris-Todaro model, some noneconomic factors could be factored into the assessment of the prospects of finding a job. While perhaps useful in looking at migration in the industrial countries of Western Europe, North America, and Australia, these theories cannot explain African migration. They ignore the impact of colonial administration, the creation of national boundaries that cut across ethnic and tribal lines, and the fact that in precolonial periods Africans moved about with their livestock in search of good pastures. Because of colonial boundaries that cut across ethnic groups and the weaknesses of administrative systems, international migration in Africa takes place whenever migrants visit relatives for any extended period. Some migrants eventually seek employment or join the informal sector abroad. Zachariah and Conde (1981) found that in the Ivory Coast there were many foreigners who worked in the informal sector as artisans or traders. In this case, motivation to migrate may not only reflect differentials in wage rates or other opportunities to find a job, but also a desire to be near relatives.

Two alternative theories look beyond the individual migrant and into the society, its internal organization and linkages with the rest of the world: Marxist and global interdependence theories. The Marxist theory views migration as a link between the capitalist industrial economies, which are at the center of the global economic system, and the traditional subsistence economies, which are at the periphery of this system. Because of technological improvements and the scarcity of capital, labor will gradually become separated from the means of production in the subsistence sector, thereby creating a reserve army of the unemployed. The weak bargaining position of labor vis-à-vis capital ensures that labor is paid less than its marginal product and that the extra surplus is appropriated by capital and reinvested to accumulate more capital. This process of capital accumulation makes the periphery dependent on the center for employment, with incomes in the form of remittances and modern goods consumed in the periphery. The Marxist analysis has been used to explain labor migration in Southern Africa and the dependency relationships between South Africa and surrounding labor supplying economies (Legassick and deClercq, 1984:140-66; Davies, 1985:57-78).

Global interdependence views migration as one of the three flows—trade, capital, and migration—that link developed industrial countries and the less developed agricultural ones. This school contends that from a global economy standpoint, the objective must be to maximize welfare through efficient resource allocation. Workers should, therefore, be permitted to move to where they can maximize their wages. If labor cannot move to where it is needed because of political constraints, capital should move to labor surplus countries. Migration is an integral part of the relationship between the more developed and the less developed countries.

The main weakness of the interdependence theory arises from the fact that the world does not operate with the objective of maximizing global welfare through trade, capital flows, and migration. There are political, social, and cultural constraints to the free movement of labor and to the closing of inefficient industries in the developed countries and their transfer to labor surplus producers. Its advantage, however, is to draw attention to the counterpart flows to labor migration, namely, remittances and their importance in removing foreign exchange constraints and ameliorating poverty in the labor-supplying countries. The policy implication is that labor-exporting countries can accelerate their domestic growth through efficient and productive use of remittances and by instituting policies that will encourage migrants to save and remit their earnings, as in the case of Korea. According to Swamy (1985:26), Korea has succeeded in maximizing benefits from migration by licensing one company to supply labor to the Middle East. This company is obligated to remit 80 percent of the monthly income of each migrant and these funds are then paid to the migrant's family in local currency by the Bank of Korea. Thus, Korea gets immediate foreign exchange benefits and reduces the chances of expenditures on luxury items by the migrants.

It is clear that international labor migration is complex and cannot be explained by one or two models or theories. While economic factors play an important role in the individual's or group's choices to move, they are by no means the only ones. Noneconomic factors, for example, social, cultural, health, educational, and political, influence in varying degrees the ultimate decisions by migrants. Although it is difficult to analyze the differential impact of all these factors on migrants' choices, examination of labor migration within a specific historical context and within a process of economic and political transformation in both the host and labor-exporting countries, can lead to a better appreciation of the phenomenon. In the case of Southern Africa, the combined Marxist and interdependence schools explain migration better than those theories that attempt to explain the behavior of migrants in terms of income differentials and the probability of getting a job.

The thrust of this paper is that international labor migration in Southern Africa can best be understood through a study of the nomadic nature of African societies before colonization; the contract for indentured labor and the subsequent contract labor system for European plantations, mines, and households during the colonial period; and the postindependence political economy of Southern Africa (Adepoju, 1984b: 441-42). The combination of historical and political economy approaches to migration permits an analysis of several important topics. Among them are the role of government in both host and home countries; the way in which recruitment is organized; the process of structural transformation in the host and home countries; demographic changes relative to land holdings and property rights; and the policy options that can be pursued to bring about expanded development opportunities in the home countries. This approach recognizes the fundamental importance of economic factors as the cause of internal and international labor migration but goes beyond them to explore the causes of increasing landlessness and the lack of health, educational, and cultural services in the labor-exporting countries. It permits questions to be raised about the types and nature of actions labor-exporting countries can take to avoid possible mass expulsion of their nationals by host countries, such as those which occurred in Ghana during the late 1960s, or Nigeria in 1983, or the sudden termination of recruitment of Mozambicans by South Africa in September 1986. Using this approach, the evolution of international labor migration in Southern Africa will be explored in the following sections.

THE SETTING

The Southern Africa region consists of the nine countries that constitute the Southern African Development Coordinating Council (SADCC), as well as Namibia and South Africa. The SADCC members are Angola, Botswana, Lesotho, Malawi, Mozambique, Swaziland, Tanzania, Zambia, and Zimbabwe. Except for Tanzania and Zambia, which banned recruitment of labor at independence, all SADCC countries export labor to South Africa, all import the bulk of their industrial and consumer goods from South Africa, and all depend on South Africa's railways and harbors for their exports and imports. With the exception of Angola, Mozambique, and Namibia, all SADCC countries had been under British colonial rule, even though South Africa enjoyed a special status from the beginning.

In 1983, the total population of Southern Africa was 107 million and growing at an average annual rate of 3.1 percent. South Africa's share of this regional population in the same year was 32 million, or 30 percent, and growing at an average annual rate of 2.7 percent. The share of the labor force in the total population for the SADCC countries and Namibia was 50.3 percent in 1983 compared to South Africa's 56 percent. The projected growth rate per annum through the year 2000 is 3.1 and 2.7 percent for SADCC countries and South Africa, respectively. These figures show that not only does South Africa have the largest population in the region, but also that its labor force participation is also the highest. This means that South Africa will have to create more jobs for its own people, thereby decreasing the number of foreign workers it can absorb.

In terms of GNP per capita, South Africa is also by far the dominant power in the region. Its GNP per capita was $2,340 in 1984 compared to the average of $610 for the six SADCC countries for which data are available. In addition to its large size, the South African economy is highly diversified, with agriculture accounting for less than 10 percent of the Gross Domestic Product in 1984, compared to 60–70 percent in the SADCC countries. Although the average growth rate of GNP per capita for South Africa in the period 1965–84 was 1.4 percent a year, compared to almost 3.4 percent for SADCC, its base was several times higher than that of SADCC members.

Because of South Africa's dominance of the region in terms of population and economic weight, and because of its central role as the country of immigration, this study will focus mainly on South Africa. The size of foreign African population in South Africa ranged from a low of 229,000 in 1911, to a high of 664,526 in 1951, and down to 406,072 in 1976. The analysis will examine developments in labor migration during the precolonial period (1652–1860), the colonial period (1860-1960), and the postcolonial period (since 1960).

PRECOLONIAL PERIOD: 1652–1860

International labor migration in Southern Africa is associated with the establishment of the first European settlement in the Cape Province in 1652. In their efforts to develop sugar plantations and other agricultural activities along the coast, the settlers encountered labor shortages that were to persist for the next two hundred years because of their inability to attract the African pastoralists that inhabited the interior of the country. During the same period, European immigration to South Africa was slow in comparison to the much larger waves of immigration to North America, Australia, and New Zealand during the same period (Stahl, 1981:8). In fact, by about 1750, the European population in South Africa was only about 200,000. To solve these labor shortages, the settlers imported slaves from the South East Asian Islands and indentured laborers from India to work on the plantations.

According to Stahl, the Afrikaners' (predominantly Dutch and French settlers) "use of Hottentot, imported slaves and Bantu to perform manual labor on their farms imbued . . . [them] with the attitude that menial physical labor on the part of whites was degrading" (1981:8). It was this attitude that later gave rise to a rigid system of occupational color bar in the mines and throughout the whole economy of South Africa. The indentured labor system was the precursor of the present system of contract labor used by the mines and of the past laws which are based on a master/servant agreement that forbids desertion during the contract period. According to Wilson, "legal curbs on the geographic mobility of labour in South Africa go back as far as 1760 when slaves were required to carry passes in moving between urban and rural areas" (1972:2).

In 1834, the British, who had by then taken administration of the Cape Province and Natal, emancipated the slaves. The Afrikaners objected so strongly to this measure that they decided to pack their wagons with their belongings and move farther north to establish their own republics. During this "Great Trek," as the movement was known, the Afrikaners came into contact with indigenous African pastoralists, with whom they fought for control of land and grazing rights. By the 1860s, the Afrikaners defeated the Africans and took over their land to establish private farms on which to graze their animals and grow crops (Stahl, 1981:9; for a detailed background, see Wilson and Thompson, 1969–1971). Dispossessed of their land, the Africans were then compelled to work on white farms, thereby relieving the labor shortage which continued to plague the settlers. The white farmers entered into all types of arrangements with the Africans living on their farms, including their payment of rent by working, share-cropping, or both.

It is thus important to note two things with regard to the evolution of South Africa's present labor system. First, labor shortages in Southern Africa in the early stages of economic development were relieved by slavery and the African dispossession of land which compelled them to sell their services as laborers. Second, there was an association of particular races with particular types of work, and there were legal barriers to labor mobility. Increasing landlessness in the rural areas generated the push factors for migration that occurred during the colonial period.

COLONIAL PERIOD: 1860–1960

As far as South Africa is concerned, the period between 1860 and 1960 was characterized by (a) the discovery and aggressive development of an extraction industry in diamonds and gold; and (b) the rapid transformation of the economy from one based on agriculture to one dominated by diversified industry and service. Diamonds and gold, discovered respectively in 1868 and 1886, required deep-mining techniques which called for power tools and skilled technicians. Capital, technology, and skilled miners were imported from Europe while black unskilled miners were recruited from South Africa and the neighboring States. A small number of white miners were used in the mining operations; they supervised large numbers of unskilled black miners. There was no attempt to train or to offer upward occupational mobility to black miners.

South Africa's neighboring states were under British and Portuguese colonial administrations which neglected economic development and focused on the adjudication of land disputes between white settlers and the Africans. In 1890, Cecil Rhodes, under banner of the British South Africa Company (BSAC), went into Zimbabwe with soldiers, a Royal Charter, and concessions for mineral rights. When mining proved difficult, these soldiers were compensated with land taken from the Matabele and Shona Kingdoms that inhabited the area. European settlement and the scramble for land between the settlers and the Africans began.

The BSAC focused its attention on land transactions and opened an Estates' Department to promote European settlement. Through lands' commissions and orders-in-council, the British government created "land reserves" for the African population. Outside these reserves land could be freely sold. The 1925 Morris Carter Land Commission, which was created to define separate land requirements for Europeans and Africans, used an interesting needs test. A European needed a "land of sufficient fertility and location to provide an income which would attract settlers and also suffice to maintain a European standard of living. For the African, however, the basis was average acreage per household—that is, enough land to provide subsistence for a family" (World Bank, 1986b:4). This creation of African reserves without regard to land fertility and the size of African populations resulted in overcrowding, soil erosion, and land degradation that compelled most Africans to seek employment as migrant workers in white farms in Zimbabwe or mines in South Africa. Similar European settlements were also taking place in Mozambique at about the same time.

Developments in South Africa

The opening of mines in South Africa exacerbated the already critical labor shortages there. The mining companies competed with each other for labor by raising wages. This reduced profits but failed to increase labor supplies. Despite various attempts through the Chamber of Mines, created in 1889 to encourage coordination of wage rates, different mining companies continued to offer competitive wages to African miners to induce them to move from one mine to another at the end of their contract. To eliminate competitive wage increases and assure adequate labor supplies both from inside South Africa and the neighbouring British and Portuguese colonies, the Chamber of Mines sought to create a monopsony system through the centralized recruitment of labor and the use of political influence to secure legislation in the supplying nations that would create sufficient "push" conditions to ensure regular flows.

Organization of Recruitment

To enhance their profitability, the mining companies sought to control wages. This was to be achieved either by enforced wage reductions, which would be resisted by both white and black miners, or by increasing black labor supplies without an increase in wages. Accordingly,

> in 1893 the Chamber of Mines established a Native Labour Department with a twofold objective of assuring an adequate and regular supply of black labour by opening up sources of supply within the Transvaal and by arranging for the recruiting of labourers from Mozambique, and of taking active steps for the gradual reduction of native wages to a reasonable level. (Wilson, 1972:3)

For the first time, the extension of recruitment into Mozambique showed that the mining companies were prepared to go beyond their traditional recruitment areas of South Africa—the High Commission Territories of Bechuanaland (Botswana), Basutoland (Lesotho) and Swaziland—to obtain laborers. By the time of the Anglo-Boer War of 1899–1902, it is estimated that there were approximately 97,000 miners from Portuguese East Africa (Legassick and de Clercq, 1984:147). Overall, between 1890 and 1900, the Chamber of Mines made many efforts to increase recruitment while keeping wages low. However, these efforts were only partially successful because white farmers still competed with the mining companies and against each other for labor and competitive wage rates.

Black miners sometimes deserted the mines after they had been recruited by touters at a high cost to mine owners. The touters often painted a rosy picture of work in the mines. After migrants arrived, many deserted and returned to their homes or became farm laborers. To counteract this problem, the Chamber of Mines persuaded the Transvaal Volkraad Parliament to adopt a "pass law" in 1894. As Stahl (1981:12) points out, during the Chamber's sixth annual meeting of 1895:

> the Chamber drafted a set of pass regulations, which provided means for the proper registration and identification of natives and for compelling them to fulfill contracts voluntarily entered into. With these regulations in force, the companies would be warranted in incurring the very considerable expense of bringing "boys" from a distance; although the initial cost would be heavy, full compensation would be found in the reduced rate of wages.

Despite the enforcement of the pass legislation, desertions and competitive wage increases continued. This was particularly true during the Anglo-Boer war when labor shortages became critical. Following negotiations among the companies, an agreement was reached in 1901 to establish a centralized African labor recruitment agency, the Witwatesrand Native Labor Association (WNLA). The WNLA was to see that:

> No company, whilst a member of the Witwatesrand Native Labor Association, will be allowed under any circumstance to engage any but white labour, except through the agency of the Association. This will apply: (1) to all natives who, from having previously worked on your mine or who from any cause may come forward and seek such work voluntarily; (2) to those who have been recruited within or without the Transvaal—in fact to all natives or coloured men employed either above or below ground on your property. (Transvaal Chamber of Mines: Annual Report, 1900-1901, quoted in Stahl, 1981:12)

Despite this centralization of recruitment and distribution of labor, shortages still persisted, and in 1904 the Chamber of Mines resorted to the recruitment of indentured Chinese from North China (Richardson, 1984:167–85). The choice of China as a source was dictated, among other factors, by the fact that natural disasters, overpopulation, diminishing land holdings, poverty, and vulnerability to changes in the international economy during the period 1890 to 1900, and the U.S. exclusion of Chinese immigrants, had created conditions in China that favored emigration. Between 1904 and 1907, 63,000 indentured Chinese miners were recruited. This program was, however, terminated because of the pressure exerted in Britain after the election of the Liberal Government in 1905. About 50,000 men were repatriated to China at the end of their contracts in 1907.

With the centralization of recruitment and distribution of labor, the Chamber of Mines was able to expand the pool of labor supplies far beyond South Africa and to keep the wages of African miners down. Between 1904 and 1978, the total mine labor increased from 77,000 to 478,600 (see Table 4.1). The proportion of South African to non–South African labor increased from 23 to 57 percent during the same period. This shift in the ratio of local to foreign labor indicates a deliberate strategy by the Chamber of Mines to reduce dependence on foreign supplies of labor over which it has limited influence or control. This change toward internalizing labor supplies poses many challenges for the labor-supplying States, many of which have come to depend on labor migration as a source of employment and income generation. These will be discussed later on in this chapter.

Table 4.1 shows the growth of employment of white and black labor in the gold mines between 1911 and 1969 and the wage differential between white and black miners. Between 1911 and 1969, white miners increased from 22,621 to 39,660 and black miners from 183,793 to 364,151. The ratio of black to white miners increased marginally from 7.7 to 1 in 1911 to 9.2 to 1 in 1969. These ratios reflected legislative requirements for a fixed employment ratio between white and black miners. Although the employment ratio between white and black miners remained relatively stable during this period, the gap between the earnings of white to that of black miners widened from 11.7 to 1 in 1911 to 20.1 to 1 in 1969. This change reflected the differential bargaining power of each group. This gap also reflects the success of the Chamber of Mines in keeping black miners' real wages under control. Using 1936 as the base (1936 = 100), the index of black miners wages was 11 percent less in 1961 than in 1911, while that of white miners rose by 29 percent during the same period.

Political and Legislative Measures

In addition to developing a single channel for the recruitment and distribution of labor, the mining companies exerted political influence to generate labor supplies both from within South Africa and from the neighboring colonial states. With regard to South Africa, the main factor affecting availability of labor was the loss of land by the Africans. In 1903, a Native Affairs Commission was set up to look into the issue of land sales between whites and Africans. In 1906, it recommended that purchases of land by "natives" be restricted to certain areas; that squatting on white farms and sharecropping be discouraged by strict enforcement of antisquatting laws; that taxation of Africans on public lands be strictly enforced; and that purchase of land for collective communal possession by Africans be prohibited. These recommendations were later enacted into law. As a result, about 60 percent of the Africans lived on and owned 7 percent of the land (Stahl, 1981:18). In 1936, an additional 6 percent of land was added to the 7 percent reserved for Africans. Despite this, the restricted allocation of land meant an increasing population density, fragmentation of land, and increasing landlessness which contributed to emigration. Strict enforcement of taxation laws further compelled many Africans to seek cash employment in the mines in between planting and harvesting seasons. This was reinforced by policies which

Table 4.1
Employment, Earnings Index, and Ratio of White to Black Labor in the Gold Mines, 1911–69

Year	White	Black	Ratio Black:White	Index of Real Earnings White (cash) 1936 =	Black (cash & food) 100
1911	24,746	190,137	7.7 : 1	92	111
1921	21,036	172,694	8.2 : 1	88	77
1931	22,654	210,238	9.3 : 1	88	91
1941	41,424	368,417	9.0 : 1	93	93
1951	44,291	298,754	6.9 : 1	114	93
1961	49,144	399,009	8.1 : 1	127	96
1969	39,660	364,151	9.2 : 1	178	108

Source: Wilson, 1973:66, 157.

gave African farmers in the reserves little access to the credit, subsidized fertilizers, and marketing support programs available to the white farmers. This led to reduced agricultural productivity for black farmers, which in turn increased pressure on them to seek supplementary income from the mines or nonmining activities in urban centres. Although the mining companies could have substituted cheap black labor for white skilled workers through training programs, the white unions used their influence to incorporate a number of color bar provisions in the Mines and Work Amendment Bill of 1926. This legislation established a list of occupations to be reserved for whites and the ratio of black miners that could be employed for every white mine worker. This color bar reservation was later extended to other nonmining sectors including railways and other industrial occupations. It made an increase in black mine employment a function of the availability of expensive white labor (Wilson, 1973:7–12; Stahl, 1981:21–27).

Developments in the Colonial States

While the collusion between the mining companies and the government created pressures that generated more labor in South Africa, parallel developments were taking place in the labor-supplying countries which also involved collusion between the colonial administration, mine owners, and white farmers. Three instruments were used in varying degrees to ensure adequate supplies of labor: (a) bilateral labor agreements with various labor-supplying States regarding such matters as the recruitment quotas, attestation fees, predeparture medical check-ups, and repatriation; (b) taxation; and (c) restriction on land acquisition by Africans.

Because of the expectations by Britain and South Africa that the three High Commission Territories of Basutoland, Bechuanaland, and Swaziland would eventually be transferred to South Africa, no bilateral agreements covering recruitment were signed with the British colonial administration. Instead, migrants from these countries were treated in the same way as South Africans until the end of the 1950s, when Britain decided to prepare these countries for independence instead of transferring them to South Africa.

Recruitment from Mozambique, on the other hand, was covered by the first Inter-State Agreements in 1901 (Rugege, 1985:148-50). The reason for this differential treatment was that Mozambique was considered a foreign country over which the British imperial government, which also ruled South Africa, had no control and over which the mine owners could exercise little influence. Yet, Mozambique had already provided 100,000 black miners to South Africa prior to this agreement (Wilson, 1972:4).

The 1901 agreement between Mozambique and South Africa provided for the licensing of recruitment agencies, attestation fees to be paid, guaranteed deposits, repatriation of miners back to Mozambique after their contracts, and the use of "best efforts" by the South African government to discourage clandestine migration. This agreement allowed Mozambique to obtain much needed revenue. In 1909, the convention was amended to require compulsory deferred pay to be remitted to Mozambique and await the miners' return. In return for the remittance of deferred pay, WNLA was given complete recruitment monopoly. The Transvaal government, in turn, agreed to a revision of the bilateral agreement in 1928 to direct certain volumes of exports and imports through the port of Lorenco Marques or Maputo.

Regarding recruitment from Malawi, the colonial administration signed a 1903 agreement with WNLA which permitted it to recruit an "experimental batch of one thousand labourers" (Tapela, 1979:74). Soon,

> labour became a major item of export and its utilization locally was implicitly discouraged. The Government assisted WNLA in its recruitment by seconding a Protectorate official to the Association but agents of local labour-needing enterprises, such as the Shire Highlands Railway Company were given no assistance and, in fact, were prohibited from seeking help from anybody. (Tapela, 1979:74)

However, from 1913 to 1938, recruitment from Malawi and other tropical countries north of latitude 22° was prohibited by the South African government because of the high death incidence among Nyasa miners. It has also been suggested that this prohibition of recruitment of Nyasa miners by South Africa was taken in consultation with the colonial government, which wanted to ensure labor availability to local white estates that were developing at the time. However, recruitment was later resumed after a royal commission of inquiry was set up by the colonial government to examine the desirability of sending men to South African mines (Wilson, 1972:69). As far as Southern Rhodesia (Zimbabwe) was concerned, no formal agreement was concluded with the mining companies. Zimbabwe was treated in the same way as the High Commission Territories.

Two additional measures used by the colonial governments to generate labor supplies were taxation and land dispossession. Soon after the discovery of diamonds and the declaration of Lesotho as a protectorate in 1868, the British government introduced the first poll tax legislation which was later also introduced in Swaziland (1896) and Botswana (1899). In 1907, Native Proclamations No. 27, in the case of Lesotho, and No. 45, in the case of Botswana, were gazetted. These provided for licensing of recruitment agents, for payment of attestation and other fees (Rugege, 1985:147-48). In Malawi, a poll tax, which was to be paid in cash by every man between 18 and 65 years old, was introduced in 1882. It was replaced in 1893 by a "Hut Tax to hit at the polygamous men. Men married to more than one wife paid six shillings for each hut occupied by a wife, for wives under polygamous marriages live in different huts" (Chilivumbo, 1985:340). The colonial government in Mozambique enacted legislation requiring proof from every man that he had held paid employment for at least six months in any particular year (Lucas, 1983:13). This forced the Mozambicans to seek domestic wage employment or go to the mines in South Africa.

The legislative measures taken in South Africa and in the labor-supplying states generated sufficient supplies of labor for the mines, the white farms, and the industrial sectors of South Africa. Over time, there developed a labor force which was dependent on paid employment and was moving between its respective home countries and South Africa for periods of one to two years. The income earned by the workers enabled them to pay taxes, acquire some modern consumer goods, and supplement their rural incomes. From the point of view of the mining companies, the system enabled them to adjust supplies to cyclical fluctuations in international demand for their commodities. It also permitted the companies to take advantage of fully developed and productive labor without investment or contribution to the costs of upbringing or training of that labor. The low wages paid to the black miners enabled the companies to maximize their profits and reinvestment.

With the coming to power of the South African Nationalist government in 1948, basic policy changes and regulations for the attraction, distribution, and repulsion of black labor were introduced. The structure of the economy also changed significantly toward more manufacturing services and transport. Nonmining and nonagricultural employment expanded rapidly and black wages increased. Some of these changes are reviewed in the section that follows.

POSTCOLONIAL PERIOD: 1960 TO THE PRESENT

By the late 1950s and the early 1960s, significant economic, political, and social changes were taking place in South Africa. Internally, the Africans began to organize themselves politically and to oppose pass laws that restricted their movement. The state reacted by adopting strong security measures that culminated in (a) the 1956 treason trial; (b) the declaration of migrants from the High Commission Territories as "foreign workers" requiring special permission to take up employment outside mining (which was not the case before); (c) the establishment of government labor bureaus from which employers needing workers could apply for permission to hire foreign workers or workers from the rural areas (homelands); and (d) the "weeding out of foreign workers who had acquired permanent residence qualifications" (Legassick and de Clercq, 1984:155). These measures established a system that regulated the demand for and the movement of migrants and other workers outside the mining and farming sectors.

On the labor-exporting side, both Tanzania and Zambia stopped labor exports to South Africa following their independence in 1961 and 1966, respectively. In 1974, a plane carrying Malawian miners crashed in Botswana, and Malawi suspended recruitment. The independent Marxist government which came to power in Mozambique in 1976 was trusted neither by the mining companies nor South Africa to continue to permit labor recruitment, and this encouraged the acceleration of the internalization of migrant labor. At the same time, the South African government intensified its laws pertaining to where different races could live. It enacted the Group Areas Act and began to implement aggressively a policy to create autonomous homelands for various ethnic groups and grant them independence with the eventual loss of South African citizenship for their people. The South African government also removed surplus population from white farms and resettled them in these homelands for security reasons.

Economically, the period from 1960 onward saw massive efforts by South Africa to accelerate manufacturing activities in line with the recommendations of the Viljoen Commission of 1958. Rapid development of manufacturing and services required more labor, which was drawn from the homelands where there was low agricultural productivity, increasing landlessness due to rapid population growth, and the deportation of unemployed urban blacks to their ethnic homelands. At the same time, wage boards granted wage increases that, in turn, encouraged mechanization by employers who took advantage of foreign capital inflows and technology. All these changes led to open unemployment among the blacks. In contrast to these restrictions on African mobility and labor migration, white immigration continued to be encouraged.

The mining companies decided to change their strategy and diversify their sources of labor supply to avoid heavy dependence on foreign supplies of labor whose unpredictability was confirmed by the Malawi suspension of recruitment in 1974. The strategy of internal recruitment of labor revealed in the 1977 Budget and Objectives of Mine Labor Organization included, among other things, maintenance of relations with as many suppliers as possible; the increase of South African recruits from 46 to 50 percent; the setting of country limits at 30,000 for Mozambique, 20,000 for Zimbabwe, and 20,000 for Malawi; and the attainment of total recruitment of 466,000 workers (Davies, 1985:88).

At the same time, the major change in many labor-supplying countries during the 1960s was their gaining of political independence. The exceptions were Angola and Mozambique, which attained independence in 1976, and Zimbabwe which became independent in 1980 after a protracted war of liberation. At independence, these countries suffered from acute poverty and lack of adequate domestic employment opportunities resulting from the colonial policy of benign neglect. Botswana, Lesotho, Malawi, and Swaziland were so poor that domestic revenues did not cover government budgets and Britain had to support them for several years following independence. In Zambia, the development of copper mining provided reasonable revenues. The Zambian mines pursued a strategy of stabilizing the labor force in the mines by building houses for the miners and their families and by providing technical training. The same approach was successfully used in Zaire, where stable communities developed around the mining areas.

Lack of adequate domestic employment opportunities, the neglect of agriculture, and the increasing need to purchase modern consumer and capital goods exported by South Africa have contributed to the continuing dependence on the migrant labor system by Botswana, Lesotho, Malawi, Mozambique, and Swaziland. This dependence was insitutionalized in the form of separate bilateral agreements between each of the five countries and South Africa, which provided, inter alia, for the voluntary remittance of deferred payments. Although these remittances reduced poverty, they created further dependence and led to the continuing neglect of agriculture and other productive activities in the labor exporters (de Vletter, 1982:1-4). According to one source, the Labour Agreement of 1964 (South African Treaty Series No. 11 of 1964) between Portugal and South Africa covered the remittances of Mozambicans and included a secret gold clause whereby the miners' deferred wages were paid in gold at the official price of $35.00 per ounce. Upon their return to Mozambique, the miners received local currency, while the gold went into Portugal's reserves and was valued at the higher international price. No such arrangements were made with the other countries and this secret gold clause was terminated by South Africa soon after Mozambique gained independence.

Studies of labor migration and agriculture in Botswana, Lesotho, and Swaziland (de Vletter, 1982) show, among other things, an absence in most households of at least one member; a high degree of dependence on remittance income by rural households; a desire among returning migrants to invest in cattle; and a growing involvement of women in farming. Thus, rural development strategies by the independent states of the region are hampered by an absence of able-bodied men to perform crucial farming tasks. Agriculture and the bringing up of children have been left to women and old men.

The roles of independent governments in the recruitment of labor were passive and facilitative because labor exports provided revenue in the form of fees and an unemployment safety valve. Labor migration bought them time to struggle with the issues of economic development with limited resources. Recently these countries have become concerned about the declining prospects for employment of migrant labor in South Africa and the deliberate strategy by mining companies to switch recruitment to domestic sources. They are also concerned about the potential disruptive political and social effects of massive expulsions of migrants by South Africa, such as those that occurred in the case of Lesotho early in 1974.

BENEFITS AND COSTS OF MIGRATION TO SOUTHERN AFRICA

South Africa's labor migration system has benefitted the development of the South African economy. It has served to relieve labor shortages which characterized the economy from its earliest settler times; it permitted the development of the mining industry; and the low wages paid by the mines enabled them to accumulate high profits which were reinvested to further accelerate capital accumulation. The South African economy neither paid for the costs of bringing up and training migrants prior to their taking up employment, nor did it incur the medical costs of caring for retired miners or for diseases contracted in the mines such as tuberculosis. (For an extensive review of the benefits and social costs of the system on the migrants themselves, see Wilson, 1972.)

South Africa's migrant labor system has had no visible costs to the South African economy that are not outweighed by significant benefits. The presence of migrant labor has not only permitted the South African economy to maintain low wages, but has also given South Africa important political leverage in its relations with its black-ruled neighbors. Threats of massive expulsion of miners have been used repeatedly in recent years in the fight against sanctions considered and instituted by the international community. At the same time, South Africa has not hesitated to use migrants as a weapon in its disagreements with its neighbors. For example, in September 1986 recruitment of Mozambican miners was suddenly halted in order to pressure Mozambique to reconsider its disagreements with South Africa. Migrant labor has also made it difficult for effectively unionizing African mine workers.

Labor Exporters

The main benefit of the labor migration system to the labor exporting countries is the partial alleviation of poverty through substantial remittances. Table 4.2 shows the estimated annual remittances to the economies of Botswana, Le-

Table 4.2
Migrant Labor Remittances from South Africa to Selected Labor Supplying States, 1973–83 (Millions)

	Botswana (Rands)	Lesotho (Rands)	Malawi (Kwachas)	Mozambique[a] (Rands)	US $	Swaziland (Rands)
1973	14.8	47.0	–	–		–
1974	6.7	63.0	12.4	75.0		4.1
1975	9.5	104.2	10.7	94.9		12.4
1976	17.9	129.0	17.5	152.2		6.9
1977	17.6	160.1	23.0	223.1		8.6
1978	15.5	187.3	31.5	287.1		9.8
1979	13.3	217.5	56.3	–	–	8.9
1980	17.9	280.3	81.1	–	53.4	8.6
1981	17.6	393.8	74.1	–	64.5	26.9
1982	22.6	457.3	74.0	–	61.7	19.4
1983	–	524.2	75.0	–	71.9	

[a]Estimates are based on monthly wage payments, a contract period of 16 months, and an average annual 100,000 migrants. Calculations by World Bank staff.

Source: United Nations, *National Accounts Statistics: Main Aggregate and Detailed Tables, 1983* (New York, 1983). World Bank, *Mozambique: An Introductory Economic Survey* (Washington, D.C., 1985).

sotho, Malawi, Mozambique, and Swaziland between 1973 and 1983. These remittances have ranged from the low of R 6.7 million in 1974 to the high of R 22.6 million in 1982 for Botswana; R 47.0 million in 1973 to R 524.2 million in 1983 for Lesotho; K 12.4 million in 1974 to K 75.0 million in 1983 for Malawi; R 75.0 million in 1973 to R 287.1 million in 1978 for Mozambique; and from the low of R 4.1 million in 1974 to the high of R 26.9 million in 1981 in the case of Swaziland. Table 4.3 presents these remittances as a percentage of the Gross Domestic Product (GDP) of each country. In the case of Botswana, the importance of remittances as a percent of GDP has declined from 8 percent in 1978 to 2.3 percent in 1982. For Malawi, remittances have increased from 2.0 percent of GDP in 1975 to 5.5 in 1983, and from 2.2 percent in 1980 to 2.8 percent in 1984 for Mozambique. The case of Lesotho is unique and shows that remittances as a percentage of GDP increased from 54 percent in 1973 to a high of 106 percent in 1983. This reflects the overdependence of Lesotho on migrant labor not only for employment but also for income to maintain high consumption levels and asset acquisition in the form of livestock and building of houses (Lucas, 1983; de Vletter, 1982). If for some reason migrants were returned to Lesotho in large numbers, a drastic decrease in the national income would result, and this

Table 4.3
Labor Income from Abroad as a Percentage of Gross Domestic Product, 1973–84

	Botswana	Lesotho	Malawi	Swaziland	Mozambique
1973	8.0	53.5	–	–	–
1974	3.2	64.3	2.6	2.6	–
1975	3.5	93.8	2.0	5.8	–
1976	5.8	90.2	2.8	2.9	–
1977	5.0	79.9	3.1	3.3	–
1978	3.1	64.3	3.9	3.0	–
1979	1.9	71.8	6.2	2.4	–
1980	2.3	67.6	8.6	1.8	2.2
1981	2.3	80.4	7.0	4.8	2.8
1982	2.3	102.1	6.2	3.4	2.7
1983	–	106.5	5.5	–	3.7
1984	–	104.4	–	–	2.8

Source: United Nations, *National Accounts Statistics: Main Aggregates and Detailed Tables, 1983* (New York: 1983). World Bank, *Mozambique: An Introductory Economic Survey* (Washington, D.C., 1985).

would reduce consumption sharply in addition to creating a large unemployment problem (Cobbe, 1982b:38).

Migrant earnings also play an important role by relieving foreign exchange constraints in the countries that maintain separate currency areas such as Botswana, Malawi, Mozambique, and Zimbabwe. In the case of Lesotho and Swaziland, which maintain a common currency area with South Africa, remittances finance the large negative trade balance between these countries and South Africa. Finally, migration has acted as an important safety valve for the chronic unemployment problem faced by the labor-exporting states.

While these benefits of migration are undeniable, the labor exporting countries also incur considerable economic, social, and political costs. First, there is the cost of raising the potential migrants. The home countries provide health, education, and other services at subsidized rates from the time the potential migrants are born to the time they are ready to enter the labor force. When they start working, they are lost from the economy except during brief periods between contracts. Their governments do not recover these costs from remittances because migrant income is not taxed. Second, during their working life, migrants generate surplus product, which is appropriated by the mining companies in the form of higher profits, which are reinvested in South Africa, thereby generating further capital accumulation there. This reinvestment of accumulated capital widens the development gap between host and labor-supplying countries. Third, when the migrants finally return home because of old age or diseases contracted in the mines, there are no pensions or insurance schemes to pay for their care. They become a burden to an economy which has not benefitted from their productive years and has, in fact, suffered from the loss of their services. Fourth, the long absences of the male migrants from home leads to a neglect of agriculture and loss of other domestic opportunities for the establishment of viable enterprises, as the burden of development is left in the hands of women, children, and old men.

One must also consider such social costs such as those associated with children growing up without fathers. This leads to many social, psychological, and delinquency problems which later trouble the labor-exporting societies. Finally, there is the political cost of loss of independent economic and political action due to the constant threat of repatriation of large numbers of miners in case of diplomatic or philosophical policy disagreements. Such policy disagreements between South Africa and its neighbors are becoming more frequent and stem fundamentally from the apartheid system.

Policy Options and Issues

The political and economic changes now taking place in South Africa have caused the labor exporting countries of Southern Africa to reconsider the short- and long-term implications of the migrant labor system which has prevailed for more than a century. It may be useful to consider first the major changes that have occurred in South Africa and have a bearing on the system, and second, the alternative options open to labor exporters.

The most significant change that has taken place since the 1960s in South Africa has been the creation of separate ethnic homelands which occupy 13 percent of the land reserved for Africans. These reserves are overpopulated and suffer from high unemployment, poverty, deteriorating agricultural productivity, and increasing landlessness. It was these factors which compelled increasing numbers of people to seek employment in the mines and industry. In order to avoid social upheavals in the homelands, the South African government, with the cooperation of the mining and nonmining business communities, has embarked on a strategy of stepping up recruitment from the homelands while reducing the quotas of recruits from foreign countries, initially Mozambique and Malawi. In addition, South Africa has offered large tax and other investment incentives to those businesses that would decentralize and locate initially around the homelands and later inside them. The intent is that once the businesses locate in the homeland where there is abundant labor, there will be no further need for recruitment of migrants from the labor exporting states.[1]

There is also a structural change in the South African economy which, coupled with the continuing recession, has resulted in substantial open unemployment among blacks. According to First, "an issue with important implications for future perspectives revolves around the question of whether the present period of recession and contraction is merely a phase, an episode or whether it will be a more lasting condition as part of the structural cores in the economy which has produced structural unemployment" (1985:11). Although the issue is still open, First and other researchers have recently concluded that demand for foreign labor in South Africa will decline over the next ten years and that the government of South Africa and its business community have the ability to accelerate the process (Stahl, 1981:24-42). The unresolved issue, however, remains whether decentralizing industry to the homelands and reducing recruitment from foreign areas will allow South Africa to counteract those factors, such as poverty and depressed living conditions, that generate migration and also to tackle its urban unemployment. As far as the labor-exporting countries are concerned, consideration of alternative strategies has become imperative. The policy options that can be pursued can be viewed in terms of short-term and longer-term measures.

Short-Run Options for Labor Senders

In the short-run, some migrant labor will continue to be recruited, although the valve can be turned on or off by South Africa at any time. Assuming no sudden cut-offs, the labor suppliers can pursue several alternative policy strategies simultaneously:

- Negotiate with South Africa on behalf of their nationals for increases in wages and improvement in working conditions and benefits. The probability of success is limited because it requires collective negotiation by the labor exporters. In the past, it has not been possible to form such a unified negotiating position, in part because the mining companies have succeeded in concluding separate agreements with the labor suppliers. The companies can also manipulate recruitment by decreasing it from those suppliers that are driving a hard bargain while increasing it from those that are willing to conclude an agreement quickly.

- Each country could negotiate directly with the mining companies to allow the sending country to supply certain items needed in the mines, for example, basic foods, blankets, and gloves. The success of this option will depend on how competitive the items identified are, vis-à-vis those produced in South Africa. The advantage of this approach is that it will stimulate local production and provide assured markets. From South Africa's point of view, the provision of such supplies would be better if undertaken in the homelands where it would reduce poverty, unemployment, and potential social unrest.

- Negotiate with the mining companies for regular contributions toward vocational and technical training of the miners' children so that they may eventually opt out of the migration cycle. In Lesotho, the mining companies have made, through their recruiting organizations and directly, sporadic donations of hospital equipment and contributions to technical education, tree planting programs, and limited scholarships. This is part of their strategy to earn goodwill. Though useful, these contributions are not sustained and have little meaningful impact.

- Withhold labor from the mines. This option would increase unemployment, cause social unrest in the labor exporting countries, reduce remittances, increase poverty, and reduce government revenue. In order to succeed, the labor exporters would have to form a strong cartel and act simultaneously; otherwise South Africa would be able to play one country against another. Moreover, the employers would just intensify their recruitment from the internal South African sources, including the homelands.

Long-Term Options for Labor Senders

In the long run, reducing dependence on migrant labor employment and earnings is the only viable option open to the labor-exporting countries. Its success requires acceleration of domestic development and alleviation of poverty in both rural and urban sectors. Such a strategy will require a policy shift toward encouraging small-scale farming and the provision of credit, extension services, marketing, introduction of high cash value crops, and applied research. In the urban areas, the strategy will require providing to local entrepreneurs operating in the informal sectors the same incentives that are granted to foreign investors. The governments would also have to improve the efficiency of their public administrations and make them both cost-effective and responsive to the developmental needs of people. Finally, the public enterprises of these states would have to be reformed so that they would contribute to the budgets, instead of draining resources from the treasury, as has been the case (World Bank, 1981:35-44). These policy approaches would need to be coupled with relevant education and curriculum reforms.

The implementation of these policies must be further complemented with cooperation among the labor exporters in order to promote trade among themselves and share research costs and the costs of financing high-level manpower training. This is now taking place under the auspices of the Southern African Development Coordination Council (SADCC), with its secretariat in Botswana. While complete economic de-linking from South Africa would be difficult for some of the countries, their dependence can be reduced through the expansion of domestic employment opportunities. Of course, clandestine migration will continue to take place and migrants will remain a formidable bargaining chip in the hands of South Africa for a long time to come. But a start toward reducing the dependence of the labor exporters on this socially, economically, politically, and culturally costly system is an urgent task facing all labor-exporting states of Southern Africa—and particularly those of Lesotho, Swaziland, Botswana, Mozambique, and Malawi.

CONCLUSION

The evolution of labor migration in all of Southern Africa is closely linked to the historical, economic, political, and social developments in South Africa, the region's most dominant country. From its early settlement days in the mid-seventeenth century, South Africa has experienced labor shortages for its plantations and other farming activities. Africans who still possessed land, and therefore had access to means of production, were unwilling to take up paid employment. The settlers' response was to bring slaves from Southeast Asia and to enslave some of the indigenous people. This was the precursor of the development of attitudes among whites that gave rise to the system of the industrial color bar whereby black Africans were barred by law from supervisory and skilled occupations.

With the abolition of slavery, a process of African disposession of land was unleashed during the Great Trek. Without access to land and other means of production, a large reservoir of black labor developed that was dependent on employment in white-owned farms, mines, industry, and commerce. Institutions were created by the mining companies and legislation passed by the government of South Africa to facilitate recruitment, distribution, and expulsion of labor. The mining companies were also instrumental in getting the "pass laws" and instituting the present contract labor system. These laws and regulations are central to the control of the movement not only of migrant workers, but also of all black people in South Africa. Having created monopsony power through the centralization of recruitment and distribution of labor among its members, the Chamber of Mines reduced black wages and increased the profitability of the mining companies. This exploitation of black miners enabled the companies to maximize their rate of reinvestment and capital accumulation.

At the same time, the government of South Africa developed legislation governing where different races could live. The Africans were confined to 13 percent of the land, in what are known as the "Native Reserves." The depressed economic conditions in these reserves gave rise to a constant flow of migrant labor and facilitated their exploitation by the mining and nonmining companies.

Over time, bilateral labor agreements were concluded with the various neighbouring states that supplied labor to the mines. The agreements provided much needed revenue to these governments and made arrangements for the remittance of deferred pay. These remittances have played an important role in the labor-exporting countries' amelioration of poverty; acquisition of assets such as livestock and building of houses; financing of the importation of essential consumer goods; and payment of school fees. They have also created economic and social dependence. In recent years it has become increasingly clear to the independent labor-supplying states that the real benefits of labor exports are elusive and politically dangerous in the long term. This is particularly true given South Africa's political system, its changing internal policies to stimulate domestic recruitment, and the changing demand in the mining sectors due to depletion of cheap mining areas.

As a result, labor-sending countries have embarked on a series of activities through SADCC aimed at reducing their extreme dependence on South Africa. In the long term, the only viable option for them is to accelerate their economic growth by adopting policies that favor small farmers and local entrepreneurs and by improving their administrations and parastatal enterprises. In the short term, they can seek to maximize the earnings from migration through negotiation with the mining companies and by making arrangements to encourage both the timely remittance of deferred pay as well as its productive investment. They can also intensify their cooperation within the framework of SADCC.

NOTE

1. It should also be noted in passing that the recently established universities in the homelands have attracted highly trained manpower from Lesotho, Botswana, and Swaziland by offering substantial salaries. This has given rise to a phenomenon of brain drain.

Part III

Labor Migration and Development in Greece and Turkey

Part III examines the effects of emigration on Greece and Turkey. In Chapter 5, Papademetriou and Emke-Poulopoulos explain how rural-to-urban Greek migration was transformed into migration to Europe in the 1960s. Greeks debated the benefits and costs of this migration, with the government defending emigration as a blessing, but this chapter concludes that migration may have aggravated as many problems as it resolved. For example, returning migrants preferred to settle in urban areas, leaving the rural areas that they left behind with a work force unattractive to industry, and aggravating congestion in Athens and Salonica. Returning migrants become investors or retire; they are not usually innovative agents of change. Remittances were often expended for housing, fueling real estate and building materials inflation.

Greece did not reap the expected dividends of migration for two reasons: too much was expected of migration, and Greek policies often hurt rather than helped migration-induced development. The authors argue that Greece should work with immigration countries such as Germany to get venture capital and technical assistance for Greek businesses started by remittances, to secure other forms of assistance from Germany and other European countries, and to develop better economic and labor market policies in Greece.

Chapter 6 reviews the reasons why emigration has not promoted development in Turkey. Gitmez emphasizes the unrealistic hopes that Turkish leaders placed on emigration and remittances; returning workers were to be the agents of socioeconomic development in Turkey during the 1960s, while their remittances would make viable Turkey's import substitution development strategy.

Turkish emigration began with the small-scale recruitment of mostly skilled urban workers in the 1960s, but Turkish and German policies soon converted Turkish labor migration into a mass flow of unskilled workers from both rural and urban areas. After the 1973–74 European bans on the further recruitment of migrant workers, Turkish migrants began to settle abroad. The Turkish population in Germany, for example, rose after 1973 despite the recruitment ban because family unification and Turkish births in Germany more than offset exits. However, the composition of the Turkish population in Germany changed from mostly workers to mostly nonworking spouses and children. Gitmez explores differences between migrants who settled abroad and those who returned, concluding that unskilled migrants from rural areas who left their families in Turkey were most likely to return.

Gitmez concludes that emigration did not lead to development in Turkey. Despite the emigration of 1.5 to 2 million workers, the return of at least 1 million, and remittances of more than $25 billion, Gitmez concludes that Turkey has not jumped up the development ladder, that is, Turkey grew, but not faster than nonmigrant countries. Migrants and their families benefitted from migration, but Turkey as a country can benefit only if it adopts economic policies which encourage and assist returning migrants to make full use of their remittance savings and skills.

5

Migration and Development in Greece: The Unfinished Story

Demetrios G. Papademetriou and
Ira Emke-Poulopoulos

Greece has experienced substantial waves of emigration for most of the twentieth century. During the first two decades of this century, more than 400,000 Greeks emigrated, mostly to the United States. During that same period, more than half returned. Between 1920 and 1940, emigration and return migration cancelled each other out, with slightly more than 100,000 people involved in the movement. An interesting feature of these two decades was that more than 70 percent of those emigrating to the United States during the second half of the 1930s were re-emigrants who had, in a sense, waited out the worst of the Great Depression (Filias, 1967a; 1975; Vlachos, 1974; Lianos, 1974). During these two decades, Greece was experiencing the social, economic, and political convulsions arising out of the Asia Minor catastrophe[1] and the subsequent population exchange with Turkey, which added almost 1.2 million Greeks to the population of mainland Greece. This event, coupled with sharply increased birth rates, saw the Greek population expand from about 5 million in 1921 to more than 7.3 million by 1940—an increase of nearly 50 percent in less than 20 years (Greek Statistical Yearbook, various years).

In response to these population pressures, Greece initiated several reforms. Among them were the expansion of administrative services, the establishment of the Agricultural Bank in 1929, several efforts to redistribute land and reduce the land monopoly of large landowners, ambitious irrigation and drainage programs, the introduction of fertilizers, and the promotion of agricultural mechanization. Such measures, however, are thought to have resulted neither in a substantial improvement in Greece's uneven regional development nor in significant changes in the country's socioeconomic structure (Filias, 1967a; 1975). Following the German occupation of Greece during the Second World War, Greece experienced a bloody civil war. Historians point to high levels of social and political mobilization during that time and note that the expectation and aspiration levels of Greeks rose so sharply that N. Polyzos, an eminent authority on Greek migration, warned of "an unprecedented emigration flow from all the social levels of the country, unless serious structural social and economic changes occur" (quoted in Filias, 1975:130).

The required structural changes failed to materialize, and the heightened social, political, and economic expectations were not met. As a result, Greece did not enjoy the economic "miracle" taking place by the late 1950s elsewhere in Europe. In the absence of social, political, and economic changes, and given the chronic unemployment in the cities and severe underemployment in the countryside, the opportunity to enter into labor recruitment agreements with France in 1954,[2] Belgium in 1957, and the Federal Republic of Germany (FRG) in 1960, were welcomed by both the Greek authorities and the unemployed peasants and industrial workers. By 1959, about 15,000 Greeks had emigrated to Belgium, nearly 5,000 to Italy, more than 1,000 to France, and 8,000 to the Federal Republic of Germany (FRG). In all, during the second half of the 1950s, nearly 38,000 Greeks emigrated to Europe. However, nearly three out of four emigrating Greeks during the 1950s continued to go to overseas countries—principally Australia (the single largest destination, receiving nearly 33,000 Greek immigrants during that period), Canada, and the United States (Greek Statistical Yearbook, various years).

A somewhat different situation began to emerge in 1959. The FRG surpassed Belgium as the principal European destination of emigrating Greek workers, despite the fact that a labor recruitment agreement with the FRG was not negotiated until 1960. During the 1960s and early 1970s more than two-thirds of Greek emigrants went to Europe. Notable exceptions were 1967 and 1968, during the height of the European recession, when, respectively, only 37 percent and 46 percent emigrated to Europe (Greek Statistical Yearbook, various years). Throughout the same period (1960-73), more than 80 percent of the Greeks emigrating to Europe went to the FRG, where they comprised between 10 and 15 percent of that country's foreign work force (Bundesanstalt Für Arbeit, various years; Greek Statistical Yearbook, various years). It is this emigration to the FRG that is the principal focus of this essay.[3]

GREEK EMIGRATION

One of the most important post–World War II Greek social phenomena has been the unremitting flight of the Greek population from the countryside to the cities, a process known in Greek as *astyphilia* (attraction to the cities, or more loosely, runaway urbanization). Astyphilia results from conditions common to developing countries: limited amounts of arable land and the subsequent poor ratio of arable land to active farmers; inequitable distribution of land; inadequate mechanization and subsequent low rates of return on labor in agriculture; socioeconomic and cultural isolation and deterioration of the countryside; and totally inadequate health and social services. As late as 1950, more than 83 percent of

Greek farms were smaller than 12 acres. Furthermore, Greece's total cultivated area in 1961 was only slightly more than 9 million acres—making the Greek arable land to population ratio very low (Fragos, 1975; Evangelinides, 1975). Greece's agricultural problems were further compounded by slow mechanization—although the number of tractors and other heavy agricultural equipment increased substantially between 1963 and 1972. (See Papademetriou, 1976, for comparisons of Greek rates of agricultural mechanization with those of other countries in the European periphery during that period.)

A second and related feature of Greek development which is of great relevance to the study of Greek emigration is the lack of balance in the country's regional development and the consequent dichotomy and polarization between center and periphery within Greece. This situation fuels internal migration which reinforces the social, cultural, and economic impoverishment of the countryside. Internal migration, in turn, overloads municipal services and leads to acute socioeconomic deprivations in the perimeters of the two major poles of attraction for internal emigrants: Athens and Salonica. Evangelinides (1975) has looked at Greece's regional development and points out the enormous distance between social, economic, and cultural levels of development in Athens vis-à-vis the rest of Greece.[4] As a result, Athens is the magnet for rural migrants and receives most of the public and private economic investments. This concentration of labor and industry in the Athens region further increases the periphery's stagnation and deterioration (Evangelinides, 1975; Fragos, 1975; Papageorgiou, 1975).[5]

Uneven development and the resulting astyphilia have been structural features of the Greek socioeconomic landscape for the past 50 years. They encouraged the growth of the Athens metropolitan area, which has two-thirds of Greece's urban population and one-third of the country's total population. These forces, and the inability of Athens to absorb effectively internal migrants, fueled international migration despite Greece's relatively low fertility rates.[6] It is not surprising, then, that Greek emigration contributed not only to slow population growth, but occasionally even to net negative growth in the 1960s.[7]

The Greek experience with labor migration demonstrates this point. Greek politics has been marked by "super power" interventions for nearly two hundred years. Such interventions have not only shaped the character of Greek social and political life, but have also defined the country's economic choices. Following the Greek civil war, successive Greek governments opted for largely successful political, social, and economic initiatives which in effect isolated the countryside by reinforcing the already deep dichotomy between the countryside and the key urban areas.[8] This "abandonment" of rural areas, together with the virtual absence of an agricultural credit market, the vagaries of international commodity markets in such key Greek agricultural products as tobacco and raisins, and the concentration of virtually all public and private investment activities around Athens and Salonica, further polarized the country economically and contributed to the periphery's continuing stagnation and isolation. A number of other social and political forces further accelerated this trend, including Greece's entrenched social and frequently repressive political structure and its overgrown, distorted, and often parasitic tertiary sector (led by state employment) which often becomes a Greek's best hope for survival and advancement.

While the contribution of these forces to international migration varies, they do seem to play an important role, as does Greece's need for the advanced industrial states' capital and technological knowledge to which emigration is believed to give Greece better access. Capital and technical knowledge are clearly both critical sine qua nons of economic growth, but are carefully controlled by, and clearly geared toward the advantage of, the advanced industrial societies.

These interrelationships make international migration a central component of the international political economy—one whose investigation requires a sensitivity to and intimacy with the forces operating in the structure and process of the world economy. At the same time, however, one must not lose sight of the many secondary factors which, to varying degrees, influence an individual's decision to emigrate and give Greek emigration its specific character. Among them are personal ambition, ease of access to Western Europe, low transportation costs (when compared with transoceanic emigration), and, *most important*, the receiving countries' labor recruitment policies.

GREEK EMIGRATION AND RETURN

In Greece, there is a relationship between low economic development, social and cultural poverty, and emigration. Leading the emigration rates in the post–World War II period have been a number of islands and prefectures from the northern provinces of Macedonia, Thrace, and Epirus. These were among the least developed regions of Greece in the 1950s and 1960s—socially, economically, and culturally—and routinely provided between 70 and 80 percent of the emigrants to Europe. Meanwhile, Peloponnesus in the south and the Aegean islands, traditional source regions for transoceanic emigration, provided only about one such emigrant in 20 (Greek Statistical Yearbook, various years).

The picture of return migration, however, is much less clear. Earlier nonrandom, small-scale surveys of returning Greek emigrants reveal a pronounced tendency to return to Greece's largest metropolitan areas (Dimitras, 1971; Vlachos, 1974). In fact, while only about one out of three emigrants came from urban areas,[9] nearly six out of ten returning migrants indicated an intention to settle there (Greek Statistical Yearbooks, 1965–73), and at least two major surveys (Unger, 1981; and Petras-McLean and Kousis, 1988) indicate that nearly half of the returning Greeks between 1970 and 1985 did in fact return to either Athens or Salonica. This tendency has been interpreted to mean that return migration was likely to provide only modest relief to the problems of depopulation, aging, and high dependency ratios of rural communities. Furthermore, the resettlement of returning emigrants in large cities would continue to apply pressure on their already distorted tertiary sector and contribute to additional un-planned urban growth.[10]

Selected Demographic Characteristics of Greek Emigrants

An examination of the age profile of Greek emigrants to Europe indicates that more than 80 percent of them belonged to the 15- to 45-year-old category. Between 1959 and 1973, there is an aging of the profile of Greek migrants, and an increase in the share of the youthful end of the cohort. Both forces are the result of the maturity of the Greek emigrant flow. Greek migrants, by virtue of the stability of their employment abroad and their demonstrated preference for stays of substantial duration (Papademetriou, 1978), were able to overcome most administrative obstacles to family reunion and bring their families to join them. This trend has mixed consequences. From the perspective of the emigrant and his family, it offers many rewards. From the perspective of the country of origin, however, it can have undesirable demographic and economic results; removing an entire family from the country increases the probability of permanent emigration and reduces the expectation of remittances.

Disaggregating the data according to sex allows for some additional observations. When both Greek and German data (see *Repräsentativ Untersuchung*, 1973) are examined, it becomes clear that Greek female emigrants tend to be younger than their male counterparts. The age groups which exhibit the largest variation between the two sexes are those under 25 (mostly women) and over 35 (mostly men) years old. Such variations can be attributed to a variety of factors. For men, compulsory military obligations usually postpone emigration until after 21, so that men under 25 tend to be those who have emigrated with their families at a younger age and who usually seek employment immediately upon attaining the minimum age requirement for legal employment. Women, on the other hand, face no military obligation and many of the service jobs they are asked to perform (such as household service and light factory work) call specifically for younger women.

Finally, data on the marital composition of Greeks in the FRG are consistent with other Greek emigration data indicating the propensity of Greek emigrants to bring their spouses along. German data show that approximately 80 percent of the Greeks in the FRG are married—a figure which exhibits a slight upward trend over time. A much more interesting statistic, however, is the proportion of Greeks who have their spouse with them. The figures are overwhelming, with Greek women reporting rates of 94 and 96 percent for 1968 and 1972, respectively (*Repräsentativ Untersuchung*, 1973).

Educational and Occupational Profile

The educational levels of migrants tend to be significantly higher than those of the nonemigrating population. Specifically, evidence from both Greek (Vlachos,

1974; Papademetriou, 1976) and German sources for 1972 indicate that about two-thirds of Greek men and 62 percent of Greek women emigrating to the FRG have had at least six years of education, while only 4 and 7 percent, respectively, were reported to be illiterate. This compares with a 16 percent illiteracy rate for the total Greek population in 1971.

The preemigration skill level and occupational profile of Greek emigrants is equally instructive. German data indicate that only 24 percent of male Greek migrants in the FRG and 15 percent of their female counterparts had some training prior to emigration. The training for both sexes was usually on-the-job apprenticeships, rather than formal technical school education, and the completion rate for both types of training was quite low. According to the same representative sample of Greeks employed in the FRG in 1972, more than 50 percent of the Greek men were employed as semiskilled workers (performing simple, repetitive tasks), while approximately one-third were employed as unskilled workers. The proportion of skilled workers, supervisors, and technicians was less than 10 percent. Female migrants, on the other hand, were absent from this last category. The qualification structure of both sexes improved significantly between 1968 and 1972, presumably as a result of the maturity of the Greek migrant flow (*Repräsentativ Untersuchung*, 1973).

The dominant activity among migrants prior to emigration appears to be workers employed in (or released from) the primary sector, followed by those previously employed in secondary sector activities. Among the other migrants, many were persons seeking employment for the first time. For example, one study found that more than 70 percent of Greece's construction workers in 1965 and 1966 emigrated as soon as their apprenticeships were completed, and the situation was often similar with graduates of Greek technical schools.

The effect of such an outflow cannot be measured only in terms of skill losses. One must also add the investment loss to Greece, which subsidized both the upbringing and education of these technicians. Viewed in these terms, one must recognize that if Greece is not to experience adverse consequences from the loss of trained individuals through emigration, such migrants must be replaced by equally trained individuals, a condition which occurs only irregularly. On the other hand, the emigration of those who have never held a job may offer Greece respite from unemployment and the potential for sociopolitical instability that unemployment engenders. To the extent that Greece has taken advantage of such relief and initiated necessary socioeconomic and political changes—and there is some evidence that the postdictatorship governments have done so—emigration may have provided an overlooked but critical benefit.

Juxtaposing the occupational data of Greek emigrants with the data for the total active Greek population for 1967 and 1971 offers some noteworthy insights. Although the data are not always comparable, it is clear that the secondary and especially the tertiary sectors are quite underrepresented among emigrants, while the primary sector tends to be overrepresented, that is, agriculture experiences the greatest net manpower losses due to emigration. Specifically, the primary sector has been losing more than 13 people per thousand annually to emigration, while it has gained only 0.2 people per thousand during the same period through repatriation (Siampos, 1976).

A final variable of interest is the type of occupations Greek emigrants perform during their stay abroad. There are striking differences between the occupations migrants performed prior to emigration and those performed in the FRG. One notices immediately that virtually no Greeks are found in Germany's small primary sector, while nearly 90 percent are employed in secondary sector jobs (including building and construction). Among the latter, most men are involved in metal production and engineering, while women are usually spread among engineering, textiles and garments, metal production, chemical work, food services, and packing—in approximately this order.[11] The rest of the Greeks are employed in various service occupations, especially transport for men and cleaning for women. Significantly, these German data are corroborated to an extraordinary degree by Greek survey data (see Polyzos, 1970; Petras-McLean and Kousis, 1988; Unger, 1981).

The importance of these data is twofold. On the one hand, they provide a record of the place of Greek workers in the German labor market and a yardstick for the performance of other guestworker groups. They also allow an objective appraisal of the match between expectations and reality in migration. During the course of the emigration debate which raged in Greece during most of the 1960s, both then Premier Karamanlis' ruling National Radical Union (ERE) and subsequent governments consistently defended emigration as a blessing (Merlopoulos, 1967; Lianos, 1977)—principally on the basis of three expected benefits: the relief of unemployment; the socio-occupational transformation of Greek workers who, *upon their return*, were expected to serve as the catalysts for Greece's own transition into the ranks of the developed states; and remittances.

The main opposition parties emphasized the negative effects of emigration and routinely accused the government of resorting to migration because of its failure to create the economic conditions that would absorb excess labor. Employers were concerned that emigration would deplete the labor reserve they felt was needed as a guarantee against future labor bottlenecks and consequent wage escalation. The presidents of the Greek Chamber of Commerce and the Greek Federation of Industries, for instance, argued repeatedly that Greece should insist on employer-financed vocational training of workers prior to and during their tenure abroad; that only unskilled workers should be allowed to emigrate; and that Greece should place an annual ceiling on the number of emigrants to Europe, while discouraging migration to overseas destinations on the grounds that repatriation from such countries is less certain. In fact, the idea of placing artificial barriers to labor emigration received legitimacy from the United Nations' Economic Commission for Europe, which warned that unless the outflow of Greek labor were restricted to 30,000 per year, Greece would risk interference with her own development efforts. Greek labor unions, finally, viewed emigration as an unwelcome but necessary consequence of poor economic conditions. On several occasions in the mid-1960s, the secretary general of the General Greek Labor Federation insisted that "migration cannot and should not be stopped at the present time," while also emphasizing the need to protect the workers while abroad (Lianos, 1977; Merlopoulos, 1967; Matzouranis, 1974; Polyzos, 1970).

GREEK EMIGRATION, RETURN, AND DEVELOPMENT

At the most general level, one finds only a tentative relationship between Greek migration, return, and development. A principal reason for the uncertain nature of the relationship is the inability to isolate the impacts of emigration and return below the national statistical aggregate. One is certainly tempted to look at Greek national aggregate data over the past twenty years, note the impressive growth in most gross indicators of economic growth, and attribute a large part of that growth to labor migration to Europe.

Greek emigration is likely to have played a potentially important role in the following areas: social demography; unemployment; educational and skill/occupational upgrading; and remittances and capital transfers.

Social Demography

The Greek population grew in the 1960s at a rate which was less than half that of the previous decade. In fact, Greece's total fertility rate fell to about 2.2 for the 1960s—from nearly 2.6 during the previous decade (Tzeugas and Tziafetas, 1988).[12] Furthermore, the age selectivity of migration and the youth of the female emigrant cohort further restricted the pool of the child-bearing population. In addition, the emigration of the younger male and female cohorts accentuated the aging of the Greek population while leading to high dependency ratios in areas of substantial emigration. Finally, the frequent separation of spouses and the leaving of children behind may have created additional problems which will not become clear until the future (Emke-Poulopoulos, 1986; Siampos, 1985).

While these social demographic effects of emigration are clearly recognized, the evidence is less clear when return migration enters the picture. In the 1970s, when the dominant direction of the Greek migration flow became one of return, the rate of increase of the Greek population was more than two and one-half times that for the previous decade—11 versus 4.3 percent (Greek Statistical Yearbook, 1983). Return, however, failed to ameliorate substantially either the depopulation or the high dependency ratios of rural communities that had experienced high emigration rates during the 1960s. A national microcensus of the estimated 298,419 households with at least one returning emigrant (a total of 625,891 returnees), undertaken by researchers at the Greek Center for Planning and Economic Research (KEPE) of the Ministry of National Economy reported in 1985 that 35 percent had settled in the Athens metropolitan area and an additional 13 percent in or around Salonica. This indicates that return to the Athens region is between two and three times larger than that region's contribution to emigration. Return to the Salonica region is nearly double both that area's contribution to the total emigration flow to Europe and the emigrants' stated intention to return (for the latter data, see Greek Statistical Yearbook, 1959-73 and Emke-Poulopoulos, 1986; on the national survey of returnees, see Petropoulos, 1985; Siampos, 1985; and Emke-Poulopoulos, 1986).

This tendency to return to the Athens and Salonica region is further reinforced by looking at another set of variables. Of those Greeks returning to urban areas (68 percent of the total), nearly 51 percent returned to the greater Athens area and its environs (eastern Sterea province), followed by a nearly 18 percent return rate to the greater Salonica area (Ministry of National Economy, 1986).

Even more important is that even among those who returned to their prefectures of origin, the overwhelming majority settled in the prefecture's capital or primary city, rather than in smaller towns or villages. This, of course, means that neither the population losses nor the dependency ratios in the countryside were likely to be reversed via return migration, nor would the sociocultural poverty of the countryside be likely to be seriously ameliorated.

Furthermore, the country's overall fertility would also not be likely to be affected by returnees who had already made their family decisions while abroad and were usually out of their prime child-bearing years when they returned. Many had become accustomed to different ideas about family size and had adopted different views about contraception from abroad—views which they are likely to pass along to relatives and friends. These new attitudes, clearly reinforced by economic uncertainty, the growth in two-income households, and the holding of additional jobs by large shares among urban dwellers, have influenced the reproductive behavior of Greeks to levels considered alarming by Greek demographers and policymakers. As a result, the total fertility rate for Greece in the 1980s is sharply lower than that during previous decades—standing at approximately 1.5 children per woman, with the rate at 1.47, 1.04, 1.82 and 1.66 respectively for 1983, 1984, 1985, and 1986 (Siampos, 1985; Tziafetas and Tzougas, 1986).

Unemployment

The relationship between unemployment and Greek emigration and return is even more complicated. During the height of Greek migration to Europe, emigration clearly played an important role in keeping Greek unemployment rates at relatively low levels—between 2.5 and 5 percent between 1960 and 1973. Furthermore, one clearly notes a trend toward less unemployment as the flow matures, from about 80,000 unemployed in the late 1950s to about 25,000 ten years later. This relationship becomes even clearer when one notes that, following the European recession of 1966 and 1967 and the resulting West German decision both to expel unemployed guestworkers and not to renew the contracts of many others, Greek unemployment for 1967 and 1968 shot upward (International Labour Office, various years; Greek Statistical Yearbook, 1959–74).

One must look beyond aggregate unemployment figures, however, in order to evaluate the relationship between unemployment relief, emigration, and development. Relief of unemployment must be juxtaposed with such variables as the types of skills emigrants had, the relative scarcity or abundance in such skills among Greek workers *in the regions where emigration has been highest*, the relevance of such skills to these regions' economies, and the availability of Greek workers of equal skills to take the place of those who emigrate. Furthermore, one must also consider the implications of the depletion of Greek manpower resources in certain politically and economically crucial regions in northern Greece and the overall losses in valuable human capital resulting both from the self- and institutional-selection processes inherent in labor migration[13] (Pepelasis, 1975). In addition, one must consider the effect of emigration in radically reducing the available pool of workers for agricultural work. The drying-up of that pool—despite data indicating that nearly 30 percent of Greeks were still employed in agriculture (Petropoulos, 1988)—has created critical shortages in agricultural labor during the harvest season (despite mechanization), in stockbreeding (see Emke-Poulopoulos, 1986; OAED, 1983), in low-level service and tourism-related occupations, and in the country's merchant-marine.[14]

A related issue concerns the effect of return migration on unemployment. It was a fact well-established in law (governed by the recruitment agreements to which Greece was party) and practice that guestworkers would be subject to repatriation if they should remain unemployed in the host country for protracted periods of time. In the complex of residence and work permits which controlled their stay in European countries during their early years as guestworkers, unemployment often led to deportation. Although tenure brought about eventual rights of establishment, substantial numbers of guestworkers repatriated, especially in the recession of the mid-1960s and in the few years immediately following Europe's "immigration-stop" of 1973-74 (see Papademetriou, 1987).

While reintegrating returning Greek emigrants into the labor market has always been problematic for Greece, the situation has worsened significantly in the past 15 years when persistent high-level unemployment began to attain a structural character.[15] In fact, returning emigrants, refugees, and second generation migrants (the children of returning Greek emigrants) have been experiencing unemployment rates which exceed those for the native population by significant margins.[16] Among the explanations advanced for this phenomenon are the returnees' age (no longer in the prime years of economic activity), inadequate labor market information, unrealistic expectations, and inability to gain quick access to the network of those who mediate and facilitate much of employment in Greece. Finally, some employers have also apparently been reluctant to employ returning emigrants because of concerns that they may have acquired a set of expectations about proper behavior and conditions at the work place (including a trade unionist mentality) with which they might "contaminate" their fellow workers (see Papademetriou, 1985b).

Educational and Skill/Occupational Upgrading

One of the most enduring expectations associated with labor emigration is that emigrants will gain educational and occupational skills while abroad and, upon their return, use those skills to spearhead their country's socioeconomic transformation. This expectation clashes with reality along a number of fronts. First, migrants possess only marginal skills before emigration and it is neither automatically part of their goal structure nor in the interest of the receivers to enhance those skills—although gradually skill and occupational advancement does occur. Data on Greek workers in the FRG based on representative samples taken in 1968 and 1972 (*Repräsentativ Untersuchung*, 1973), and again in 1979-80 (Mehrländer et al., 1981), show that some skill enhancement had occurred, but mostly in the later years when tenure in the FRG had been quite lengthy. Despite documenting advancement, however, these studies show that only relatively modest proportions of Greeks had attained the coveted rank of "skilled worker" while the majority had only experienced "some" occupational advancement as they moved from entry-level positions to "semiskilled" ones. This rather routine "advancement" occurs almost entirely in the context of on-the-job training and should not be seen as a significant measure of occupational upgrading. These studies also indicate, however, that as Greeks gain permanent domicile status in the FRG, they spread out across the job hierarchy and begin to be found both in services (sales and ownership of small business establishments) and in "professional/technical" occupations.[17]

Preliminary data on the profile of returning Greek migrants from the previously mentioned microcensus shed some additional useful analytical light on this cohort of Greek workers (Ministry of National Economy, 1986). Nearly nine out of ten of the study's respondents (*n*=862) had worked in industrial occupations in the FRG—about two-thirds of them in heavy industry. This is comparable to the almost 90 percent of the Polyzos (1970) sample of 2,249 emigrants[18] and the 82 percent figure reported by the German authorities in 1973 (*Repräsentativ Untersuchung*, 1973). The similarities do not end here. The microcensus also reports a 51 percent rate of semiskilled workers, while the proportion of skilled returnees stands at about 15 percent. In addition, one also finds among returnees a sprinkling of foremen (.5 percent), white collar workers (3.2 percent), and self-employed (1.4 percent).

A substantial majority of returnees (70.3 percent) captured in the Greek microcensus held only a primary school certificate—as compared with only about 50 percent of all Greeks in the FRG in 1973 having only that level of education (*Repräsentativ Untersuchung*, 1973).[19] An additional 1.6 percent had a technical school or post-secondary school diploma. The microcensus results also indicate that 19 percent of those interviewed had received additional education in the FRG.

Returning Greek migrants fall into the following categories. Some are clearly those who failed to make more than a marginal adjustment to their new environment—those whom Cerase (1974) would classify under his label of "return of failure." Others, equipped with only modest educational and skill resources prior to emigration and assigned only low-skilled repetitive tasks while abroad (in a process Kudat [1975] calls skill "homogenization"), return with few significant new job skills that are largely irrelevant to Greece which has only nascent heavy and advanced industries.

Very few returning Greeks apparently belong in Cerace's "return of innovation" category. This category includes those most likely, and best equipped, to make an impact on and effect some socioeconomic changes upon their return. Even they, however, are at best only influencers, rather than architects, of such changes (Böhning 1975; 1976a; Papademetriou, 1978; Polyzos, 1970). The reason for this paradox is that while such gifted returnees may have the *potential* to provide a significant impetus for change if they return to the smaller towns and rural areas of their origin, their efforts are likely to be stymied by antiquated, but well-entrenched, socioeconomic hierarchies there. When considering that only about one in four returning Greek workers actually return to "rural" areas, even returning "innovators" can be expected to have only a marginal impact on the socioeconomic structure and power relations of their regions of origin. Thus, even when the return flow is substantial, unless sending regions have been making some progress toward structural social, economic, and political adjustments, their returning emigrants are likely to deny their native country the benefits of their professional experience and withdraw to, or be compelled to seek refuge in, the tertiary sector.

Data from the 1985 microcensus on the labor market behavior of returning Greek workers support this analysis (Petropoulos, 1985; Petras-McLean and Kousis, 1988). Specifically, more than four out of ten returning workers who settled in urban areas worked in services, as compared with only one in five among those returning to rural areas. Among the latter, two-thirds continued to engage in agriculture, although not as a principal economic activity. In fact, large proportions of the sample reject both agricultural work and work in the manufacturing sector in favor of employment in the service sector and self-employment, and, in many instances, informal sector employment and unemployment.

Remittances and Capital Transfers

While investment in housing satisfies one of the migrants' most basic reasons for emigrating, even a cursory look at Greek real estate data will note the extreme distortion of the real estate market and the leading role played by building materials in fueling inflation. Furthermore, and despite the employment opportunities and multiplier economic effects which housing generates, its intermittent character and its distortions in labor and material costs make for mixed economic consequences.[20]

Between 1955 and 1985, *officially registered* Greek remittances from all sources exceeded $15 billion dollars (see Table 5.1).[21] They comprised nearly 22 percent of the country's invisible receipts during that period. Until 1973, remittances paid for approximately between one-quarter and one-third of the

Table 5.1
Emigrant Remittances, Invisible Receipts, and Balance of Trade (in Millions of U.S. $)

Year	Balance of Trade (1)	Invisible Receipts (2)	Remittances (3)	(3)/(1) (4)	(3)/(2) (5)
1955	−158,3	153,8	50,6	31.9	32.8
1956	−255,7	182,6	60,9	23.8	33.3
1957	−286,1	235,7	75,0	26.2	31.8
1958	−267,0	217,6	76,7	28.7	35.2
1959	−237,8	237,2	88,6	37.2	37.3
1960	−296,3	273,2	92,7	31.2	33.9
1961	−332,9	319,6	107,5	32.2	33.6
1962	−397,7	379,6	139,1	34.9	36.6
1963	−435,7	454,3	168,1	38.5	37.0
1964	−555,0	479,5	176,8	31.8	36.8
1965	−685,6	549,4	207,0	30.1	37.6
1966	−745,4	635,9	235,0	31.5	36.9
1967	−693,6	659,0	232,1	33.4	35.2
1968	−767,8	719,0	239,4	31.1	33.2
1969	883,7	788,2	277,3	31.3	35.1
1970	−1,084,2	949,2	344,6	31.7	36.3
1971	1,302,3	1,292,3	496,6	36.0	36.3
1972	−1,605,9	1,606,6	559,6	34.8	34.8
1973	−2,816,7	2,195,9	714,6	25.4	32.5
1974	−2,885,3	2,460,5	624,4	21.6	25.4
1975	−3,042,3	2,850,3	757,4	24.9	26.6
1976	−3,333,1	3,187,8	777,2	23.3	24.4
1977	−3,902,8	3,700,1	899,2	23.0	24.3
1978	−4,342,8	4,422,6	951,4	21.9	21.5
1979	−6,177,8	5,663,0	1,136,9	18.4	20.0
1980	−6,809,6	6,159,4	1,059,4	15.6	17.2
1981	−6,696,8	6,482,0	1,057,1	15.8	16.3
1982	−5,926,8	6,097,6	1,015,6	17.1	16.7
1983	−5,385,9	5,529,2	911,7	16.9	16.5
1984	−5,350,7	5,288,7	898,1	16.8	17.0
1985	−6,268,0	5,260,5	774,5	12.3	14.7
Total	--	--	15,203,1	--	--

Source: Bank of Greece, The Greek Economy (annually); Bank of Greece, Monthly Statistical Bulletin (various)

country's trade deficit. Since 1974, however, remittances have been able to pay only between 15 and 25 percent of that deficit—despite substantial increases in their size. The relationship between remittances and all invisible receipts largely parallels that between remittances and the trade deficit, reflecting the extraordinary growth both in the size of Greek invisible receipts (which include tourism, income from shipping and seamen's remittances, foreign pensions, and income from convertible deposits) and the trade deficit.

The relationship of remittances to the Greek national income is equally revealing: in the 1970 to 1977 period, for instance, remittances stood at between 3.5 and 5 percent of national income, a figure which fell to well under 3 percent in the 1980s (Emke-Poulopoulos, 1986:304).

Table 5.2 shows the relationship of remitted income to three of Greece's hard currency expenditures: expenditures by Greeks who travel abroad and imports of foodstuffs and of manufacturing goods. Expenditures by Greeks travelling abroad has more than tripled in the post-military-dictatorship years, while the importation of foodstuffs has grown about three and one-half times during the same time. Similarly, the importation of manufacturing goods has experienced a comparable growth of more than 300 percent since the 1973-74 period. These indicators, taken together, probably point to Greece's increasing prosperity— and returning Greek migrants and worker remittances have certainly played and continue to play an important role in that prosperity.

Returning Greek migrants usually bring with them savings estimated in one recent survey of returnees to be between 1 and 6 million drachmae (Unger, 1981).[22] Routinely, these sums are used for buying or fixing-up real estate, purchasing agricultural land and farm machinery, purchasing small service establishments (such as restaurants, small hotels and shops, and service stations), and investing in the transportation industry—principally as taxi owners and operators in major cities or owners/operators of small-scale rural and semiurban transportation companies. Finally, returning emigrants also use their savings to supplement their income, especially when they return to rural areas and continue to engage in farming.

Returning migrants also bring with them household goods. These goods receive duty-free entry into the otherwise highly protectionist Greece as part of a one-time-only opportunity to return to Greece with one's entire household. Unger (1981), in a survey of 574 returning Greeks in several prefectures of northern Greece, found that 89 percent of the respondents brought with them washing machines, 85 percent television sets, 75 percent stoves, 77 percent refrigerators, 71 percent furniture, 59 percent stereo equipment, 26 percent automobiles, and 8 percent trucks. A few respondents also reported bringing farm machinery.

Of even greater importance among observers of the return migration process, however, is the impact these expenditures have on local economies. It is clear that in Greece the increased ability and propensity of remittance-assisted households to become major purchasers in what is an otherwise limited consumer

Table 5.2
Hard Currency Income from Remittances, and Hard Currency Expenditures for Imports and Foreign Travel (in Millions of U.S. $)

Year	Hard Currency Income Emigrant Remittances	Imports of Foodstuffs	Imports of Manufacturing Goods	Hard Currency Expenditures Hard Currency Used by Greek Tourists Abroad	Total	Relationship of: (percent) (5/1)	(6/1)
1963	168,125	13,799	84,413	27,535	125,747	14.8	58.4
1964	176,836	15,388	106,405	38,629	160,422	90.7	68.8
1965	206,940	22,332	131,089	41,454	194,875	94.1	74.1
1966	234,967	22,682	169,769	40,613	233,058	99.1	81.9
1967	232,067	24,896	179,188	40,755	244,839	105.5	87.9
1968	239,381	24,433	182,084	42,445	248,962	104.0	86.2
1969	276,997	27,955	188,433	47,905	264,293	95.4	78.1
1970	342,892	26,886	224,981	55,297	307,164	89.5	73.4
1971	457,984	33,164	264,529	73,655	371,348	81.1	65.0
1972	559,632	39,619	314,541	95,798	449,958	80.4	63.2
1973	714,633	70,917	477,483	113,297	661,697	92.5	76.7
1974	624,409	64,736	406,613	130,052	601,401	96.3	75.4
1975	757,365	68,736	575,499	154,624	798,859	105.4	85.0
1976	777,208	87,270	726,328	150,668	964,266	124.0	104.6
1977	899,185	115,189	944,324	164,016	1,213,529	136.0	117.8
1978	951,427	146,894	1,142,828	223,844	1,513,566	159.0	135.5
1979	1,136,915	173,730	1,455,708	302,391	1,931,829	169.9	143.3
1980	1,059,427	170,215	1,099,570	309,111	1,578,896	149.0	119.8
1981	1,057,094	204,419	1,357,168	361,125	1,922,712	181.8	147.7
1982	1,015,599	212,572	1,370,372	374,223	1,957,177	192.7	155.8
1983	911,734	203,642	1,260,011	362,176	1,825,829	200.2	160.5
1984	898,066	197,022	1,230,777	338,689	1,766,488	196.6	158.9
1985	774,469	217,486	1,385,206	367,542	1,970,234	254.3	206.9

Sources: Bank of Greece, Monthly Statistical Bulletin (various).

market has been a contributor to broad demand-pull and, gradually, cost-push inflation across the entire economy. The decision of the Greek military government (1967-73) to withdraw the public subsidies on basic foodstuffs transformed Greece from a country with one of the lowest inflation rates among members of the Organization for Economic Cooperation and Development during the 1960s, to one with one of the highest such rates during the past 15 years (Papademetriou, 1976). Demand by remittance-assisted households for durable imports (both Table 5.2 and a look at trade data between Greece and the FRG over time [Papademetriou, 1984a] attest to the vitality of such trade) have without a doubt raised the appeal of imported consumer goods for all households. This, in turn, contributes to the further depression of the appeal of locally produced durable goods and leads to the increasing allocation of foreign currency to import such products.

It is in the social realm, however, that the impact of migration becomes even more controversial. An examination of data disaggregated to the level of prefecture shows few discernible patterns between levels of emigration and either economic growth or a more equitable distribution of income. In fact, one of the most "redistributive" effects of emigration appears to be the addition of a new layer to the middle class: the remittance-supported household. Whether such socioeconomic advancement is permanent or not, the implications of this new social class configuration, and the size of this "new" class (it includes only a fraction of those families with a member abroad), are important changes to which the migration process has apparently contributed but which require additional study.

The demographic effects of emigration discussed earlier (especially the altering of regional demographic profiles and the skewing of sex and age cohorts in semiurban and rural areas) have significant, *though not necessarily always negative*, implications for the social organization and power relationships in the life of villages and small towns. In view of evidence that many migrants opt to return to the rural/small town communities from whence they originated (regardless of whether they emigrated directly from there or with an intermediate stop in a larger city), one must investigate the linkages between remittances and actual returns, on the one hand, and changes in the social and political power structure of these communities, on the other. While the impact of individual returnees on such relationships has been routinely discounted in the literature, a significant and regular return flow might be found to strengthen migration's cumulative potential for change by creating an atmosphere initially of confrontation, and eventually of change, as modernity clashes with tradition.

There are no Greek studies which test this hypothesis—probably because Greek researchers have been slow in focusing on the effects of "permanent" return migration (rather than emigration) on communities. This void is probably also the result of the rather recent character of substantial return flows. In any event, the preconditions for a return movement to become an agency for change are hypothesized here to include that the return should be voluntary, it should be to the community of origin, and it should be part of a regular return flow. Furthermore, returnees need to have maintained an active interest in the affairs of the community, reinforced both by regular visits and through the proxy of an activist family. Finally, and once a tradition of return is established (where only one of emigration existed before), the architects of the transition in social and power relationships will probably need to demonstrate both financial success abroad and financial responsibility upon return.

This summary of observations and selected key findings might tempt one to join the chorus of those who are apt to discount even migration's *potential* contributions to development. We will not do so. Instead, our investigation of Greek emigration and return leads us to the conclusion that the Greek "investment" on migration has not yielded the expected dividends—but principally because the expectations were unrealistic and analysts have often been impatient with the length of the process and the depth of the impact (which has been small), and have frequently focused on aggregate indicators of change (where the net impact of emigration often gets lost). Furthermore, in the absence of the structural social and economic changes necessary to allow Greece to take full advantage of the opportunities which migration offers, relief of unemployment and remittance income could only play a minor, and essentially passive, role in Greek growth. Migration's most pronounced impact has thus been in agricultural mechanization, the housing boom, the proliferation of small service establishments, and the growth of tourist-related infrastructure. The beneficiaries of the process have been emigration households that have seen their socioeconomic position improve substantially.

CONCLUSIONS AND RECOMMENDATIONS

Greece has made very substantial progress in the last quarter century along most indicators of economic development. The role of emigration and return on this growth, however, has neither been isolated nor studied systematically at the local or household levels. In the absence of evidence to the contrary, then, Greek migration has entailed lost opportunities and resulted in fewer benefits than expected. Enhancing these benefits requires measures that will gradually make Greece more of a partner with individuals and receiving countries in migration-related matters.

At the interstate level, Greece needs to explore and exploit all opportunities offered by the special relationship that migration implies for sending and receiving countries. For instance, access for Greek products to German markets cannot be shown to have been markedly influenced by the large presence of Greek workers in the Federal Republic—over and above what distance and the European Community (EC) relationship might predict.[23] Neither can German investments in Greece be shown to have been influenced more by the worker connection than the opportunity to capture the relatively small but highly discriminating and active Greek internal market. Both relationships seem to be better explained by the "laws" of asymmetrical relations which distribute benefits from the contact between unequally developed states unevenly and in favor of the dominant state. Hence, Greece must try to enhance its benefits from migration in areas where public intervention is both possible and likely to have an impact, namely, in the areas of remittance utilization and return migration.

One such area merits particular attention. Greece and the FRG concluded negotiations and in 1982 ratified an agreement to assist repatriating Greek emigrants with industrial ventures in Greece. The agreement (Public Law 1262/ 1982) was largely the result of initiatives undertaken by the *Verband zur Förderung Griechischer Arbeitsnehmergesellschaften* (Federation for the Advancement of Greek Worker Companies) in Stuttgart. The federation, modeled after similar Turkish and Yugoslav organizations, was able to persuade German authorities to institutionalize procedures which had operated unsystematically for several years. The process is as follows: once a group of investors has been formed and an investment idea has been developed (often with the assistance of the federation), the federation undertakes preliminary feasibility and market assessment studies in an effort to appraise the proposed venture's prospects for success and the likelihood of investor interest from sources beyond Greek workers employed in the FRG. A federation committee of experts then meets to decide whether to recommend the project. If the committee's recommendation is positive, independent consultants are engaged to conduct first a full market study and then a full feasibility study. If these results are also encouraging, a corporation is chartered. The federation then sponsors a series of intensive seminars designed to train the principals of the corporation and potential investors in the intricacies and principles of investment, management, and related activities. At the same time, there begins a several-month-long series of technical training regiments covering every aspect of organizing and managing an industrial concern.

Most expenses incurred throughout the course of this process are borne by the German and Greek governments on a 70/30 percent formula.[24] The financing of the investment venture is in accordance with the following terms: the minimum investment by the workers is set at 30 percent of the total; for the remaining funds, investors must obtain loans from a variety of quarters, such as commercial sources, preferential-term loans under the terms of Greece's industrial investment programs, and other sources. These sources may also include the European Economic Community—if the project falls under that organization's priorities. Finally, up to 20 percent of the total investment funds can be obtained from special preference loans from a joint Greek/FRG investment fund supported equally by the two governments.[25]

This program has evolved slowly: in 1981 only three such companies were in operation, involving 122 investors having committed less than half a million dollars in projects employing 46 workers (Papademetriou, 1983c). But by early 1986, 247 companies had been created. The total investment exceeds $110 million (14.2 billion drachmae) of which returning workers contributed about 20 percent in foreign currency. Nearly two-thirds of the total investment has been in tourism-related activities and an additional one-quarter in manufacturing.[26] The remaining investments have been in primary sector activities. The entire program employs 4,238 persons. The total amount invested represents about 5 percent of total investments in Greece for the 1982–85 period (Bank of Greece, Annual Statistical Bulletin, various years; Alexandris, 1985; Papantoniou, 1985; Emke-Poulopoulos, 1986).

Greece's overall slowness in turning remittances into an effective development instrument reflects shortcomings in both public and private management arenas *and the distortions which the country's constant political and military preoccupation with Turkey has caused.* The latter problem seems destined to continue to preoccupy Greece. The former one, however, includes errors both of omission and commission. At the private level, Greek domestic capital markets have offered few of the incentives essential to channeling remittance capital toward productive sectors/activities. This failure comes on the heels of repeated failures by a heavily subsidized and indebted private sector to take advantage of opportunities offered it. At the same time, the public sector has also been slow in providing either the required direction in such areas as tax credits and abatement, preferential exchange rates, and such policies as relocation incentives and accelerated depreciation schedules for new industrial ventures, or the guidance of industrial investment within the parameters of a coherent industrial decentralization and regional development program. It is interesting to note that these voids contrast sharply with government initiatives in the construction sector. For reasons which include tradition, calculations about social peace, and extreme policy inertia, that sector is the recipient of a series of incentives and concessions by successive Greek governments.

Furthermore, the Greek failure to capitalize on return migration reflects a lapse in articulating and implementing an economic and social development strategy *in the context of the phenomenon of migration.* In this matter, Greece is equally responsible with other labor exporting countries for expecting the "promised" benefits from migration to materialize without thoughtful state intervention. Besides a lesson in the frequent incompatibility between public and private goals, one also observes the perils of benign neglect and the need for developing initiatives designed to facilitate the conversion of the migration process into a more effective development instrument. In view of the fact that for nearly 15 years now the dominant direction of the Greek migrant flow is that of return, the remaining remarks will focus on that component.

Greece needs to continue to pay attention to the following areas: the protection of the social and economic rights of its nationals abroad and the maintenance and strengthening of cultural, linguistic, religious, and educational ties with migrant communities—two matters that can now be addressed effectively within the framework of the European Communities. Greece must also recapture the initiative with regard to the size and composition of the return flow and the reinterpretation of returnees and their families. In order to do so most effectively, it must focus on obtaining a reliable skills' inventory at home and abroad, assessing the needs of Greek workers interested in repatriation, and trying to match those skills with the country's employment needs (see Papademetriou, 1985a and 1985b for a discussion of this point).

There are two necessary prerequisites to effectively implement such measures: making measurable progress toward developing a comprehensive manpower planning and employment policy and, within that context, the development of a reliable job information system. This system must be tied in both to major employers in Greece and to the network of the dozen or so labor offices which the Greek Department of Labor operates in key German cities. This area has been largely neglected by Greece, although it is quite susceptible to policy manipulation. It requires, however, a reliable system with effective communication channels to reach Greek nationals in Germany. Furthermore, Greece should also continue to lobby the German government to subsidize training programs for Greek migrants in skill areas in which Greek manpower planning indicates future labor demand is likely to develop. A final component of this concerted effort would be the implementation of programs designed to effectively reinsert returnees, and especially children, into the country's social, cultural, and educational mainstream.

Of particular interest in this regard is the reintegration of returning Greek children. Children face problems ranging from insufficient knowledge of the Greek language and differences between German and Greek curricula, to inadequate preparation in formal written Greek, and negative attitudes on the part of teachers and fellow students. The Greek Ministry of Education appears to be making extensive efforts to facilitate the reintegration of these children, especially in the form of special education classes, bilingual education, and extensive supplementary education courses after school hours (see Emke-Poulopoulos, 1986; Haris, 1980; Kasimatis, 1984; Petropoulos, 1988).

A final group of possible initiatives could focus on influencing the investment behavior of returning migrants. Greek policy makers should understand that in returning, the migrant responds to a variety of forces. The economic one is not necessarily dominant among them. Hence the need to address the issue in a comprehensive fashion. An area which can pay handsome dividends for both individuals and country lies in assisting those contemplating return with investment ventures—particularly in employment-generating activities. A necessary prerequisite to implementing programs in this area again involves a coherent strategy of development which recognizes the benefits of industrial decentralization and seeks to promote economic activity in the context of the nation's political and social objectives. Recent Greek governments seem to be conscious of this need. Once the nation's directions have been debated and agreed upon, tapping the resources of migrants and using them as one of many vehicles to spearhead development should become a priority item. Public Law 1262/1982 is an appropriate beginning point in this regard.[27] It can become an important instrument for development, however, only when the Greek government adopts a policy attitude which respects the entire set of aspirations of Greek migrants—instead of simply engaging mechanistically in high profile activities whose main intent is to repatriate the emigrants' resources, but *not* the emigrants themselves (Papademetriou, 1985a).

With this caveat in mind, Greece might offer, in conjunction with the German authorities, additional assistance with the planning, designing, financing, technical product development, marketing, and managing of such projects. It is in these areas where most industrial initiatives have been most deficient. It is also in these areas where both migrants and the country as a whole are deficient. If policy efforts focus in these areas, success can be most rewarding. The results from such cooperation may be most promising because they rest on a most solid—but frequently forgotten—dictum of migration: that the home community often remains the migrant's primary reference point and principal determinant of behavior (see Piore, 1979). With this in mind, a last area of continuing policy intervention might be on the one infrastructure item which appears to dominate the interests of most migrants: housing. The purpose here must be not only to influence and direct the migrant's investment decisions but also to integrate housing construction better within the context of each region's structural, service and employment needs—and thus bring it into conformity with the country's overall development.

NOTES

1. This refers to the Greek-Turkish War of the early 1920s which resulted in the routing of the Greek armies by Ataturk's armies in 1923. The catastrophe refers not only to that defeat, and the chaotic retreat of the Greek army out of Asia Minor (mainland Turkey), but also to the massacres of Greeks in such historically "Greek" cities as Smyrna (Izmir) and to the disorderly abandonment of such cities by hundreds of thousands of Greek nationals. These events were followed by more orderly exchanges of populations between Greece (of mostly Turkish nationals from Northern Greece) and Turkey.

2. The formal agreement with France lasted for less than two years.

3. Nearly 650,000 Greeks emigrated to the FRG in the post–World War II period—more than half of *total* Greek emigration. (See Petropoulos, 1988.)

4. Petropoulos (1988) notes that, in 1981, Athens had 56 percent of the Greek health personnel, as well as disproportionate shares of the gross national income and a large number of goods and services. Salonica exhibited similar patterns.

5. Since the late 1950s, the greater Salonica area has also benefitted from significant public investments.

6. For the past three decades, Greece's fertility levels have been at replacement level (1970s) or slightly above replacement levels (1960s and 1950s). (See Siampos, 1967; 1976; 1985.)

7. When rates of return migration are computed, however, annual net population growth rates are always positive. In fact, even during the decade of the 1960s—which witnessed the heaviest outflow of Greeks—Greece's population increased by 404,000.

This was less than half that for the previous decade. (See Greek Statistical Yearbook, various years.)

8. The countryside, and particularly the less-developed provinces of western Greece, had been the communist insurgents' power base during the Greek Civil War.

9. More precisely, they reported an urban residence as their residence prior to emigration.

10. Return migration in the 1960s and early 1970s contributed to an additional redistribution of the population as northern Greece, which had contributed about one-third of total emigrants, saw only a fraction of returnees settle there. In fact, most returnees planned to settle in central Greece and the greater Athens and Salonica areas. (See Greek Statistical Yearbook, various years.)

11. Petras-McLean and Kousis (1988, Table 6), in a report on two surveys of returning immigrants, indicate that the industrial profile of returnees approximates these data. Between half and two-thirds of returnees had been employed in four industries: iron and steel, automobiles, chemicals, and electronics.

12. The Greek total fertility rate has continued to deline. It is estimated that by the year 2000, Greece will have a negative population growth ($-.18$). (See Petropoulos, 1988:23-24.)

13. In what has been described as "skimming-off" and a "double-selection-out" process (Baucic, 1974), labor importers were extremely selective in recruiting workers and, after the initial year abroad, renewed only the contracts of those workers who had exhibited the greatest promise for social and occupational adjustment. (See also ILO, 1973.)

14. In a rather typical response to such shortages, a thriving market for illegal aliens has developed in Greece over the past 15 years. Conservative estimates place the size of that illegal work force at about 70,000 workers, mostly Africans and Asians. In two areas, placement of domestics and the merchant-marine, few make any pretenses about these industries' heavy reliance on illegal workers. In fact, in the case of domestics, thriving "offices for the assistance of foreigners" have sprouted up in major cities supplying "household assistants" for very substantial fees. The conditions of work for illegal aliens are generally exploitative and include low wages, poor working conditions, and lack of protection by unions (see Soulis, 1985; Hadjipanayotis, 1985).

15. Registered urban unemployment in Greece has stood at about 10 percent throughout most of the 1980s. Rural unemployment and underemployment are thought to be considerably higher. (Greek Statistical Yearbook, various years.)

16. The 1985 microcensus found that formal unemployment rates among returnees stood at about 25 percent higher than those for the entire population (Petropoulos, 1988; Petras-McLean and Kousis, 1988).

17. The results of such studies are not always consistent. Hadjipanayotis, for instance, places the proportion of skilled Greek workers in the FRG in 1980 at an extraordinary 30 percent (1982).

18. Only about one-third of them had reported that they held jobs in the manufacturing sector prior to emigration.

19. Subsequent German surveys indicate higher levels of education among Greeks there. This can be attributed to higher levels of education among Greeks reaching the FRG after 1972, to the higher educational achievements of Greeks born and growing up in the FRG and, apparently, to the fact that Greeks returning to Greece had disproportionately low levels of education.

20. One positive byproduct of the housing boom in Greece, on the other hand, has been the creation of an extremely active, though now ailing, cement industry which was for a time at the heart of an industrial building materials international conglomerate generating significant export earnings.

21. Substantial additional cash amounts are transmitted informally during the emigrants' frequent home visits while noncash transfers in the form of such durable goods as electronics, house appliances, and automobiles are also extremely significant. Informal estimates by the first author indicate that these last two types of "transfers" may be as large as the officially registered transfers. Significantly, survey data indicate that the majority of returning Greeks continue to deposit their savings in Germany (see Petropoulos, 1988:37).

22. In the 1980s, the exchange rate for drachmae has been about 140 drachmae to $1.00.

23. Greece became an associate EC member in 1962 and a full member in 1981.

24. Of the 30 percent contribution by the Greek government, one-third is in the form of an outright grant while the remaining two-thirds are in the form of long-term, low-interest loans with repayment schedules commencing after the company is in actual operation. The cost of technical training is divided among the investors (50 percent), the German federal government (35 percent) and the Greek government (15 percent)—the latter two contributions being in the form of low-interest loans. (For a detailed description of these agreements see Papademetriou, 1984a.)

25. This elaborate scheme is intended to anticipate most of the problems associated with setting up foreign-worker-led industrial ventures. Foreign participation, for example, is limited to 40 percent of each venture so as to preempt potentially negative local reaction; and a balance is struck between preparing the investor/management/technical team and facilitating the take-off of projects with generous grants and loans. Yet, investors are asked to carry a financial burden substantial enough to dissuade all but the most serious candidates.

26. A large proportion of tourism-related activities have focused on the Aegean islands. Northern Greece, by contrast, has the lion's share of industrial initiatives. As Papantoniou notes (1985:14), many of these concerns are small-scale shops which act as "extended work benches" for companies in advanced industrial countries. As such, they depend on another firm abroad for both orders and the marketing of their product.

27. The Greek government has been experimenting with several additional small-scale, but innovative, programs. Among them are a loan program that would encourage young professionals to set up their practices in rural/less-developed regions; special loan provisions that focus certain agricultural bank loans on returning migrants who commit some of their own resources on agricultural enterprises; and assistance with resettlement costs for returnees who choose to settle in underdeveloped areas. (See Petropoulos, 1988:38-43.)

6

Migration without Development:
The Case of Turkey

Ali S. Gitmez

Northwestern Europe's rapid growth in the 1950s and 1960s led to the massive recruitment of migrant labor from the less-developed countries of the Mediterranean basin. Italians, Portuguese and Spaniards were among the first to appear in advanced Europe's labor markets, followed by Greeks, North Africans, and Yugoslavs. Turks joined rather late in the labor flow. They began to appear in the early 1960s, and grew most rapidly in the second part of the 1960s until the recruitment bans of 1973–74.

Post–World War II European labor migration differs from earlier international migration flows in at least three respects: it was a mass phenomenon; it was presumed to be temporary; and it was regulated and controlled mainly by the recipient countries. In the Turkish case, these characteristics are evident in the following facts: hundreds of thousands of workers were recruited within about a decade; they were recruited on a contractual basis for short periods initially; and regulation and control was evident in every step, from recruitment to remittances to return.

The Turkish experience with international labor migration includes migration for work both to northwestern Europe (in the 1960s and 1970s) and to the oil-rich Arab countries since the 1970s. Migration helped Turkey to enter fully the world politicoeconomic and monetary system, with its increasing control of finance, production, and distribution by transnational corporations. Turkey's incorporation into that system began with the introduction of the Marshall Plan in the late 1940s, and was followed by membership in NATO, OECD, and, in 1963, associate membership in the European Communities.

The Turkish economy also became more integrated with the world economy during this period through loans by such international credit organizations as the World Bank and the International Monetary Fund (IMF), and its political stability became increasingly tied to the continuous flow of foreign money from foreign loans and remittances. The latest step of this integration has been the restructuring of the Turkish economy in 1980 and its export-promotion and outward-oriented industrialization strategy. Seen in this broader world context, Turkish labor migration is a tangible example of the international circulation of capital and the changing division of labor, it is not a simple response to a convenient coincidence of interests between the countries of emigration and immigration.

This chapter addresses three questions: (a) why did Turkey have "false expectations" about labor migration—expectations which were shaped by the labor-importing countries? (b) how did conditions of emigration change? and (c) how did workers return and reintegrate? The organizing principle of the effort will be to evaluate Turkish international labor migration on the basis of the "expectations" about migration; no "cost-benefit" analysis is attempted. The focus of the chapter is on the impacts and contributions of emigration and return migration to Turkish development in light of earlier expectations.

BACKGROUND

The 1950s and 1960s were a period of significant change in the structure of Turkish society. In the 1950s, the Anatolian peasants, who for hundreds of years were tied to the land, began to migrate to urban centers in great numbers. Internal migration changed both the peasants' life style and the structure of Turkish society. The results were a rapid transformation of both the rural and urban economies and social structures, and the establishment of several key state initiatives on land distribution and employment creation. These were the years in which "peripheral capitalism took hold, bringing with it the social transformation entailed by the dissolution of traditional structure" (Keyder, 1988). The large scale internal migration that began during this decade increased Turkey's urban population from 18.5 percent in 1950 to 25.2 percent in 1960. Istanbul, the most attractive receiving region, grew by more than 50 percent from 1950 to 1960.

Turkish development during the 1950s was haphazard at best. As Griffin describes: "From 1955 to 1960 Turkey was in a permanent economic and political crisis. . . . Symptomatic of these difficulties was the rapid rate of inflation: prices rose 60 percent between 1954 and 1958. In the end the IMF was invited to help prepare a stabilization programme" (1976:230-31).

Following the 1960 military intervention, the "Planned Economic Development" period began with its emphasis on "industrialization based on import-substitution." The problems attendant to the import-substitution strategy had significant economic manifestations which included balance of payment difficulties and high levels of inflation. This meant more dependence on foreign currency and, in turn, on international capital.

"Planned Development" assigned foreign exchange and international capital a special role in promoting Turkey's economic development and preserving political stability. Foreign exchange bottlenecks were the focus of economic development in the 1960s (Gulalp, 1983:51), and migration of workers was viewed as one tool for obtaining foreign exchange.

Turkey's decision to sign bilateral agreements with northwest Europe's labor-short countries was thus prompted as much by the need for remittances as by the fear of unrest among the ever-increasing unemployed masses. The deal was simple, straightforward, and presumably beneficial for both sides: "employers hire foreign workers, and workers migrate to jobs abroad," (Kindleberger, 1967:196). Migration was to be a fair exchange: a flow of foreign workers to advanced European economies, and a flow of foreign capital into Turkey.

The reason for this exchange was the underlying structural imbalances of the Turkish economy in its peripheral role in the international division of labor. As with all cases of labor migration, however, contemporary "European labor mobility, its volume and its forms, are determined to a great extent by the recruiting countries" (Schiller, 1976:363) or more specifically, by the recruiting employers. The private firms that benefit most from the employment of foreign workers determine the number and characteristics of such workers.

EXPECTATIONS FROM EMIGRATION AND RETURN

Labor migration was expected to benefit Turkey at two levels. On one level, migration would reduce unemployment in Turkey, help Turkish workers achieve new qualifications and values abroad, and provide remittances. On a second level, returning workers would make important contributions to Turkey's economic progress. By transferring the technological knowledge, experience, and the social values of Europe, the returning workers would become social pioneers in their native country (Lutz, 1963). The transfer into developing countries of technological know-how, work discipline, technological culture, and remittances would thus minimize inequalities between developed and developing countries (Kindleberger, 1967; OECD, 1978a).

Turkish planners, government officials, and social scientists fully accepted this scenario (Tuna, 1967). Exporting labor came to be viewed as an opportunity to meet the need for economic and social development, and the individual migrant would be an agent of economic and social change. The most important social benefits of migration would be the learning of modern work discipline, the acceptance and assimilation of the Western social and cultural values, and the development of a new social and political consciousness. Armed with these ideas, Anatolian peasants would then become the pioneers for social change.

EMIGRATION OF TURKISH WORKERS

Turkish migration to northwest Europe began with a German offer in the late 1950s to train technical manpower to operate German machinery, thus promoting West German investments in Turkey. This German training offer received a positive response from the Turkish Chamber of Commerce and Small Industries, and a liaison was formed independently of the respective governments.

Not until October 1961 did Turkey conclude the first formal agreement to supply manpower to the Federal Republic of Germany (FRG). What began in 1961 as a relatively small movement (11,185 workers) grew, after similar agreements with Austria, Belgium, the Netherlands, France, and Sweden, into an emigration flow of 103,975 in 1972, and 135,820 in 1973. The stock of Turkish workers in West Germany jumped from 7,000 in 1961 to 18,500 in 1962, to 615,827 after the stoppage of migration in 1974. As Table 6.1 shows, 804,917 Turkish workers were officially sent to Western Europe between 1961 and 1975. In addition, between 120,000 and 150,000 people emigrated illegally, mainly as tourists.

Despite a large number of returning workers during the 1966–67 economic recession, and a smaller number of returns thereafter, there were still about 900,000 Turkish workers in northwest Europe at the end of 1973, when mass migration to the FRG was stopped. These workers were accompanied by about 200,000 children and 250,000 spouses. The worker flow was reversed in 1974, with a net repatriation of some 20,000 to 30,000 Turks annually (Gökdere, 1978; Gitmez, 1984). Despite this, the Turkish population in western Europe at

Table 6.1
Characteristics of Turkish Emigration, 1961–75

| Years | Applicants | Emigrants | Emigrant Characteristics | | |
			Rural Origin	Skilled	Male
			%	%	%
1961	45,050	1,476	45.8	45.0	96.9
1962	77,495	11,185	32.9	31.9	96.1
1963	143,434	30,328	22.4	24.5	91.5
1964	322,402	66,176	47.7	36.9	93.6
1965	333,449	51,520	45.3	39.0	78.3
1966	119,151	34,410	49.7	25.7	71.6
1967	105,323	8,947	45.7	30.5	60.5
1968	126,735	43,204	46.4	28.8	73.7
1969	253,946	103,975	43.4	24.5	80.0
1970	372,959	129,575	42.5	27.0	83.9
1971	267,403	88,442	47.6	35.5	83.9
1972	202,510	85,229	49.4	33.7	78.1
1973	263,608	135,820	51.1	42.0	80.1
1974	77,090	20,211	45.5	39.2	93.4
1975	125,546	4,419	45.3	54.3	91.0
Total	2,847,136	804,917	—	—	—

Source: Turkish Employment Service (TES) figures.

the end of 1980 was around 2 million; only 40 percent of these were economically active, the rest being spouses and children. This means that although many workers returned since the 1973 recession, the Turkish population in Europe has increased because of family reunion and births abroad.

The number of Turks in western Europe increased by 36 percent between 1975 and 1980. Widespread unemployment and unfavorable conditions in northwest Europe in the early 1980s forced some Turks to return home, but the total Turkish population did not decrease. Table 6.2 shows the Turkish population in northwest Europe in 1980 and 1985.

About 2 million Turkish people now live in northwest Europe, constituting the third largest immigrant group there. There are an additional 300,000 Turks in other immigration countries, in the Middle East, and Australia. As Table 6.2 shows, the stock increased in all countries from 1980 to 1985, but there was a slight decrease in the Federal Republic of Germany, a result of the 1984 German return incentives during which 213,469 people returned to Turkey.[1]

There has also been an unreported and unofficial emigration of Turks to the FRG since 1976: over 100,000 Turks have sought political asylum there since 1976. Their number peaked in 1980, with 57,913 young people seeking asylum in the Federal Republic.

Table 6.2
The Stock of Turkish Population in Europe and in the Oil-Rich Arab Countries, 1980 and 1985

| Country | Stock of Turkish population | |
	1980	1985
West Germany	1,462,400	1,400,400
Netherlands	121,714	155,579
France	92,772	154,862
Austria	65,000	80,000
Belgium	66,563	77,069
Switzerland	35,875	49,259
Scandinavian countries	34,298	43,316
Other Europe	n.a.	153,480
Europe total	1,885,102[a]	1,988,965
Middle East(2)	95,200[b]	206,778
Australia	38,532[c]	87,000
Total:	2,018,834	2,282,743

Sources: Turkish Ministry of Labor and Social Security figures; OECD, SOPEMI estimates: 1980-1985

Notes: [a] Lack of sufficient information; underestimate.
[b] Includes Libya.
[c] Lack of information; underestimate.

Turkish labor emigration to the oil-rich Arab countries of the Middle East and North Africa began in 1973 and increased after 1975, especially after 1980. Libya was the first country to rely on Turkish construction firms, although only a small number of workers (664) were employed by these firms in 1973. The stock of Turkish workers in the Middle East and Libya was about 95,000 in 1980, and reached an estimated 207,000 in 1985 (Martin, 1990). Table 6.3 shows the official emigration of Turkish workers to both northwest Europe and to the Middle East and Libya.

This table also includes estimates for illegal migration and for asylum seekers. There were some genuine asylum seekers, especially after the 1980 Turkish military intervention, but the majority of asylum seekers entered the FRG for economic reasons.

THE CHANGING CHARACTER OF EMIGRATION

Official Turkish emigration to northwest Europe lasted from the early 1960s to 1973—when the receiving countries unilaterally halted it. The temporariness of emigration during this period drew almost exclusively single emigrants.

Table 6.3
Emigration of Turkish Workers, 1961–85[a]

Destination country	1961-1973	1974-1980	Number of persons 1981-85
W. Germany	648,029	9,412	432
France	45,366	10,668	23
Austria	34,461	5,003	211
Netherlands	23,359	1,836	47
Belgium	15,309	834	27
Switzerland	6,360	2,794	930
Australia	4,668	3,785	1,022
Saudi Arabia	4	26,739	107,994
Libya	664	48,457	106,735
Others[b]	12,069	15,729	36,348
Illegals[c]	--	--	150,000
Asylees	--	80,555	22,785
Total	a) Official:		1,169,325
	b) Unofficial:		203,340

Source: Turkish Employment Service (various)

Notes: [a]Includes only officially dispatched workers, and not those going abroad on their own or those who joined their spouses/families abroad.
[b]Probably an underestimation.
[c]Only a rough estimate; true figure should be much higher considering the total of 25 years and a high number of illegal immigrants in the oil-rich countries.

After 1973, labor emigration took on a new character in three important respects.

First, its composition changed and it became nonselective. International migrants are usually a select category of the native population. They originate usually from more urban and industrial regions, and they have higher education, skill, and training levels than the population at large. These characteristics were very much in evidence during the initial period of Turkish migration (Abadan-Unat, 1976). For instance, of the 55,000 Turkish workers in West Germany in 1963, 41 percent had lived in Istanbul prior to emigration, and an additional 6 and 4 percent were from Ankara and Izmir, respectively. Only 18 percent had come directly from villages, and the remaining 27 percent were from other cities (Abadan-Unat, 1976).

By 1974, however, the characteristics of the Turkish immigrant stock in Europe had changed considerably: the proportion of those coming from Istanbul had dropped to 21 percent, while that of those coming from other major cities increased to 34 percent. The proportion of those coming from the poorer rural regions increased correspondingly to 26.5 percent (Gökdere, 1978:178).

The change in the composition of Turkish emigration reflected changing public perceptions of and state concern over migration, as well as changing conditions in the socioeconomic organization of international migration. Various internal and external factors contributed to the change in the composition of the migrant population and helped to create new and unconventional channels of emigration. One internal Turkish factor involved a change in public attitude. In the early years, rural people were reluctant to migrate, since emigration conjured images of an unknown "journey" comparable with the fearful Ottoman army draft to fight in foreign wars from which there was little chance of returning alive. But after a few years of observation, and many instances of success, the rural population began to emigrate in larger numbers.

Among the external factors affecting the nature of the migrant population was a change in western European recruitment. In the early period, recruitment mainly focused on workers from northern, western, and southern Anatolia, Turkey's more developed regions, with the representation of eastern Anatolian migrants increasing only after 1970 (Kudat, 1975:44). Only about one-quarter of the workers came from the agricultural sector (Abadan-Unat, 1976).

This pattern was the result of state policy reinforced by labor importer preferences for younger, better educated, skilled workers with some industrial experience, thus largely excluding the rural population. However, European recruitment policy was soon altered to favor the more rural, unskilled, naive, and easily manipulable immigrants. During the second half of the 1960s, the German recruitment system especially tended to recruit unskilled Turkish peasants for work in large industrial firms where they performed unskilled and semiskilled jobs. This system worked via the practice of nomination; an immigrant could personally request the recruitment of family members, relatives, friends, or neighbors (after 1973, only spouses could be sponsored). Thus, Turkish migration became the migration of families, relatives, and friends. Strong and extended family ties and kin relationships in rural Turkey made the practice almost exclusively a channel of rural migration.

Large numbers also joined the migrant flow as tourists, finding employment by themselves and legalizing their status at a later time. This practice also required preestablished relationships, as well as the supporting facilities which are found among rural populations. In addition to the 701,333 workers who emigrated via the Turkish Employment Service (TES) between 1967 and 1974, some 100,000 to 150,000 emigrated as "tourist workers" (Gitmez, 1984). In both cases, rural-origin emigrants constituted the majority.

An additional influence on rural migration, and thus on regional chain migration, was the Turkish government's decision to give priority to persons who were either members of village development cooperatives, through a set-aside of 15 percent of all out-migration-visas, or from areas which had been hit by natural disasters or affected by unfavorable weather conditions. From 1967 to 1973, some 752 cooperatives were able to send 42,500 rural workers abroad. When emigration came to a halt in 1973, there were some 4,550 cooperative establishments at various stages of development which had formed to take advantage of the quota system (Gitmez, 1984). By allocating an additional 15 percent of the quota to people from natural disaster areas, the Turkish government intended to use emigration as a form of relief to residents of regions struck by earthquakes, floods, and drought.

The result of these policies was that later migrants were generally not as skilled as earlier ones. Although there was a sample survey only in 1964, the proportion of those originating from rural parts of the country probably increased considerably after the 1966–67 economic crisis, and especially immediately prior to the 1973–74 bans on immigration. A recent sample survey found that nearly two-thirds of migrants came from rural backgrounds and from the central and eastern parts of the country.

The second respect in which the character of Turkish emigration to Europe changed in the post-1973 period was that it became settlement migration. This was partly due to policy changes. The guestworker policy of temporariness gave way to integration. Both the workers and the recruiting country initially viewed the process as one where migrants would earn the largest amount in the shortest time in order to return home with savings and status. Labor recruitment was never intended to become backdoor immigration.

The possibility of staying longer or even settling permanently began to emerge even before the 1973–74 labor recruitment ban. The recruitment ban, however, marked the beginning of a period of large-scale stabilization. In subsequent years, family reunion policies were introduced and there were discussions of the full integration of foreign workers. By 1980 there were 298,434 Turkish families in the FRG, and they had 733,366 minor children. The Turkish population in Europe had thus undergone a radical transformation: the ratio of the

0–18 age group to the total Turkish population in the FRG was one-to-five in 1973, and it rose to one-to-three in 1980.

The final change in the character of Turkish emigration involved a change of direction from Europe to the oil-rich Arab countries. As emigration to northwest Europe was changing character in the early 1970s, a new wave of migration, this time to the Middle East and North Africa, began to form. It began with 664 single construction workers in 1973, increased to 1,015 in 1974, and 2,210 in 1975. Libya was the first oil-exporting country to recruit Turkish construction workers, followed by Saudi Arabia in 1975. Several other Gulf states recruited Turks, but smaller numbers. The nature of emigration to the Arab countries differs greatly from that to Europe. Workers for the Arab region:

1. were recruited mainly by the Turkish construction firms doing contract work in these countries;

2. were recruited strictly on a temporary-contractual basis and usually for short periods;

3. were single workers who were housed in dormitories in labor camps and isolated from the host societies; and

4. worked and lived in poor conditions, were controlled tightly, and were often denied basic social rights—conditions which were not comparable to those in Europe.

In 1980, there were about 100,000 Turkish workers in the Arab countries. In 1985, that number doubled to 211,000, about 70 percent of whom were in Saudi Arabia and 20 percent in Libya (Martin, 1990).

The changing direction of Turkish emigration to the oil-rich Gulf states reflects both the changing character of international migration and the restructuring of the global economic and monetary systems. The labor flow from Turkey has broader implications for, and is the consequence of, the socioeconomic and political reorganization of international migration in the context of the world economy.

RETURN MIGRATION

While Turkish migrants to northwest Europe evolved stable and relatively permanent immigration communities, some workers and their families returned home. Contrary to the earlier expectations and despite efforts to send large numbers of Turks home, there has not been a mass return or repatriation. Although there was a considerable increase in the number of repatriating workers following the 1973–74 recession, the returns have been stable. Net return estimates were about 30,000 persons each year from 1967 to 1974 (Gökdere, 1978:99). In 1975 and 1976, returns rose to between 55,000 and 60,000, but have since dropped to between 20,000 and 30,000 per year.

The number of returning Turks exceeds the number of entries in almost all northwest European countries, but the stock of Turkish population in these countries (except in the FRG) is still increasing. Table 6.4 shows the number of

Table 6.4
Entries and Departures of Turkish Workers in Selected Countries, 1980–84

Country		1980	1981	1982	1983	1984	Stock in 1985
				Numbers (000)			
W. Germany	Entries	212,3	84,0	42,7	27,8	34,1	1,425,8
	Departures	70,6	70,9	86,8	100,4	213,5	
Netherlands	Entries	17,3	8,4	5,1	3,7	4,1	155,6
	Departures	2,4	3,2	4,8	5,6	6,2	
Oil producers	Entries	28,4	58,8	49,4	52,5	45,8	206,778[b]
	Departures[a]	--	--	--	--	--	

Source: Turkish Employment Service (TES); OECD-SOPEMI, 1980-85

Notes: [a]Unknown due to shifts from one country to another and to lack of
          information
          [b]Excluding Syria

entries into and returns from two major labor-receiving countries, the FRG and
the Netherlands, as well as the oil-rich Arab countries. The return data reveal
that there has not been a mass return and that it is mainly the first generation
migrants who return, not the whole family.

RETURNING MIGRANTS: IS THERE NEGATIVE SELECTION?

The migrant worker is frequently a target worker who intends to return home
after achieving a savings goal. The worker and his family base their expectations
and plans on the assumption that they will reassemble in Turkey after a certain
period of time, making homecoming the natural termination of the trip. Why do
some migrants stay longer and settle abroad?

A number of theories offer conflicting explanations as to what distinguishes a
returned worker from a stayer. Functional theories view homecoming as the result of social disintegration; they emphasize that family conditions play an important role in homecomings, and that workers who belong to minority groups in
their native country are less likely to return.

System analyses see a close relationship between homecoming and social integration. The tendency to stay in the receiving country and the period of residence
there is related to the existence of strong family ties and satisfaction with life
abroad, so that, for example, workers who are highly skilled and well trained but
live in ethnic enclaves exhibit less integration and more inclination for returning.

In a recent Yugoslavian survey, for instance, returned workers were found to have lower initial social and economic status in their native country, less upward social mobility in the country of destination, strong family ties, and be less integrated in the receiving country. There is some evidence that a migrant's propensity to return is a powerful factor in determining the degree to which he will become integrated and assimilated in the host society, but some researchers view return as a regressive response to unsuccessful integration and assimilation.

Studies by Kudat (1975) and Kudat and Kallweit (1976) have found that most returned workers share the following characteristics: they were from rural backgrounds, they had not brought their families abroad, and they stayed abroad for shorter periods of time. They were also found to have had lower earnings and savings than nonreturnees. Finally, they were found to be working in factories that were either about to close or were on the verge of introducing new technologies that displaced workers.

Reasons for the return of migrant workers such as family problems, inadequate assimilation, and health impairment fall in the category of what Cerase (1974) calls the return of failure. What is meant by failure in this context is the individual's choice of personal security over economic benefits. It is evident that an industrially skilled worker who integrates into a foreign society is more in demand due to his skills, prefers a longer stay in a foreign country, and is less affected by economic crises. The unskilled rural worker, on the other hand, tends to stay for a shorter time in a foreign country due to his difficulties of adaptation, lesser skills, and the likelihood that he will lose his job during economic crises.

REASONS FOR RETURN: THE TURKISH CASE

Despite the fact that more than half of all Turkish workers who emigrated to Europe have returned home, there have been only three major government-sponsored studies of return migrants. As a result, many aspects of return migration are not understood. Major reasons for Turkish returns are family problems (Tuna, 1967; Abadan-Unat, 1976) and achievement of economic goals. Penninx and Van Velzen (1976), on the basis of interviews with a small group of returning workers of rural origin, report that returning migrants stayed abroad for shorter periods than settlers. A comparison of Turkish workers in Berlin in 1974 with 1,632 who had returned to Turkey in 1975–76 led by Kudat and Kallweit (1976) to conclude that returning workers stayed abroad for a shorter period of time and therefore were less experienced regarding life abroad; they were mostly from rural areas; and the majority did not have their families with them while abroad. Family separation appears to be the single most important difference between returned workers and those who remain abroad (Entzinger, 1978). Returned migrants include a higher percentage of workers who were less tolerant of depression and who had experienced more undesirable conditions than those who remained in the FRG. Other studies have also connected return of migrants of rural origin with family and health reasons, as well as inadequate adaptation (see Abadan-Unat, 1976; Gitmez, 1989), and these conclusions are consistent with the results of various studies which suggest that the probability of return increases when an immigrant retains close links to the home area.

A Turkish State Planning Organization (SPO) study in 1971 showed that the period of stay for unskilled workers was, on average, 2.2 years, versus 2.6 years for the semiskilled and 2.8 years for the skilled. A survey in West Germany found that only 13 percent of unskilled migrants showed a tendency to settle abroad, as compared with 17 percent of the semiskilled and 28 percent of the skilled (Böhning, 1972). These results support the contention that workers of urban origin tend to adapt better to the new society and to stay longer.

Although it may be undesirable to reduce all reasons for return to a single variable, such as lack of integration in the host society, one of the main reasons to return seems to be indeed "not feeling at home" in the host country. This "feeling" seems to be more prevalent among the unskilled, the less integrated, the less secure, the less tolerant of difficult work and social conditions, and those who do not have their families with them.Such factors do not explain post-1980 returns sufficiently. Workers who return to retire, however, are not innovative missionaries. They do not return as entrepreneurs or as agents of social change in the countryside.

REINTEGRATION AND EFFECTS OF RETURN MIGRATION

It is difficult to detect exact behavioral patterns or clear-cut modes of readaptation among returning migrants.[2] The dominant characteristic of Turkish migration has been its diffusion, starting with the haphazard organization of emigration and culminating with the laissez-faire approach toward reintegration. As a result, individual migrants use the opportunities they encounter, rather than proceeding according to a clear set of economic and personal priorities. In this sense, worker choices may coincide neither with individual attributes and priorities nor with the expectations of Turkish officials.

MODAL PATTERNS OF REINTEGRATION

In this study about one-half of the migrants returned to a village, approximately the same proportion as before migration. The percentage of those moving to urban or semiurban settlements who used to live in villages before migration is only 8 percent. About 5 percent reported an urban settlement as their last place of residence before migration but returned to live in villages.

Second, 61 percent of the respondents went abroad via official channels, while 18 percent went first as tourists and later won legal status. The proportion of those going abroad as tourists is much higher among respondents from less-developed regions than for those from developed regions.

Third, one-third of the sample completed some technical and vocational training while abroad. Those reporting such training, however, received it on the job and were working full time in production jobs while learning the skills they gained.

Fourth, respondents reported spending about 37 percent of all remittances for housing and building lots; 34 percent spent savings for agricultural land or for machine shops; and 23 percent invested in service sector activities with some job creation potential. About one-third of all business ventures were made in villages and 59 percent on the perimeters of urban centers and towns. Expenditures typically reflected the perceived needs of return migrants and their families and appear to be an attempt by migrants to realize their earlier expectations.

Fifth, the dominant activity among those sampled was involvement in small-scale self-employment. Agriculture still remains the largest single sector of self-employed economic activity for returnees: 28 percent of the respondents were engaged in agricultural work after they returned. An additional one-third worked in small businesses, retailing, services, and industry. An unexpectedly high 20 percent were not working, were unemployed, or not interested in working—a proportion that is higher for those returning to industrialized regions.

Finally, although there was little change in the proportion of people living in villages, the proportion who owned land and the average size of land holdings increased. Participation in agricultural production, however, decreased. About 44 percent of the sample owned land, but only 28 percent appear to be actually working in agriculture.

The picture painted by these survey data is that there is a return of the retired. Most returning migrants are middle aged; most complain about health problems and feel tired; and most have little ambition for new achievements and successes in Turkey. Many say that they have not come back to work or to start a new life, but to rest, to spend their remaining years in peace, and be buried in the home country instead of "being sent back via Frankfurt".[3] The majority are simply not prepared to reestablish an active economic life in Turkey.

Returned workers retire and live from savings, income from investments, or pensions (20 percent). Returning to a village either as a retired person or to get involved in familiar and relatively risk-free small activities is a pattern followed by more than 65 percent of returned workers. Small-scale commercial activities are easy and relatively risk-free, and the majority seem to have chosen them. It seems impossible to create a dynamic army of new entrepreneurs from worn-out masses.

Migration's most positive effect has been on the well-being of the migrant family. Labor migration significantly improved the economic fortunes and social status of most families. More than two-thirds of the sample expressed full satisfaction with what they had done and gained, and only a small minority thought that their economic condition was worse.

External migration does not seem to have accelerated urbanization: a majority of returned workers of rural origin return once again to villages and small towns, especially in less-developed regions. Indeed, some of those who have returned have headed for the villages after a short period of urban life, especially in the more underdeveloped regions. About 14 percent of urban residents before migration returned to villages in Turkey. International migration seems to be a slow irreversible process of rural to urban migration.

This finding has implications both for migrant employment and the investment. Experience shows that migration does not have a profound effect on the structure of employment. The proportions of those working in the various sectors of the economy after return are not very different compared to the proportions prior to migration. Although there is a considerable amount of job changing at the individual level, there has been no great flow of labor from one sector of employment to another and the relative weights in the general structure have been relatively stable.

Returning to the original place of residence after migration usually means a return to the same work or profession, but returning to old jobs is an indicator of regression; it means that the skills learned abroad are not used upon return (Paine, 1974). There are several reasons. Villages and small towns lack the necessary infrastructure to use returning workers' skills and experiences. Considerable savings go into agriculture, but mostly in land ownership, and this results in dramatic increases in land prices (Penninx and Van Velzen, 1976; Gitmez, 1989).

The size of one's resettlement community is one determinant of the type and productivity of the investment made. Businesses started in small communities are likely to be smaller in size, demand less resources, and be ineffective as job creation ventures. Returned workers usually allocate only a portion of their savings to each business venture to decrease risks.

Most migrant investments are intended to create a place of employment where the worker can work independently. Establishing a private business is a major reason for migration. State Planning Office and Turkish Employment Service studies show that a substantial majority of the workers interviewed prior to migration plan either to have a private business, or, after buying some land, to settle in the village. Establishing their own businesses allows them to gain a more respectable status in society (Penninx, 1982).

Turkish workers clearly exhibit the universal inclination toward safe small enterprises with low productivity, toward consumption rather than productive investments, and toward making investments in trade and services rather than in industry. Similar tendencies are also observed among returned workers in other countries.

THE OUTCOME: FAILURE OR SUCCESS?

Sending countries regarded the export of workers as a "safety valve" for unemployment relief and a means for obtaining hard currency and the upgrading of the skills of their workers—both necessary ingredients for development. From the available data and experience, we can conclude that these expectations are largely unrealistic and unattainable.

First, more than one-quarter century has passed since emigration began and Turkey's relative position on the world development scale has not improved. Altogether, about one and one-half million Turkish workers have worked abroad and well over $20 billion of hard currency have been injected into the home economy, but the experience appears not to have left the country in a significantly better position than it was 25 years ago. Turkey does not seem to have derived many benefits from migration, and there is not much reason to expect this picture to change.

Migration and remittances have peaked. There will not be another million Turkish workers in Europe remitting foreign currency. Migrant workers remit the largest share of their earnings during the first few years abroad when the families are left behind. After they have united their family abroad, they may remit some money for investments, but this dries up after settlement abroad. Settlement means that migrants cease to be a potential source of manpower for Turkey because their return will be for retirement, not to participate in the work force.

Turkey's Integration into the World Economy

The migratory cycle and remittances have played a major role in Turkish integration into the world economy. This is evident by Turkey's dependence on foreign capital and foreign markets both for its products and its excess labor. Economic development policies emphasize the development of export industries aimed at specific markets abroad. Turkey's world integration is irreversible; the whole economic and social life has been restructured, and the debts to the international lending organizations are so high that their repayment is almost impossible. Migration has played an important role in this process. It enabled a primarily self-sufficient but closed society to open its windows, leading to more international relationships. This effect should not be dismissed as secondary in a society which had for centuries been predominantly rural and static.

Remittances and the Social and Political Status Quo

Remittances played a major role in reducing the country's trade deficit. However, how was this foreign income used? It is often assumed that remittances are used efficiently (Ebiri, 1985), but this is a misleading assumption. Some researchers argue that if remittances raise the domestic savings rate, and savings are used for capital formation, then the productive capacity, employment, and growth rate should be raised. Remittances and savings, however, are largely used in family consumption, not in productive and employment-creating investments. Thus, the positive balance of payments effects of remittances may be negated by the purchase of consumer items and by expenditures on housing, land, and ceremonial celebrations.

There are other negative effects of remittances. Remittances have played the role of system-maintenance, and they helped to perpetuate the existing system of low productivity. They have helped successive Turkish conservative governments avoid adapting rational development plans and radical, but necessary, restructuring efforts. In this sense, remittances are a conservative economic force for maintaining the status quo. Without foreign exchange, Turkey might have been forced to change its productive techniques, alter its social structure, and search for other means of accomplishing the necessary social change (Martin, 1990).

Returnees as Developmental Initiators

The return of workers does not seem to confer significant development advantages on the sending economy. There is ample evidence that returned workers are not a stimulus for development. Furthermore, the conditions to which they return neither encourage nor allow their resources to be of major productive use. Savings are not used in capital outlays and productive and employment-creating investments; instead they are used for small-scale trade and service establishments. Such small, nonproductive, and inefficient ventures accelerate the development of a service economy, and thus have a distorting effect on the overall home economy.

Returning migrants do not seem to be a significant source of industrial skills, since they are reluctant to enter the wage-earning labor market as factory workers. Many come home for retirement rather than to work. Furthermore, returned workers are not innovators or the carriers of skills, entrepreneurial spirit, and Western attitudes toward work and life. The majority have only one dream: to start a small business and become self-employed. It is therefore clear that the major asset which most returned workers bring with them is their savings. However, their small-scale investments do not represent a significant contribution to economic development.

THE HUMAN ASPECT

The export of well over 1 million workers from 1960 to 1974 has clearly had an effect on relieving some of Turkey's unemployment and underemployment. Emigration was important to the industrially infant Turkish economy and to hundreds of thousands of unemployed Turks. Despite the migrants' significant personal sacrifices and the psychological and societal implications of these sacrifices, the individuals involved and their families clearly enjoyed significant economic benefits from migration. In this respect, the process has to a large extent accomplished an important goal by providing an alternative for large num-

bers of people. The material benefits of migration to the migrant and his family
are real.

Migration has provided new and interesting life experiences for a large section of the society. It has allowed people of the bottom-stratum of the society to
experience a new and different world. In purely human terms, this in itself has
been a great event for the migrants and their families.

In short, poor Anatolian Turks have had a chance to come into contact with
advanced societies. Wealthy and educated Turks as well as Anatolian peasants
travel abroad, become exposed to other cultures, and have the material means to
participate in the larger world economy. Without labor migration, this would not
have been possible.

Migration has also provided important options, alternatives, and opportunities to groups which might not have otherwise had them. Among them are
women who had an opportunity to move outside their assigned regions and
roles, enter the labor market for wage employment, and exercise their independence, all of which would have been unimaginable otherwise (Kiray, 1976). In
fact, women migrants have undergone the greatest geographical, occupational,
and status changes; most have moved from domestic activities to participation in
the international work force in rather complex job and cultural settings. Among
other social and personal complexities and implications, such an experience has
had a liberating and emancipating effect that might be of great value in itself. In
the Turkish case, the proportion of women migrants before 1965 was only 7 percent, but it rose to 22 percent in 1965, then increased further, so that 146,681
women were officially recruited between 1961 and 1974 (Abadan-Unat, 1976).
The number of women workers abroad increased even more after the recruitment ban due to the large number of women entering the labor-receiving countries for family reunion.

Labor emigration also opened previously unavailable options to the dissatisfied and adventure-seeking individuals. For them, emigration provided an alternative to a traditional, limiting, and discouraging environment. This category
includes not only industrial workers and peasants, but also various professionals,
such as teachers, artists, nurses, doctors, and asylum-seekers and refugees.

It is obvious that migrants have had to pay a high price in hardships and sacrifices for the improvement in their economic fortunes. Such sacrifices often have
long-term effects. Separation from the family, family dislocation and fragmentation, discrimination, and many other social and psychological pressures all affect
the migrant worker's physical and mental health. In this respect, migration has
many negative effects on both the family and the mental well-being of migrant
workers. Such sacrifices and hardships are not peculiar to external migration;
they are the inevitable result of change. However, migration yielded general satisfaction; most migrants say that they would migrate again.

Was emigration the only viable option? As Rogers asks (1985:298), "Did he
[the migrant] merely choose between going abroad and staying put? Or was it a
choice between going abroad and staying and accepting the status quo?" Left to

choose between survival under undesirable conditions and starvation, it is certain that the former would be chosen. This does not change the fact, however, that many first and second generation migrants abroad experience depression and unhappiness and are torn between the home and receiving societies. They feel they belong simultaneously to both and to neither.

What is the outcome of migration? Work abroad was expected to produce a successful "secondary socialization" for migrant workers. This expectation has "assigned" a role for returning migrant workers which involved making use of the savings and technical and social skills acquired abroad in the development at home. Migrant workers were recruited for specific low-level jobs that required little skill and afforded workers few opportunities for personal growth. The social conditions are equally unstimulating. Migrants were often segregated in settings similar to those at home, and thus were only marginally exposed to real "secondary socialization" abroad.

Migrant workers, perhaps because of their rural background, have had great difficulty adapting to the new environment, the norms of life, and complex employment organizations of the receiving societies. Since their aim in emigrating was not to obtain training and learn new industrial and social skills, they see themselves as transients and build all their plans on the basis of their perception of "temporariness." Together with the unfavorable conditions in which they live, and in view of their limited ability and experience, they expend little effort toward freeing themselves from the working and living conditions offered them. The result is that migrants do not benefit from the experience, and develop more passive and conservative attitudes. What is left for them to do is to work and save money so that they can lead an independent life back in Turkey. They build their expectations and future plans around the ultimate goal of owning a small business in Turkey.

The expected "secondary socialization" does not take place. In such a "distorted social setting," the migrant cannot improve himself and learn the technical and social skills to effect real social change in his place of origin. Instead, the small business at home becomes his "village culture" and a security symbol. An independent business as a symbol of self-assertion on return is a universal tendency (Martin, 1990) toward gaining status, praise, and recognition. It is also a sign of psychological and social success, and seems the best way to self-actualization. Returning workers become more conservative, more individualistic, more family-oriented, and more traditional in their thoughts and actions; their expectations of change are expressed through individual and family achievement.

CONCLUSION

Sufficient time has passed since the beginning of labor emigration from Turkey to be able to evaluate the impacts of emigration and return, as well as the arguments concerning the contribution of migration in the fulfillment of the initial expectations of the process. For a period of time in the past, exporting labor played an important role in the relief of Turkey's unemployment. Migrant worker remittances constituted the major benefit to Turkey from international migration. Unemployment relief and injections of foreign currency have played only a minor role in the growth of Turkey's economy. Judged by present conditions, Turkey needs workers' remittances as much as ever. The Turkish economy, in fact, does not seem to have benefited from the experience by using remittances to improve its development potential, and there is little reason to believe that this will happen in the future.

Labor migration's impact on the material, social, and psychological well-being and satisfaction of the individual migrant has not been studied extensively. Individuals emigrated to escape economic hardships and poverty and to be able to build a better future for themselves and their families, not necessarily to contribute to their country's economic growth. Considering the migrants' educational and skill limitations, it is unrealistic and unjustified to expect migrants to aspire to become innovators, entrepreneurs, and agents of change. Since this burden is not placed on intellectuals and professionals who work abroad and earn substantially higher incomes, it makes little sense to assign this role to the migrant workers with their limited resources and qualifications.

The individual migrant and his family benefited from emigration. Social and psychological obstacles notwithstanding, emigration was an alternative to poverty and misery. It provided a material, social, and psychological outlet to hundreds of thousands of people and has contributed to their satisfaction. Given the conditions at their home, the alternative to emigration for many Turkish migrant workers would have been to remain underemployed and totally unsatisfied. The offer of employment and a secure income abroad would have been chosen even if the returns were smaller.

The interests of the *home country* and the *migrant worker* often conflict with each other. The choices and aspirations of individual migrants are unlikely to be the choices that would most augment the process of development; in fact, they may distort development. While individual migrants free themselves from poverty, the emigration economy becomes more dependent on the advanced industrial countries. In other words, to match the interests of Turkey and its migrant workers, Turkey must make enough social and economic progress to attract migrants to return home and, once home, returned migrants must make productive investments that use their skills.

NOTES

1. There has been an increase in the number of Turks in other European countries after 1983. Some of those leaving Germany may have moved to other European countries so that not all Turks who left Germany returned to Turkey.
2. About 1,365 returned migrants, drawn from three regions differentiated on the

basis of economic development, were interviewed in 1978 and 1979. About 30 in-depth interviews asked about the experiences of the returned workers (Gitmez, 1989).

3. This is a common expression among the Turks in Berlin which reflects the fact that coffins carrying dead Turks on the way to Turkey for burial are allowed to travel only via Frankfurt (Berlin-Frankfurt-Turkey).

Part IV

Labor Migration and Development in Asian Emigration Countries

Part IV reviews the effects of emigration on the development of countries which sent workers to oil-exporting Middle Eastern nations, especially after the 1973 oil price hikes. In the early 1980s, there were an estimated 2.5 million Asians working in Middle Eastern nations and an annual emigration of one million more (Arnold and Shah, 1986:3). Asian countries—including Pakistan, India, Bangladesh, the Philippines, Korea, Thailand, and Sri Lanka—began to assume that Middle Eastern labor markets would remain available to their citizens. The safety valve and remittance effects of emigration overrode the caution about embracing emigration voiced by researchers. However, the displacement of more than one million Asian workers caused by Iraq's invasion of Kuwait in August 1990 underscores the vulnerability of countries that rely on foreign labor markets for jobs. Chapter 7 examines the effects of temporary worker migration on Pakistani development. Pakistan sent a larger fraction of its work force abroad in a shorter period of time than did Turkey, but the 2 to 3 million Pakistani migrants went primarily to Middle Eastern oil exporters after 1974, while most of Turkey's 1.5 to 2 million migrants went to European nations before 1974.

Burki notes that Saudi Arabia's second five-year development plan in 1975 launched a Middle Eastern labor migration which eventually involved 2 to 3 million foreign workers, 10 to 15 times more than Saudi Arabia planned to import. Of an estimated 2 million foreign workers in Saudi Arabia in 1978, Burki reports that two-thirds were Arabic-speaking workers from places such as Yemen and that 20 percent or 400,000 were from Asian countries, including 100,000 Pakistanis. Burki asserts that these estimates of Pakistani and other migrants are low; by 1979, Burki estimates that there were 750,000 to 1 million Pakistani migrants in Middle Eastern countries.

Most Pakistani migrants came from the northwest, a relatively poor area which was sending one-third of its annual work force growth, or 150,000 migrants, out of the area. Burki explains that construction projects during the 1960s led to a system in which crews of young male and often unmarried workers were recruited from various villages, and these workers became familiar with migration to do construction work for multinational firms. Labor migration to the Middle East continued this pattern; Pakistani migrants from North West Frontier province were not hard to recruit because they had a history of leaving the area and living in labor camps to work for three to five years on construction projects within Pakistan. Up to half of Pakistan's migrants were from the northwest.

Burki describes how the changing demand for labor in the Middle Eastern countries affected the characteristics of Pakistani migrants. As construction jobs gave way to maintenance and service sector jobs, Pakistan responded with training centers that taught the skills needed abroad.

By the mid-1980s, Burki estimates that 2.5 to 3 million Pakistanis were employed abroad and that these migrants remitted $3 billion annually through official channels and an additional $1.5 to $2 billion unofficially. Burki notes that Pakistani migrants to Middle Eastern countries appear to save and remit more than did Turkish migrants to Europe. Poor migrant households, which devote two-thirds of their incomes to food, spent over half of their remittances to improve day-to-day living, the Pakistani migrants also invested in land, doubling land prices in some areas. Similarly, investments in housing helped to triple brick and cement prices during a period when the overall price rise was 40 percent. Burki recounts the benefits of emigration to migrant households: incomes doubled in the one-fourth of all households which included migrants, and young household members got more food, health care, and education. The households without migrants, which were one notch above these migrant households in income, became relatively worse off.

What of the future? Burki does not believe that Middle Eastern oil exporters can quickly or significantly reduce their need for foreign labor. There may be a change in composition, for example, from construction to maintenance, and such a change will likely lead to the settlement of migrant families abroad. Burki argues that Pakistani migrants are not likely to flood home, but neither is another foreign labor market likely to offer Pakistan a safety valve for its rapid work force growth.

Chapter 8 shifts the focus to the Philippines, Thailand, Sri Lanka, Bangladesh, India, and Pakistan. Stahl and Habib review first the effects of emigration on unemployment and conclude that, for instance, the emigration of 2.5 percent of the Filipino work force has relieved unemployment pressures and has not generally caused skill shortages that were severe enough to limit production and thus lead to second-round layoffs in the Philippines. This generally optimistic conclusion rests on the observation that the massive surpluses of even skilled labor in most Asian countries make complaints of emigration-induced production disruptions rare.

Stahl and Habib present evidence that suggests that migrants often use the skills they already have while abroad. The relatively few migrants who acquire new skills abroad prefer self-employment upon their return, so that emigration and return have not generally increased human capital stocks in labor-exporting countries.

The authors argue that the magnitude and effects of remittances on development are the litmus test of the benefits of labor migration. Remittances increase the incomes of migrant households, increase national income and savings, and generate foreign exchange. In the early 1980s, an estimated 2.5 million Asian migrants remitted $8 billion, or over $3,100 each. Generally, migrants use remittances to buy necessities and luxuries, to pay off debts, and to purchase (or construct) housing and buy land. The remittances that are saved can be invested to expand the emigration country's capacity to produce and to export. Stahl and Habib briefly discuss attempts to estimate the overall effects of remittances on a sending country's economy and note that, by one estimate, each Bangladeshi migrant in 1983 created about three jobs at home with his remittances.

Stahl and Habib conclude that labor migration is neither a panacea nor a Pandora's box for development. Emigration does not automatically translate into development because migrants do not acquire new skills. Remittances, while useful, do not launch investment by themselves. However, neither has emigration from Asian countries led to skilled worker shortages causing production bottlenecks, nor did emigration keep poor labor exporters poor. Exporting labor is, in Stahl and Habib's conclusion, a useful tool to promote development that works best if an economy is primed for development.

7

Migration from Pakistan to the Middle East

Shahid Javed Burki

Migration has been an important factor in Pakistan's economic, social, and political development. The movement of people into and out of Pakistan from 1947 to 1951 influenced attitudes in the country and prepared the government and the people for subsequent migratory movements. This chapter deals with the emigration of Pakistani workers to the Middle East in the 1970s and early 1980s; it also discusses briefly the movement of Afghan refugees into Pakistan after the Soviet invasion of Afghanistan.

Over the past decade, Pakistan has emerged as a leading labor-exporting country. In 1983, it was estimated that between 2 and 3 million Pakistanis had secured jobs overseas, primarily in the Middle East and North Africa. However, with the severe 1983 to 1985 economic downturn in the Middle East oil-exporting countries, there is now some fear that the migrants may return (Burki, 1985). The outflow of professional, skilled, and unskilled labor—and the possibility of their return—has and will continue to have profound social and economic impacts on the country and may also shape its future political development. This chapter reviews the nature of Pakistani migration from both a macro and a micro perspective, the impact of migration on the domestic economy, the relationship of worker migration to concessional aid and to exports, and the prospects for future labor exports. A concluding section explores the relationship between migration's effects and government policies.

A purely economic analysis of Pakistani overseas migration would distort the total impact of this human movement. In order to present a more complete and accurate picture, this chapter evaluates the social and economic dynamics of the migration movement, as well as the potential political implications, given what we know of the 1947 migration and its consequences.

THE IMPACT OF THE 1947 MIGRATION FROM INDIA

In order to understand how migration to the Middle East impacts Pakistan, it might be useful to recapitulate what we know about the impact of the movement of people that occurred in 1947 and 1948. Less than a year after Pakistan became independent, one out of every four persons in its western province—present-day Pakistan—was a refugee from India. This refugee influx was the result of a population movement almost unparalleled in human history.[1] The movement took place between June 1947, when the British announced their intention to leave the Indian subcontinent, and the middle of 1948, when the successor regimes of India and Pakistan began to actively police the border between them. Estimates of the number of people who moved across the Indo-Pakistani frontier range from 12 to 14 million.

A comparison of the population estimates made in the censuses of 1941 and 1951 for what is now Pakistan suggests that the larger of these two numbers may be more accurate. If this is the case, it would appear that in 1947–48 Pakistan gained 8 million Muslims, while losing 6 million Sikhs and Hindus to India.[2] After this exchange, West Pakistan (present-day Pakistan) had an estimated population of 32 million, one-quarter of whom had arrived from India. The 1951 census showed that in a number of large cities, the refugees were a majority: in Karachi, the new country's capital, they accounted for 57 percent of the population. The census also showed that refugees dominated a number of professions. For instance, the proportion of positions they held at all levels of the government was far greater than their share of the population.[3]

The refugee community's influence on the development of the state of Pakistan has been analyzed in depth elsewhere (see Burki, 1979). The refugees contributed to the extraordinary economic dynamism of the 1950s and 1960s and played a critical role in the rapid modernization of some sectors of the society. But assimilation of this large refugee population did not occur without tension. The refugee community attempted to shape Pakistan's political and administrative institutions in the images of Westminster and Whitehall. But the landed aristocracy, the traditional leaders of the states and provinces that now constituted the state of Pakistan, could not readily accept the curtailment of its power, which the acceptance of such institutions would have necessarily entailed. Although the Constitution of 1956 closely followed the Westminster and Whitehall models, these contributed very little to Pakistan's second (1962) and third (1973) constitutions. Between 1956 and 1962, the country went through a process of indigenization which reduced the power of the refugee community and reestablished the landed interests as an equally important political and economic force in the country.

The economic dilemmas that have confronted Pakistan since its inception can also be traced to this conflict between the refugees and the indigenous population. Economic development is one of the issues around which the kaleidoscope of fissures and splits in the recent Pakistani leadership has revolved. Refugees from India generally favor free enterprise, while the landed aristocrats favored state guidance. This issue was important in 1948 when the refugee-dominated administration of Prime Minister Liaqat Ali Khan announced an industrial policy that put the private entrepreneurs in charge of developing Pakistan's manufacturing sector. It was also important in the 1972–76 period, when a coalition of urban intellectuals and landed interests persuaded Prime Minister Zukifar Ali Bhutto to enlarge the state's role by nationalizing important parts of the industrial sector (Burki, 1979).

Refugees from India played an important role in Pakistan's development, particularly in freeing an extremely conservative society of some of its social and cultural inhibitions. Once uprooted from their environment, the refugees from India were ready to modernize and change their attitudes regarding the role of the family, the status of women, and worker's mobility. These new attitudes were passed from the migrants to the indigenous population and facilitated a quick response to the economic opportunities that emerged in the Middle East in the 1970s.

MIGRATION TO THE MIDDLE EAST: ITS OVERALL IMPACT

The large scale migration of Pakistanis to the Middle East began early in 1974. Between 1974 and 1984, some 2.5 to 3 million people may have been involved in this movement, or 10 percent of the total Pakistani labor force. The full significance of this migration requires studying both the people who are involved and those affected indirectly. Those affected indirectly include the migrant workers' 12 to 15 million dependents, who receive remittances form the Middle East, which probably quadrupled the recipients' per capita incomes. The spending of these remittances, as well as the skills that Pakistan is losing to the Middle East, have in many ways affected those not directly involved in this movement of people.

We first explore the characteristics of the typical Pakistani migrant to the Middle East: Who is he, where does he come from, what are his skills, how much is he remitting back to his dependents, in what ways are his beneficiaries using remittances, and what is he likely to do when he returns to Pakistan? These are "micro-questions" about the individuals involved in this movement of people, but some of the answers lead to "macro-questions." For instance, what is the impact of migration on the family and the larger community from which the migrants came? Would this impact be limited only to the economic sphere, or would it also have some political, social, and cultural consequences? If so, what would be the nature of this larger impact?

A great deal of quantitative information is needed to answer the micro-questions and more time must elapse before anything definite can be said about the influence of this migration on the society at large, the macro perspective. Furthermore, the economic, political, and social impact of this movement has begun to be felt only very recently. Even though some of the analysis presented here is speculative, these speculations should help us more meaningfully observe and anticipate further developments. The profile of the migrant constructed in this analysis is based on scattered bits of information, some of which are anecdotal (Perwaiz, 1979; and Burki, 1980).

The Middle East Demand for Expatriate Labor

In the fall of 1973, OPEC quadrupled the price of its petroleum exports. The price increase had an immediate impact on the export receipts of this group of countries. In 1970, OPEC exports of goods and nonfactor services was estimated at $10 billion; in 1974, this increased to $115 billion. In 1970, the OPEC had a trade deficit with the rest of the world of $3 billion; in 1974, this amount was turned into a surplus of $60 billion. Such a sharp improvement in economic fortunes affected both the oil-exporting countries and countries on their periphery. The oil-rich countries in the Arabian peninsula—Saudi Arabia, Kuwait, United Arab Emirates, Oman and Qatar—saw a profound economic change which, within a very short period, began to impact the neighboring countries in northeastern Africa and western Asia.

In 1975, Saudi Arabia launched its second five-year development plan. This plan envisaged an expenditure of $143 billion by 1980, a large proportion of which was earmarked for developing physical infrastructures (Wilson, 1978). It was estimated that the kingdom would need 450,000 unskilled workers to implement this program, only 300,000 of whom were available locally (Ahmad, 1978). The shortfall of 150,000 was to be met by importing workers from the neighboring labor-surplus countries. In order not to tarnish Saudi Arabia's Islamic way of life, emphasis was placed on importing Muslim workers. Although neighboring Yemen provided the vast majority of the unskilled workers needed for the rapidly growing construction industry, Pakistan had a large reservoir of manpower available for export. Soon after the five-year program was launched, the flow of migrants from Pakistan to Saudi Arabia began.

It soon became obvious that the construction industry's demand for labor had been underestimated, and Saudi Arabia's ability to provide a large proportion of the needed labor from its own population was seriously overestimated. The planners had hoped to use highly capital-intensive methods of construction, but given the overall backwardness of the society it was not possible to limit the use of labor on construction sites. They had also hoped to draw a large number of nomads to work in construction, but more than half a million out of a population of 6 million continued to remain as pastoralists. The result was a sharp increase in the demand for expatriate workers.

It is difficult to estimate the number of workers who actually migrated to Saudi Arabia to help implement the first phase of this ambitious development program. Estimates range from 2 to 3 million, with the Saudi government inclined to accept the lower figure. Even the lower estimate is some 13 times the number expected when the country's second five-year plan was launched. Migrants from the Middle East's Arabic-speaking countries accounted for the vast majority of workers during this period. According to one estimate, they numbered 1.3 million, or 65 percent of the migrant work force. The second largest contingent came from Asia. Of the estimated 400,000 Asians, about 100,000 were Pakistanis. Many more foreigners entered Saudi Arabia than these estimates indicate. A large number entered illegally. Glubb (1978) points out that many illegal immigrants stay on after the annual Muslim pilgrimage to Mecca and live in shanties in the major cities, always hoping to obtain a work permit. The very large increase in the number of foreign pilgrims entering the kingdom is explained in part by this search for work. For instance, in 1973 about 607,000 pilgrims entered Saudi Arabia for Hajj. A year later, after the Saudis began to implement some of their ambitious infrastructure schemes, the number of pilgrims increased to 919,000. But ships from various countries "which had arrived with a thousand or so pilgrims were said to be leaving with only a quarter of their complement" (Glubb, 1978).

Geographic Origin of Pakistani Migrants

Most of Saudi Arabia's foreign workers were recruited by western construction firms working on such large projects as the Damman-Jiddah highway, a highway linking the North Yemeni port of Hudaida with Jizan on the Red Sea Coast of Saudi Arabia; redevelopment of the cities of Mecca and Medina; and construction of new oil pipelines. With these projects scattered over large tracts of inhospitable land, the contractors demanded workers capable of hard manual labor in very difficult climatic conditions. Such workers could be found in large numbers in the northern areas of Pakistan.

A number of economic, social, and cultural factors turned Pakistan's northwestern districts into a vast pool of labor available for the Middle East. These districts in the early 1970s had a total population of about 15 million and a labor force of some 5 million. Agriculture in these districts depends on rainfall which is irregular and not sufficient to sustain the large labor force. The rate of population growth has been high over the last two decades—on the order of 3.3 percent a year[4]—with the result that the labor force is now increasing at the rate of 3 percent or 450,000 a year. More than 150,000 workers who annually join the labor force must look for opportunities elsewhere.

There are even fewer work opportunities in the region's towns and cities. Cotton, Pakistan's most important industrial raw material, is cultivated in the southeastern districts. The southeast also produces natural gas, the country's most important energy resource. There are no comparable resource endowments in the northwest. The interest groups that dominated economic decision-making during Pakistan's early days had little political incentive to get industries established in the northwest. The result is that the urban economy in the northwest is as backward as the rural economy, a fact that explains the area's relatively low rate of urbanization. For more than two decades the population of Peshawar, one of the region's main cities, increased at a rate even lower than that of the natural increase, which suggests that some people emigrated. It was only with the migration of Afghans into northern Pakistan that this region's urban population began to grow at a rate higher than that of the natural increase.

Both supply and demand factors have contributed to the large-scale migration of labor from Pakistan's northwest districts. It is in part the poverty of these districts and in part their social structures that have turned them into net exporters of workers to the outside world. Although a number of different people inhabit this region—Pathans in the districts bordering Afghanistan, and Rajputs and Jats in the districts between the Indus and Jhelum Rivers—there is some similarity in community structures. The Pathans belong to acephalous, or "headless," tribes in which each small group has its own leader (Ahmed, 1977). There are no tribal leaders, or *sirdars*. The agriculturists and pastoralists of the northern Punjab districts are similarly organized. Such an organization suits employers, especially when the workers are hired in large numbers. In these situations, the agreements (generally oral) are drawn up between the contractors and the leaders of worker groups. These groups are not particularly large—no more than 10 or 12 workers come from the same village or locality. When they move, their leader, or *malik*, moves with them.

There is a long history of long distance migration among the people of the northwestern districts. The Mughuls, the Pathans, the Sikhs, and the British found willing recruits from these districts for their armed forces, a practice that continued after the establishment of Pakistan. When Pakistani contractors began seeking construction workers to help them build Karachi into the country's new capital, they turned once again to the labor force from this area. Karachi's construction boom lasted just over a decade. It began in 1948 and subsided in the early sixties, when the government of Ayub Khan decided to move the capital to the northwest, adjacent to the city of Rawalpindi. At about the same time, Pakistan began the vast Indus "replacement works," a system of dams, rivers, reservoirs, and link-canals intended to compensate the country for the water it would lose to India under the terms of the Indus Water Treaty.

The construction of Islamabad, the new capital, and of the Indus replacement works provided workers with opportunities they had never experienced before. Islamabad and some of the more important dams and canals were being constructed in the northwestern districts. For the first time in this region's history, large construction works were being carried out close to home. This meant that the number of jobs available to them was much larger than those lost in Karachi. What ultimately proved even more important to local workers was the fact that the larger construction contracts for building Islamabad and the Indus replacement works were won by well-established foreign firms; the workers were thus exposed to the firms which were later to play a significant role in the Middle East construction boom. Workers also became familiar with the modern construction industry.

The Middle East boom started precisely at the time that the construction activity connected with Islamabad, Mangla Dam, and Tarbela Dam was winding down. The workers who were being laid off in the early 1970s began to find jobs in Saudi Arabia, mostly with the same firms that had employed them in Pakistan. What began as a small trickle from 1969 to 1973 became a flood in the 1974–82 period (Table 7.1). The movement of labor between Pakistan and Saudi Arabia during the 1974–82 period, then, involved mostly workers from the northwestern areas. These migrants had the same characteristics as those who had established the Pathan colonies in Karachi and had filled the labor camps maintained by the foreign contractors that built Islamabad and the Indus Basin replacement works. They were young, mostly in their late teens or early twenties, and with little or no education. A large number of them were unmarried. They moved as members of villages, communities, or tribe-centered groups,

Table 7.1
Labor Supply in the Northern Districts of Pakistan, 1978 (in Thousands)

Population[a]	17,728
•of which male[b]	9,160
•of which rural male[c]	7,328
•of which rural male between 15 and 29 years	1,605
•of which rural male between 15-29 years and in labor force[d]	1,445
•of which rural labor force between 15-29 years and in labor force with no skills[e]	1,017
•of which migrants to the Middle East	375-500

[a]Population of 1978 was calculated assuming a rate of increase of 3 percent of the 1972 population of the northern states (Division of Peshawar, Malak and Dera Ismail Khan, centrally administered tribal areas and the Districts of Rawalpindi, Campbellpur, and Jhelum) of 14,857 million. The areas account for 27.1 percent of the total Pakistani population.

[b]Same as note a. Male population was 7.672 million.

[c]Calculated as 21.9 percent of the total male population - the ratio in 1972 for males between the ages of 15 and 29 for all rural areas in Pakistan. By way of comparison it may be noted that the ratio for urban areas was much higher—25.8 percent.

[d]Calculated using the participation rates of 88.9, 97.5, and 93.7 percent respectively for rural males in the age groups of 15-29, 20-24, and 25-29 years, giving an overall rate of 90 percent.

[e]Calculated as 66.1, 69.9 and 75.6 percent of the total labor force respectively for the ages 15-19, 20-24, and 25-29 years, giving an overall percentage of 70.4 percent.

Source: These estimates are made from the data from the population census of 1972.

mostly with their own headmen. They were essentially temporary migrants expecting to return home after no more than five years of construction work.

The only substantial bit of evidence available on the origin of these migrants is from a random check, by Pakistan International Airlines, of the addresses of the workers who flew to various Middle Eastern destinations during one week in the month of March 1979. Of the three hundred addresses examined, representing about 10 percent of the total number of persons flown by the airline during that week, nearly one-half had their homes in the northern districts. The proportion of migrants from the north was even larger among those who traveled to the Middle East by sea.

Even if we work with the lower proportion, it seems that by 1979, some 375,000 to 500,000 migrants originated from Pakistan's northwestern districts; this was out of a total stock of some 750,000 to 1 million migrants working by that time in the Middle East. A very large proportion of this work force appears to have been recruited initially by representatives of the large construction firms that had operated in these parts of Pakistan in the 1960s and early 1970s.[5] Later recruitments were also done by a number of local entrepreneurs (Table 7.2).

Table 7.2
Number of Persons Recruited for Foreign Employers (in Thousands)

Year	Private	Public	Direct	Total
1971	3	2	–	5
1972	4	1	–	5
1973	8	5	–	13
1974	15	2	–	17
1975	22	1	–	23
1976	39	3	–	42
1977	78	3	60	141
1978	79	4	48	131
1979	81	10	35	126
1980	91	14	25	130
1981	120	15	33	168
1982	99	35	38	172
1983	74	8	46	128
1971-1983	713	103	285	1,101

Source: Government of Pakistan, Pakistan Economic Survey, 1983-84 (Islamabad: Finance Division, 1984, p. 109, Table 3, based on the data provided by Bureau of Emigration and Overseas Employment and Overseas Employment Corporation.) The statistics do not include the stock of Pakistanis abroad prior to 1971 or dependents and students.

The construction workers drawn from the northwestern districts comprise by far the single most important group among the Pakistani migrants to Saudi Arabia. In the smaller Gulf States (UAE, Oman, Qatar, Bahrain), however, the number of Pakistani urban professionals, mostly from the cities of Karachi and Lahore, matches that in construction labor. The events that influenced migration to these countries differed somewhat from those that resulted in the Pakistani labor movement to Saudi Arabia.

The small Gulf States also made a significant contribution to the Middle East's construction boom during the 1970s. Since they also needed foreign construction workers, the firms that had contracts in these countries turned to Pakistan again to obtain a significant proportion of the work force they required. But there was relatively little formal hiring of workers directly from Pakistan. Instead, a very large number of workers "from the [South Asian] sub-continent [made] illegal crossings to the east coast of UAE, sometimes paying hundreds of dollars to the Dhow owner. Some arrivals [were] not even aware that their entry [was] illegal" (see Thomas, 1978; see also Tingay, 1978). The relative ease with which boat crossings could be made from the Mekran coast of Pakistan to the largely unattended landing points on the Gulf coast meant that organized migration of the type that occurred to Saudi Arabia was less important in this case.

Like Saudi Arabia, the small Gulf states also needed skills other than those specific to the construction industry. However, with a population base considerably smaller than Saudi Arabia's, these countries turned to foreigners to fill a variety of jobs in the rapidly expanding modern sector. As Thomas (1978) points out, "because of the lack of education among UAE nationals and the development of local and federal bureaucracies, almost all the skilled clerical and administrative staffs are foreigners, mainly Levantine Arabs." Arabs, however, were not the only people filling these positions. Once again, Pakistan met a part of the need. Pakistan's economic slowdown in the early seventies had considerably reduced the absorption rate of skilled manpower. As a result, there were considerable surpluses of such skilled personnel as doctors, engineers, bankers, business managers, accountants, and economists. Beginning in 1976, the number of such migrants destined for the Middle East increased sharply. By mid-1979, they accounted for nearly 10 percent of the total, compared with less than 1 percent in 1974.

In the early 1980s the slowdown in the Middle East's construction activity affected migration from Pakistan. The Middle East needed workers to maintain the large physical infrastructure that was built between 1973 and 1983. Maintenance is more labor-intensive than construction; it requires a number of very different skills, most of which were not locally available to the Middle East. Pakistan responded to this change in demand by setting up a number of training institutions which turned out large numbers of carpenters, plumbers, electricians, and other skilled workers. These skills became prominent among the workers that migrated.

The Stock of Migrants

In response to the opportunities offered by these rapidly expanding economies, the scale of migration from Pakistan to the oil-surplus countries of the Middle East has risen dramatically since the mid-1970s. Between 1973 and 1975, employment in these economies rose at the rate of 5 to 6 percent a year. Since 1983, job creation has slowed down, but the dependence on imported labor has not diminished significantly. As discussed above, much of the labor response from Pakistan was spontaneous, not government-sponsored, and the workers seeking Middle East employment proceed abroad through various channels, public and private. The two official agencies responsible for providing workers for foreign employment are the Bureau of Emigration and Overseas Employment (BEOE) and the Overseas Employment Corporation (OEC). The BEOE (since 1971) works through labor attaches in the Middle East and a network of roughly 500 privately licensed agents, processing state-to-state labor contracts. The OEC (since 1977) handles applications in response to private sector demand from abroad. The bulk of emigration, particularly in the earlier years, was channeled partly through private promoters registered with the government and partly through direct contact with overseas employers. Illegal employment is also alleged to have been widespread, particularly in the mid-1970s.

Since a substantial flow of migrants do not go through government channels, official statistics from the BEOE tend to understate the true outflow by a significant margin, particularly prior to 1977. According to official estimates, the labor force stock working abroad is currently about 1.1 million. However, estimates of the number of workers outside the country in the mid-1980s from the ministry of manpower, based on the judgment of labor attaches in the Middle East, suggest a total of more than 2 million. This is roughly similar to another estimate of 2.25 million obtained from a nationwide survey carried out by the Pakistan Institute of Public Opinion. That the stock of migrants is likely to be in excess of two million is finally borne out by the amount of remittances received back in Pakistan. Remittances reached $3 billion in 1983, before declining somewhat. This is the amount sent through official channels; an additional $1.5 to 2.0 billion comes in through the informal (*hundi*) system. Given the wages migrants receive and even considering their high propensity to save, this volume could have been generated only by a stock of people in excess of 2.5 million. For the purpose of this paper, therefore, the stock of Pakistanis working in the Middle East (the Gulf States, Iran, Iraq, Syria, and the countries of North Africa) is estimated to be between 2.5 and 3.0 million.

The typical migrant in the 1970s was a man who left his wife and family behind. He usually worked abroad for two to four years, visiting home once a year. Most of the workers had little or no formal vocational training, but instead had long years of experience on the job. The informal sector has played a prominent role in Pakistani migration. This is not surprising given that more than 75 percent of those employed in Pakistan are classified either as self-employed or as helpers in the family business. In recent years the small-scale industrial sector has expanded steadily, contributing significantly to production and export growth; hence, it has been a major source of trained labor.[6]

As mentioned above, the large stock of Pakistani migrants in the Middle East was built during the ten years of the construction boom in the Gulf states, from about 1973 to 1982. In this stock, manual workers comprised 83 percent of the migrants, of which 43 percent were unskilled and 40 percent were skilled (Table 7.3). Professional, clerical, and service categories made up the remainder. Most of the manual workers were in the construction sector. The average length of stay for the workers in the construction industry was just over four years.

THE ECONOMIC IMPACT OF MIGRATION ON THE DOMESTIC ECONOMY

To understand the full short- and long-term social and economic impact of Pakistani migration to the Middle East requires reasonably firm information about the number of people involved; their social, economic, and cultural backgrounds; the amount of remittances they send to their families in Pakistan; and the use the benefitting households make of these additions to their incomes.

During the first wave of migration, the majority of emigrating workers came

Table 7.3
Characteristics of Migrants' Broad Occupational Structure of the Labor Force and Provincial Origin, 1979–80

	Migrants (%)	Labor force (%)
Skill composition		
Manual workers	83.2	73.8
(a) Unskilled	42.6	–
(b) Skilled	40.6	–
Professionals	4.3	4.7
Clerical	1.5	5.0
Service	2.2	7.9
Salesmen/business	6.0	8.6
Others	2.9	–
Total	100.0	100.0
Provincial breakdown		
Punjab	70.4	n.a.
Sind	14.0	n.a.
NWFP	11.7	n.a.
Baluchistan	3.9	n.a.
Total	100.0	n.a.

Source: Gilani et al., 1981: 10, Table 5.

from the poorer districts in the Northwest Frontier Province and the northwestern districts of Punjab. The migration that occurred at that time tended to draw
several members from the same household, particularly when the migrants came
from extended households with many male members. Farag (1976) estimates that
437,000 unskilled workers (the mid-point between the range of 375,000 and
500,000 estimated above) migrated from this region, involving some 337,000
households. In 1978, the region had 3.22 million households with an average of
5.5 members, and it was primarily the poorest, the bottom 20 percent, that joined
the migration stream. In other words, about one out of every two poor households
in this region had members working in the Middle East. The poor households did
not have to raise resources in order to send their workers abroad because, in most
cases, the workers were given passage by the contractors who hired them. For
this reason, more people from poor households went to Saudi Arabia than to the
Gulf States. The labor market was much more organized in the case of the former
and much more fragmented in the case of the latter.

To understand the full significance of what this migration meant for the poor
households, their social and economic status before they sent workers to the
Middle East must be examined. However, once again we run into data problems.
Disaggregated data are not available, so we must rely on aggregate data. According to a recent study, rural Pakistan in 1961 had 6.5 million households, and
4 million or 60 percent were poor. Of the poor households, 71 percent had some
land, 15 percent were landless, and 14 percent drew the bulk of their income
from nonfarming occupations. However, all poor households received some income from labor on farms other than their own (Naseem, 1977).

Households were classified as poor if they did not grow enough food on their
own or did not have enough income to buy sufficient food from the market to meet
the minimum daily requirement of their members. Poor households spent 68 percent of their incomes on food, 11 percent on clothing, and 12 percent on housing
(Burki and Hicks, 1977). Poor households also had high rates of illiteracy, infant
mortality, and morbidity; these rates were particularly high for women.

Migration has had a profound impact on the economy of this region. A significant and long-lasting impact of migration may be produced by the flow of remittances directly to the families whose members are working in the Middle East.
The full significance of this impact can only be understood in terms of the pre-
and post-migration incomes of the affected households. While Pakistan does not
publish data on the contribution of different geographical areas to the national
product, some rough estimates can be made.

In 1978 the population of the areas which contributed the majority of migrants accounted for 23 percent of the migrants, but their share of the Gross
National Product was about 18 percent. This implies regional product of $3.4
billion, which in turn means an average per capita income of $191 and a house-
hold income of about $1,050. Accepting annual earnings of $2,000 per migrant
worker, a savings rate of 66 percent, and 1.3 workers per recipient family, it appears that households which have sent out migrants received average remit-

tances of $2,145 per annum. While the average household income in this area was about $1,200 a year, the migrants have come from the poorer sectors of the population. Income distribution studies for Pakistan suggest that the share of total income going to the bottom 20 percent of households is approximately 9 percent (see Guisinger and Hicks, 1978). Assuming that this is the segment of the population that has sent workers to the Middle East, pre-migration family incomes would be around $700 a year. This means that every year workers are remitting to their households amounts equal to three times as much as the premigration family income. Such a boost in household income must have had a significant impact on these families' economic well-being, unless a good proportion of the remittances received was squandered on unproductive consumption.

Analysis of the possible expenditure patterns of families receiving remittances should be done in the context of the gross increase in income over the period that the migrants stay abroad. There was considerable turnover among the migrants to the Middle East; the work in which they were engaged was physically exacting, as was the working environment. It appears that construction workers remained outside Pakistan for an average of four years, a period during which a total of about $8,600 per family is likely to have been remitted back home. This means that over a four-year span, these households received remittances totaling more than 10 times their annual premigration incomes.

Semiskilled workers and those working in sectors other than construction appear to have stayed for longer than four-year periods, in part because their actual work and the working environment were somewhat less exacting. This is true for the workers in the service sector as well as for semiskilled workers hired to maintain physical infrastructures. Average wages earned by these new groups of migrants were much higher than those construction workers received, although their savings rates were probably lower. Even so, the amount remitted per year is probably higher than that of construction workers.

How are the families using this windfall income? Two types of evidence are available: direct and indirect. Analysis of the expenditures of the average migrant household reveals that it consumes 62 percent of remittances, invests roughly 20 percent, and spends 15 percent on residential real estate (Table 7.4). If the invested portion is productive, then migration will have a long-term beneficial impact on both private consumption and the productive potential of the economy as a whole. Only 2 percent purchase financial instruments; the low percentage is indicative of the relative unattractiveness of financial instruments as real returns on institutional savings have been negative. The Pakistanis' unfamiliarity with managing financial instruments may be an additional reason, since a significant portion of migrants are unskilled and probably illiterate, given Pakistan's 24 percent literacy rate.

It would be of interest to compare the Pakistani migrant with other migrant groups. Some interesting similarities and differences are apparent in considering the case of the Turkish migrant—a case which has been extensively researched. Compared to the Turkish migrant's remittance behavior, the Pakistani migrant

Table 7.4
Average Income, Savings, and Remittances by Skill Category, 1979–80 (in Thousands)

Skill Category	Average Income	Savings	Remittances	Ratio of Remittances to Savings
Unskilled	45.6	31.75	23.74	0.75
Skilled	53.80	34.36	28.30	0.82
Professional	117.70	86.08	53.68	0.62
Service/Clerical	60.16	39.36	33.84	0.86
Salesmen/Business	77.92	49.21	31.94	0.65
Others	82.50	63.25	46.10	0.73

Source: Gilani et al., 1981: 105

tends to save and remit a higher proportion of his earnings (Paine, 1974). The average Turkish migrant saved 46 percent of total earnings, of which he remitted 24 percent for family maintenance; the typical Pakistani migrant saves 70 percent of total earnings, of which he remits roughly 75 percent for family maintenance. One possible explanation for this difference is that the Pakistani remits relatively more because the Pakistani exchange rate is not thought to be significantly overvalued. In the Turkish case, remittances increased markedly when the Turkish lira was devalued in 1970. With respect to the structure of remittance expenditures both migrant groups appear to spend significant proportions on the following (1) recurring consumption; (2) residential real estate; and (3) work-related investments.

Lacking direct information from the families, one must again rely on indirect data. The movement of the price indices for various types of goods and commodities provides some helpful hints about the expenditure pattern of the households receiving remittances from abroad. The *patwaris* (village clerks) in the villages around Rawalpindi report a doubling of agricultural land prices. This probably means that a portion of remittances is going into land purchases. A significant portion is also being spent on constructing new houses or remodeling old ones. In nine out of ten cases, new construction or remodeling work in the villages close to Rawalpindi was being carried out by families with workers in the Middle East.[7] This construction activity has had an impact: in 1979, the price of bricks in Rawalpindi had increased to Rs 500 per thousand versus Rs 300 in 1974. By 1984, bricks were selling at more than Rs 1,000 per thousand, a rate of increase since 1974 that was three times the rate of increase in the commodity price index, and an even sharper price increase was registered for cement. The price of bicycles—another popular purchase for the new rich in the rural areas—has registered a similar increase, from about Rs 400 in 1974 to between Rs 1,000 and 1,500 in 1984. This 300 to 400 percent increase in the prices of certain goods, when compared to a 40 percent increase in the price index of the basket of goods purchased by poor families, suggests that a sizeable amount of this new income was spent on these items (Burki, 1984a).

The poor spend nearly two-thirds of their income on food. The sharp increase in the incomes of the poor households which receive remittances should have resulted in improved food intake. This should be the case especially when these households were initially consuming less than the minimum daily requirement. Though relative food prices did not increase significantly between 1974 and 1984, food consumption in Pakistan, including imports and changes in stocks increased, at the rate of nearly 5 percent a year. When compared to an increase in population of about 3 percent, this signifies a substantial improvement in per capita food consumption.

There is also evidence of an increase in expenditure on health and education by households from labor-exporting regions. A large number of private schools have opened in the districts of Peshawar, Altock, Mardani, and Rawalpindi. The number of physicians and hospital beds per 1000 people in these districts has increased at a rate higher than the country average, and evidence also points to a faster increase in the sale of medicines in these areas than in the rest of the country.

The foregoing analysis points to three conclusions about the economic and social impacts of remittances on households receiving incomes from migrants working in the Middle East. First, the sharp increase in the current incomes of labor-exporting households (which accounted for nearly one quarter of all households by 1984) meant a significant permanent change in their economic and social status. Even if these households were able to invest only a third of their total windfall gain in productive activity, that investment activity could result in a 50 percent increase in their incomes. In doing so, these households would have leap-frogged over those that did not have members working abroad. Second, by being able to meet their basic health, education, nutrition, and shelter needs, the remittance-receiving households would be better able to improve the development of their human capital. We should expect the young migrants themselves to be better nourished and, in some cases, somewhat more literate when they return home. The next generation should benefit even more. Improvement in health and education would further increase the long-term prospects of the families with migrants. Third, it is possible that the changes in the circumstances of the families with migrants may come about at the cost of those households that do not have access to these additional incomes. This could happen if the economy is not able to provide the new rich with the goods and services in the quantities they need. This is a sufficiently important outcome of migration to merit further consideration. If there are serious constraints on increasing the supply of essential commodities such as food, clothing, bicycles, and the like, their prices would rise in response to the additional demand. The noticeable boom in urban consumption in Pakistan has had a redistributive impact, increasing the relative prices of goods and services consumed by families made wealthier by migration (Perwaiz 1979:85–87).

Households with workers in the Middle East have seen a quantum leap in their incomes and now have the capacity to bid away these goods from the less fortunate consumer. Despite price increases, households receiving remittances may still be able to improve the levels of their consumption for these items, but this would happen at the cost of other households. In other words, the economy's inability to expand the supply of these consumption items could cause serious tension between those who are benefitting from the remittances and those who are being hurt by them. The beneficiaries are households that, before migration began, were among the poorest in the country. Those that have been hurt are those previously one notch above on the income distribution scale. The price increases discussed above suggest that such a development may well be occurring. However, a significant increase in agricultural output and the resulting stability in food grain prices has saved the society from feeling the full force of this potential negative impact of migration.

Indirect Consequences of Migration

Migration to the Middle East has also had a number of indirect consequences, the most important of which are changes in the labor market. Migration has been a significant factor in the sharp rise in domestic wages of skilled and unskilled labor in recent years, although this link cannot be established quantitatively due to lack of data. Data on the daily wage rates of different categories of construction labor show an annual increase of 20 to 30 percent since the mid-1970s. Official estimates of inflation during this period yield an average annual rate of 9 to 10 percent, meaning that real wages rose significantly. The increase in real wages was not confined to the urban sector of the economy. Sparse data on rural wages also indicate a 25 percent annual increase in the late 1970s. Since roughly 10 percent of the estimated labor force is in the Middle East, migration has contributed to these rising wages not only by moderating the growth of the domestic manual labor supply, but also by increasing purchasing power via remittances at a time when economic recovery was under way and the GDP was growing by 5 to 6 percent a year.

Whether the improvement in income which brought about changes in the labor market is permanent will depend upon a number of factors, the most important of which is the way present and potential employers react to this sharp increase in their labor costs. The first reaction to the wage increases has been to mechanize some of the operations that have been traditionally carried out by unskilled workers. For instance, 16,000 tractors were imported in 1978–79—the largest number and sharpest increase registered in any one year—to help landowners facing labor shortages (Muhammed, 1979). In 1984–85, farmers acquired an estimated 24,000 new tractors. There is also a brisk demand for threshers and other types of simple agricultural machinery. Machinery is also being introduced into the construction industry.

A definitive assessment of the distributional impact of migration is not possible, since no recent data exists on income distribution or on the consumption structure of major income groups. However, given the migrants' occupations, it is likely that rising wages have involved a redistribution of income from the owners of capital to labor. If so, and given the government's concern for fulfilling basic needs, this income transfer is socially desirable. But, while rising wages need not constitute a problem, the government is concerned about losses in the quantity and quality of output. It is alleged, for instance, that as the experienced workers leave for the Middle East, the unskilled step in, rendering lower quality services at higher unit costs. Withdrawal of technical and managerial talent disrupts production, thus lowering productivity.

The public sector has also been adversely affected as larger numbers of its managers and skilled workers have been attracted to Middle East jobs. One example of this drain of highly skilled manpower is found in the exit of engineers employed by the Water and Power Development Authority (WAPDA). As new power plants were commissioned in the Middle East, WAPDA found it difficult to retain its highly trained staff—"the people in whom we had invested a great deal of time and resource," in the words of WAPDA's chairman. In an effort to mitigate such damage, the government has expanded its formal training system activities. The planned output of trainees from government institutions until 1985 was 30,000 a year, a threefold increase over the 1978–79 level. Informal and private-sector institutions are estimated to contribute roughly 20,000 skilled/ semiskilled workers a year. However, even this substantial expansion is unlikely to fill the need for skilled and semiskilled labor, which was conservatively estimated at 50,000 new positions a year until 1985.

Rough estimates of training costs indicate a substantial private return from vocational training: on average, annual costs range from Rs 2000 to 4000, depending on the training center, and remittances can average Rs 31,600 a year for three to four years. With managerial and financial constraints on further expanding government involvement in vocational training, the scope for increasing private-sector involvement can be explored. Therefore, even when considering the cost to the society of improving the skills of the work force and the cost that results from the disruption to production that inevitably results from migration, it is hard to say that the country has not gained even from the export of highly skilled people.

Balance of Payments

The most tangible benefit of Pakistani labor exports to the Middle East has been the substantial inflow of remittances, which, as we already noted, increased from $449 million to nearly $3 billion in 1982–83. During this period, gross imports of oil products increased fourfold, from $359 million to $1.5 billion, and roughly 30 percent of the increase in the total gross import bill was due to oil price increases. Since 1977–78, remittances have exceeded disbursements of foreign assistance. By 1984–85, remittances constituted almost 80 percent of merchan-

dise export earnings and they financed 35 percent of merchandise import expenditures and reduced the current account deficit by more than half (Table 7.5).

It is widely believed that official estimates of remittances grossly understate
the true magnitude of remitted funds and represent only a fraction of the total.
Recent surveys of migrant households indicate that the bulk of remittances flow
through banking channels, although there is a portion that flows through the traditional system of exchange through private agents, the so-called hundi system
(Table 7.6). Some 86 percent of migrants use banks in remitting earnings; excluding migrants from the Northwest Frontier Province, this rises to 94 percent. The average Pakistani migrant chooses to bring with him on his annual
home visit roughly 25 percent of his remittances in cash and 10 percent in kind.
Thus, out of an annual average remittance of Rs 31,600, RS 7,700 is brought in
cash and Rs 2,600 in kind. It appears that roughly 25 percent of savings are not
remitted: a percentage that varies between occupational groups, the highest

Table 7.5
Remittances: Comparison with Selected Foreign Exchange Flows
(Million U.S. $)

Account:	Remittances	Disbursements of Foreign Assistance	Exports (fob)	Imports (cif)	Current Balance
1975/1976	339	1059	1162	2341	−947
1976/1977	578	961	1132	2647	−1052
1977/1978	1156	856	1283	3039	−601
1978/1979	1398	948	1644	4154	−1110
1979/1980	1748	1469	2341	5177	−1120
1980/1981[a]	2128	1174	2716	6168	−1566
1981/1982					
1982/1983					

[a]Estimate

Source: State Bank of Pakistan

Table 7.6
Proportion of Immigrants Using Unofficial Remittance Channels

	Rural	Urban	Total
Punjab	3.8	5.1	4.8
Sind	–	4.3	5.3
N.W.F.P.	51.8	42.0	47.7
Baluchistan	13.6	25.0	21.0
Azad Kashmir	5.3	0.0	4.2
Pakistan	24.1	10.4	14.5

Source: Gilani et al., 1981: 111

being for the business category and lowest for the professionals. The wide-spread belief that the bulk of migrant savings remains abroad is not supported by the evidence.

Changes in the Direction and Composition of Exports

The impact of worker migration upon the Pakistani export sector may be examined in terms of (a) migrants' remittances acting as a complement for export earnings, and (b) migrants creating a special market for Pakistani exports.

As discussed above, migrants' remittance provided a valuable source of external resources at a time when the value of imports was increasing rapidly largely due to the increase in the price of petroleum and related products, as well as to a sharp increase in the price of capital goods. Furthermore, the export sector was performing rather poorly due to the recession in the industrialized countries.

Between 1973 and 1984, the total value of goods and commodities imported by Pakistan was about $31 billion. During the same period, remittances through official channels totaled about $13 billion. Therefore, worker's remittances paid for 42 percent of total imports over this period, and by complementing export earnings, they effectively financed the trade gap between export earnings and expenditures on imports.[8]

The approximately two and a half million Pakistani workers in the Middle East also created a large market for the kinds of goods and commodities that normally would not have been exported to the Middle East. This new development was reflected in the share of oil-exporting countries in Pakistan's total exports, a share which increased from 2 percent in 1960 to 23 percent in 1984.

What about the future? The sixth Pakistani five-year plan (1983–88) made some ambitious predictions about the influx of remittances into the country. But the plan's projection had to be revised. In the first of the series of rolling three-year plans, workers' remittances were expected to grow at only 5 percent instead of 10 percent annually.

ARE THE MIGRANTS RETURNING HOME?

It has been argued that Middle East countries no longer have the capacity to absorb additional foreign workers. In fact, because of the downturn in economic activity experienced by all Middle East oil-exporting countries, a return flow of migrants is conceivable. According to some indications, such a flow may already have begun; there are fewer Pakistanis emigrating now than are coming back home. In other words, the pool of Pakistani workers in the Middle East has begun to shrink. With this reduction will come a decrease in the amounts remitted back to the country.[9]

The 1983–85 decline in remittances was not the first. Pakistan's recent economic history suggests that a decline in the level of remittances in one month or even one quarter need not establish a new trend. A downturn in remittances should not lead to the conclusion that the time has arrived when Pakistani workers will begin to return home in large numbers.[10] For instance, the remittances received in the second quarter of 1981 ($504 million) were 6 percent below those received during the year's first quarter ($537 million); the declining trend then continued into the third quarter, when remittances went down another 4 percent. Consequently, in the second half of 1981, remittances were more than 3 percent less than in the first half. The flow began to increase again during the fourth quarter of 1981, however, and there was a steady growth from one quarter to another in 1982. Then 1983 brought another significant drop; in the second quarter of that year, remittances declined by 9 percent, from $801 million to $728 million.

Some of the pessimism about the Middle East's economic prospects stems from its recent performance. High income oil exporters of the Middle East, after registering a GDP growth rate of 7.5 percent a year from 1973 to 1980, saw their economies stagnate from 1981 to 1984. With stagnation came a decline in incomes per capita, and, consequently, a reduction in the demand for the services which migrants have traditionally provided. If recession continues in the Middle East, a decline in the number of foreign workers could certainly occur. The important question then is whether the present slump will last into the future, or whether the recovery of the industrial economies will finally begin to affect the Middle East. Apart from the effect of recovery in the Western world, there are other reasons why one should expect some improvement in the economic growth rate in the Middle East oil-exporting countries.

There is a minimum economic growth rate that is essential to Middle East political tranquility. This rate may be anywhere between five and ten percent of GDP a year. Having suffered declines in GDP growth rates in the last several years, the Middle East countries are likely to pursue some expansion in the future. Although a revival in the economies of the Middle East is expected, there is a serious question about the availability of resources for bringing it about. The oil market remains soft. Even if oil prices rise, the Middle East may not reap an immediate benefit. The first benefit within the OPEC group would go to the economically weaker states of Nigeria and Indonesia. Also, as has happened in the past, other oil producers not subject to OPEC discipline may increase their production, thus making it difficult for the Middle East to increase production.[11]

If oil does not generate the resources required for a Middle East economic revival, other avenues might be explored. These could include floating bonds in the expectation that the glut in the oil market will dissipate and provide a sufficient amount of export earnings to service the new debt. Investment policies could be changed in favor of using the return on the financial assets owned by the Middle Eastern governments for domestic purposes, rather than for reinvestment in the industrial world. The total value of these investments is estimated at between $400 and $500 billion, and this investment should be generating some $40 to $60 billion a year, which is equivalent to a significant proportion of oil export earnings.

The Middle East is also acquiring new and perhaps more secure channels for obtaining resources for future development. Already, Middle Eastern fertilizer, chemical, and petrochemical industries are competitive with the older North American and European industries. There is a rapidly maturing industrial revolution in the Middle East. As more plants are brought into production, the earnings of the Gulf countries from non-oil sources will increase further, and the Middle East will have access to sufficient external resources to begin to reinflate its economies. Allowing the present recession to continue much longer into the future poses some very serious political risks.

There is a third reason why the Middle East demand for foreign labor is not expected to decline precipitously, even if the construction boom that generated it in the first place does not revive or collapses. The physical capital that has been created with the help of foreign labor will need to be maintained by foreign labor. The composition of skills required may change—construction workers may be replaced by maintenance workers—but the share of national income of the Middle Eastern countries that is claimed by foreigners might not decline.

In this respect, the Middle East is very different from Europe. In Europe, the remarkable economic boom of the 1960s was made possible in part by the import of guestworkers. Once the pace of economic growth slowed down in Europe—as it did in the mid-1970s—the need for foreign workers declined rapidly. This was one reason why several labor-exporting countries faced such economic difficulties in the early 1980s. In fact, many in Pakistan feel that their country should learn from the Turkish experience and reduce both its dependence on exporting workers to solve its surplus labor problems, and its dependence on migrant workers' remittances for meeting its perennial foreign exchange gap. It is difficult, however, to see why the Middle East's labor-short economies, still lacking in basic physical and human infrastructure, should suddenly reduce the stock of expatriate labor. Within a quarter century—from 1950 to 1975—the economies of Europe matured; the Middle East has a long way to go before it enters the same phase of development.

Finally, some subtle demographic changes are also taking place that could have a profound impact on the Pakistani population in the Middle East. Notwithstanding the policies adopted by the Middle East governments, the demographic composition of the migrant population will change as more women and children join the male workers. This is more likely to happen as transient construction workers are replaced by the more permanent maintenance workers—a trend that has already begun. This will help stabilize the migrant population as has already happened with the Pakistanis in Britain, although perhaps not on the same scale. While such a development will retard the return of migrants, it will adversely impact remittances, since single workers save a larger proportion of their earnings than those whose families are with them. With time, a good proportion of migrants will be absorbed in Middle Eastern economies, societies, and cultures. There are signs that this might be happening already in some countries of the Gulf, particularly in Kuwait and in the UAE. Saudi Arabia may eventually follow suit.

The conclusion to be drawn is that the flow of remittances from the migrants may not increase at the high rates of the last decade, but there is little reason to believe that the flow will decline precipitously. Remittances might increase by about 5 percent per year, as envisaged by the planning commission, or they might remain at their present level in nominal terms. At the same time, the social, economic, and political dynamics set into motion by migration will continue to change the Pakistani socioeconomic landscape.

CONCLUSIONS

What are the main conclusions to be drawn from this case study of a nation in which migration of people, especially to and from the Middle East, has played such an important role in economic and social development? The main conclusion is also the most obvious one: In labor-surplus economies, manpower is an important asset which can add to national wealth, improve income distribution, and provide resources for development—provided no constraints are placed in the way of labor mobility. Factor mobility was a critical assumption made by classical economists in developing their ideas about the effective use of resources.

In the post–1947 years, Pakistani refugee manpower was a key to restoring the country's economic well-being. At the same time, Pakistan also benefitted from Britain's open labor market in the 1950s and 1960s; its sudden closure in the early 1970s, however, would have hurt a great deal had the Middle Eastern economic miracle not occurred simultaneously. For about a decade, the Middle East provided enormous benefits. Now the Middle Eastern labor market also threatens to close, at least in terms of increasing the number of migrants. However, the growth in Pakistan's population, and hence the growth in its labor force, continues at a very high rate—perhaps by as much as 3.2 percent a year. While Pakistan has been exceptionally fortunate in using labor migration as one way to solve the problem of economic backwardness, the option of labor export might not be available to it in the future. The demographic problem must be addressed directly, not through the safety valve that migration provided during the four decades of its independent existence.

NOTES

1. Perhaps the best account of this migration from a historical perspective is that of J. B. Schechtman, *The Refugees in the World* (New York: Barnes, 1963).

2. The 1951 census estimated that 7.22 million refugees were living in Pakistan at the time of the remunerations. See J. Russell Andrus and Azizali F. Mohammad, *The Economy of Pakistan* (Stanford, Calif.: Stanford University Press, 1958), p. 464.

3. For an analysis of the political role of the refugees, see Theodore P. Wright, Jr., "Indian Muslim Refugees in the Politics of Pakistan." *Journal of Comparative and Commonwealth Politics* 12 (1974):189-205.

4. The northwestern districts have had a higher natural rate of population growth than the rest of the country, 3.3 percent a year versus 3.0 percent.

5. If the 12 percent which goes for the purchase of residential real estate is further invested by the seller of the real estate, then the proportion invested rises to 32 percent. "Investment" for the average migrant is defined in Table 7.4 as purchase of industrial machinery, commercial buildings, agricultural machinery and other modern inputs, and improvements in liquid/semi-liquid financial instruments.

6. Based on 1986 data collected by the ILO on Pakistani return migrants from the Middle East, it appears that a part of the increase in the number of small-scale industrial sector enterprises in recent years can be attributed to investment in the same by return migrants. For the group surveyed, the proportion in nonagricultural self-employment activities such as manufacturing, trade, service, and transport enterprises increased by a factor of 2.5 after migration. New businesses set up by return migrants generate, on average, 1.4 additional jobs, with manufacturing concerns generating as much as six additional jobs. See Nadeem Ilahi, "Occupational Choice and Investment in Guest Worker Context: The Case of Return Pakistani Migration from the Arab Middle East" (Ph.D. dissertation, Department of Agricultural Economics, University of California, Davis).

7. Based on the author's assessment of a sample of villages near Rawalpindi in May 1979 and June 1984.

8. The Consumer Price Index with 1975/1976 = 100 was as follows: FY76: 111.7; FY77:122.0; FY78:130.0; FY79:141.3; FY80:156.0. Government of Pakistan, Ministry of Finance and Economic Affairs.

9. See Shahid Javed Burki, a series of three articles entitled "Pakistanis in the Middle East," in *The Muslim*, December 19 and 27, 1984, and January 4, 1985.

10. Although the trade gap increased from $1.5 billion in 1977–78 to $3.4 billion in 1982–83, the payments deficit averaged four percent of GNP, due to the remittances.

11. Better information on recent trends became available with the completion of an ILO study of returning migrants. According to Dr. Moinuddin Baqai, Secretary Planning Commission, a survey using exit and entrance data at the international airports in Pakistan indicates that by the fall of 1985 migration had turned negative, i.e., the number of people returning to Pakistan exceeded those leaving for the Middle East. (Interview with Dr. Baqai on January 15, 1986).

8

Emigration and Development in South and Southeast Asia

Charles Stahl and Ansanul Habib

This chapter discusses the impact of contract labor migration on the economies of the labor-exporting countries of South and Southeast Asia. Such a focus is not to deny that a number of Asian countries, particularly Pakistan, India, the Philippines, and Sri Lanka, have been exporting high-level manpower for years. Nor is it to deny that this "brain drain" has been costly for these countries. Rather, the reason for the focus on contract labor migration is that it involves more people than the brain drain and has a much greater impact on the economies of the emigration countries, as well as a potential to effect social change. The brain drain has received attention in the literature, but the issue of contract labor migration is very much underresearched.

Contract migration has not received its due research emphasis. Because of the severe shortage of empirical information, and also because of the methodological shortcomings of most of the studies that have been undertaken, we do not have an information base of sufficient detail to warrant unqualified conclusions regarding the overall developmental value of contract labor migration for any specific Asian country. What we do have are bits and pieces of empirical information which, when assembled, do afford some insight into the impact of labor emigration in Asia.

LABOR EXPORTING POLICIES

The labor emigration policies of most of the Asian labor exporters are essentially the result of governmental reaction to the massive increase in labor demand in the Middle East (brought about from increased oil export revenues) in the face of limited indigenous labor supplies. To supplement these limited labor supplies, the oil-exporting countries turned initially to the poorer Arab states. After excess supplies of labor in these countries were absorbed, additional workers were recruited, first in the South Asian countries, and later in Southeast Asia. The governments of these countries generally favored emigration, but were concerned about the possible exploitation of their workers because of, inter alia, recruitment without contracts and contract violations. These countries sought to regulate the recruitment of their workers, usually by licensing employment agencies and specifying model contracts to be entered into between the citizen worker and his employer. It is also the case that in some of the countries, bureaucrats and entrepreneurs envisioned profits to be made through the regulation of labor recruitment. Thus, driven by a combination of profit incentive and humanitarian concern, the governments of all the Asian labor-exporting countries eventually established a set of regulations aimed at specifying procedures for recruitment and rules for the protection of workers.[1]

Implicit in the design of these recruitment policies was the assumption that exporting labor was of significant benefit to the sending country. The reasoning was that labor export would serve as a "safety valve," reducing pressures on the domestic labor market. In addition to relieving unemployment, exporting labor would result in the formation of "human capital" as overseas contract workers learned new skills on the job. Other important benefits were thought to arise from the cash sent home by the overseas workers and the savings with which they returned, which are collectively referred to as remittances. These remittances were viewed as a valuable source of foreign exchange which could help reduce pressure on the balance of payments, a perennial problem for the countries of South and Southeast Asia. It was also considered that these remittances would be a stimulus to capital formation, the sine qua non for economic development. Thus, unemployment relief, skill acquisition, balance of payments relief, and capital formation were the assumed developmental advantages of labor emigration that underpinned the development of labor emigration policies in South and Southeast Asia.

But to what extent have these assumed developmental advantages been realized? And at what cost? In the first section of this chapter we will focus on labor export as a source of unemployment relief. The second section will concentrate upon the issue of skill acquisition, while the third section will evaluate the developmental impact of remittances in terms of their effect on balance of payments, output, and employment. The final section will pull together the information presented in the preceding sections so that some generalizations might be ventured regarding the consequences of labor emigration.

EMPLOYMENT CONSEQUENCES OF LABOR EMIGRATION

Table 8.1 provides information regarding the number of overseas workers from Asia's various labor-exporting countries, in addition to information concerning the size and sectoral distribution of their labor forces. Several caveats apply to these figures. The stock figures are only rough estimates, with very wide margins for error. They are essentially informed guesses using information

Table 8.1
Annual Placements and Stocks of Emigrant Workers, and Labor Force Size and Sectoral Distribution of the Asian Labor-Exporting Countries

	Annual Placements	Stock	Percentage of Migrants in Middle East	Labor Force and Sectoral Distribution[a] (millions)			
				Total	Agriculture	Industry	Services
Bangladesh	1978: 23,481 1980: 30,573 1983: 51,925	1978: 60,000 1980: 100,000 1983: 200,000	97	51.6	38.2	5.7	7.7
India	1978: 69,000 1980: 236,200 1983: [119,000][b]	1977: 214,000 1979: 350,000 1982: 800,000	n.a.	417.9	296.7	54.3	66.9
Pakistan	1978: 130,525 1980: 129,847 1983: 140,000	1981: 800,000	n.a.	47.5	27.1	9.5	10.9
Philippines[c]	1978: 88,241 1980: 214,590 1983: 434,207	1983: 732,000	85	29.2	13.4	5.0	10.8
South Korea	1978: 101,998 1980: 146,435 1982: 196,855	1981: 192,000	77	25.6	8.7	7.4	9.5
Sri Lanka	1979: 20,980 1981: 40,311 1982: 62,500	1981: 50,000	n.a.	9.2	5.0	1.3	2.9
Thailand	1978: 15,500 1980: 21,049 1983: 67,311	1983: 195,000[d]	96	38.3	29.1	3.5	5.7

[a]Size of labor force is for 1983; sectoral distribution is for 1981

[b]January-June only

[c]Annual placement figures include both land-based workers and seamen.

[d]This figure is an average of the low and high stock estimate for 1983.

Sources: Labor force figures for all countries are from World Bank (1985:174,214). Bangladesh: Habib (1983:29,76-77). India: Gulati (1986:195); Demerey (1986:20). Pakistan: Demerey J(1986:20,27). Philippines: Stahl (1984 :4). Thailand: Stahl (1984a:9,29).

from a variety of sources, for example, annual placements, average length of contract, average earnings, percentage of earnings remitted, and total remittances. Unfortunately, most of the major labor-importing countries do not provide information on the number of foreign workers in their countries, principally because of the political sensitivities toward labor import. Nor do the sending-countries keep accurate records of returning migrants which, when subtracted from annual outflows, could be used to estimate stocks abroad. The annual placement figures, while more accurate than the stock figures, are also subject to error arising from illegal and hence unrecorded recruitment, the extent of which varies among countries.

The information contained in Table 8.1 also highlights the importance of the Middle East as the principal destination of most Asian emigrant workers. Although figures are not available for India, Pakistan, and Sri Lanka, the greatest portion of migrant workers from these countries have also found employment in the Middle East. In the case of Sri Lanka, the figure would be in excess of 90 percent.

Although the Table 8.1 figures are soft, they do indicate that labor emigration is very big business in several of the Asian countries. The question to be addressed is: how do these large numbers impact the labor markets of the sending countries?

The labor market information in Table 8.1 permits comparison between the size of a country's labor force and the number of migrants employed abroad. On the basis of this information, it is evident that labor migration is relatively more important to the Philippines than to the remaining Asian labor exporters. For the Philippines, the estimated stock of migrants abroad amounted to roughly 2.5 percent of the country's labor force and to 4.6 percent of its combined industry and services labor force. The corresponding figures for Pakistan were 1.7 percent and 3.9 percent. For the remaining countries, the stock of migrant workers abroad amounted to less than 1 percent of the work force.

The literature addressing the issue of emigration and employment appears to be sharply divided between those who argue that emigration alleviates unemployment and those who argue that the evidence refutes this hypothesis. Numerous studies from countries throughout the world have concluded that emigration has reduced unemployment, if only by a modest amount. Those disagreeing with these conclusions argue that the conventional view of emigration and its relationship to employment is a gross oversimplification. They argue that the contribution of emigration to unemployment relief cannot be measured by simply subtracting the number of worker migrants from what total unemployment would have been in the absence of migration. Basically, the argument is that labor emigration may actually contribute to unemployment as a result of the contraction of productive activities caused by the loss of irreplaceable or difficult to replace emigrant workers.

There have been some reports from the Asian labor-exporting countries that emigration has not had a totally beneficial effect on the domestic labor market.

Bottlenecks have emerged in development projects in Sri Lanka as a consequence of the shortages of skilled workers. In 1980, a number of industries in the Philippines, especially oil refineries, claimed to have experienced skill shortages. Wilson (1979:39) quotes the concern of a Pakistani official that "we are losing our skilled engineers, our best construction managers, our most energetic and imaginative men to the Middle East." Three years later Ahmad (1982:17) reported that serious shortages still existed in Pakistan for masons and carpenters and, to a lesser degree, for welders and plumbers, plus noteworthy shortages of electricians, steel fixers, and painters.

Pakistan estimated that 83 percent of its migrants were production workers and blamed declining workmanship in new building construction and in textile products on emigration. Ahmad (1982:46) also refers to the low construction skill standards now prevalent in Pakistan which cause delays in that sector, inadequate maintenance of equipment, and rising costs. Gilani et al. (1981: pt. 2, 39) argue that the decline in productivity in Pakistan occurred not because of the unavailability of replacement workers, but because skilled workers who departed were replaced by hastily trained, formerly unskilled workers.

There is also concern in Pakistan that the predominance of production and related workers in the emigration stream may create bottlenecks for the non-agricultural section. Sarmad (1985:22-23) reviews the findings of a report by the Manpower Division which estimated manpower requirements for Pakistan's Fifth Five Year Plan (1978–83). The report claims that for the majority of occupational groups experiencing emigration, only marginal shortages were anticipated. Those occupational groups with the greatest anticipated shortages were in the "production workers" category, specifically machine tool setters and operators, plumbers and welders. These were also the occupations experiencing the highest level of emigration.

Jayme (1979:85, 88-93) cautioned that it was unlikely that the Philippines could sustain the heavy drain on professional, technical, and other skilled workers without incurring some costs. In Bangladesh, Siddiqui (1986:247) suggests that overseas employment may have caused some dislocation in the production process due to the loss of skilled labor, but that this could have been minimized by proper management practices.

On a more positive note, a study on Thai emigration argues that Thailand has not reached the point of serious shortages of skilled labor, let alone the unskilled (Roongshivin, 1982:26). For the Philippines, Tan (1983) found little evidence that labor emigration had caused any dislocations. Despite the fact that large numbers of Filipino construction and transport workers were recruited for overseas work, Tan reported that high rates of unemployment still prevailed in these sectors.[2] A similar note is present in a study by Addleton (1984:586-87), who maintains that the relative abundance of labor in Pakistan made it possible for the labor markets to respond relatively easily to the migration of large numbers of unskilled workers, although he recognized the possibility of some bottlenecks occurring in the supply of some categories of skilled production workers.

Perwaiz (1979:22) strongly condemns the planning commission's unqualified complaint of labor shortages in Pakistan as conveying the "erroneous impression of a general labor shortage."

For Bangladesh, Ali et al. (1981:159-71) assess the effects of labor migration on the manning of production and service establishments. They conclude that Bangladesh is unlikely to lose anything substantial because of the migration of unskilled and semiskilled workers, since the time and cost involved in training replacements is small. Siddiqui (1983:37) reports that there was a surplus of doctors and engineers in Bangladesh despite emigration within these occupational categories. For India, Weiner (1982:5) claims that emigration has reduced unemployment in the states of Kerala, Karnataka, Goa, Maharashtra, and Gujarat, as well as in the Punjab. This is particularly true for the educated unemployed. While there is evidence of skilled workers shortages in the construction sector in the state of Kerala, "emigration from India has not produced the kind of loss of human resources experienced by some of the Mediterranean countries" (Weiner, 1982:5). Smart (1984:17) makes the more general observation that the Asian labor-exporting countries have met both foreign and domestic demand for manpower through formal and informal training with "relative ease." This was particularly easy with regard to service workers who, because of their low level of skill, presented few replacement problems.

The evidence seems to suggest that the overall effect of out-migration in reducing unemployment has both a positive factor contribution and a negative indirect contribution. The latter results from the departure of difficult-to-replace skilled workers, so there is a reduction in output and an increase in unemployment among those workers who are complementary to the departing skilled workers. It might also be argued that the indirect reduction in output following the emigration of skilled workers may, through interindustry linkages, cause further reductions in domestic employment. However, this pessimistic view of the labor market consequences of exporting labor hinges on the assumption that emigrating workers are very difficult to replace. At least in the context of the overpopulated, labor abundant countries of Asia, where highly educated persons often find employment difficult to obtain, it is unlikely that the emigration of skilled manpower is having a decisively detrimental developmental effect. It may be true that at certain times in specific industries, firms may have difficulties filling vacant positions in particular occupations, but it would seem unlikely that this is a general problem among the Asian labor exporters. However, these generalizations are advanced with caution because, as Abella has pointed out (1984:495), inadequate labor market statistics throughout Asia make it difficult to gauge the labor market consequences of emigration.

EMIGRATION AND SKILL FORMATION

The opportunity that workers may get to enhance their skills while abroad is a potential benefit of temporary emigration. It is assumed that temporary and circular labor migration can result in a net addition to the emigration economy's stock of human capital if the skills learned abroad contribute more to the home economy's development than the skills the worker would have learned at home.

But are these expectations realistic? It appears that three criteria have to be met before return migrants can make a skill contribution to the sending country. First, migrants must learn skills while abroad. Second, those skills must be relevant to the needs of the sending country. Third, the returning migrants must use those skills upon return.

A recent study of Pakistani migrants revealed that while some 25 percent of returnees claimed to have learned new skills, only 7 percent thought that these skills were of any use to them once they returned home (Gilani, 1983a:18). A study of India found that the "skill component" of overseas employment was only 24 percent and concluded that the skill acquisition rate was not very encouraging (Mathew and Nair, 1978:1149). Smart et al. reported that new skills were acquired by just over 24 percent of Filipino workers going to the Middle East, but that the skills could have been acquired just as easily within the Philippines. Stahl (1984a:35) compared the premigration skills of Thai overseas workers with those necessary to perform their overseas job. He found "probable skill acquisition" in the case of almost 37 percent of migrant workers. Using a similar approach, Habib (1985) found that fewer than 1 percent of Bangladesh migrants took up occupations abroad which required a higher degree of skill than they possessed before departure. In another Thai study, Roongshivin (1982:18) claimed that the Middle Eastern countries normally use state-of-the-art technologies in almost every area of industrial activity, and that Thai workers who have been engaged extensively in these activities should have acquired new skills.

A related issue in skill acquisition is the question of how often previous skills match overseas job requirements. It was found that almost 80 percent of Filipino workers in the Middle East were employed in jobs that required the same skills the workers used prior to emigration (Smart et al., 1983:11). Another study on Filipino migration reports an occupational continuity figure of almost 73 percent, and a new skill acquisition rate of 14 percent (Teodosio and Jimenez, 1983:133-34). For Bangladesh, Habib (1985:295) estimates that more than 75 percent of overseas migrants appear to have a postmigration skill level no different from that possessed prior to migration. In his study of Thai overseas workers, Stahl (1984a:35) found that almost 57 percent pursued the same occupation abroad as they did at home.

Successful transfer of skills acquired abroad to the home country requires that the migrant's occupations—the one practiced abroad and the one assumed upon return—be closely related. The debate as to whether migrants learn new skills and whether such skills are appropriate becomes academic if the migrants prefer not to employ their acquired skills upon return. In view of the fact that the wage rate at home in the occupation pursued abroad is often five to ten times less, it is quite possible that the returning migrant will not take up work at home which uses skills acquired abroad. In general, a number of studies have found that returning workers prefer independent employment and very often employment that uses neither the skills they acquired abroad nor those they possessed before emigration. This aversion of the work force and strong preference to establish small independent businesses, mainly in the tertiary sector, appears to be the dominant characteristic of return migrants throughout the world. With regard to the Asian countries' emigration, Smart (1984:23) reports that 75 percent of Filipino migrants see themselves starting a business when they return home. The percentage of returnees interviewed in Pakistan who wanted to return to their former occupation was reported to be quite low (Ahmad, 1982:44). Another study on Pakistan reported that only 5 percent of the returnees expect to take up a salaried job (Gilani, 1983a:14). But this information only reveals intentions, and it remains to be seen to what extent returnees will or will not take up occupations relying upon skills used abroad.

Thus, empirical evidence on the question of migrants' skill gain does not appear to be very encouraging. Although there is scattered evidence of Asian migrants acquiring skills abroad, it does not appear that this is the general outcome of labor emigration. Moreover, evidence indicates that even if skills are acquired abroad, it is questionable whether they will be employed upon return. However, it is important to note, as Smart (1984:23) observed, that while emigration may not lead to skill acquisition for the migrant, it does provide the migrant's replacement at home with an opportunity to acquire skills.

THE MAGNITUDE, USE, AND IMPACT OF REMITTANCES

According to Martin (Chapter 2), the magnitude and use of remittances provides the litmus test of the benefits of a labor export policy. To the labor-exporting countries, remittances from their nationals working abroad can provide benefits in a variety of ways.[3] First, remittances are likely to lead to an increase in the real income of both the worker and his family. Second, abstracting from any direct negative consequences of labor export for indigenous industries, remittances should lead to an increase in real national income, savings, and investment. Third, remittances provide an increasingly important non-traditional source of foreign exchange, which is often scarce and a constraining factor on development. Remittances can, therefore, lead to (a) increased welfare through enhanced consumption, (b) increased investment through increased saving, and (c) increased imports of strategic producer goods through an augmented supply of foreign exchange.

In this section we explore the consequences of remittances by first looking at their contribution to alleviating the balance-of-payments problems of the Asian labor exporters. Following this we will review empirical information pertaining to the expenditure remittances with a view toward discerning their developmental impact on the sending countries' economies.

Estimates of remittances from emigrant workers are reported by the sending countries' central banks. However, these estimates are subject to a considerable margin of error since they record only those remittances that are reported by receiving banks and hence flow through formal banking channels. A portion of remittances enter the sending country through informal financial channels and are thus not counted by the central bank. Also, recipient banks within the formal financial sector may choose not to report their receipt of foreign exchange, using the funds instead for purposes which contravene regulations on the use of foreign exchange. Nevertheless, remittances make a substantial foreign exchange contribution to the economies of the Asian labor exporters. For example, it has been estimated that in 1981 more than 2.5 million Asian workers remitted $7.9 billion to their home countries, which amounted to 2.3 percent of their GNP (Abella, 1984:496).

Table 8.2 provides information on the magnitude of remittances received by the Asian labor-exporting countries for selected years.[4] Although the pattern of change differs somewhat among the countries, the period 1980 to 1983 saw a significant growth in remittances in every country for which data are available. Bangladesh experienced a growth in remittances of 137 percent over this period; the Philippines, 23 percent; Sri Lanka, 115 percent; and Thailand, 182 percent. Over the period 1981 to 1983, Pakistan experienced a 48 percent growth in remittances. Table 8.2 also shows the magnitude of remittances relative to merchandise exports and imports. In 1983, remittances amounted to 84 percent of Bangladesh's merchandise exports and paid for more than 28 percent of its imports. In the same year, remittances to Pakistan were almost as large as merchandise exports and paid for more than 50 percent of imports. While the figures for the other Asian labor emigration countries are not quite so dramatic, they also indicate that remittances make a substantial contribution to those countries' balance of payments. Remittances from overseas workers are also large relative to the value of foreign aid received by the Asian labor-exporting countries. For instance, remittances were well in excess of foreign aid in Pakistan and the Philippines.

The evidence presented in Table 8.2 makes it clear that remittances are an important source of foreign exchange for the Asian labor exporters. In these countries in recent years, a substantial portion of imports has been financed by money sent home by overseas workers. Undoubtedly, this has been a welcome relief for those labor-exporting countries facing foreign exchange constraints on development brought about partly by OPEC's monopoly pricing of oil. However, while remittances have helped to alleviate foreign exchange shortfalls, there is still considerable debate about the overall impact of remittances on development. An analysis of the use to which remittances have been put should be helpful in an analysis of the benefits of a policy of labor export.

Use of Remittances

Evidence from the Asian labor-exporting countries indicates that there are several major expenditure priorities to which the lion's share of remittances are

Table 8.2
Remittances from Migrant Workers to Selected Asian Countries, 1980–85

Country	Total (Millions of US Dollars)	Percentage of Merchandise Exports	Percentage of Merchandise Imports	Percentage of Gross National Product	Percentage of Foreign Aid
Bangladesh					
1980	257	33.9	9.9	2.7	12.0
1981	280	35.5	10.3	2.8	16.9
1982	515	66.8	21.0	5.2	29.4
1983	610	84.2	28.2	5.6	42.2
India					
1980	1,600	19.3	11.5	1.3	56.7
Pakistan					
1981	1,900	69.6	33.6	7.7	159.8
1983	2,810	97.7	50.3	10.9	209.4
1984	2,405	91.4	37.3	8.6	n.a.
1985 (Jan.-Sept.)	1,800	n.a.	n.a.	n.a.	n.a.
Philippines					
1980	774	13.4	10.0	2.8	171.9
1981	798	13.9	10.0	2.5	168.0
1982	810	16.1	10.6	2.4	163.5
1983	955	19.1	12.8	3.6	178.2
1984	625	11.6	10.3	2.2	n.a.
1985 (Jan.-May)	296	n.a.	n.a.	n.a.	n.a.
South Korea					
1980	1,102	6.3	4.9	2.0	343.7
1981	1,359	6.4	5.2	2.2	344.7
1982	1,538	7.0	6.3	2.3	2,050.7
Sri Lanka					
1980	137	12.9	7.4	4.7	19.9
1981	229	21.0	12.0	5.2	30.7
1982	237	23.4	13.2	5.6	47.0
1983	294	27.7	17.0	5.8	62.9
1984	301	20.6	15.6	5.1	n.a.
Thailand (from Middle East)					
1980	240	3.7	2.9	0.9	48.6
1981	480	7.0	5.4	1.6	86.6
1982	446	6.5	5.9	1.3	71.0
1983	676	10.7	7.4	1.8	109.4
1984 (Jan.-Sept.)	441	8.0	6.3	1.6	n.a.

n.a. = not available

Source: Abella (1984), Arnold and Shah (1984), Asian Development Bank (1985), unpublished
data from Pakistan's Habib Bank, International Monetary Fund (1985), Kim (1986),
Korale (1986), Stahl (1984a).

devoted.[5] These are current consumption of both basic necessities and luxury
goods, the payment of debts, and the purchase of nonproductive assets, most importantly housing and land. That a considerable portion of remittance income is
devoted to the purchase of basic necessities is consistent with evidence from remittance studies elsewhere in the world. It is also consistent with the more gen-

eral empirical finding that in poor countries, low income households spend additions to their income on basic necessities more than do households at higher income levels. The same applies to the expenditure of remittances for housing. One of the few studies which used a control group (Ali et al., 1981) found that in households with the same income levels, remittance recipients spend significantly more on housing than did households without migrants.

That an important use of remittances is the payment of debts can be explained both by the poor background of the emigrants' households and the fact that most overseas contract workers incur considerable expenses in acquiring their jobs abroad. The finding of a low propensity to undertake productive investment on the part of remittance receiving households and returnees is not surprising. It would be naive to expect that the work experience abroad will transform a poor rural peasant into a modern farmer, or a poor working class urban dweller into an industrial entrepreneur. Rather, remittance receivers and returnees choose to direct their hard-won earnings into "safe" investments, for example, savings accounts, land, and jewelry. However, these findings are no basis on which to conclude that the developmental value of remittances is negligible.

Economic Impact of Remittances

The majority of poor labor-exporting countries have to rely on imported capital goods, technology, and sometimes raw materials and intermediate inputs to expand national output. The conventional way to acquire these is to expand exports. If, however, the export sector is operating at full capacity, then an expansion of exports will require an addition to export capacity, that is, investment in the export sector. In contrast, remittances are a relatively costless way to acquire additional foreign exchange, in that the export of labor services requires no addition to export capacity. Of course, remittances are a costless source of foreign exchange only if migrant workers are in excess of a country's labor needs.

If remittances are to have a more lasting impact on a country's real income, then they must stimulate productive investment, either directly or indirectly. Direct investment occurs when the returned migrant or the recipient of the remittance income invests it. However, as discussed above, empirical evidence demonstrates that in the Asian context, recipients invest very little remittance income. Instead, that income is destined to serve immediate consumption needs, pay debts, and build a new home or improve an existing one. However, if such additional demand is met through expanding production facilities, the overall impact on output, and hence employment and investment, should be favorable. This stimulus to investment from the demand side is an often ignored factor in the development process (see Stahl, 1982:873; 1984:76-78; 1986:88).

It is unlikely that the increased demand for investment goods deriving from the remittance-induced expansion in aggregate demand will be fully funded from increased profits. Rather, part of the new investment will have to be financed with loans from banks or other financial intermediaries. The inflow of foreign exchange remittances into the sending country's banking system can collectively expand its loan portfolios. A number of constraints may limit the extent to which the banking system can do this (see Stahl, 1984), but remittances should contribute to investment from the supply side through their contribution to the expansion of loanable funds.

The Output and Employment Consequences of Remittances

The loss of manpower through emigration could adversely affect domestic output. However, perhaps with the exception of certain industries and occupations in Pakistan, it is unlikely that labor emigration has, to any serious extent, disadvantaged the labor-exporting countries of Asia. On the other hand, remittances have the definite potential of increasing the level of output in the emigration country. Remittances constitute an addition to real income which will expand aggregate demand. This expanded demand arises not only from the consumption expenditures of remittance recipients, but also from the consumption expenditures of those who have sold assets such as land and houses to remittance recipients, and those who have received funds for the repayment of personal debts incurred by remittance recipients. While some of this additional demand will be met by imports, the remainder will be satisfied by an expansion of domestic output. In some industries, this demand will be met by fuller use of existing capacity, with a consequent improvement in profitability as a result of improved economies of scale. In those industries operating at full capacity, the new demand should induce an expansion of capacity, that is, investment, which will now be less constrained by foreign exchange and credit availability in the wake of the inflow of remittances. In either case, the expansion of output will generate more domestic employment.

There are several methods of modeling the economy-wide effects of an inflow of remittances. One could employ a price endogenous, computable general equilibrium model (CGE) usually built around the country's social accounting matrix. Such a model could be used to trace the impact of remittances on the various productive sectors of the economy, taking into account interactions among these sectors. Since the models are price endogenous, they could also afford insights into the impact of remittances on prices, indicating which sectors of the economy are likely to experience price rises due to supply rigidities. Such models also incorporate an investment response function on the part of different industries, so that one could gauge the likely impact of remittances on investment. Depending on data availability, the CGE model can also be used to analyze the impact of remittances on the distribution of income. The CGEs are also capable of modeling the effect of any changes in the monetary base which result from the inflow of remittances, assuming such changes are permitted by the monetary authorities.

An alternative approach which is less demanding, both in terms of the analytical and statistical skills required and the information needed, is input-output analysis. Although less sophisticated than the price endogenous CGE models, it is nonetheless a general equilibrium model capable of tracing the path of remittance expenditures and predicting the output, employment, capital, and foreign exchange requirements of a remittance-induced increase in aggregate demand. Although less sophisticated than price endogenous CGE models, it may be that input-output analysis gives predictions which are as accurate as those of the CGE model.

Within the Asian context, only one study has employed a general equilibrium model to analyze the interindustry impacts of remittance expenditures (Habib, 1985). The model was built around the input-output tables for the economy of Bangladesh and relied on expenditure survey data from remittance-receiving households collected by a World Bank study (Ali et al., 1981). This latter expenditure information was broken down to conform broadly to the intersectoral framework used in the input-output table. In this way the percentage distribution of remittance expenditures among the various sectors (of the input-output table) was calculated. This percentage distribution was then applied to remittance inflow data between 1976 and 1983 to obtain the sector by sector consumption expenditures due to remittances. These figures were then fed into the input-output model and their expansionary effect, net of imports, was calculated. Bearing in mind that the results are very much assumption-dependent, the expenditure of remittances for consumption purposes had both a direct and an indirect impact on output. The effect on output is due to the fact that to supply more of its products, an industry will have to purchase inputs from other industries.

The indirect effects estimated by Habib (1985: Chapter 7) would have been considerably greater if his model had taken into account the further effects of the initial expenditure. These latter effects arise when the suppliers of the factors of production who produced the consumption goods purchased by remittance recipients and those factors which produce the intermediate inputs necessary to produce those consumption goods, in turn, spend their newly acquired earnings. The indirect effects would have been further augmented if account were taken of the economy-wide impact of the increased investment expenditure in those industries experiencing a rise in demand for their products. A further underestimation of the output consequences of remittance inflow arises because no account is taken of how those who sold land to remittance recipients spend their money, nor how the emigrants' creditors used the funds they received in retirement of the emigrants' debt.

Using the input-output framework, Habib (1985: Chapter 8) also calculated the employment consequences of remittance expenditure. He estimates that in 1983, just over 200,000 Bangladeshi migrant workers remitted some $610 million which gave rise to a level of final demand (for Bangladeshi goods and services) of $351 million. This final demand, in turn, would have directly generated 440,000 jobs and another 137,000 indirectly, for a total of 576,000 jobs. For the same reasons discussed above in relation to the underestimation of the output effects of remittance expenditure, this is a substantial underestimate of the actual employment creation potential.

These models generate estimates of the employment generating potential of remittance expenditures. There are a variety of possible constraints which industries may face in their attempts to respond to an increased demand for their output. These constraints mean that the full potential of output and employment expansion will not be realized. In some instances, an industry can be severely constrained, so that price increases might be the result of remittances.

CONCLUSIONS

The emigration countries of Asia have actively pursued a policy of labor export with the expectation of the following benefits: skill acquisition by migrants, relief of unemployment, and balance of payments relief. These countries also anticipated that by increasing savings and providing scarce foreign exchange, remittances would stimulate investment, the sine qua non for economic development. However, a number of studies have cast doubt on the extent to which labor export has achieved these goals. It appears that the most significant discrepancy between anticipated and actual benefits is in the area of skill formation. Empirical evidence indicates that Asian migrants, in general, are not to any significant extent experiencing skill formation. In some instances, deskilling might be occurring as skilled and semiskilled workers take up unskilled positions abroad because those were the only jobs available at the time. But on the whole, the majority of migrants work at jobs that require the skills they possessed at the time of their emigration. If newly acquired skills are not employed upon return, then their acquisition makes little difference. In this regard, some studies have found that returned migrants are reluctant to rejoin the labor force as wage employees, preferring instead to use their accumulated savings in small businesses in the service sector.

Other studies of Asian labor emigration have provided evidence, albeit often anecdotal, that in some countries at least a few industries have complained of shortages in particular occupations as a result of labor emigration. Some writers argue that these shortages can result in a contraction of domestic economic activity and promote unemployment among those workers and other factors of production complementary to those scarce skills lost through emigration. Thus, rather than alleviating unemployment, emigration may actually promote unemployment. Others have argued that Asian labor emigration has not, in general, resulted in labor shortages. Generally, those studies concerned with the negative employment consequences of labor emigration have ignored the positive contribution to domestic employment that the expenditure of remittances can make. In one study which has attempted to model this impact, the potential contribution of remittances to domestic output and employment is considerable. Thus, at least in the Asian context, any negative output consequences due to the loss of workers through emigration is likely to be offset by the positive stimulus to employment that the expenditure of remittances will provide. There is another consideration regarding the employment-creation effects of labor emigration that few studies have recognized. That is, insofar as an emigrant would be unemployed at home, when he emigrates the home country is saved the cost of providing the necessary complementary inputs necessary to provide a job for that worker in the domestic economy.

Empirical studies on Asian labor emigration have revealed that remittances and returnee savings are spent largely on basic necessities, some luxury consumer goods in the form of electrical appliances which are usually imported, debt repayment, housing, and education. Very few remittances are used for real investment purposes. This finding has led many to conclude that the development value of remittances is negligible. We have seen that such a conclusion is not warranted and actually reflects a lack of understanding of the complex economic processes set in motion by remittances. In fact, remittances can augment the supply of loanable funds while indirectly stimulating the demand for those funds with a consequent increase in the level of real capital formation.

It seems relatively certain that labor emigration has, on the whole, provided substantially more benefits than costs to Asian labor-sending countries. However, these findings do not imply that labor emigration will stimulate development in all or even most poor countries. They do imply that if certain conditions exist, for example, that a country's economic structure is relatively diverse, that it has an adequate supply of labor, and that there is a financial system capable of mopping up small amounts of savings from a wide variety of sources and channeling them to businesses willing and able to respond to rising demand for their output, then remittances will promote economic growth as should any other external stimulus to the economy. In the absence of these conditions, neither remittances nor any other stimulus will be of much value to national development.

In short, the failure of remittances to provide a positive stimulus to development in a number of labor-exporting countries is due largely to the structural features of underdevelopment. Thus, our findings do not contradict the view that "while emigration may secure a more adequate standard of living for at least some migrants and their families, it is rarely a solution to the problems of national impoverishment" (Swanson, 1979:21). Indeed, the solution to the problems of underdevelopment is also the key to ensuring that remittances serve as a stimulus to development.[6]

As discussed above, remittances will be advantageous to those countries with sufficient productive flexibility to respond to their stimulus. This raises the question of whether labor emigration can result in such a large-scale loss of labor or a depletion of critical skills that an economy loses it productive flexibility. There are a few countries that have experienced such large-scale emigration. Lesotho, in southern Africa, and the Yemen Arab Republic are cases in point.[7] In effect, the cream of these countries' labor force has been skimmed off by their wealthy neighbors. Left with a sparse and relatively low-skilled labor force, these economies have been unable to respond on a broad front to the remittance stimulus. Consumption needs other than house construction and some services have been satisfied through imports. These cases suggest that there may be a level of labor emigration beyond which a country risks impairing the productive flexibility of its economy that is necessary to transform an external stimulus into a positive growth-promoting force.

In the cases of Lesotho and the Yemen Arab Republic, massive emigration is both an effect and a cause of severe underdevelopment. If these small countries had been on a path toward development before emigration began, then remittances might have boosted development which, in turn, would have expanded domestic employment opportunities sufficiently to curb emigration. We argue that the larger, more diversified, and more developed an economy is, the greater will be the contribution of labor emigration to development. This description characterizes the economies of the labor-exporting countries of Asia, which explains our generally sanguine evaluation of the potential contribution of labor emigration to development in that region.

This is not to suggest that all of the labor emigration countries of Asia are on a path toward meaningful development. Indeed, in the Marcos era, emigration from the Philippines was viewed as a safety valve to relieve the pressures of unemployment due to the government's inability or unwillingness to undertake the economic, social, and political reforms necessary for broad-based development. In such cases we would argue that the developmental value of remittances will be correspondingly reduced. To reiterate, the more rigid, inflexible, and underdeveloped a country's socioeconomic system, the less labor emigration and remittance inflow will be of developmental advantage.

One final issue merits mention. The recent collapse in world oil prices must necessarily reduce the magnitude of Asian participation in the oil-exporting countries' labor markets. In particular, we can expect that demand for construction workers will fall dramatically. Thus, we should anticipate substantial return migration with a concomitant decline in the inflow of remittances. To some extent the Asian labor exporters' drop in remittances will be offset by reduced oil prices. It is important for planning purposes that the labor emigration countries be able to anticipate which sectors of their economies and which occupations will be most affected by these significant changes. It is our view that the types of general equilibrium models briefly discussed in this paper hold the key to evaluating the impact of these changes.

NOTES

1. Details of regulatory policies for Bangladesh can be found in Siddiqui (1986). For India, see Tandon (1983). For Pakistan, see Hoda (1983) and Zar (1984). For the Philippines, see Lazo et al. (1982). For the Republic of Korea, see Kim (1982). For Sri Lanka, see Korale (1984). Finally, for Thailand, see Prompunthum (1983). For an overview of migration policies and programs in the Asian labor-exporting countries, see Shah and Arnold (1986).

2. The findings of Tan (1983) were referred to in Abella (1984:494).

3. For a good overview of the importance of remittances to the sending country, see Ecevit and Zachariah (1978:36), Harris (1979:15), and Finkle and McIntosh (1982: 160-64).

4. This table and the discussion of it is derived from Stahl and Arnold (1986:7-8).

5. Empirical studies which contain some information on expenditure patterns of remittance receiving households are for Bangladesh: Mahmud et al. (1980), Ali et al. (1981), and Habid (1985). For India: Commerce Research Bureau (1978), Mathew and Nair (1978), Prakash (1978), Oberai and Singh (1980), Radhakrishnan and Ibrahim (1981), and Gulati (1986). For Pakistan: Gilani et al. (1983a), Pakistan Institute of Public Opinion (1983), and Abbasi and Irfan (1986). For the Philippines: Institute of Labor and Manpower Studies (1983), and Go et al. (1983). For Thailand: Pitaynond et al. (1982) and Singhnetra-Renard (1983).

6. It does merit emphasis, however, that many of the studies Swanson reviewed suffer from the same theoretical shortcomings as have many of the Asian country studies. As a result, they mostly underestimate the broader national gains attributable to labor emigration.

7. For a discussion of the impact of emigration on the Yemen Arab Republic see Fergany (1982); for Lesotho, see Cobbe (1982).

Part V

Labor Migration and Development in Latin America, Mexico, and the Caribbean

Part V summarizes studies of the effects of emigration on countries in Latin America, the Caribbean region, and Mexico. In Chapter 9, Diaz-Briquets examines the effects of emigration from Latin America at national, regional, and individual levels. He notes that several countries have experienced substantial emigration flows, including Paraguay, Colombia, and Mexico, and that emigration from some of the smaller countries has been sufficient to slow or stop population growth.

The effects of emigration and remittances on national labor markets and economies are harder to disentangle, but Diaz-Briquets concludes that the emigration of unskilled workers is not a serious problem for the larger emigration countries, while remittances contribute substantial foreign exchange to sending countries. He also notes the negative macro consequences of emigration: stagnation if internal markets become too small to achieve economies of scale, the draining off of protest which permits entrenched leaders to stay in power, and the often permanent loss of young, vigorous, and better educated workers.

Diaz-Briquets turns next to the regional consequences of migration, noting that border cities are especially sensitive to changes in migration flows. However, the most important negative effect of a recession in a destination country, such as Venezuela for Colombian migrants, is the decreased trade which affects a variety of industries and cities. The border city pain of recession-reduced migration is real, but macroeconomic effects in the emigration country are much larger.

Diaz-Briquets reviews studies of the effects of emigration on the villages migrants depart from and concludes that remittances in Latin America are spent to improve living standards, to build housing, and to buy land and livestock. Most investments generate rents for their owners; only the minority of investments in services such as restaurants or stores generate jobs, and most of these remittance-created jobs go to local family members or relatives of the migrant. Remittances alter the structure of rural communities, creating a new class of rich residents, and the resulting tension between the traditional and migrant elite can inspire development or resentment. Migrant households clearly benefit from remittances, but their effect on villages is more complex.

Diaz-Briquets concludes that emigration can reduce unemployment pressures in small countries or those with high emigration rates, that migration and remittances can have limited effects in rigid societies with unequal incomes that are not primed for development, and that the major losses associated with emigration are of the brain-drain type. He does not believe that this generally pessimistic picture of emigration's failure to generate development will be altered until labor importers work cooperatively with labor exporters.

Chapter 10 examines emigration and development in the Caribbean. Pessar traces contemporary migration patterns to the adaptation patterns of ex-slaves after emancipation: ex-slave owners continued to own the land, and ex-slaves responded by migrating. Migration from island to island was a way to escape discrimination and inferior status at home, to earn higher wages, and eventually it became a rite of passage for youth.

Pessar traces middle-class emigration to development policies which favored low-wage export industries and did not leave a place for the middle class. The middle class consequently migrated to the United States, Canada, and the United Kingdom. There has been enough emigration from some Caribbean islands to reduce population growth despite high fertility and longer lives. Pessar argues that middle-class emigration is deleterious; it leads to production bottlenecks, provokes rapid turnover in managerial and professional jobs, and requires local educational institutions to train more people than will be employed locally.

Emigration has also feminized agriculture and promoted more land speculation than investments which increased food and fiber output. Pessar notes that, in many cases, migrants let land lie fallow because there is a shortage of farmworkers. Pessar concludes that Caribbean nations should turn away from low-wage export industries and emigration because these policies do not promise to effectuate development. Instead, education and training systems should be reoriented to satisfy domestic labor needs, small-scale agriculture should be strengthened, and the return intentions of emigrants should be reinforced.

9

The Effects of International Migration on Latin America

Sergio Diaz-Briquets

Although emigration within and from Latin America has increased during the last few decades, we have only a partial understanding about its determinants and consequences. There have been studies which examined the causes of emigration from sending countries and the consequences of immigration into destination countries, but most dealt with only a few countries—generally those experiencing the highest relative volume of immigration or emigration, such as Argentina or Mexico. Other studies have focused on somewhat atypical situations (but increasingly common during the 1970s and 1980s) in which massive emigration was linked to political repression and instability or to economic downturns.

Little is known about the consequences of emigration for sending countries, although in particular instances, such as Mexico, these consequences have been studied in some detail. This is partly because of the difficulties and costs associated with conducting research in areas from which migrants depart, and partly because until recently these consequences were assumed to be of only marginal significance. These studies have generally focused on the in-depth analysis of selected migrant-sending communities whose experience may or may not be representative of the situation in a country at large. Another genre of studies examines selected effects of international migration by analyzing highly aggregated data sets that permit only broad interpretations. This chapter examines a sampling of this literature and provides a general overview of the consequences of international migration on countries of migrant origin in Latin America.

In Latin America, international migration is a highly complex process involving not only population transfers among Latin American countries themselves but also between Latin America and several developed countries. The determinants of these migrations, and the reasons behind the increase in emigration since the Second World War, are complex. What is important is to point out that consequences for the countries and regions from which migrants depart depend on the type of emigration (e.g., permanent, long-term, seasonal, rural to rural, urban to urban), and whether the countries of destination are developed or developing.

These migrations, in most instances, are unregulated. Often they involve spontaneous flows from one rural area to another in search of unoccupied land, but frequently their genesis can be found in unofficial labor recruitment. In the latter case, they can be regarded as conventional labor migration flows. Within Latin America itself, many of these migrations have deep historical roots and are facilitated by ethnic and language commonalities. In particular cases, as in Mexican emigration to the United States, Colombian emigration to Venezuela, and Bolivian emigration to Argentina, they are the product of official labor recruitment programs that in combination with spontaneous, economically and socially driven undocumented movements have given shape to the contemporary migratory landscape of the region. This complex configuration of migration determinants helps explain why several countries in the Western Hemisphere decided to implement amnesty programs to regularize the status of large undocumented immigrant populations. Since the 1950s, Argentina has had several such programs. Venezuela and the United States each had one during the 1980s.

It is equally important to differentiate analytically among the various levels on which the consequences of emigration can be evaluated. The broadest and most global is the nation state; I will refer to these consequences as macro effects. Among these effects are alterations in the absolute size and rates of growth of national populations, changes in national market size and aggregate demand, and the impact remittances have on gross national product. In relative terms, the macro level effects tend to be almost insignificant when compared to the consequences emigration can have on selected regions within a country, particularly in regions experiencing high emigration rates. At the regional level, consequences similar to those seen at the macro level can be observed, with a greater or lesser intensity, depending on the degree and character of migration from the region in question. Along this continuum, the consequences of emigration are experienced even more acutely at the community level. Finally, emigration consequences are felt most poignantly at the household and individual levels.

These distinctions are of more than academic value since what may prove to be advantageous to a regional or national aggregate may prove to be detrimental to an individual or household, or vice versa. Likewise, it is necessary to distinguish between the short- and long-term consequences or emigration and to define how these consequences can vary as a result of emigration rates, the socioeconomic characteristics of emigrants and of the regions from whence they depart, and the nature of emigration and its duration. Emigration has become an accepted, even expected pattern of behavior in some areas, and an emigration mentality affects the consequences of emigration in areas of origin. It is neither simple to make distinctions between areas, nor is it easy to evaluate the consequences of emigration at the various conceptual levels.

NATIONAL OR MACRO CONSEQUENCES

At the most general level it is evident that emigration has had major demographic effects in the Latin American countries experiencing the greatest absolute or relative rates of emigration. Current and future rates of population growth are most heavily impacted in countries which migrants leave permanently, although the effects of temporary emigration are also perceptible. Mexico, Colombia, Paraguay, and Uruguay are some of the countries where the demographic effects of emigration have been greatest. Such has been the case more recently in several Central American countries, particularly El Salvador, Nicaragua, and Guatemala, in part as a result of that region's instability (Peterson, 1986). In 1973, approximately 15 percent of Paraguay's population lived abroad (Gillespie and Browning, 1979). According to estimates reviewed by Balan (1985:50), 7.5 percent of the Uruguayan population emigrated between 1963 and 1975.

In absolute terms, millions of people have migrated throughout the Latin American region (e.g., 500,000 Paraguayans, 1 million Colombians) while the number of people who have left Mexico is in the millions. Just under the Immigration Reform and Control Act (IRCA) of 1986, some 2.3 million Mexicans, or 3.1 percent of Mexico's 1990 population, applied for permanent residence in the United States (see Table 9.1 for figures on Western Hemisphere applicants). The corresponding figures for El Salvador were 173,000 applicants, or 3.2 percent of the country's population in 1990 (INS, 1989). In overall terms, however, for the region as a whole as well as for most individual countries, the share of intrahemisphere emigration as a percent of the total population (regionally, or of receiving or sending countries) is relatively small (see Table 9.2). Mexico, Paraguay, and some of the Central American countries (as well as the majority of the island nations of the Caribbean) are obvious exceptions.

The demographic effects of emigration extend beyond those associated with changes in population size and growth rates over the short term. The delayed effects may turn out to be more important. A disproportionate number of migrants tend to be in their family-formation years. To cite one case, the emigration from Colombia of more than 150,000 women of childbearing ages is believed to have been an important factor in the fertility decline recorded there.

The demographic consequences of temporary and circular migration, on the other hand, are not well understood. It can be hypothesized that temporary migration is capable of reducing birth rate since the time of cohabitation is reduced, often for long intervals. Even more powerful demographic effects may result from the changed world views migrants are prone to acquire while residing in other countries. Such exposure could lead to changes in either reproductive behavior or in family size desires. The strength of these behavioral and attitudinal changes is likely to be influenced by the character of destination countries. Rural migrants moving into other agricultural areas are not likely to be exposed to new normative elements capable of bringing about behavioral changes

Table 9.1
**Applications for Legalization under the U.S. Immigration Reform and
Control Act (IRCA) of 1986 Submitted by Western Hemisphere
Unauthorized Immigrants by Country of Origin**

Country	Applicants
Mexico	2,287,400
El Salvador	173,400
Guatemala	72,200
Haiti	65,100
Colombia	33,000
Dominican Republic	27,100
Jamaica	19,800
Peru	18,000
Honduras	17,600
Nicaragua	16,800
Ecuador	15,400
Canada	11,700
Belize	6,300
Argentina	6,100
Brazil	5,400
Chile	4,800
Bolivia	4,400
Guyana	4,300
Trinidad and Tobago	4,200
Costa Rica	3,700
Venezuela	2,500
Bahamas	2,400
Panama	2,200
Uruguay	2,200
Antigua-Barbuda	1,400
Barbados	1,200
Grenada	1,100
Dominica	900
St. Vincent & Grenadines	800
St. Lucia	700
Cuba	600
St. Kitts-Nevis	600
Paraguay	400
Turks & Caicos Islands	400

Source: U.S. Immigration and Naturalization Service, Statistical
Analysis Branch, Office of Plans and Analysis,   "Provisional
Legalization Application Statistics," Washington, D.C., January 27,
1989, Table 1.

of this nature. This is not the situation with temporary workers who come in
contact with the lifestyles found in a modern city, be it in a developing or developed country.

There is little doubt that the macro demographic consequences of international migration for countries of origin in Latin America are substantial. In a few

Table 9.2
Foreign-Born Population and Share of the Foreign-Born Population of Latin American Origin Enumerated in Recent Censuses: Selected Latin American Countries

Country	Census Year	Percent Foreign Born	Percent of the Foreign Born of Latin American Origin
Argentina	1980	9.4	26.4
Brazil	1980	.9	9.7
Costa Rica	1984	3.7	82.9
Chile	1982	.7	45.8
Ecuador	1982	.9	72.0
Guatemala	1981	.7	74.9
Mexico	1980	.4	10.8
Panama	1980	2.6	62.4
Paraguay	1982	5.6	88.6
Peru	1981	.4	36.2
Venezuela	1981	7.4	59.9

Source: Data from the files of the Programa de Investigacion de la Migracion Internacional de Latinoamerica (IMILA) of the Centro Latinoamericano de Demografia (CELADE) presented in Adela Pellegrino, *Migracion Internacional de Latinoamericanos en Las Americas*, Universidad Catolica Andres Bello, Caracas (undated), Cuadro 2, p. 30.

countries (Paraguay, El Salvador), emigration rates have been high enough to offset natural increase rates. The long term consequences on population growth are also notable since return migrants tend to acquire attitudes less conducive to high fertility, and migrants who do not return bear their children abroad.

Whether these demographic changes are beneficial or detrimental to the development process appears to be a function of various factors, including the intensity of emigration and the national context in which emigration occurs. In Latin America, where unemployment and underemployment rates are high, it is generally assumed emigration relieves unemployment. In Bolivia, for example, labor emigration removed approximately 9 percent of the labor force increase anticipated between 1960 and 1970 (Marshall, 1981:240). In Montevideo, the Uruguayan capital, the unemployment rate rose from 8 to 13 percent in early 1976 as emigration to Argentina declined due to a severe contraction in the Argentina economy (Marshall, 1981:257). However, many studies have found that most migrants do not come from the ranks of the unemployed. While this assessment is generally correct, it should not be forgotten that because of high population growth rates, there are continuous new additions to the labor force. Emigration may also remove from the domestic labor force individuals with skills in short supply, and their departure represents a major loss. However, emigration can be said to have generally beneficial effects on the labor market. In some cases, however, the benefits are only marginal given the poor employment conditions prevailing in the region and the limited volume of emigration relative to the total labor force.

There are other macroeconomic effects of emigration. Emigration can have an appreciable impact on aggregate demand and on the size of internal markets. Remittances can increase the purchasing power of migrant households and can significantly augment national incomes. In Costa Rica, for example, Bogan (1985:222) estimates that, in 1979, remittances sent and savings brought home from the United States amounted to a sum equivalent to more than two percent of the country's total exports. This is a surprisingly large percentage in view of the relatively small number of Costa Ricans abroad. The comparable figure for countries where the number of migrants is larger is much more substantial. During the mid-1980s, for instance, Salvadoran migrants in the United States were remitting between $350 and $600 million a year, or 9 to 16 percent of GDP for 1985 (Pear, 1987:1, 5). In Mexico, documented and undocumented workers remitted more than 7 billion pesos (or approximately 1 billion dollars) during the "bracero" program.[1]

As large as that figure is, it might underestimate the true extent of remittances by between 50 and 90 percent (Cross and Sandos, 1981:44). In 1989, the Dominican Republic received some $350 million dollars in remittances, making this source of foreign exchange as significant as the earnings produced by traditional exports. Only tourism receipts exceeded those of remittances (Portes and Guarnizo, 1990).

In some of the countries with high emigration rates, some concern has been expressed that the departure of so many workers may have detrimental effects for socioeconomic development. Cross and Sandos (1981:45) note that migrants tend to be among the more enterprising of Mexico's people. In their view, the more ambitious Mexican bracero workers were the most likely to stay permanently in the United States, thus representing a serious loss to Mexico. In some countries, economic activities are constrained by limited population size; future economic development is thereby jeopardized (Balan, 1985). In the smaller countries, the internal markets are already too limited to sustain adequate production levels, and they stagnate as potential consumers and producers emigrate, as in Uruguay (Filgueira, Veiga, and Petruccelli, 1978) and Bolivia (Alegre, 1974). Even infrastructural development is obstructed since, due to the small population base, the per capita cost of constructing facilities is higher than it would otherwise be.

Even more troublesome can be the emigration of disproportionately large numbers of skilled professionals and technicians. Data reviewed by Pellegrino (undated) suggest that the skill composition of Latin American emigrants has gradually become more heterogenous. According to data compiled by Torrado (1980), between 1961 and 1975 approximately 60,000 such skilled persons emigrated from Latin America and the Caribbean to the United States alone.[2] In some of the least developed countries, especially in Central America and the Caribbean, Torrado estimates that between 20 and 40 percent of all university graduates emigrate. The losses of human capital are particularly severe in selected specialties such as engineering, medicine, and in some of the social and natural sciences. Within Latin America itself, net transfers of human capital from country to country can also be substantial, as with Uruguayan skilled migration to Argentina (Marshall, 1981:244–45).

Such a massive hemorrhage of trained talent bleeds labor-exporting societies of some of their most talented workers. Not only has the migrants' training been subsidized by their native countries, but the migrants then fail to pursue productive activities at home during their most economically active years. It is not uncommon to find serious production bottlenecks associated with the absence of needed skills. It is also not uncommon to find expatriate technicians performing tasks native professional migrants employed abroad are qualified to do. It is no less true that intellectually and financially rewarding employment opportunities are often lacking for those choosing to emigrate, so that their departure may entail a lesser cost since the prospective migrants at home are unable to attain their highest potential productivity. The opportunity cost of their migration, therefore, may not be so high. Conversely, the emigration of the more skilled may result in a significant increase in the volume of remittances received from abroad.

Selective emigration appears to be very costly, since a disproportionate number of migrants, particularly to the United States and other developed countries, have skill and educational levels well above national regional averages. The manpower losses associated with unskilled emigration, on the other hand, are much less substantial in most cases because of high unemployment rates and other factors. These workers' productivity is rather low; the loss of their labor can be compensated by the remittances and savings migrants accumulate. Their departure may help reduce economic and political tensions, but the effects of these developments may be negative or positive, depending on the consequences emigration has on the evolution of political and socioeconomic institutions.

At the political level, emigration may help preserve archaic and nonparticipatory political systems and postpone, if not always avoid, political change. Political change often goes hand-in-hand with political instability and can derail socioeconomic development. Over the long term, however, the absence of structural change may interfere with development. Some authors believe that emigration has helped Mexico cope with a series of economic shocks since the early 1980s, as well as with earlier difficulties (Cross and Sandos, 1981). In the view of Gillespie and Browning (1979:516), the political "constancy" of Paraguay, a country authoritatively ruled by Alfred Stroessner for over thirty years, may have been made partly possible by emigration:

> If population growth were to become too rigid, sooner or later this might increase discontent and lead to political activity. Emigration draws off young adult workers

from areas where job prospects are poor. . . . Whether or not the effects of this
policy are explicitly recognized by Stroessner and his associates is not known, but
such a policy is quite consistent with the pattern of domination.

Petruccelli (1979:525) also notes that emigration tends to preserve political
stability and hinder development by reducing tensions caused by "structural
weaknesses." The focus on emigration detracts from considering alternatives capable of leading to necessary changes in the fabric of society. In El Salvador, to
cite another case, social peace was maintained for many years in the semifeudal
rural sector through migration to cities and emigration to neighboring Honduras. With the closing of the emigration option for landless peasants and
minifundistas (as a consequence of the El Salvador-Honduras War of 1969), and
the ignoring of calls for changing the existing land tenancy patterns, a revolu-
tionary situation emerged and the political explosion engulfing El Salvador since
the late 1970s became a predictable phenomenon.

Finally, in some countries where the population is divided along clearly defined racial lines, emigration can produce social dislocations capable of inciting
political instability and interfering with development, as in Guyana and Belize. In
the former, differential emigration and return migration rates have tended to
alter the racial composition of the population (Strachan, 1983). In Belize, high
emigration rates of the black population, together with large influxes of immigrants who speak Spanish and indigenous languages, are leading to changes in
the country's ethnic composition. This realignment is a source of concern to the
politically dominant blacks (Everitt, 1984). The potential for political confronta-
tions among the various ethnic groups, never far below the surface, could contribute to severe economic dislocations. The chances for conflict increase if
emigration weakens the political and economic power of given ethnic groups.

Through remittances and savings brought home by returning migrants, emigration may contribute to economic activity by increasing demand for locally
produced goods and services as aggregate purchasing power rises. Remittances,
conversely, may undermine the production of locally produced goods by increasing the demand for imported items. Whether or not other consequences of emigration are regarded as positive or negative depends on the size of the country in
question, the rate of population growth, the emigration rate, and the prevailing
socioeconomic conditions.

In the least populous countries, where internal markets are small and the
number of potential consumers limited, emigration, particularly of the more
energetic and potentially productive young members of the middle class, has a
detrimental impact on development. Skewed national income distributions ag-
gravate the situation further since the share of the population living above a bare
subsistence level, and therefore capable of participating in the country's modern
economic life, is limited. Population losses also result in increases in the relative
per capita cost of providing social services and of developing economic infra-

structure, since the number of potential users is smaller than it would otherwise have been.

REGIONAL CONSEQUENCES

The demographic and associated impacts of emigration are not felt with equal intensity in all regions of a country. Many studies have established that international migrants are drawn predominantly from selected regions rather than randomly from throughout a nation's territory. In Colombia (Barrera, 1986) and Mexico (Cross and Sandos, 1981) the evidence indicates that most migrants, respectively to Venezuela and the United States, originate in a few regions, although migrants from all regions can be found in the emigration streams. Whether or not most international migrants come from urban or rural regions appears to depend on the socioeconomic characteristics of each of the sending countries, as well as on the history of each migratory flow. There are indications that most Colombian migrants to Venezuela, for example, were of rural origin, but more recent flows might be dominated by urban-origin migrants. Mexican migrants, while still mostly rural, increasingly emigrate from less agricultural and more urbanized areas (Ranney and Kossoudji, 1983). The case of Uruguayan emigration to Argentina appears to be unique in that most migrants come from the Montevideo metropolitan area.

Regional differentials in emigration rates can result in a situation in which some regions of a country are heavily impacted by emigration while others are hardly affected. There are only a few studies that have attempted to establish the magnitude of such regional consequences. One of the most interesting was conducted by Ungar Bleier (1986), who evaluated the consequences of the Venezuelan economic crisis of the 1980s on return migration to Colombia. While her study fails to establish with precision the relationship between emigration and its consequences at the regional level, it does suggest some mechanisms through which local socioeconomic characteristics may influence the nature and extent of those consequences.

By focusing on several indicators of economic activity, Ungar Bleier examined how the five Colombian cities of Cucuta, Bucaramanga, Medellin, Cartagena and Cali had fared in view of the Venezuelan recession of the early 1980s. Each of these cities differs in terms of its distance from the Venezuelan border, and each has developed its economy along different lines. Bleier's principal finding was that the impact of the crisis was far more severe in Cucuta and Bucaramanga, the two cities closest to Venezuela. Cucuta was devastated by the Venezuelan recession. This border city was the main entry point for Colombian migrants to Venezuela and had large contingents of floating workers. The city's economy was highly dependent on trade and services, with a limited industrial base. As long as Venezuela prospered, so did Cucuta, as trade across the border expanded and the city benefited from the never-ending traffic of migrants.

That picture changed rapidly as economic conditions in Venezuela began to deteriorate. The volume of exports to Venezuela and the number of foreign visitors declined dramatically as the devaluation of the Venezuelan bolivar increased the relative value of Colombian goods and services. Unemployment rates rose, as more and more commercial enterprises went out of business and tourism declined. Unemployment was exacerbated further by the return of migrants, who discovered that the less valuable bolivar could buy less in Colombia than before. Other migrants returned simply because they could not find or hold jobs in Venezuela. As the value of the bolivar declined, so did the amount of remittances migrants were sending home.

The effects of the Venezuelan recession in the other cities were commensurate with the degree of each city's dependency on Venezuela. In Cartagena, for example, where most economic activity was oriented toward the internal Colombian market, the impact was limited to a decline in tourism.

One interesting conclusion of this study is that return migration rates were not as high as were feared. Emigration rates to Venezuela did decline, but they did not decline as much as anticipated, due to the poor employment prospects in Colombia, both in terms of unemployment and wage levels. A reversal in migratory tendencies, therefore, had only a relatively minor effect in Colombia. This led to a substantial reduction in bilateral trade, to a considerable decline in migrants' remittances, and to a contraction in the internal demand for Colombian goods.

Ungar Bleier's most important finding is unmistakable: the emigration-related consequences of the Venezuelan recession were dwarfed by the direct economic effects (the losses associated with the reduction in trade between Colombia and Venezuela) of the contraction in economic activities. What her analysis indicates, however, is that at the regional level the emigration-related consequences can be severe, especially in border areas where growth and prosperity are in many ways linked to migratory activities. Since the early demographic and economic growth of Cucuta was linked to migratory flows, and its continued economic prosperity depended at least partly on the services the city provided to migrants, any curtailment of emigration negatively affects the local welfare. The cause and effect relationship weakens with the distance of a city from Venezuela and the reduction in the links of the local economy to that country. In essence, what Ungar Bleier has described is a "border effect" whose best known parallel can be found in the Mexican cities along the United States-Mexican border.

LOCAL CONSEQUENCES

At the local or community level the effects of emigration are particularly visible. Although the accumulated evidence is insufficient to make definite generalizations, some of the available assessments reach judgments that run contrary to what could have been expected on a priori grounds. Some of the evidence, while inconclusive, suggests that emigration tends to help preserve the status quo or reshape the socioeconomic environment in a manner that derails the development process. Other assessments suggest the opposite: although the benefits of emigration for sending communities are limited, events are set in motion that eventually accelerate development.

It has been noted that in sending communities, living conditions improve perceptibly as the additional income earned by migrants contributes to household resources. Improved standards of living, however, do not necessarily translate into the establishment of solid foundations from which socioeconomic development can proceed. In fact, some of the community-level changes may give rise to new forces that interfere with the economic and social transformations associated with development.

In their broadest outlines, the findings from Latin America tend to be similar to those reported for other major regions of the developing world (Massey et al., 1987:216–17). Migrant remittances and savings in rural areas are used to improve housing, purchase consumer goods, and acquire land and livestock. In urban as well as in rural areas, many migrants use their newly acquired resources to establish small business enterprises. These enterprises tend to be concentrated in activities with only a marginal development impact, at least over the short term. These small businesses usually demand only limited skills and small amounts of capital; most are service establishments such as restaurants and bars, retail stores, and transportation-related activities, such as taxis and trucks; and most employ few workers other than members of the household. Most of these small businesses fall within the informal sector but by no means all.[3]

Despite their low productivity, informal sector activities play essential social and economic roles in developing economies. Current common wisdom suggests, in fact, that in many countries the informal sector is one of the most dynamic components of the economy (Portes and Benton, 1984). The apparent inefficient use of migrants' earnings in their home communities may be the seeds of future development that would not have germinated were it not for the emigration experience. The long-term and perhaps significant payoff may be in the future, but the informal sector may be a breeding ground for entrepreneurial activity. Massey and his associates (1987:231–36) found these investments to be very significant in the business life of the four Mexican communities they studied. Assessments that minimize the effects of these investments on development often ignore the structural constraints retarding Third World investment, in particular the advantages the concentration of business activities confer to large urban centers to the detriment of small urban and rural communities. Once these constraints are taken into account, migrant investments serve as important stimuli for the economic development of sending communities.

Cornelius (1990:16), in a study of three Mexican communities, found that of 250 nonagricultural businesses, 63 percent were owned by present or former migrants in the United States. Nearly half of the migrant businesses still depended at least partially on a continued flow of remittances. This finding is similar to that reported by Lopez and Seligson (1990:20) in their study of a small sample of migrant-related businesses in San Salvador, El Salvador. Up to one-third of the Salvadoran enterprises were opened thanks to the availability of remittances. The survival of these businesses in the war economy of El Salvador depends on the continuous inflow of migrant's savings. Portes and Guarnizo (1990) report that remittances in the Dominican Republic play a more significant role in entrepreneurial activities than has been generally assumed. An important finding of their study is that migrant entrepreneurs are capable of mobilizing substantial amounts of resources earned while engaged in business activities in the New York City area.

What all these studies suggest is that migrant-related entrepreneurial activities are contingent on and in fact help perpetuate the continued ebb and flow of migratory flows. Savings accumulated abroad provide the initial capital to finance a business venture; foreign earnings are also instrumental in sustaining these businesses and provide working capital for the growth of the more successful of these ventures. While in general these enterprises provide only limited employment opportunities, they often represent one of the few sources of jobs other than those found within the local traditional economies. Occasionally one of these migrant businesses meets with considerable success and becomes an important source of local employment opportunities.

How migrants invest their savings is indicative of the interplay of how migrants perceive opportunity structures in countries and localities of destination and in communities of origin. Goldring (1990) offers an interesting discussion of how these perceptions help shape differential investment patterns in the two Mexican communities with long traditions of United States-bound emigration that she studied. Her conclusion is that the nature of the investments varies according to how committed the migrants are to their home communities. These perceptions affect the development prospects associated with remittance inflows which in turn are a reflection of the role the home communities have in the life of migrants who spend considerable periods of time in the United States.

Most evidence suggests that internal and international migration can help bring about a gradual but profound transformation in the rural economy. As Balan (1985:75) points out, it leads to "a more elaborate division of labor within the domestic community" and introduces, in many rural localities, new or enhanced economic relations based on the exchange of money. While traditional social structures are transformed, however, it is not always for the better. In their studies of Mexican sending communities, Reichert (1983), Mines and Massey (1985), and Massey and associates (1987) found one of the consequences of emigration to be increasing social class stratification. Families with migrants have more access to resources than families without migrants abroad The former are apt to invest some of these additional resources in such traditional symbols of wealth and power as land but, in the process, drive land prices up. Nonmigrating households no longer can afford to own land. Migrant families also have better homes and access to a greater array of modern comforts and amenities than families with no migrants. New housing or improvements to existing housing stocks, whether for family use or as investment property, give some dynamism to local economies. Building new housing creates employment opportunities and establishes linkages with other sectors of the economy, but strong housing demand can lead to inflationary pressures (Massey et al., 1987:219–25).

Land and other wealth becomes more concentrated in the village, sometimes giving rise to social differences not found before the onset of emigration. Reichert (1983) also identifies a process whereby formerly stable social systems are disrupted as a result of the social stratification brought about by emigration. Some of these changes compound existing structural inequities by widening the prevailing income distribution differentials, while other may be seen as eventually favoring the development process. Among the latter are profound changes in world views, which emphasize the predominance of personal effort and hard work over fate.

Land is purchased more for the security and status it confers than to increase family income through farming. Since households with migrants abroad tend to have high propensity to acquire land and their subsistence is less directly tied to farm income, farms owned by households with migrants abroad may be only partially cultivated, left fallow, or worked through sharecropping or rental arrangements. However, the farm land owned by households with migrants is often more productive. As Massey and his associates (1987:247, 249) note:

> Migration . . . bears a complex relationship to factors that influence agricultural productivity. Increasing migration is associated with less commitment by family workers to the tasks of farm work, but also with increasing use of other inputs such as hired labor, machinery, and scientifically improved seed. . . . Migration thus appears to affect the level of agricultural production in two different directions simultaneously. On the one hand, increasing migration brings about a decline in the number of households engaged in cultivation; on the other hand, through the application of capital it increases productivity and production among those migrant households still engaged in farming.

What the net effect is on total agricultural production depends on how much land is owned by migrant households, the intensity with which these farms are cultivated, and other factors.

A somewhat different perspective suggests that in rural communities emigration is regarded as a mechanism for preserving antiquated social structures. The stability of the small land-holding system is made possible by the supplemental income minifundio households derive through the wages earned by migrant workers (Gillespie and Browning, 1979; Gomez Jimenez and Diaz Mesa, 1983; Arizpe, 1983). This relative stability, however, is won at a price. At the household and individual level, emigration introduces numerous social and economic disequilibria. Seasonal and long-term migration disrupts family life. When the conditions under which emigration occurs are uncertain, families are separated, since most male migrants leave their spouses and children behind. In regions where agricultural activities have traditionally been the prerogative of males, productivity suffers as women, children, and elderly are the ones left behind to cultivate the family farm.

In some other instances entire communities benefit from emigration. Mines and Massey (1985), and Massey et al. (1987) report that in migrant sending communities in Mexico, living standards have risen well above what they could have in the absence of emigration. Mines and Massey (1985:115) argue that:

> the standard of living of towns people has been greatly elevated through wage labor in the United States because families with migrant members have been able to buy better housing, medical care, food, and more consumer goods than ever before. In addition each community as a whole has been able to collect contributions from U.S. migrants to make improvements in local infrastructure.

These findings, and those of other researchers who have worked in Mexico, however, may not be applicable to many other Latin American emigration countries, except those that have sent sizable contingents of migrants to the United States. Workers migrating from one Latin America country to another are less likely to generate as much in savings as emigrants to the United States. The reason is obvious: wage rate differentials between Latin American countries are not as wide as between Mexico and the United States. Results from a survey conducted among Bolivian migrants in Argentina in the early 1970s, for instance, suggest that migrants' savings and remittances were minimal, mainly because of the low salaries received by the migrants (Diaz-Briquets, 1982:36). More recent evidence shows savings and remittances among Bolivian migrants to be indeed important for the welfare of many households. The disparity of the findings might be explained by the differential character of the types of Bolivian emigration analyzed. The earlier data refer to migrants employed in rural areas, while the more recent data deal with return migrants who had been engaged in urban activities in Buenos Aires.

EMIGRATION AND DEVELOPMENT

Given the high levels of unemployment and underemployment prevailing in Latin America, it is reasonable to conclude that emigration benefits sending societies, at least over the short term, especially when it is the unskilled who emigrate. This generalization may not be as valid when a disproportionate number of skilled workers are part of the emigration stream. The effects of emigration in reducing unemployment in many countries are of little consequence given the high rate of population and labor force growth and the relatively modest amount of emigration which most countries in the region experience. In countries with lower labor force growth rates, such as Uruguay or where emigration rates are high, such as Mexico, Colombia and El Salvador, emigration can reduce unemployment.

In Latin America, in most countries the effects of emigration on aggregate demand are generally of only marginal significance. Highly unequal income distribution patterns overshadow every other consideration. Because of low incomes, a very large proportion of the population is virtually excluded from the market economy. The effects on aggregate demand tend to be more substantial in countries with smaller populations and less skewed income distribution, such as Uruguay. They are also quite significant in countries with relatively large numbers of emigrants abroad such as Colombia, the Dominican Republic, El Salvador, and Mexico. Migrants remit to these countries hundreds of millions of dollars.

The effects of emigration on social, economic, and political changes appear to be mixed. Over the shorter term, emigration seems to favor the maintenance of the status quo by providing a social safety valve. As some studies indicate, emigration deflects attention from many of the problems confronting these societies. Over the longer term, however, the effects might well be different, since exposure to alternative ways of doing things may impel people to tackle old dilemmas differently. Whether social and economic changes result, however, and the nature of these changes, depends on the political and socioeconomic environment from which emigration occurs and the destination migrants seek. Emigration can exacerbate some of the social, economic, and cultural problems found in sending societies and may even give rise to new problems. Other findings suggests that the knowledge and resources migrants acquire abroad may eventually become vehicles for social and economic change. The immediate effects of return migration may be limited. Some studies suggest that few migrants invest their savings in productive activities because migrants prefer to use their savings in expenditures to improve living conditions. Massey et al. (1987) claim that the specific socioeconomic context of developing countries must be taken into account when evaluating the development impact of migrant investments. Once allowance is made for this factor, it seems that migrants' investments do have a significant effect on economic development.

In the Latin American context, the loss of human talent associated with emigration seems to be restricted to the highly skilled—the so-called brain drain—although in some instances it is assumed that the emigration of skilled blue-collar workers is equally detrimental. The losses are especially severe for the smaller and least developed countries in the region, where emigration rates of the skilled are high. Even more significant may be losses in selected professions experiencing heavy net emigration. The emigration of highly trained workers is costly since these are the workers who can potentially make the biggest contribution to their home country's development.

Attempts to influence emigration in Latin America have been few and generally ineffective (Pastor, 1985b). Very few countries have even considered whether it is desirable to attempt to intervene in the migratory process (Colombia is the major exception).

Most governments of emigration countries recognize that there are severe limits to what they can do, and that far more crucial roles are played by economic and political forces and the unilateral actions of receiving countries. Despite this realization, it is not uncommon for governments to call for the implementation of specific policies, such as procedures to regulate labor flows, that take into account the interests of sending countries. In practice, these policies are rarely implemented because receiving countries are seldom willing to accommodate and give priority to the needs of sending countries. Recent disagreements between the Mexican and U.S. governments concerning the issue of illegal Mexican migration to the United States are the best known instances of the difficulties associated with reaching bilateral understandings.

Of all the Latin American nations with high levels of emigration, Colombia tried the hardest to implement an elaborate and comprehensive set of policy initiatives to try to manage emigration. These policies included manpower planning and the provision of information and assistance to prospective migrants and returnees. The success of these initiatives are modest at best.

Multilateral efforts are also not promising, as the experience of two of the major regional integration schemes in the region, the Andean Pact and the Central American Common Market, demonstrate. One of the thorniest issues in these integration attempts was the question of labor mobility. The Andean Pact includes a labor agreement, the Convenio Simon Rodriguez, whose intent is to facilitate and regulate labor flows among participating countries, but it never reached the implementation stage, although it is claimed that the 1980 Venezuelan Amnesty program was implemented, at least in part, to comply with the spirit of this agreement. Increases in officially sanctioned labor mobility were not among the accomplishments of the now nearly defunct Central American Common Market.

Sending countries are virtually powerless in their efforts to manage the forces leading to and arising from international migration. Benefits arising from emigration will exert their influence regardless of any policy initiatives, although selected policy interventions may maximize their effects. Detrimental consequences of emigration could be minimized by the right mix of policies. The structural difficulties with which sending countries must contend, and a generally poor economic environment, severely limit their freedom of action. The main hope for the future is that receiving countries might be willing to coordinate efforts with sending countries in the implementation of selected policies. This may happen as regional economic integration schemes continue to be tried in Latin America, and as traditional labor exporting countries seek to negotiate the opening of their national markets contingent on the orderly export of at least part of their surplus labor. Mexico, for example, raised the labor flow issue when in 1990 it declared its interest in negotiating a free trade agreement with the United States. Many barriers stand on the way of Mexico's request, however. The same question is sure to arise as well in Central America and the Caribbean as fresh initiatives are proposed to reactivate the Central American and Caribbean common markets.

Up to now, the scope for policy coordination between migrant-sending and migrant-receiving countries has been only limited. Countries receiving undocumented immigrants have been prone to ignore or to pay only lip service to these flows, as long as there was the perception that the benefits exceeded the costs. When receiving countries have acted, they have generally done so on the basis of political pressures exerted by some groups who perceive that it is in the national interest to control migratory flows. These initiatives have seldom taken into account the impact they might have on the economic development of the countries whence emigrants originate. This attitude appears to be changing as it is becoming increasingly clear that border controls and law enforcement measures are inadequate measures to cope with powerful emigration pressures. This new vision may lead to the formulation of proposals to maximize the potential developmental benefits sending countries could derive from emigration.

NOTES

1. The bracero program, the result of renewable bilateral agreements between Mexico and the United States between 1942 and 1964, brought 5 million Mexican seasonal laborers to the United States; some returned year after year, so perhaps 1 million Mexicans participated. It was unilaterally terminated by the United States in 1974.

2. Skilled migrants from Cuba excluded.

3. The informal sector is the segment of the economy characterized by small enterprises with limited access to capital, simple technology, and labor-intensive production methods. Wages in informal sector activities are generally low. The informal sector shows a great deal of flexibility in adapting to economic changes, produces a wide range of goods and services, and plays a key role in generating new employment opportunities in developing countries.

10

Caribbean Emigration and Development

Patricia R. Pessar

"Caribbean peoples have always been, and still are, a massively uprooted people."
So reads Arthur W. Lewis's "tenth commandment" for understanding the ethnic
and colonial heritage of the Caribbean (Chaney, 1985:12). To understand the
role that migration has played and continues to play in the lives of Caribbean people, we must recognize that migration emerges from and feeds back into the political, economic, social, and cultural fabric of the region. This review seeks to
examine the complex nature of contemporary Caribbean migration.

In describing the multiple facets of Caribbean migration, I eschew a popular
line of migration research that attributes international migration to unicausal
factors. Favorite candidates are population pressure (Fox, 1982), and changes in
the dominant mode of production which displace segments of the populace and
attract new workers to new locales (Standing, 1981; Piore, 1979).

Caribbean migration demands more refined and multiple explanations than
are found in unicausal propositions. For example, large-scale migration within
the English-speaking Caribbean began in the 1840s, long before the islands
were beset by overpopulation. The second causal argument ignores the fact that
emigration more commonly proceeds from Caribbean rural areas that struggle
with agricultural stagnation than from areas which have experienced the imposi-
tion of capital-intensive modes of production. A holistic explanation of Caribbean
migration must begin with a discussion of origins.

EMANCIPATION AND LABOR MIGRATION

For much of the Caribbean, the origin of "free" labor migration can be traced
to emancipation and the constraints placed on the newly liberated ex-slave population by the plantation economy. On many of the smaller islands, the elite
refused to relinquish their near monopolistic control over land, finances, and

markets. For example, local land laws in the British Leewards allowed planters to keep their land "leading to an early migration adaptation by all the new freedmen" (Richardson, 1983:7). With their material options constrained locally, many ex-slaves set off to the larger islands seeking employment and an eventual stake in a parcel of land.

On the larger islands, such as Jamaica and Trinidad, freedmen were able to purchase land. Some used savings they had accumulated from their independent cultivation and trade prior to emancipation (Petras, 1981); others labored for wages and then invested in land. While ex-slaves gained access to small parcels of land, few were able to establish themselves as full-time subsistence farmers. Rather, a "proto-peasantry" emerged (Mintz, 1974). This group was characterized by a need to combine self-employment of family members in agriculture with occasional wage employment. Since opportunities were scarce in the countryside, most individuals sought employment in towns off the islands.

On a few of the Caribbean islands, most notably Haiti and the Dominican Republic, a true peasantry emerged after emancipation. Smallholders flourished by growing food for household consumption and for sale (Mintz, 1974; Bosch, 1978). The development of a "peasant adaptation" rather than a "migration adaptation" meant that these islands would not experience large-scale emigration until a much later date than their neighbors in the English-speaking Caribbean.

From emancipation to the present, migration has been a vehicle for social mobility in the Caribbean. In migration, blacks have found a way to escape the social and material constraints operating in societies rigidly stratified by race and color. The early interisland migrations can be interpreted in this light. On islands where the Europeans monopolized all arable land, many ex-slaves rejected the ignominious alternative of working for past masters and headed for relatively more open island communities.

The "caste system" has remained an influential force in emigration. Scholars note that while the black population has sought higher education as a vehicle for social mobility, education alone has rarely proved sufficient. Many Caribbean people of color have had to emigrate from their home island in order to receive social acknowledgement for their improved status (Mills,1987).

Another legacy of the plantation economy was that in most islands there was insufficient fertile land and markets to create an independent peasantry. As noted earlier, this situation fostered a labor reserve disposed to migrate in search of wage-employment. It also encouraged the creation and maintenance of workers who endeavor to keep their employment options open through what has been labeled "strategic flexibility" (Carnegie, 1982:10). By learning and practicing many unskilled and semiskilled trades—which do not demand long term commitments—individuals are able to take advantage of diverse opportunities locally and abroad. For members of this labor reserve, Caribbean migration tends not to "mark an individual's progress through a series of income brackets" (Richardson, 1974:152); rather it is a household subsistence strategy.

Finally, in much of the Caribbean, migration has been woven into the cultural system. Especially for the lower classes, migration has emerged as a "rite of passage": "Foreign travel was accompanied by such an aura of accomplishment that it came to be regarded as a necessity in order to 'become a man,' to know the world and to understand life" (Thomas-Hope, 1978:77).

Turning to the demand side of this intraregional migration, researchers have observed a pattern in which laborers of the poorer islands migrate temporarily to the larger islands to fill casual jobs which have been vacated through the occupational mobility of the domestic work force. For example, Shell Oil Refinery jobs in Curacao were filled by the local population, while migrants from St. Eustatius and Saba assumed new vacancies in Curacao's port and shipping industries (Bor, 1981, cited in Chaney, 1985:60). Another illustration is Haitian migration for the sugar and coffee harvests in the Dominican Republic.

CARIBBEAN MIDDLE-CLASS MIGRATION

Just as the plantation system and its social and cultural legacy must be examined to understand the interisland migration of the poor, so contemporary export-oriented industrialization must be probed to understand middle-class migration to North America and Western Europe. To place this middle-class migration in a demographic context, let us consider the case of Jamaica. During the 1970s, professionals, skilled, and other white-collar workers accounted for 70 percent of the employed emigrants who left the country (Anderson, 1985). The same pattern holds for eastern Caribbean countries (Marshall, 1985).

Larger islands, such as Puerto Rico, the Dominican Republic, and Jamaica, have sought to benefit from the comparative advantage they possess within the international division of labor. They have made their large stock of cheap, underutilized labor available to foreign investors. This step has been taken in order to offset the islands' comparative disadvantage—the lack of capital for local investment.

Critics have argued that Caribbean societies have unwittingly suffered in this exchange. They have purportedly forfeited most of the value produced by their labor forces to wholly owned foreign subsidiaries (Petras, 1980; Bray, 1984b). For example, between 1975 and 1980, remitted profits from Dominican trade zones quintupled from U.S. $7 million to U.S. $35 million (Duarte and Corten, n.d.:7). As for the Caribbean economies, "low-wage sourcing by the multinationals and great retail merchandisers of the advanced countries, and free-trade border zone inducements, reduce the contribution to domestic value added to little more than wages" (Felix, 1977:9).

While export-oriented industrialization has brought some employment benefits to the Caribbean working class, it has threatened the economic security and social mobility of the middle sectors. Since foreign investors commonly import their own materials, capital goods, and management, there is little demand for local raw materials or finished goods and few opportunities for local entrepreneurs and administrators. Thus, one effect of foreign-dominated export industrialization is that Caribbean capitalists and petty bourgeois sectors have experienced a reduction in access to, and participation in, the economic opportunities generated by industrialization (Bray, 1984b). Furthermore, due to its low wage structure, the export-oriented sector has not appreciably increased the domestic market for products or services provided by the middle class. It has been argued that the growth of the low-wage export sector has had an especially depressive impact on wages for the lower middle class, since the work place demands and potential agitation of this group are muted by real or anticipated competition for their jobs by the large mass of more poorly paid workers (Bray, 1984a).

A "middle-class bottleneck" is the way David Bray (1984a) characterizes the negative outcome of the Caribbean of export-based industrialization. This bottleneck is by-passed by many members of the Caribbean middle class through emigration to more advanced industrial societies. In these societies, Caribbean immigrants commonly bolster near-exhausted internal labor reserves and are often employed at the bottom tier of the labor markets (Piore, 1979).

Development policies adopted in the Caribbean have encouraged middle-class emigration over the last 30 years. These policies have increased the dependency of Caribbean countries on "core" economies, such as the United States. The consequences of this dependency have been detrimental to the Caribbean during the worldwide recession of the 1970s and 1980s. During this period, members of the middle class have been motivated to emigrate owing to a sharp decline in the standard of living. This decline can be traced to high inflation and wage freezes. For example, in the Dominican Republic between 1969 and 1978, real wages dropped from U.S. $80 a month to $54 (NACLA, 1985:9).

To summarize, there are political, economic, social, and cultural roots of Caribbean migration. The first migration flow draws mainly upon semiproletarianized, rural workers and it is destined primarily to neighboring islands within the Caribbean. This migration flow is in part a byproduct of economic, social, and cultural imprints left by the plantation economy, slavery, and emancipation. The second migration flow draws upon a very different population—the Caribbean middle class. This middle class migration is directed to countries outside the Caribbean—primarily the United States, Canada, and Great Britain. To account for this second migration flow, we looked to the economic and social constraints for the Caribbean middle class created by export-oriented industrialization.

POPULATION GROWTH

As in many parts of the Third World, rapid population growth and a resultant young-age structure create pressures on Caribbean labor markets that cannot be satisfied under the limiting conditions described above. Many Caribbean countries have, nonetheless, experienced very low intercensal growth rates during recent decades. In many cases, this moderate population growth has not been achieved through direct family planning intervention, but rather through emigration. Despite high fertility and dramatic improvements in life expectancy, the populations of Montserrat and St. Kitts have been shrinking because of emigration (Marshall,

1985). Moreover, she found that only Guyana and Trinidad and Tobago had population growth rates of more than 2 percent in recent years. Roberts calculates that between 1960 and 1970, net emigration "canceled out" 52 percent of the natural increase of the Caribbean region (cited in Chaney, 1985:37).

While emigration plays an important role in controlling population growth in the Caribbean, the large-scale emigration of men and women in their peak working years does have certain negative consequences. Let us consider the cases of the Dominican Republic and Jamaica—two countries with high rates of emigration. In 1970 their dependency ratios were 103 and 106, respectively. In contrast, the ratio for Argentina was only 57 (Chaney, 1985:29, Table 3.4). In practice, such high dependency ratios translate into fewer persons working for a longer number of years to support the very young and very old. Often, elderly women must assume the responsibility for raising and maintaining small children who are left behind by their migrant parents. Researchers have observed that this practice sometimes contributes to childhood delinquency and crime.

UNEMPLOYMENT AND SKILL DEPLETION

Conventional wisdom holds that migration can export poverty and unemployment. This view may be congruent with the temporary, intraregional migration patterns described above. It does not, however, capture the reality of the middle class migration stream between the Caribbean and North America and Europe, since the majority of the emigrants were employed prior to their departure (Pastor, 1985a; Chaney, 1985).

The failure to make the distinction between unemployed and employed migrants leads analysts to overestimate the impact of migration on rates of unemployment. For example, in the case of the Dominican Republic, Morrison and Sinkin (1982) claim that if only 200,000 instead of 500,000 had emigrated, open unemployment today would be 42 percent instead of 24 percent. The authors overlook the fact that the majority of Dominican immigrants (at least those destined for the United States) were employed prior to emigration; or as Grasmuck puts it, Dominican migrants "do not represent a reduction in the size of the hardcore, unskilled unemployed" (1984:169). Furthermore, Morrison and Sinkin disregard the fact that some of the migrants were themselves employers or capitalists whose property and investments created economic opportunities for others (Pessar, 1982).

Not only are the majority of people who emigrate from the Caribbean employed at the time of their departure, but they are workers who are skilled and semiskilled. The emigration of these workers from the Caribbean (Anderson, 1985; Marshall, 1985; Chaney, 1985) is a matter of grave concern. Critics note that:

> (1) small states like Grenada with low and slowly growing per capita income experienced emigration rates among the highest in the world, (2) human resources were the key to development, and (3) skilled and professional workers were par-

ticularly mobile and were most likely to migrate permanently. (Cole, n.d., cited in Marshall, 1985:103)

A study of Grenadian graduates of the regional University of the West Indies (U.W.I.) during the years 1953 and 1972 showed that 81 percent of the 149 graduates were residing outside Grenada. The situation was particularly dire for medical graduates: for all disciplines, five Grenadians had to be sent to U.W.I. to get one back, but to obtain one doctor through the university, 22 had to be trained (Marshall, 1985: 103).

The large-scale emigration of administrators, managers, and technically skilled workers (e.g., accountants and bookkeepers) has had deleterious effects on Caribbean public and private sectors. A common pattern finds public administrators filling the higher-paid, private sector jobs vacated by the outflow of professionals and managers. A study conducted in Jamaica (Mills and Robertson, 1974, cited in Anderson, 1984) reported that rapid turnover of staff affected 67 percent of the professional, technical, and middle-level grade in the civil service. Another Jamaican study (Greene et al., 1983, cited in Anderson, 1984) noted a problem in the retention of experienced personnel at the height of their professional capacities (ages 35–44).

Problems of skill depletion through emigration also affect the private sector. Officials of large national and multinational companies in Jamaica complain that "they often train people for employment abroad." According to one official, the emigration of key managers can set off chain reaction emigration: "It seems that the decision of the top management staff to emigrate signals a message throughout an organization." The subsequent raiding and pirating of remaining managers causes salaries to escalate, increasing inequalities, and permits persons with little education and training to be promoted.

Many students of Caribbean migration would agree with the claim that "those who are able to migrate are not the 'redundant' but those who cannot be easily replaced" (Bray, 1984b:24). Nonetheless, the problem of skill depletion is superceded by the larger issue of whether there is truly a demand for the professionals and highly skilled workers who emigrate.

It can be argued, as Patricia Anderson (1984) does for Jamaica, that the Caribbean countries' manpower problem is not one of jobs looking for people. Factors of production, such as capital and physical facilities, are rarely lying idle, awaiting new infusions of manpower. Rather, large-scale out-migration would suggest it is the lack of these other factors of production that leads to domestic underutilization of manpower, and ultimately to migration. As Anderson observes: "The inflow of managers, directors, accountants, and engineers is very largely determined by the flow of capital, as their role is primarily to manage, implement or service foreign investment. Without this capital inflow, the management inflow ceases or is reversed" (1984:37).

According to Anderson, within the public sector, the demand for professional and other high skill workers must be analytically differentiated between "social need" and "effective demand." For example, in Jamaica in 1985 there was one doctor to 5,240 persons, and one dentist to 20,000 persons. These figures are far below the Pan American Health Organizations' recommended ratio for doctors and dentists. These are, respectively, 1:910 and 1:2, 857 (Anderson, 1987). "Social need," of course, does not translate readily into "effective demand." From the perspective of the potential migrant, the lack of effective demand is experienced as employers' and consumers' inability to employ the service provider at levels of renumeration commensurate with the provider's own investment and expectations about appropriate standards of living. The dilemma is reflected in the fact that for this population the motive for migration is not the absolute gap between home and host country wages, but the fact that with spiraling costs of living, the income received at home is increasingly inadequate to meet middle class consumption standards.

MIGRATION AND AGRICULTURE

Emigration from agricultural communities in the Caribbean and elsewhere has occasioned great expectations. Some observers anticipated reduced land pressure; more investment in advanced, capital-intensive agriculture; increased agricultural production; and greater opportunities for employment in farming (Griffin, 1976). Inspired by an equilibrium view of migration, some analysts predicted a time would come when conditions would be sufficiently improved in rural areas to stop migration. Empirical research in agricultural communities in the Caribbean has proved these predictions wrong.

Caribbean migration—of both the temporary and more long-term varieties—commonly results in older women being left behind to carry on domestic, child care, and farming duties. This "feminization of agriculture" often has negative outcomes for smallholder farming. Agricultural production suffers for many reasons. Women are sometimes forced to abandon full-time farming to supplement household incomes with wage-work. There is also evidence that women find it more difficult than men to hire competent day laborers. Women do not usually have title to the land and may not be eligible for government development and credit programs. Else Chaney (1985) suggests that emigration and the increased feminization of agriculture has contributed to the decline of smallholder farming in the Caribbean. According to Chaney, the reduction of "food for the poor" has forced already strained Caribbean governments to expend limited foreign exchange revenues on food imports.

Contrary to the common sense view that emigration would reduce land pressures, migration has often led to the opposite outcome. Migrants commonly engage in land speculation. This activity inflates land values beyond the reach of most nonmigrant families and often removes valuable land from production. In one Dominican migrant community, for example, land speculation by migrant households had contributed to a 1,000 percent inflation in land prices over a 15-year period (Pessar, 1982:353).

This pattern is repeated throughout the Caribbean. Research conducted in 1962 in Montserrat, for example, revealed that plantation lands had been subdivided and sold to migrants in North America and Britain. These lots were frequently removed from cultivation and held for speculative purposes or for future house building (Philpott, 1973). In St. Vincent, overseas investment in house lots and farmland inflated land values beyond the reach of landless peasants. Off-island purchases also led to increased land fragmentation—a process that renders uneconomical the commercial cultivation of the one or two acre plots that are normally purchased by migrants (Rubenstein, 1976; 1979).

There is little evidence that migration and remittances and savings spur agricultural production and productivity. Land speculation and absentee landholding often contribute instead to a reduction in production. Second, evidence from many Caribbean islands indicates that migrant households cut back on their commercial and subsistence farming activities as they become more reliant on remittances for consumption needs. In Nevis, emigration was accompanied by a 70 percent decrease in cotton acreage and a 50 percent reduction in sugar cane acreage between 1955 and 1962. Richard Fruct attributes this decline in production to an unwillingness to farm when remittance income is available (1968:204).

In a Dominican migrant community, only 41 percent of migrant households with access to land cultivated all of their land as compared to 71 percent of the nonmigrant households with land. Among landholding migrant households, the majority reported that they cultivated one-half or less of their property. Among nonmigrant households, such limited land use was reported by only 26 percent of the respondents (Grasmuck, 1982).

Third, in the wake of migration, estate owners have frequently found it difficult to find wage laborers. In Montserrat, cotton production on estates disappeared as remittances made agricultural workers reluctant to accept the low wages offered to them (Philpott, 1973). A recent study of St.Kitts-Nevis finds a cadre of "remittance men" is being created on both islands. As a consequence, farmers are having great problems procuring labor, and management's incentives to increase productivity are often ignored (Mills, 1987).

These findings indicate that migration often has negative consequences for agricultural production and productivity. In their study of Dominican immigration, Grasmuck and Pessar compared two agricultural communities which differed according to size, proximity to markets, and access to credit. In the smaller, more remote community, the researchers observed a pattern of agricultural land being left fallow, cultivated less intensively, and converted into pasture. In the larger and more advanced community, by contrast, migration was not associated with agricultural decline. Instead, migrant households with access to land were more likely than nonmigrant households to report that their agricultural production had increased over the last ten years, 50 percent compared to 40 percent. In this advanced community, migrant households were more likely than nonmigrant households to have cultivated all of their land—92 percent to 84 percent, respectively (Grasmuck, 1982). These comparative findings caution against generalizations about the deleterious effects of migration on agricultural areas. The same unfavorable conditions that favor emigration from remote underdeveloped rural communities may also constrain migrant households from investing their labor and limited capital in farming.

REMITTANCES AND RETURN MIGRATION

An intention to return to the home country is virtually a truism of Caribbean migration. This predisposition to return has obvious implications for remittances, since this transfer of funds is one way in which emigrants sustain contact with their home community. According to Elizabeth Thomas-Hope (1985), the return is constituted not only by people and money, but also by a variety of producer and consumer goods, attitudes, and ideas.

Research throughout the Caribbean has shown that remittances are most commonly directed to household consumption. With the exception of housing, there is little evidence that remittances and savings are put directly to productive uses with multiplier effects (Brana-Shute and Brana-Shute, 1982). Several authors have documented that remittance income and increased commodity consumption by migrant households exacerbates inequality in Caribbean communities (Pessar, 1982; Rubenstein, 1983). Other researchers have pointed to the anomaly wherein large-scale emigration may simultaneously raise living standards while undermining the local economy and increasing its dependence on the external economy (Lowenthal 1972; Thomas-Hope:1985).

The foreign exchange benefits of remittances can be great, however, and this is one feature that makes Caribbean governments cautious about developing policies to restrict emigration. Reliable statistics on remittances are extremely difficult to obtain. A preliminary study of government and banking statistics for seven Eastern Caribbean countries revealed that in 1978, they received a total of U.S. $12.5 million in remittances. Nonetheless, the Brana-Shutes "strongly suspect" that these amounts are underestimates (1982:275–76). In a recent study of St. Kitts-Nevis, Frank Mills (1987) estimates that approximately U.S. $18.6 million entered the twin-island nation during 1984. The magnitude of this contribution is clear when compared to the 1984 Gross National Product total of U.S. $60 million (World Bank, 1987).

Turning to the returnees themselves, there is little evidence that they are able to introduce change into their home societies. Some suggest that returned migrants with improved skills are blocked from innovation by those who have not been abroad and resent the returnees' "new ways." Writing about Surinam, Frank Bovenkerk (1981) observes that return migrants have become a "new minority" who have difficulty in applying their new knowledge and skills. Another problem noted for Surinam and the Dominican Republic (Hendricks, 1974) is that migrants return from more industrialized countries with skills that are unmarketable in their home countries. Many migrants who work temporarily on other islands acquire little or no additional training (Myers, 1976).

MIGRATION AND POLICY

Perhaps a Caribbean region where each country could productively retain its own population is impossible to achieve. Nonetheless, the region must strive to reduce its reliance upon two highly dependent, economic pillars: export-oriented industrialization and labor export. This redirection implies economies based on a strong indigenous core as well as export-oriented sectors. Such a reorientation would require greater regional cooperation to broaden the financing and markets for locally produced goods and services. Incentives would also have to be created to retain a cadre of skilled managers and technicians needed for Caribbean development.

It is a positive development that Caribbean scholars are joining their North American and European counterparts in challenging the conventional view that labor migration represents a solution to many of the Caribbean's social and economic problems. Dawn Marshall (1985) and Frank Mills (1987) are but two Caribbean nationals who have called for Caribbean governments to make explicit statements of policy concerning emigration. Marshall and Mills urge Caribbean nations to examine whether the immigration policies practiced by receiving countries produce adverse effects on immigrants. These two researchers also advise officials to explore whether the Caribbean nations can afford the loss of so many of their citizens, irrespective of training and skills.

In the short run, there are certain steps that Caribbean countries can take to lessen the negative effects of migration. Educational and training systems need to be more closely geared to the needs of the developing countries so that these systems are more carefully related to job opportunities. Such reform will reduce the loss that occurs when those persons most expensive to educate and train—and hardest to replace—leave their home countries.

New policies should reduce the decline of smallholding agriculture encouraged by out-migration. If we accept the premise that small-scale agriculture in the Caribbean brings the benefits of self-employment, some wage employment, the production of needed food crops, and a resultant decrease in expenditures of hard currency for food imports, then efforts must be taken to assist the women and men left behind. These individuals need clear titles to land and access to inputs, credit, and extension assistance. To increase the viability of rural migrant households and communities, small income-generating projects should be developed. Promising avenues include food processing, repair and manufacture of agricultural equipment, production of agricultural input, and small businesses and service enterprises in the informal sector (Chaney, 1985).

Most of the migrants from the Caribbean region intend to return to their homes, so programs to attract them home should be developed. Such programs might include the promotion of small businesses that combine migrant remittances with start-up funds from labor-receiving countries and international agencies.

Part VI

The Unsettled Relationship between Migration and Development

Part VI reviews the unsettled relationship between migration and development. Chapter 11 notes that migrant families clearly benefit from remittances, but it is less clear whether their communities and societies benefit as well. Labor importers hold the key to future labor flows, and a recognition by them that labor migration cannot be simply a temporary borrowing of another country's unneeded workers would be a first step toward developing bilateral and multilateral policies which promote development as well as migration.

Chapter 12 is a lagniappe for readers. The Immigration Reform and Control Act of 1986 created a commission to "examine the conditions in Mexico and such other sending countries which contribute to unauthorized migration to the United States." In the language of this book, why didn't several decades of recruitment, remittances, and returns promote stay-at-home development in the countries sending migrant workers to the United States? What types of "mutually beneficial" policies could promote such development?

After three years of studies and hearings, the commission concluded that migrants come to the United States illegally for economic reasons and that, although more development is the long-run solution to emigration pressures, in the short and medium terms development is more likely to increase migratory pressures. Nonetheless, the commission called for expanded trade and more development assistance to promote the economic growth which will eventually reduce emigration pressures.

Despite this J-curve effect of first more and later less emigration, the commission called for expanded trade and more development assistance to promote the economic growth which eventually reduces emigration pressures, asserting that "expanded trade between the sending countries and the United States is the single most important long-term remedy" for such pressures.

The commission report emphasized that promoting stay-at-home development is a formidable task. Since 1950, the populations of Mexico and the Central American nations have tripled, so that Mexico alone adds almost 1 million job

seekers to its labor force each year. These job seekers find few jobs in modernizing agriculture, so they flock to urban areas and strain infrastructures and labor
markets. The commission recognized that an integrated and long-run oriented
program which includes programs for family planning, rural job creation, and
export-led manufacturing growth will be needed to create economies and labor
markets which keep potential migrants at home. To coordinate U.S. policies toward migration areas and to assess the migration impacts of proposed U.S. policies, the commission recommends the creation of an independent Agency for
Migration Affairs.

11

Migration and Development: The Unsettled Relationship

Demetrios G. Papademetriou

This book has painted a sobering picture of international labor migration. Re-searchers who have examined the effects of emigration on a particular country are skeptical about the potential of labor migration to become a vehicle for development. What lessons can be drawn from the literature on migration and development? The lessons will be examined at three levels: migrants and their families or households; the sending community and the larger society; and the receiving society. Finally, the prospects for increased sending- and receiving-country cooperation in the context of migration will be explored.

MIGRANTS AND FAMILIES OR HOUSEHOLDS

Migration entails numerous personal sacrifices. Migrants often suffer a variety of physical and stress-related ailments while abroad. Suspended between two cultures and often living at the very margins of the host society, most temporary and circular migrants have few of the skills required to adequately understand and adjust to their new environment. At the same time, because of the assumption of temporariness (an assumption frequently shared by both the host society and the migrants themselves), there is little incentive on either side to invest in the migrant's secondary socialization. Even when a migrant is able to extend the stay abroad and reunify with his family there, the adjustment process is a lengthy and difficult one, and the social and psychological tensions which inhere in all migration, particularly the generational ones, will continue to affect family cohesion. The existence or formation of ethnic communities may palliate but does not eliminate these problems.

At the same time, families left behind have to adjust to the sharply restricted interactions and the social and psychological problems attendant to the breadwinner's prolonged and repeated absence. As a result, family bonds and solidarity erode—the implications of which range from changes in social norms and the terms and locus of decision-making and control (Adepoju, Chapter 3), to new gender-differentiated economic roles and child-rearing practices. Although not all of these changes are undesirable, many of them create serious readjustment problems for the returning migrant.

Against these negative effects of emigration one must balance the undisputed social and economic gains which most migrant households realize. Whether their families emigrate with them, come to join them at a later time, or stay behind and receive the remittances from the household member who is abroad, the economic benefits are substantial. Burki (Chapter 7) estimates that the income of Pakistani families with an unskilled member in the international labor migration stream is multiplied by a factor of three; if the migrant is a skilled worker or a professional, the gains are proportionately higher.

Differences in migrant type, migration stream, length of stay abroad, and whether the migrant's status is within or in violation of a country's immigration laws result in often substantial variations in remittances. For instance, rural-origin migrants involved in the frequently unauthorized migration streams in Africa and the Americas have to pay their own transportation expenses and smuggling fees; they may have trouble finding regular employment; and they usually work in low wage industries, at least initially. As a result, they tend to earn and remit less than the many South and East Asian and Southern European migrants who are part of more organized migration systems in which employers are responsible for transportation costs and employment and wages are guaranteed for the duration of the contract.

The differences in the earning, saving, and remitting ability of these types of groups is often significant. In a recent study of irregular Caribbean Littoral (but not Mexican) migrants in the United States; Papademetriou and DiMarzio (1986:111) found that nearly three out of four of the sample's subjects had remitted funds during the previous year averaging slightly under $1,200 per emigrant.

THE SENDING COMMUNITY AND SOCIETY

The human capital characteristics of individual migrants, their legal status, and the migration stream of which they are a part strongly influence their earnings and, hence, their ability to remit; the propensity to remit and the use to which remittances are put are shaped by a different set of variables. The propensity to remit varies with available opportunities for family unification and permanent settlement abroad. The more accessible these opportunities, the less regular the remittances are likely to be. Remittances are likely to dry up when specific investment goals back home have been met and the decision to settle abroad is made.

While the size of remittances is shaped by the interaction of the variables just outlined, their disposition conforms closely to the individual's and the household's original goals for emigration. From a development perspective, mobility migration is presumed to be more important than survival migration. Mobility migrants not only earn more; they are also more likely to have higher human capital characteristics *before* migration and to be able to take advantage or initiate opportunities to enhance those characteristics while abroad. At the same time, however, they are also more likely to be offered more opportunities to stay abroad. If they do so, the sending society gains very little from the migration process. If they return home, however, these former migrants come closest to the ideal of the "innovator," that is, the returned migrants whose skills and investment behavior are most likely to have a positive influence on their community and, if a critical mass can be attained, their region.

The possibility of return migration having a positive developmental impact, then, is tied directly to two processes: first, the *permanent* return of successful migrants and, second, the success of sending societies in taking at least the first tentative steps toward making the structural social and economic adjustments which are the sine qua non of sustained development. Only then will return migration stand a chance of making a positive impact beyond the migrant household and the immediate community.

The review of the vast literature on this topic offers only occasional, largely isolated, and usually conflicting evaluations of such impacts. The reasons are very complex and often tied to the types of return one is likely to encounter in each specific migration flow. Unplanned returns, such as those associated with mass expulsion, changes in immigration laws, plant closings, or protracted economic recession in the host society are the least likely to lead to lasting positive consequences for the migrant, his household, and his community. Voluntary returns after relatively short periods abroad, motivated by family considerations and the inability to adapt to the new environment, are also likely to be largely inconsequential to the home country. It is the longer-term and more successful migrants, however, who choose to return because of a combination of reasons, including special repatriation inducements and programs and success in reaching human capital enhancement[1] and savings goals abroad and investment goals at home, that carry the greatest potential for personal success and possible community and larger society gains.

These gains, however, are neither inevitable nor without unanticipated negative consequences. The often double-edged sword of investments in housing and agriculture have been discussed in this volume's introductory essay, as have the conflicting reports on the impact of migration and remittances on agricultural productivity. The impact of emigration on social change in rural communities is equally inconclusive. As Diaz-Briquets points out (Chapter 9), on the one hand, emigration may help preserve the status quo in a manner which may make for stability, but which basically derails the development process. El Salvador's stability-through-emigration "model" (an approach shattered by the 1969 war with Honduras) is not unique in terms of the degree to which many labor-sending countries indirectly rely on emigration to postpone needed social and economic changes and help preserve antiquated socioeconomic and authoritarian political systems. On the other hand, return migration in particular may help set into motion local processes which eventually help accelerate development.

One additional controversy about return migration involves the propensity of returned migrants to engage in small-scale service and informal sector activities. One school of thought views this propensity with alarm—especially when a country's tertiary sector is felt to be inflated and thus "distorting" and even "parasitic." Many students of the European, African, and South Asian return migration process view tertiary and informal sector activities in this manner. Another school of thought, however, views informal sector activities with considerably less anxiety and sees in them not only the survival of large numbers of a society's least fortunate members, but also a breeding ground for entrepreneurial activity where the seeds for further development are sown (Portes and Walton, 1981; Massey et al., 1987; and Diaz-Briquets, Chapter 9).

It is not necessary to enter this debate here to appreciate that some of the small-scale service activities in which returning migrants often engage perform an important social and economic role both in themselves, as with the establishment of rural transportation systems, and in their role in the maintenance and reproduction of the middle classes, providing such services as deliveries, repairs of every nature, gardening, housekeeping, and babysitting. Most of these activities are neither vestigial, nor anachronistic, nor transitional in the sense that they are about to become extinct. They are in fact a dynamic development which often plays crucial political and socioeconomic roles (see Berger and Piore, 1980, for a discussion of the role of this sector in France and Italy).

The extensive discussion of return migration and remittance undertaken throughout this volume suggests that these are the areas where more research and most policy initiatives must focus. There is the need to investigate and test the effectiveness of incentives to attract returned migrants to their areas of origin through such programs as set-asides for relocation, assistance with setting up small businesses of types and in areas where they are needed the most, and related activities. In addition, incentives intended to attract remittances through such programs as preferential exchange rates, special foreign-currency denominate bonds, and foreign currency accounts are worth exploring. Finally, reception and reintegration services for returning migrants and their families must be instituted or expanded and must offer returned migrants reliable relocation and labor market information, as well as a full array of educational services for returning children (Conde, 1987). Channelling remittances and influencing the relocation choices of returning migrants makes obvious a point explicitly and implicitly reiterated in the various essays: the contribution of labor migration to the development of a migrant's country is directly related to that economy's size, sophistication, and diversification and to the quality of that society's overall social, physical, and administrative infrastructure.

RECEIVING SOCIETIES

The structural problems associated with underdevelopment create a fertile ground for the emigration of the less-developed countries' citizens in search of work. Such expulsive conditions, although necessary, are not sufficient conditions for labor emigration. This is neither to say that all labor migration flows in the long, historical view have been receiver induced nor to deny that migration streams often acquire lives of their own which may at times be at variance with the actual needs of a receiving country's labor market. The occasional dissonance between the needs of host labor markets and the behavior of migration flows usually means that the receiving society, but not capital itself, has lost control over the migration process and that ethnic networks have developed and matured to the point where they are able to frustrate the host society's official immigration policies and in effect act as independent migration forces.

These developments are common to all but the most highly organized and controlled migration flows. Recognition of this fact does not seem to be motivating most labor receivers enough for them to take initiatives to correct the problem. Among the possible reasons for this failure to act may be the following: first, even during periods of economic downturns, advanced industrial societies continue to need the services of foreign workers whose economic presence has become structurally central to them. As a result, large scale repatriations would be extremely disruptive for the host economy, as discovered by Nigeria which, for political reasons, has opted twice for expelling its foreign work force—in 1983 and again in 1985.

Second, receivers are content not to risk the damage to their image which even limited expulsions entail. Instead, they allow attrition and the market to regulate the disposition of those foreign workers who have become redundant. It is the failure to understand the structural dependence on foreign labor which migration engenders (and the resilience and maturity of ethnic communities who, together with their allies among churches, civil rights groups, and much of the political left, have been able to provide a social and economic safety net for their members) that has led many analysts to predict that receiving societies would attempt to "export their unemployment." These dire predictions have failed to materialize.

Finally, despite much rhetoric (especially in Europe in the mid-1970s) about taking the jobs to where the labor is, there has been only a trickle of investment in labor-supplying countries. The private investment behavior of a number of major labor-receiving countries indicates that they choose countries for investment on the basis of their favorable investment climate and potential for profitability. Even industries heavily dependent on foreign labor did not typically invest in the countries from which most or even some of their foreign workers came. Most of the foreign investments of these industries were in countries considerably poorer than the labor exporters.

COOPERATIVE BILATERAL AND MULTILATERAL
APPROACHES TO MIGRATION

International migration movements are rooted in the structural character of economic disparities between and among states. Solutions must be sought in policies which address the place of the migration process in the global political economy. Migration must be examined in the overall development process while also devising and expanding initiatives intended to protect the human and labor market rights of migrants (see Goodwin-Gill, 1989).

Such initiatives can have only modest expectations of successful implementation. They can have only marginal impacts on the development of sending countries. Furthermore, key actors in the international migration system (such as South Africa, Nigeria, and numerous other countries) cannot be expected to subscribe to them, while several types of migrants (such as those outside of a country's immigration laws) will benefit only marginally. However, discussions of such initiatives should not be avoided either because of the uncertain outcomes of development, or because of reservations about the international community's ability and interest in promoting economic equality among nations.

For instance, it is not at all obvious how migration and development might become related, nor how the aid, trade, and investment policies of receiving countries might be coordinated so as to have a sufficiently pronounced impact on the development of recipient countries. It is equally uncertain how these policies might lead to the abatement of emigration pressures, or how to convert return migration into an instrument of social and economic change. Foreign economic policies, finally, may have a rather complex and essentially weak relationship to migration and development (Pastor, 1985a). In addition to the array of political difficulties at both ends of the process, many options would also run afoul of the complex international treaties to which most advanced industrial societies are signatories. Sidney Weintraub (1980) has pointed to many of those difficulties, especially with regard to U.S. obligations under the General Agreements on Trade and Tariffs (GATT).

Such initiatives may not stem migration. The evidence suggests (Temple, 1981) that migration pressure could be stimulated during the early stages of economic growth. It is, of course, at least theoretically possible that migration pressures will attenuate when "development" crosses an as yet empirically unknown threshold. Initiatives such as the U.S. Caribbean Basin[2] may in fact have considerable symbolic political significance and, presumably, may even assist in the marginal improvement of the living standards of some of the people in that area. What such initiatives should not be expected to have, however, is a measurable impact on overall emigration pressures, at least for the foreseeable future. A number of studies which examine the feasibility of and prospects for "substituting" trade for migration in Europe reach similar conclusions. (For the Federal Republic of Germany, see Hiemenz and Schatz, 1979).

CONCLUSION

Advanced industrial societies have been able to draw on the human and other resources of the less-developed countries almost at will, and receiver-country-regulated migration is a subsidy to the rich from the poor. Current migration patterns are neither historically unique nor likely to dissipate in the near future. As a result, the challenges that migration flows pose for the global system will continue. As the recent U.S. Select Commission on Immigration and Refugee Policy (SCIRP) recommended (1981), comprehensive initiatives are needed to address the multiple dimensions of the international migration problem. What SCIRP and the Commission for the Study of International Migration and Cooperative Economic Development recognize is that policy makers must address persistent problems with the politics and economics of the sending countries, and with regional and global economic conditions which reinforce economic inequalities. One starting point may be assessments of the sources and dynamics of international migration. The motivation for such assessments is already present: immigration policies have become inextricably intertwined with and will increasingly affect the ability of major labor-importing countries to articulate and implement even their most basic economic, foreign, and defense policies.

Labor importers have relied on foreign workers without regard to how migration might affect the development of the countries of worker origin. Increasingly, however, the beginnings of a convergence between domestic and foreign policy interests with regard to migration are becoming more obvious in a number of regional settings. Aligning the two and allowing each set of interests to inform and guide the other is much more likely to yield desirable policy responses for both than would the complete submergence of one into the other. Domestic policy arenas will continue to be the forum for immigration reform debates— at both ends of the migration flow. Mexico, despite its understandable interest in the outcome of the most recent U.S. policy debate on immigration, has repeatedly refrained from openly trying to influence these deliberations. Thahane (Chapter 4) also points to the delicacy of the situation in Southern Africa. Such an attitude, however, while recognizing the receivers' sovereign right to control membership into what Zolberg (1989) calls that "most comprehensive of corporate organizations, the state," does not make the consideration of sending-country interests on this matter any less compelling.

In making immigration-related decisions, receiving countries could become more sensitive to the implications of such policies for the sending societies. This is especially important when policies might lead to the abrupt repatriation of foreign workers. Such policies also have the potential of playing havoc with the advanced industrial societies' own economic and implied foreign policy goals. Reforms in the international migration system must take extreme care to be consonant with other, perhaps even more important, tactical and strategic receiver-country interests.

In the final analysis, only when receivers and senders work together can the latter address some of the problems which are known to give rise to large-scale international migration: inequality, persecution, war, hunger, and poverty. To do so would first require a fundamental rethinking of the entire process by receivers—a rethinking based not on altruism but on rational self-interest. If receivers are to be successful in implementing well-conceived domestic initiatives in social, population, and economic matters, they must effectively address the one component which has an often critical impact on all these areas: immigration, and especially unauthorized migration. However, recognition of interdependence implies mutual responsibilities. To neglect these responsibilities not only calls attention to the advanced industrial societies' frequent role in promoting and maintaining such inequalities but may also deprive them of an opportunity to continue to have a role in influencing future political development in their respective regions.

NOTES

1. Enhancing the skills of migrants is not a priority for receiving economies. Even more important, however, is that many foreign workers may not be interested in deferring immediate economic goals in favor of a personal investment in an uncertain future.

2. The Caribbean Basin Initiative offers limited trade concessions and investment incentives to U.S. investors who invest in certain Caribbean island states.

12

Immigration and Economic Development

Commission for the Study of International Migration and Cooperative Economic Development

The Commission, in consultation with the governments of Mexico and other sending countries in the Western Hemisphere, shall examine the conditions in Mexico and such other sending countries which contribute to unauthorized migration to the United States and (shall explore) mutually beneficial, reciprocal trade and investment programs to alleviate such conditions.

Section 601 of the Immigration Reform and Control Act,
Public Law 99-603, November 6, 1986

The last two decades witnessed unprecedented levels of global migration—much of it unauthorized—from developing to developed countries. Unexpected movements of people created regional tensions, exacerbated economic and social problems in host countries, taxed international humanitarian support systems, and created what some refer to as "compassion fatigue" in many receiving countries.

The bipartisan Commission for the Study of International Migration and Cooperative Economic Development was created to address the "push" factors that motivate unauthorized immigration to the United States from Western Hemisphere countries. Extensive consultations abroad, domestic hearings and research confirmed two fundamental conclusions:

—although there are other important factors, the search for economic opportunity is the primary motivation for most unauthorized migration to the United States; and

—while job-creating economic growth is the ultimate solution to reducing these migratory pressures, the economic development process itself tends in the short to medium term to stimulate migration by raising expectations and enhancing people's ability to migrate. Development and the availability of new and better jobs at home, however, is the only way to diminish migratory pressures over time.

These conclusions led the Commission to focus on measures that the United States and sending countries might take cooperatively to provide jobs in their home countries for increasing numbers of potential unauthorized immigrants. This Report addresses recommendations to both the United States and sending countries that, when taken together, would contribute to mutually beneficial economic growth, thereby easing the undocumented migratory flow over time.

INTRODUCTION

The United States adopted significant changes in immigration policy when it enacted the Immigration Reform and Control Act (IRCA) in November 1986. Breaking tradition, it addressed the problem of unauthorized immigration in both domestic and international terms, simultaneously targeting the "pull" and the "push" factors that motivate undocumented migration to the United States.*

The Act sought to diminish the pull of American jobs by penalizing employers who knowingly hire undocumented workers. To address the push factors, the Act created the Commission for the Study of International Migration and Cooperative Economic Development to study the causes of undocumented migration. The Congress thereby sought for the first time to deal with the issue in nonenforcement terms.

U.S. immigration policy has long been ambivalent and often incoherent, reflecting in large measure public sentiment on the subject. If our laws closed the door to some, our legal system assured others that there were always cracks that could be slipped through. If it was illegal to enter without proper documentation, it was not illegal for employers to hire undocumented workers. Our inconsistency is constantly reflected in foreign policy decisions which are driven by considerations often at odds with immigration concerns, and this sends a host of contradictory signals to actual and potential immigrants.

There is a direct or indirect migration consequence to most important foreign policy decisions. Thus, U.S. intervention in Central America during the 1980s had direct migration consequences. Unstable political conditions in Central America and substandard living conditions in some Caribbean countries motivated many people to emigrate without authorization to the United States. Official U.S. passivity towards the foreign debt burdens of sending countries affected migration by contributing to diminished economic growth. In Mexico, a severely depressed economy resulted in a continued flow of migrants, including much undocumented migration to the United States. The degree to which access to the U.S. market is available to developing country exports has clear positive or negative migration fallout.

The Commission is convinced that expanded trade between the sending countries and the United States is the single most important long-term remedy to the problem it was mandated to study.

The possible effect on migration of other official actions has never figured in the formulation of economic or foreign policy. Emphasis is usually on immediate goals—resolution of the crisis of the moment—rather than on the long-term trends in human migration that generate their own momentum, ultimately producing millions of new and permanent residents of the United States.

- Migration consequences should not necessarily override other considerations in policy formulation, but they must be given explicit attention.

This is our principal institutional message: that a government structure be designed to assure that the issue of migration policy receive as much attention as do the consuming but often transient day-to-day concerns that otherwise dominate the process. The philosophy that guides this report is that immigration policy requires constant study and attention at a senior level of government. This can best be achieved by centralizing the current widely dispersed government structure for handling immigration and refugee affairs in a single agency whose head reports directly to the President.

The Commission was charged with seeking effective approaches to economic cooperation between the United States and key migrant-sending countries of the Western Hemisphere, based on the conviction that greater economic opportunity at home will reduce the pressure to emigrate. The driving force behind the Commission's work is thus to promote mutually beneficial economic development so as—over time—to diminish the need for unilateral enforcement measures to control unauthorized immigration.

The complexity of our mandate is illustrated by a basic contradiction revealed in the research. While greater economic opportunity at home is an essential element for reducing pressures to emigrate, development is a long-term process, measured in decades or even generations. There is thus a very real short-term versus long-term dilemma. Any serious cooperative effort to reduce migratory pressures at their source must be pursued over decades, even in the face of immediate contrary results. This applies equally to the United States and to the sending countries, which have primary responsibility for their own development. Enforcement measures should become less necessary over time as economic development succeeds.

The Commission interpreted its mandate not as being hostile to immigration—immigrants have constantly renewed and revitalized American society—but rather as seeking to reduce our undocumented population and the attendant potential for its continued exploitation. Our work was also one of hope—of how to promote development, not of enforcing restrictions. The work was accomplished through a three-track program of consultations abroad, domestic hearings and research. The geographic focus of our activities was Mexico, Central America and the Caribbean—the area from which most unauthorized immigrants come.

RECOMMENDATIONS

The Commission is well aware of our national fiscal situation and sought wherever possible to make recommendations that would not have immediate budgetary impact. The unresolved migratory pressures generated by over two million uprooted Central Americans make that area an exception. We firmly believe that the best way the United States can contribute to economic growth and job creation in sending countries is to put its own fiscal house in order. Recognizing the practicalities of the situation, however, we call for shifts in choices between certain domestic and international interests. For example, limitations on foreign assistance impose a need for more generous treatment of imports from Caribbean Basin countries to stimulate job creation to reduce emigration. The issue for many countries is stark: they either export goods and services to create jobs at home, or they export people. Everything we suggest is aimed at reducing pressures over time for unauthorized immigration. Implementation of our recommendations would also assist in the protection of our national security interests by contributing to stability in the region and to the furtherance of our commercial interests by improving markets for our exports.

TRADE AND INVESTMENT

The Commission is concerned that the pace and pressure of events in Eastern Europe will consume official U.S. attention at the expense of development efforts to our south. This outcome is not foreordained, and U.S. policy can assure that the Western Hemisphere will benefit from global political and economic changes. It would be especially tragic to allow conditions in Central America—where our help is most needed—to deteriorate as resources and attention are directed elsewhere.

The Commission makes numerous recommendations aimed at stimulating economic growth and job creation in sending countries. The most important are reviewed below. We stress the primary responsibility of the countries themselves to provide opportunity for their populations. The Commission acknowledges the considerable headway that has been made in Mexico, and efforts that are underway in other countries. The Commission emphasizes, however, that appropriate adjustments in certain U.S. economic policies are essential to sending countries' ability to achieve sustained economic growth. This is particularly true in the trade area.

U.S. Trade Policy and Foreign Development

A decade of World Bank research confirms that countries with industries capable of meeting foreign competition at home and abroad fare better than countries with industries protected by import barriers and where development strategy looks primarily inward. The faster migrant-sending countries can improve their economies, the shorter will be the duration of pressures to emigrate to the United States.

There has been a dramatic transformation in Latin American development policies from protectionism and state control to reliance on market forces, competition and maximum participation in the world economy. Exports have now become a major factor in the economies of the region with the United States being their dominant foreign market.

But increased exports require access to international markets. Export policies of migrant-sending countries can succeed only to the extent that economic policies in the industrial countries complement them. If efforts at export promotion are frustrated by trade restrictions, entire development programs may falter.

U.S. actions that frustrate the development of the economies of migrant-sending countries in the Western Hemisphere will ultimately encourage emigration. The Commission recognizes that the U.S. market is one of the most open in the world to both foreign products and investment, and that trade issues are socially sensitive when imports from low-wage countries compete head-on with U.S. production. The United States, under these circumstances, has the dual role of protecting the jobs and living standards of its citizens and of fostering economic conditions that discourage unauthorized immigration. U.S. economic policy should therefore promote an open trading system.

Regional Economic Integration

Improved access to U.S. and other developed country markets is the key to the economic future of the area. The United States recognized this in 1983, when the Caribbean Basin Initiative (CBI) was enacted; in 1987, when the U.S.-Mexico Framework Agreement on Trade and Investment was negotiated; and again—on a grander scale—in 1989, when the U.S.-Canada Free Trade Agreement (FTA) came into effect.

Mexico is an important competitor in the world marketplace. The smaller economies of the Central American and Caribbean countries do not have that potential. The Commission strongly advocates their integration—and Mexico's—into larger trading areas.

Toward North American Free Trade

The U.S.-Canada Free Trade Agreement (FTA) opened real prospects for a North American free trade area including Mexico. Over 60 percent of Mexico's exports come to the United States (more than 80 percent excluding oil). Mexico already competes with Canada in a number of sectors in the U.S. market.

Mexico has made clear its desire to negotiate a free trade agreement with the United States. As a result of the meeting in June 1990 between Presidents Bush and Salinas, preparations for negotiations on free trade are now under way between the two countries.

Mexico seeks greater assurance of access for its products in the U.S. market. The U.S. interest in a free trade agreement with Mexico is to enlarge the potential for U.S. exports, based on complementarity of production in the two countries. The United States also has a strategic interest in Mexican economic growth and political stability. However, the Commission has serious concerns about runaway industries seeking low Mexican wages. This requires the United States to move deliberately.

- The United States should expedite the development of a U.S.-Mexico free trade area and encourage its incorporation with Canada into a North American free trade area.

- The United States should examine the effect of North American free trade on the trade of other Western Hemisphere countries in order to minimize any damage. It should also support wide free trade within the Hemisphere, but should allow the initiative to come from interested countries.

Accelerating the Momentum of the CBI

The Caribbean Basin Initiative is a unilateral U.S. tariff preference scheme intended to provide incentives for economic growth and political stability in Central America and the Caribbean. (It does not include Mexico.) Its centerpiece is duty-free access to the U.S. market for 12 years (until 1995) for most products exported by the 23 beneficiary countries.

The CBI has been moderately successful. Its fundamental purpose—broadening and diversifying the region's production and export base—is slowly being achieved. But it has been hamstrung by factors beyond the control of beneficiary countries. Markets for traditional exports have been weak and CBI benefits have, at best, barely offset declines in such sectors. Many of the area's most competitive products have been excluded from the benefits. In some countries, political instability and conflict have impaired the climate for foreign investment.

The return of peace in Central America and events in Eastern Europe may diminish the availability of official resources for the Caribbean Basin region. This would be most unwise and shortsighted. So long as economic distress continues, so will potential instability on our doorstep, aggravating the flows of unauthorized migrants to the United States. Both Houses of Congress have approved the permanent extension of the CBI, but with other less significant improvements.

- In addition to its indefinite extension, the CBI should be enhanced by significantly easing limitations on beneficiary products.

- Moreover, the Commission believes that the CBI should be transformed into a contractual arrangement between beneficiary countries and the United States, modeled after the Lomé agreement.

Revitalizing the Central American Common Market

The Central American Common Market (CACM)—formed during 1958–63 by Guatemala, El Salvador, Honduras, Nicaragua and Costa Rica—was once the most successful regional integration initiative in Latin America. A tenfold increase in regional trade peaked at $1.1 billion in 1980. Industrial production doubled. But intra-regional imbalances, oil price shocks, falling commodity export prices, political conflict and tensions, and heavy external debt service burdens brought CACM to a virtual standstill by 1986. Growth possibilities based on CACM's past protected import-substitution strategy are exhausted. Yet trade has somewhat recovered and CACM still plays an important role in the region's economy, which has a combined market of almost 27 million people. Most of CACM's free trade and cooperative institutional arrangements remain in force.

Resumption of the integration process based on a strategy of developing efficient, globally competitive production not dependent on a high degree of protection is essential to Central America's economic recovery and job creation, and therefore to the alleviation of migratory pressures.

- The United States and, with its encouragement, the international financial institutions and other international donors should contribute to the revitalization of the Central American Common Market.

CARICOM—Slow in Coming Together

The 13 small English-speaking countries of the Caribbean Basin have been moving toward regional integration since formation of the Caribbean Free Trade Association (CARIFTA) in 1965 and, later, the Caribbean Community and Common Market (CARICOM) in 1973. However, members did not begin to trade freely among themselves until late 1988, and 8 countries are still permitted to protect key products. CARICOM's governing body has set July 4, 1993, as the deadline for fully activating the Common Market. Members are concerned that further delay would adversely affect their trading prospects in light of the emergence of major developed-country trading blocs, i.e., the European Community and the U.S.-Canada Free Trade Agreement.

- The U.S. should actively support CARICOM efforts at integration.

Encouraging Exports of Manufactured Goods

Many of the migrant-sending countries have emphasized the export of manufactured goods. In order not to make these exports too expensive, they have lowered import tariffs and eliminated nontariff restrictions that had previously excluded foreign input necessary to produce for export. This is particularly true of Mexico. To a great extent, the United States has already benefitted from the unilateral lowering of barriers by these countries. At the same time, however, U.S. import restrictions weaken legislative initiatives aimed at promoting economic growth and political stability in the Caribbean region. For example, the allocation of U.S. import quotas on manufactured goods such as textiles, apparel and steel is based on historical precedent rather than current U.S. priorities. This favors established suppliers such as the newly industrialized East Asian nations.

- Quota allocations for textiles, apparel and steel should be progressively shifted in favor of Mexico and CBI beneficiary countries.

The United States encourages Western Hemisphere countries to export their products through a number of programs, such as the CBI, the Generalized System of Preferences (GSP) and the practice of levying duties only on the value added abroad on products made with U.S. components. For some migrant-sending countries, other U.S. import barriers, such as restrictions on sugar, outweigh all the foregoing benefits combined.

- The United States should make a special effort in the current Uruguay Round of Multilateral Trade Negotiations of the General Agreement on Tariffs and Trade (GATT) to reduce trade barriers that affect exports of Western Hemisphere migrant-sending countries.

Agriculture

The development process in Mexico and Caribbean Basin countries has resulted in large-scale rural outmigration over the past 30 years. Some migration has been directly to the United States. Most, however, has been in-country to urban areas, continually reinforcing emigration pressures from these overcrowded cities to the United States.

The Commission recognizes that the United States is limited in what it can do directly to halt or reverse these processes. But the United States can contribute indirectly through its advisory, lending and training programs in the agricultural sector and, most importantly, by improving access to its markets for sending country agricultural products. The Commission strongly supports ongoing technical assistance being provided by the U.S. Agency for International Development (AID) and the Department of Agriculture to raise agricultural, agro-industry and non-agricultural employment in rural areas.

The Commission supports the Administration's initiative seeking eventual elimination of all trade-distorting agricultural policies. As a first step, the United States proposed in the Uruguay Round of the GATT that all quota restriction and other non-tariff distortions be converted to their tariff equivalent. These tariffs could then be gradually reduced or eliminated. The Commission recognizes that attainment of the U.S. objective will entail a difficult negotiating process. Meanwhile, the United States should give special consideration to two commodities of critical importance to most sending countries in the Caribbean Basin: sugar and coffee.

After seven years of open markets, Congress in 1981 restored a sugar price support program to protect a relatively small number of U.S. sugar growers and processors. The sugar support system is a classic use of protection benefitting domestic producers at the expense of U.S. consumers and lower-cost foreign suppliers. This has had an adverse economic effect on both lower-cost sugar-producing countries in the area—whose exports to the United States dropped drastically—and the U.S. consumer, for whom the cost of sugar rose. Legislation before the Congress would partially restore Caribbean Basin sugar quotas.

- The Commission supports partial restoration of Caribbean Basin sugar quotas pending a phased return to a free market situation.

The United States should also assess other potential uses of sugar cane derivatives, with particular attention to the use of ethanol as a less polluting fuel.

With regard to coffee, the absence since July 1989 of worldwide quotas under the subsequently-lapsed International Coffee Organization (ICO) has caused serious drops in the export earnings of some key migrant-sending coffee producers, e.g., Colombia and El Salvador. The situation reflects the culmination of years of disagreement between the United States and major coffee-producing countries over coffee quotas and discount sales. Talks seeking a consensus for a renewed and reformed ICO began in late 1989 after President Virgilio Barco of Colombia made a special appeal to President Bush, who promised to review the situation.

- Discussions on coffee trade issues should be continued with a view to stabilizing prices.

The Commission recognizes that this is not a free trade solution.

Job Creation Through Section 936

Section 936 of the Internal Revenue Code was designed to enhance Puerto Rico's attraction as a manufacturing site and to encourage employment-producing investments by U.S. corporations there. The law exempts certain income from their Puerto Rican operations from U.S. taxes. The Tax Reform Act of 1986 expanded the exemption to include interest on loans for projects in CBI countries. Funds on deposit in Puerto Rico can now be used for loans at favorable interest rates to qualifying projects, including complementary (twin plant) and stand-alone operations. The Section 936 Program has been an important development and job-creation tool for Puerto Rico.

- Section 936 should be continued. Puerto Rico should remain its primary beneficiary, but efforts should be made to expand its employment-generating effect in CBI countries through greater utilization of 936 funds in labor-intensive operations in such countries.

The Co-Production Partnership

Co-production strategies enable developing countries to generate jobs, earn foreign exchange, modernize plants, and undertake self-sustaining industrial development. In Mexico, *maquiladora* (assembly) operations originated in 1965 to attract investments to generate jobs for returning workers when the Bracero Program (1942–64) was terminated. U.S. companies send American-made components to plants on the Mexican side of the border for further processing, and then import the assembled goods paying duty only on the value added in Mexico. In 1989, maquiladoras accounted for over 15 percent of Mexico's manufacturing jobs, earning about $3 billion in foreign exchange. If successful, today's assembly operations will evolve into a full-fledged manufacturing industry, enabling Mexico to develop its own capability to generate technology.

In order to maximize the benefits of maquiladora activities and to increase local inputs, Mexico must persevere in its efforts to integrate the maquiladora industry more fully into the national economy. Facilitating the location of maquiladoras in the interior of Mexico will accelerate this process.

- The United States should support Mexican requests to international financial institutions for funds to improve infrastructure in interior Mexican locations capable of hosting maquiladora activities.
- The Commission strongly urges the two governments, and the governments of other migrant-sending countries, to be vigilant about protection of worker rights and labor standards in maquiladora and other assembly plants.

Free trade zones (FTZs), patterned after Mexico's maquiladoras, have developed in Caribbean Basin countries. FTZs are essentially in-bond assembly operations that produce finished or semi-finished goods from largely imported components. By 1989, offshore assembly activities accounted for close to 200,000 jobs, 112,000 of them in the Dominican Republic alone. Offshore assembly offers the smaller Central American and Caribbean economies the opportunity to accelerate growth and increase employment.

Co-production assembly and manufacturing has had spectacular growth throughout the migrant-sending region. However, many foreign assembly plants are alleged to be sweatshops where poorly paid workers toil under exploitative conditions. By local standards, working conditions and wages in foreign assembly operations are generally above the national average. There has been considerable debate about the extent to which Mexican maquiladoras and offshore assembly operations in the Caribbean Basin affect employment levels in the United States. Regardless of one's views on these issues, increased economic interdependence suggests that growth in foreign assembly carries its own momentum.

Technology

Increased foreign direct investments can do more for technological development in migrant-sending countries than any other measure. The acquisition of modernizing technology which accompanies foreign direct investment is essential to development. Technology transfer and adaptation require not only a hospitable climate for foreign direct investment, but adequate protection of intellectual property through patents, trademarks and other safeguards for trade secrets.

- Migrant-sending countries should encourage technological modernization by strengthening and assuring intellectual property protection and by removing existing impediments to investment.

Worker Rights

The linkage between trade policy and worker rights began with the enactment of the CBI legislation in 1983. Congress later included worker rights provisions in legislation authorizing the GSP, the Overseas Private Investment Corporation, and U.S. participation in the Multilateral Investment Guarantee Agency of the World Bank. Most recently, Congress provided, in the Omnibus Trade Bill of 1988, that linkage between labor standards and trade must be a principal U.S. negotiating goal in the current Uruguay Round of the GATT, and that the denial of internationally recognized worker rights constitutes an unfair trade practice.

- Consistent with U.S. law, the Commission supports linking trade benefits to respect for worker rights.

- The United States and international development agencies and financial institutions should become more actively involved in promoting labor welfare.

TARGETING MIGRANT-SENDING REGIONS FOR ECONOMIC GROWTH

The pattern of concentrated migratory flows from specific regions within countries suggests it may be possible to reduce undocumented immigration to the United States by targeting economic development in those areas.

For regional development programs to succeed, it is essential that development policies be sustained, sectoral policies be coordinated and resources be allocated carefully. Regional development efforts should not be targeted to resource-poor areas with meager development prospects. They should instead be oriented to nearby regions with greater development potential that may offer improved economic alternatives to prospective migrants.

Regional development is particularly appropriate for Mexico, where considerable numbers of undocumented migrants are known to originate from specific areas in a few states. Mexico should itself take the initiative by improving the physical infrastructure of regions containing migrant-sending communities, and providing incentives for domestic and foreign investors to locate there.

- International financial institutions should give priority to development projects that focus on decentralized growth in Mexico's poorer regions.

DEVELOPING SMALL BUSINESS

Small businesses in the formal and informal sectors are a major force in the economies of Mexico, Central America and the Caribbean. The small enterprise sector provides employment for about a third of the region' economically active population. Small businesses tend to be family owned and operated, hire few employees, and are generally undercapitalized and technologically disadvantaged. Their access to credit is limited, as is their choice of managerial, marketing and production techniques.

Bureaucratic requirements often constrain entry into the formal sector and pose major problems for small firms already within it. The informal sector thus often serves as a refuge for the urban poor, and provides employment to an increasing number of women. However, remaining outside the legal framework increases risks and vulnerability to exploitation.

In recognition of their income and employment potential, credit and technical assistance to the small business sector are currently the focus of many development organizations, including AID, the World Bank, and the Inter-American Development Bank. These agencies work in cooperation with local, nongovernmental groups at the grassroots level. The programs are intended to generate additional income and employment, but are precarious because of high default rates.

- National and international development agencies should work with sending-country governments to reduce legal and bureaucratic impediments to small business development.

- Local and foreign private business sectors should increase support for small business assistance programs. Ways should be sought for greater participation of private commercial banks in financing small businesses, including those owned by migrant households.

Remittances

In countries with significant emigration, most migrant remittances are used to pay for basic necessities and little goes to productive investment. But remittances have great potential as an investment resource, particularly in the migrant-sending communities to which they are sent. Millions of legal residents in the United States have close ties to areas where undocumented migrants originate and have a strong commitment to assisting their families and communities. If remittances were to be channeled into productive small businesses and these succeed in generating jobs and higher incomes, emigration pressures should eventually abate in those areas.

Migrant remittances could be used to help capitalize national or regional development banks serving small business. By voluntarily pooling their savings with other financial resources, migrants could maximize their returns and at the same time invest in the development of their homelands.

- Individual migrant investments should be complemented by other financial resources from official and private institutions and tied to programs supporting the small business sector. AID should take the lead in fostering cooperative mechanisms to carry out this objective.

STRUCTURAL ADJUSTMENT PROCESS

The guiding development strategy in Latin America and the Caribbean in the decades following World War II was to create domestic industries whose output could substitute for imports. Because many domestic markets were too small to support an efficient industrial base, especially in the Caribbean and Central America, regional integration schemes developed to widen the scope for import substitution. These organizations stressed protected regional markets.

The program had mixed results. Imports did not generally decline; instead, they shifted from final consumer products to intermediate goods needed in the new industries created. Because the programs were financed at the expense of agriculture, its output usually suffered. In most areas, the concentration on overall economic growth translated into increasingly unequal income distribution. While Mexico, the Dominican Republic, Trinidad and Tobago and some Central American countries achieved high rates of economic growth, they were not prepared for the shift from producing simple consumer goods to more complex products requiring higher levels of technology.

Development strategies have now shifted to de-emphasize protectionism and stress competition. Most migrant-sending countries in the Western Hemisphere—with Mexico in the forefront—are restructuring their economies. Private initiative is increasing. Private foreign direct investment is avidly sought. Export promotion is taking its place alongside the production of goods for the domestic market.

The process of structural adjustment involves the transition of an economy from a state-dominated model to one in which the market plays the major role, where prices rather than administrative decisions determine the allocation of most resources, and where regulation is designed primarily to foster rather than stifle competition. Undertaking the steps needed to decrease price distortions and allocate resources to the most efficient areas of a country's economy is always a painful process. It entails such actions as devaluing the currency, eliminating subsidies and increasing interest rates. Imports usually become more expensive. The cost of borrowing increases.

- The United States should condition bilateral aid to sending countries on their taking the necessary steps toward structural adjustment. Similarly, U.S. support for non-project lending by the international financial institutions should be based on the implementation of satisfactory adjustment programs. Efforts should be made to ease transitional costs in human suffering.

- U.S. policies should complement and not frustrate adjustment mechanisms in migrant-sending countries. In practical terms this means, for example, that a move toward export promotion should not be negated by U.S. import barriers.

IMPROVING THE FINANCIAL OUTLOOK

Western Hemisphere economies have been seriously burdened during the past decade by an outflow of capital. Oil price increases during the 1970s transferred resources to oil-exporting countries which became the basis for the petrodollars used by commercial banks to underpin much of the buildup of foreign debt. The United States during the 1980s became the largest single user of foreign savings, thereby diminishing its availability and raising its cost to developing countries. Overvalued exchange rates and political instability stimulated capital flight in many countries. Investment needed to create jobs has lagged and public infrastructure has deteriorated. The need to service internal and external debt has drained public budgets of funds for social services, causing substantial personal hardships.

Responsibilities for action to correct the financial environment must be shared. The single most important cooperative measure the United States could take is to correct its own fiscal deficit. The Commission has no illusions as to the difficulties involved, but must acknowledge this reality. Migrant-sending countries are themselves responsible for internal policies to establish development programs and create a domestic environment that attracts foreign investors.

Servicing External Debt

By reducing resources available internally, the burden of servicing external debt has aggravated the economic distress of migrant-sending countries and caused extensive suffering among their people. It has also limited some of the potential benefits to the United States of increasingly open access to Western Hemisphere markets, largely because debt-service payments are limiting the foreign exchange available for imports. The degree of debt has varied by country, but interest payments have typically been about 25–50 percent of exports of goods and services.

The transfer of resources from debtor countries has placed a major burden on their budgets and balance of payments. Investment in public works and services have had to be drastically curtailed. The quality of life has eroded for large segments of the population, particularly the poor and those persons already prone to emigrate.

The Baker Plan of 1985 recognized the failure of a policy that forced countries to contract their economies in order to pay interest on foreign debt, but it foundered for lack of substantial new commercial bank lending. The Brady Plan of 1989 recognized this shortcoming and proposed a menu of choices for commercial banks that includes reductions of principal or interest on old debts, as well as new lending. While the Commission commends the effort made by Secretary Brady to change the negotiating context for debt restructuring, it doubts the Brady plan will be sufficient. The United States and other industrial countries should keep the debt issue under constant scrutiny and be prepared to take new initiatives.

- The key consideration in addressing the debt problem is to assure that the painful efforts of debtor countries to restructure their economies not be frustrated by excessive debt service burdens which entail a major cost in human suffering.

PROMOTING HUMAN RESOURCES

Many of the problems migrant-sending countries face are aggravated by high population growth rates and low levels of educational achievement. Voluntary family planning and improved educational systems are essential to socioeconomic development.

Rapid Population and Labor Force Growth

Most of the world's developing regions experienced a phenomenal acceleration in population growth rates following World War II. Immunization through

modern public health programs, large scale sanitation measures, and the introduction of chemical insecticides and antibiotics dramatically reduced mortality,
particularly of infants and young children. In the absence of offsetting declines in
births, the rate of natural increase soared.

Mexico's population more than tripled between 1940 and 1980, from 20 to 67
million people. An additional 21 million added during the last decade bring the
total to 88 million. This pattern was much the same in Central America, whose
population (including Panama) increased from about nine million in 1950 to over
28 million in 1990. With minor variations, these trends were repeated elsewhere in the Western Hemisphere.

With a delay of one to two decades, such growth in population produces
equally rapid growth in the labor force. One million persons now enter Mexico's
labor market each year, compared with two million new jobseekers in the United
States, which has almost three times Mexico's population. In the entire Caribbean Basin region and Mexico, the number of people in the labor market will
have almost quadrupled from 24 million in 1950 to 92 million by the year 2000.

In response, almost all migrant-sending countries have fostered voluntary
family planning programs. A secondary but equally important objective of these
programs is to promote maternal and child health.

- The Commission endorses the continued financing of voluntary family planning
  efforts, including those which promote natural family planning. If they are to be
  effective, such efforts to foster responsible parenthood must take into account
  the Latin American moral and cultural atmosphere in which they are
  implemented.

Education

Raising educational levels is essential to socioeconomic development and reduction of migratory pressure. An educated population is key to raising productivity. Increasing education is correlated to declining fertility and improved
nutritional standards. Vocational education is a prime necessity. Better paid
skilled manual workers—badly needed in migrant-sending economies—are not
as prone to emigrate as less trained workers earning lower wages.

Educational programs in localities with high migration rates could emphasize
development of skills, vocational and white collar, for which there is a relatively
high demand in the broader economic region. This would entail assessing prospective labor demands by skill levels and gearing regional school systems to
provide students with appropriate training. This goal is attainable in a large
country such as Mexico, which has a well-developed system of rapidly growing
secondary cities.

One way to overcome the shortcomings of the limited resources and relatively
small populations of the smaller Central American and Caribbean countries is to
create or strengthen existing regional training institutions to serve the needs of

more than one country. These training centers have already been effective in helping reduce shortages of highly educated workers.

- Congress and AID should program assistance funds for increased vocational education in migrant-sending countries.

Following the 1984 recommendations of the National Bipartisan Commission on Central America (Kissinger Commission), the United States funded programs to provide educational opportunities in the United States for disadvantaged persons from Central American and Caribbean countries. Such programs not only enhance educational opportunities and employment potential when students return to their home countries, but expose them to the culture and democratic ideals of the United States as well.

- The Congress should continue to fund such programs, include Mexico as a participant, and expand the scope of scholarship programs in the United States.

EFFORTS TO SAVE NATURAL RESOURCES AND THE ENVIRONMENT

Rapid population growth in the migrant-sending countries and measures leading to economic development often have led to considerable environmental degradation and erosion of the natural resource base. As available natural resources have diminished, competition for them has intensified pressures for people to migrate across borders.

Although damage is already severe, some patterns of destruction could be reversed by sustainable agricultural practices and measures to preserve natural ecosystems. The latter are not incompatible with economic growth as long as development activities are consistent with sustainable resource management. Environmentally sound development projects that generate employment include agroforestry, agricultural practices based on traditional agroecosystems, and multipurpose use of the forest, including ecotourism.

- The Commission strongly endorses the current practice of requiring environmental impact statements for all projects funded by international development assistance agencies.
- Further, regional centers cooperating with existing international agricultural research networks should be established to encourage the development of techniques to minimize ecological damage in agriculture.

The Mexican side of the U.S.-Mexico border is a special case in point. An area of booming economic growth, it is also characterized by poverty and severe pollution. Rapid industrialization has created serious concern for environmental degradation. Poor water quality, untreated sewage, agricultural runoffs damaging to local water supplies, air pollution, and improper disposal of hazardous and toxic substances affect both sides of the border.

- The Commission urges a concerted effort by both governments to improve the quality of life in border areas.

REDIRECTING ASSISTANCE FLOWS

The Commission is concerned that the U.S. foreign assistance program does not enjoy wide public support. Conflicting rationales and unclear objectives, unrealistic Congressional directives, the visibility of funds for foreign assistance at a time of budgetary stringency, and a widespread public perception that the money is not well spent contribute to popular opposition.

Foreign Aid

Evaluations in 1989 of the foreign assistance program by AID itself and by a House Foreign Affairs Committee task force emphasized the need for dramatic changes in direction of the program in order to make it politically viable and an effective instrument for global development.

Foreign assistance must be streamlined by eliminating bureaucratic red tape as well as redundant, unnecessary and conflicting objectives. The Commission is convinced that a more effective and targeted aid program and one which is sensitive to migration considerations would help in securing public and political support.

More U.S. development assistance should be channeled through private voluntary organizations (PVOs) because of their understanding of local conditions, needs and demands. PVOs are apt to stress long-term development and humanitarian concerns instead of the short-term political goals often imposed by Congress and the State Department.

- Efforts to involve local organizations in the project preparation phase of development assistance should be increased.
- AID should be required to assess the potential migration impact of development projects and then evaluate the actual impact after they are implemented.
- AID should channel more funds through private voluntary organizations.

Development Strategies and Funds for Central America

Of the two million people in Central America who have been uprooted by conflict and instability, about one third are displaced within their own country. The others have crossed into neighboring countries. Another 500,000 to one million have emigrated to the United States. The plight of these migrants and displaced persons poses one of the most difficult challenges facing Central American governments and is one of the most volatile political problems related to the peace process. These people have been identified by Central American governments and the international community as the priority group for receiving assistance.

There is a growing international consensus that development-oriented programs, rather than just short-term humanitarian assistance, can better address the needs of refugees and displaced persons in Central America. This is a welcome and needed change in focus. For it to succeed, greater cooperation by the United States and other donors is essential.

- The United States should support the process adopted by the United Nations-sponsored International Conference on Central American Refugees in Guatemala in May 1989 and channel more funds through the U.N. High Commissioner for Refugees (UNHCR), the U.N. Development Program (UNDP) and other relevant international organizations dealing with migration and development.

- Most importantly, the United States and the UNHCR should focus more attention and resources on voluntary repatriation and reintegration efforts, including counseling and the establishment of appropriate mechanisms to monitor the well-being and safety of returnees.

BILATERAL AND MULTILATERAL COOPERATION

Sending countries are generally unconcerned about the impact their migrants may be having on receiving countries. They often view emigration as a necessary escape valve. The United States has not made this issue a high priority and has been reluctant to raise it in bilateral discussions with sending countries. Neither the United Nations nor the international community as a whole has paid much attention to the issue of international migration, except in the context of refugee or refugee-like movements. In many cases, migration has been viewed by both sending and receiving countries as a foreign policy irritant. In others, it is not considered important enough to be on bilateral agendas.

- The International Organization for Migration (IOM) should play a larger role in Western Hemisphere migration discussions by convening meetings and seminars with high-level participation from the United States and Latin American member governments.

- The United States should give higher priority to the issue of unauthorized migration and seek greater cooperation on the part of sending countries regarding certain enforcement measures (for example, to curtail smuggling rings or fraudulent document activities).

BORDER DEVELOPMENT AND COOPERATION

A unique culture has developed among Mexican and U.S. border communities, which have become economically interdependent. Hundreds of millions of legal border crossings take place each year—for shopping, work, entertainment or medical treatment—creating an amalgam of U.S. and Mexican society. Extended families often live on both sides of the border. Economically, border areas are highly diverse, containing some of the poorest localities in the United States and some of the fastest growing areas in Mexico. Public and private infrastructure is deficient on both sides.

Many common border problems are now addressed by joint commissions or other bodies. For example, the International Boundary and Water Commission (IBWC) operates quietly and efficiently to deal with boundary disagreements and the quality, quantity and sharing of surface water. The environmental agencies of the two countries—the Secretaría de Desarrollo Urbano y Ecología (SEDUE) and the Environmental Protection Agency (EPA)—chair the national delegations that work together successfully on environmental issues throughout the year. Yet some border issues are handled only in ad hoc fashion. Funds for border infrastructure and economic development are lacking in both countries.

- The perennial issues dealing with border development, development funding, cross-border commerce, cultural exchange, and emergency needs should be assigned to a new Border Development and Cooperation Commission, modeled along the lines of the IBWC.

- To facilitate cultural interactions and encourage economic development, more border crossing points should be created and action expedited on those now under consideration.

CREATING AN AGENCY FOR MIGRATION AFFAIRS

Migration responsibilities are currently diffused among several different Cabinet departments and agencies. No mechanism exists within the U.S. government to assess the impact of U.S. policies and actions on migration, to rank migration against other priorities or to bring it to the attention of decisionmakers. Failure to pay sufficient attention to the effects of U.S. policies and actions on migratory flows has over many years contributed to a large influx of unauthorized people.

The Commission believes that a reorganization of the current structure within the Executive Branch for handling migration is urgently needed to ensure that migration be given a high priority on the U.S. domestic and foreign policy agendas, and that migration consequences be carefully considered by policymakers involved in trade, development and international economic matters.

- Immigration and refugee matters should be centralized and streamlined into a new Agency for Migration Affairs.

- Relevant federal agencies should be required to prepare and disseminate immigration impact statements (similar to environmental impact statements) to accompany major U.S. government decisions regarding development assistance and trade with migrant-sending countries.

U.S.-MEXICO POLICY COORDINATION

The official U.S. structure for cooperative consultation on economic development issues between the United States and migrant-sending countries in the Western Hemisphere is rudimentary, even with Mexico. U.S. relations with Mexico are more important in economic and strategic terms than with most other nations with which well-developed consultative arrangements exist, e.g., through the Organization for Economic Cooperation and Development. Mexico requires constant attention at the highest levels of the U.S. government.

- If a U.S.-Mexico free trade agreement is concluded, or a North American free trade agreement develops, the question of structure should be addressed in the negotiations and be part of the agreement.

- The Commission supports the creation of the position of Assistant Secretary of State for North American Affairs, to include Mexico and Canada.

AFTERWORD

Summing up, the Commission is convinced that expanded access by sending-countries to U.S. and other markets through increasingly free trade is the most promising stimulus to their future economic growth. The more able they are to sell their products abroad, the less their people will feel the need to seek economic opportunity away from home.

The major paradox the Commission found, however, is that the development process itself tends to stimulate migration in the short to medium term by raising expectations and enhancing people's ability to migrate. Thus, the development solution to unauthorized migration is measured in decades—even generations. Any serious cooperative effort to reduce migratory pressures at their source must stay the course in the face of short-term contradictory results.

Primary responsibility for their own development rests with the sending countries themselves. But if the United States is to cooperate in a long-term search for a mutually beneficial outcome, it must recognize that achieving it requires steadfastness of dedication and purpose over many years. If this message is understood, the Commission will have fulfilled its mandate.

NOTE

*The term "undocumented" is used interchangeably with "unauthorized" throughout this Report and refers to persons in the United States without legal authorization.

Appendix: Social Indicators of Development

Ghana	*page*	244
Greece		248
Jamaica		252
Lesotho		256
Malawi		260
Mexico		264
Nigeria		268
Pakistan		272
Philippines		276
Turkey		280

Ghana

	Unit of measure	25-30 years ago	15-20 years ago	Most recent estimate (mre)	Same region / income group		
					Sub-Saharan Africa	Low-income	Next higher income group
HUMAN RESOURCES							
Size, growth, structure of population							
Total population (mre = 1988)	millions	7.83	9.84	14.04	466	2,881	629
14 and under	% of pop.	..	..	..	46.8	35.4	38.3
15-64	"	..	..	..	50.4	60.2	57.4
Age dependency ratio	unit	..	..	..	0.98	0.66	0.74
Percentage in urban areas	% of pop.	26.2	29.8	32.3	31.7	34.2	56.1
Females per 100 males							
Urban	number	..	..	..	..	..	..
Rural	"	..	..	..	..	..	..
Population growth rate	annual %	1.8	2.2	3.4	3.1	2.0	2.2
	"	4.0	2.7	4.8	6.1	3.7	3.5
Urban/rural growth differential	difference	3.0	0.7	1.7	4.1	2.2	2.5
Projected population: 2000	millions	..	..	19.85	673	3,625	805
Stationary population	"	..	..	59.62	..	..	..
Determinants of population growth							
Fertility							
Crude birth rate	per thou. pop.	47.0	45.4	46.2	47.2	30.4	31.5
Total fertility rate	births per woman	6.85	6.56	6.40	6.56	3.89	4.08
Contraceptive prevalence	% of women 15-49	..	1.0	..	..	57.4	..
Child (0-4) / woman (15-49) ratios							
Urban	per 100 women	..	..	..	..	..	..
Rural	"	..	..	..	..	..	..
Mortality							
Crude death rate	per thou. pop.	16.6	15.5	13.3	15.8	10.0	8.6
Infant mortality rate	per thou. live births	118.5	104.0	90.0	113.6	72.6	59.1
Under 5 mortality rate		..	..	145.0	173.4	174.8	96.5
Life expectancy at birth: overall	years	47.5	50.6	54.0	50.6	61.4	63.8
female	"	49.2	52.4	55.8	52.3	62.3	66.1
Labor force (15-64)							
Total labor force	millions	3.26	3.81	5.40	189	1,343	232
Agriculture	% of labor force	61.0	57.1	..	..	..	..
Industry	"	15.3	17.2	..	..	..	..
Female	"	43.0	41.9	40.0	38.0	36.0	31.2

	units						
Females per 100 males							
Urban	number	:	:	:	:	:	:
Rural	"	:	:	:	:	:	:
Participation rate: overall	% of labor force	41.9	38.9	35.8	41.6	49.2	39.0
female	"	35.5	32.2	28.5	30.8	34.9	23.5
Educational attainment of labor force							
School years completed: overall	years	:	:	:	:	:	:
male	"	:	:	:	:	:	:
NATURAL RESOURCES							
Area	thou. sq. km	239	239	239	22,242	36,997	17,083
Density	pop. per sq. km	33	41	57	20	76	36
Agricultural land	% of land area	25.8	26.1	26.3	32.7	36.1	38.3
Agricultural density	pop. per sq. km	127	158	216	62	211	94
Forests and woodland	thou. sq. km	98	91	84	6,634	9,154	5,449
Deforestation rate (net)	annual %	-0.7	-0.8	-0.8	-0.5	-0.3	-0.7
Access to safe water	% of pop.	35.0	56.0	36.5	..	73.4	76.7
Urban	"	86.0	93.0	75.5	..	..	..
Rural	"	14.0	39.0	24.2	..	..	46.3

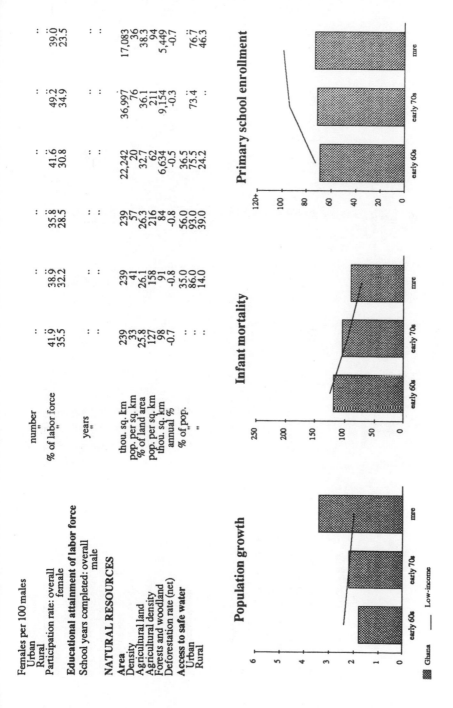

Population growth

Infant mortality

Primary school enrollment

Ghana ▦   Low-income ──

Ghana

	Unit of measure	25-30 years ago	15-20 years ago	Most recent estimate (mre)	Same region / income group		
					Sub-Saharan Africa	Low-income	Next higher income group
INCOME AND POVERTY							
Income							
GNP per capita (mre = 1988)	US$	230	280	400	320	310	1,270
Total household income	% of income						
Share to top 10% of households	"	:	:	:	:	:	:
Share to top 20% of households	"	:	:	:	:	:	:
Share to bottom 40% of households	"	:	:	:	:	:	:
Share to bottom 20% of households	"	:	:	:	:	:	:
Poverty							
Absolute poverty income: urban	US$ per person	:	:	:	:	:	:
rural	"	:	:	:	:	:	:
Pop. in absolute poverty: urban	% of pop.	:	:	:	:	:	:
rural	"	:	:	:	:	:	:
Prevalence of malnutrition (under 5)	% of age group	:	:	35.5	:	:	:
EXPENDITURE							
Food	% of GDP	:	39.3	:	:	:	:
Staples	"	:	:	:	:	:	:
Meat, fish, milk, cheese, eggs	"	:	:	:	:	:	:
Cereal imports	thou. metric tonnes	82	85	223	8,252	27,738	36,712
Food aid in cereals	"	:	32	110	3,786	7,122	7,851
Food production per capita	1979-81=100	125.9	135.4	105.1	94.4	116.4	97.0
Share of agriculture in GDP	% of GDP	43.5	47.7	50.6	35.1	33.0	16.0
Daily calorie supply	calories per person	1,950	2,162	1,759	2,095	2,392	2,767
Daily protein supply	grams per person	38	49	39	52	57	70
Housing							
Average household size	persons per household	:	8.4	:	:	:	:
Urban	"	:	:	:	:	:	:
Fixed investment: housing	% of GDP	:	:	:	:	:	:

Fuel and power

Indicator	Unit						
Energy consumption per capita	kg of oil equivalent	75.9	186.6	129.1	103.7	323.7	886.3
Households with electricity	% of households						
Urban	"	..	..	..	..	..	..
Rural	"	..	..	..	..	..	..

Transport and communication

Indicator	Unit						
Population per passenger car	persons	286	160	349	..	..	27
Fixed investment: transport equipment	% of GDP	..	2.4	1.2	..	..	..
Total road length	km	..	1.3	28,400	..	..	..
Population per telephone	persons	..	164	173	..	..	16

INVESTMENT IN HUMAN CAPITAL

Medical care

Indicator	Unit						
Population per: physician	persons	13,737	12,900	14,894	..	1,462	1,547
nurse	"	3,730	693	640	..	1,746	..
hospital bed	"	..	800	..	..	756	..
Access to health care	% of pop.	..	..	64.0	52.9	43.4	62.6
Immunized (under 12 months): measles	% of age group	..	..	51.0	45.7	41.3	64.7
DPT	% of age group	..	..	37.0	18.4	21.6	28.2
Oral Rehydration Therapy use (under 5)	% of cases	..	..	36.0	..	..	..

Education

Indicator	Unit						
	% of GDP	..	3.3	..	..	..	..
Gross enrollment ratios							
Primary: total	% of school-age group	69.0	71.0	73.0	78.0	99.3	106.8
female	"	57.0	62.0	63.0	67.6	87.8	101.3
Secondary: total	"	13.0	37.0	35.0	22.0	33.4	52.0
female	"	7.0	28.0	27.0	12.3	26.1	51.8
Tertiary: science/engineering	% of tertiary students	22.5	20.7	14.5	..	..	..
Pupil-teacher ratio: primary	pupils per teacher	32	31	24	40	10	28
secondary		20	23	16	35	19	18
Pupils reaching grade 4	% of cohort	..	82.3	85.6	..	..	81.0
Repeater rate: primary	% of total enrollment	..	2.3	..	..	..	8.0
Illiteracy rate: overall	% of pop. (age 15+)	..	..	46.8	53.4	43.3	26.2
female	% of females (age 15+)	..	..	57.2	64.0	56.5	32.5
Newspaper circulation	per thou. pop.	28.7	50.8	37.8	5.2	20.4	79.3

Source: World Bank International Economics Department, September 1989.

Greece

	Unit of measure	25-30 years ago	15-20 years ago	Most recent estimate (mre)	Same region / income group		Next higher income group
					Europe, Middle East, North Africa	Upper-middle-income	
HUMAN RESOURCES							
Size, growth, structure of population							
Total population (mre = 1988)	thousands	8,550	9,047	10,030	502,676	424,306	782,801
14 and under	% of pop.	25.5	23.9	20.3	38.3	34.1	20.5
15-64	"	65.7	63.9	65.9	56.8	60.2	66.6
Age dependency ratio	unit	0.52	0.57	0.51	0.75	0.65	0.49
Percentage in urban areas	% of pop.	47.5	55.3	61.4	49.7	68.8	78.3
Females per 100 males							
Urban	number	:	105	106	:	:	:
Rural	"	:	106	101	:	:	:
Population growth rate							
Urban	annual %	0.5	0.9	0.3	2.0	1.8	0.5
Urban	"	2.4	2.0	1.4	3.4	3.1	0.8
Urban/rural growth differential	difference	3.7	2.3	2.6	2.2	3.8	0.3
Projected population: 2000	thousands	:	:	10,258	661,662	521,035	829,402
Stationary population	"	:	:	9,375	:	:	:
Determinants of population growth							
Fertility							
Crude birth rate	per thou. pop.	17.7	15.7	11.9	33.5	26.4	13.7
Total fertility rate	births per woman	2.30	2.37	1.70	4.58	3.39	1.78
Contraceptive prevalence	% of women 15-49	:	:	:	:	:	:
Child (0-4) / woman (15-49) ratios							
Urban	per 100 women	:	33	32	:	:	:
Rural	"	:	42	35	:	:	:
Mortality							
Crude death rate	per thou. pop.	7.9	8.8	9.6	10.6	8.3	9.3
Infant mortality rate	per thou. live births	34.3	24.0	12.6	70.9	46.9	9.6
Under 5 mortality rate				14.0	100.2	58.4	19.7
Life expectancy at birth: overall	years	70.4	72.9	76.4	62.7	67.2	76.0
female	"	72.2	74.8	79.2	64.5	69.8	79.3
Labor force (15-64)							
Total labor force	thousands	3,414	3,460	3,823	173,176	156,018	365,613
Agriculture	% of labor force	47.2	36.6	:	:	:	:
Industry	"	23.7	27.5	:	:	:	:
Female	"	25.0	25.9	26.5	25.6	29.5	37.8

Females per 100 males	number						
Urban	"	..	105	107	..	..	..
Rural	"	..	108	99	..	..	..
Participation rate: overall	% of labor force	39.9	38.2	38.2	37.7	38.2	47.5
female	"	19.4	19.4	20.0	19.0	22.1	35.0
Educational attainment of labor force							
School years completed: overall	years	3.2	4.3	7.9	..	..	..
male	"	..	..	..	..	..	..
NATURAL RESOURCES							
Area	thou. sq. km	132	132	132	12,216	20,337	33,827
Density	pop. per sq. km	65	69	76	40	20	23
Agricultural land	% of land area	65.7	69.1	69.7	29.7	31.6	37.0
Agricultural density	pop. per sq. km	99	99	109	135	65	62
Forests and woodland	thou. sq. km	26	26	26	926	7,587	8,548
Deforestation rate (net)	annual %	0.3	0.0	0.0	0.2	-0.4	0.0
Access to safe water	% of pop.	..	65.0	..	62.0	79.4	..
Urban	"	..	88.0	..	88.4	90.1	..
Rural	"	..	37.0	..	44.2	62.7	..

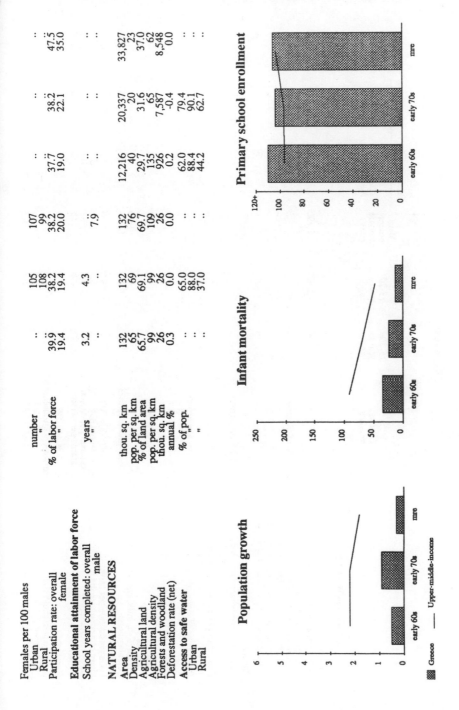

Population growth

Infant mortality

Primary school enrollment

Greece   —— Upper-middle-income

249

Greece

| | Unit of measure | 25-30 years ago | 15-20 years ago | Most recent estimate (mre) | Same region / income group | | |
					Europe, Middle East, North Africa	Upper-middle-income	Next higher income group
INCOME AND POVERTY							
Income							
GNP per capita (mre = 1988)	US$	700	2,370	4,790	1,660	2,940	17,080
Total household income	% of income						
Share to top 10% of households	"	..	..	..	..	..	..
Share to top 20% of households	"	..	..	..	..	..	..
Share to bottom 40% of households	"	..	..	..	..	..	..
Share to bottom 20% of households	"	..	..	..	..	..	..
Poverty							
Absolute poverty income: urban	US$ per person	..	..	..	..	..	..
rural	"	..	435	..	..	..	..
Pop. in absolute poverty: urban	% of pop.	..	..	..	..	..	..
rural	"	..	..	..	..	..	..
Prevalence of malnutrition (under 5)	% of age group	..	..	..	..	..	..
EXPENDITURE							
Food	% of GDP						
Staples	"	..	..	22.7	..	..	..
Meat, fish, milk, cheese, eggs	"	..	..	1.8	..	..	..
Cereal imports	thou. metric tonnes	277	1,013	11.0	..	..	..
Food aid in cereals	"	..	..	1,074	40,185	35,596	70,360
Food production per capita	1979-81=100	74.0	99.2	95.0	103.7	104.3	102.1
Share of agriculture in GDP	% of GDP	24.5	18.7	15.8	15.4	12.3	2.6
Daily calorie supply	calories per person	3,049	3,465	3,688	3,014	2,980	3,376
Daily protein supply	grams per person	96	108	115	83	80	101
Housing	% of GDP			8.9			
Average household size	persons per household	4	3	..	..	..	..
Urban	"	4	3	..	..	..	..
Fixed investment: housing	% of GDP	..	5.6	4.2	..	..	..

	Units						
Fuel and power							
Energy consumption per capita	% of GDP	..	..	2.4	..	..	..
	kg of oil equivalent	615.4	1,421.7	1,970.4	1,157.7	1,427.7	4,885.1
Households with electricity	% of households						
Urban		..	..	..	..	..	..
Rural		..	..	..	..	..	..
Transport and communication							
Population per passenger car	% of GDP	..	..	9.4	..	..	..
	persons	82	21	8	29	14	3
Fixed investment: transport equipment	% of GDP	..	1.6	1.9	..	..	..
Total road length	km	..	..	..	..	..	..
Population per telephone	persons	5	5	3	16	9	2
INVESTMENT IN HUMAN CAPITAL							
Medical care							
Population per: physician	% of GDP	..	..	4.8	..	..	..
	persons	710	600	351	1,009	1,021	530
nurse	"	600	990	454	798	602	168
hospital bed	"	..	200	162	446	..	..
Access to health care	% of pop.	..	..	..	..	..	..
Immunized (under 12 months): measles	% of age group	..	..	81.0	69.7	..	82.4
DPT		..	..	82.0	68.7	..	..
Oral Rehydration Therapy use (under 5)	% of cases	..	..	3.7	30.1	..	..
Education	% of GDP	..	..	..	..	..	..
Gross enrollment ratios	% of school-age group						
Primary: total		110.0	104.0	106.0	87.4	103.5	101.9
female	"	109.0	104.0	106.0	78.4	99.4	101.8
Secondary: total	"	49.0	78.0	88.0	47.5	57.8	94.3
female	"	41.0	69.0	87.0	38.7	56.7	93.7
Tertiary: science/engineering	% of tertiary students	18.2	23.6	27.3	..	..	..
Pupil-teacher ratio: primary	pupils per teacher	36	30	23	31	27	20
secondary	"	31	28	17	18	..	..
Pupils reaching grade 4	% of cohort	..	96.3	98.0	77.5	76.8	97.7
Repeater rate: primary	% of total enrollment	6.5	2.9	0.2	7.4	18.1	..
Illiteracy rate: overall	% of pop. (age 15+)	19.6	15.6	7.7	49.5	21.8	..
female	% of females (age 15+)	..	..	12.2	56.8	25.6	..
Newspaper circulation	per thou. pop.	103.0	103.0	119.7	68.1	86.5	315.6

Source: World Bank International Economics Department, September 1989.

Jamaica

| | Unit of measure | 25-30 years ago | 15-20 years ago | Most recent estimate (mre) | Same region / income group | | |
					Latin America, Caribbean	Lower-middle-income	Next higher income group
HUMAN RESOURCES							
Size, growth, structure of population							
Total population (mre = 1988)	thousands	1,760	2,043	2,429	416,138	629,214	424,306
14 and under	% of pop.	43.4	45.2	35.1	36.9	38.3	34.1
15-64	"	51.2	49.0	58.4	58.6	57.4	60.2
Age dependency ratio	unit	0.95	1.04	0.70	0.71	0.74	0.65
Percentage in urban areas	% of pop.	37.6	44.1	50.9	72.6	56.1	68.8
Females per 100 males							
Urban	number	..	..	..	104	..	..
Rural	"						
Population growth rate	annual %	1.0	1.6	1.2	2.0	2.2	1.8
Urban	"	3.1	2.8	2.8	3.2	3.5	3.1
Urban/rural growth differential	difference	3.3	2.1	2.9	3.7	2.5	3.8
Projected population: 2000	thousands	..	..	2,659	516,308	805,063	521,035
Stationary population	"			3,608			
Determinants of population growth							
Fertility							
Crude birth rate	per thou. pop.	38.2	29.9	25.7	28.7	31.5	26.4
Total fertility rate	births per woman	5.42	4.53	2.86	3.59	4.08	3.39
Contraceptive prevalence	% of women 15-49	..	38.0	52.0	..	..	..
Child (0-4) / woman (15-49) ratios							
Urban	per 100 women	..	..	..	..	..	..
Rural	"						
Mortality							
Crude death rate	per thou. pop.	8.4	7.0	5.5	7.5	8.6	8.3
Infant mortality rate	per thou. live births	48.6	29.4	18.0	54.2	59.1	46.9
Under 5 mortality rate	"			20.0	65.0	96.5	58.4
Life expectancy at birth: overall	years	65.5	68.5	73.9	66.4	63.8	67.2
female	"	67.3	70.5	76.7	69.2	66.1	69.8
Labor force (15-64)							
Total labor force	thousands	703	803	1,186	146,446	232,336	156,018
Agriculture	% of labor force	37.2	32.1	..	..	..	..
Industry	"	19.9	17.2	..	..	..	..
Female	"	41.0	44.6	45.8	26.6	31.2	29.5

	units						
Females per 100 males							
Urban	number	..	..	..	106		
Rural	"	..	..	..	88		
Participation rate: overall	% of labor force	39.9	39.3	48.4	35.0	39.0	38.2
female	"	31.3	34.3	44.0	18.5	23.5	22.1
Educational attainment of labor force							
School years completed: overall	years	..	..	..	..	..	..
male	"	..	..	..	..	..	..
NATURAL RESOURCES							
Area	thou. sq. km	10.99	10.99	10.99	20,396	17,083	20,337
Density	pop. per sq. km	160	186	218	20	36	20
Agricultural land	% of land area	44.4	43.2	42.2	36.3	38.3	31.6
Agricultural density	pop. per sq. km	361	430	517	55	94	65
Forests and woodland	thou. sq. km	2.10	2.00	1.89	9,776	5,449	7,587
Deforestation rate (net)	annual %	-0.5	-0.5	-0.5	-0.5	-0.7	-0.4
Access to safe water	% of pcp.	..	86.0	..	73.2	76.7	79.4
Urban	"	..	100.0	..	83.5	90.1	90.1
Rural	"	..	79.0	..	52.7	46.3	62.7

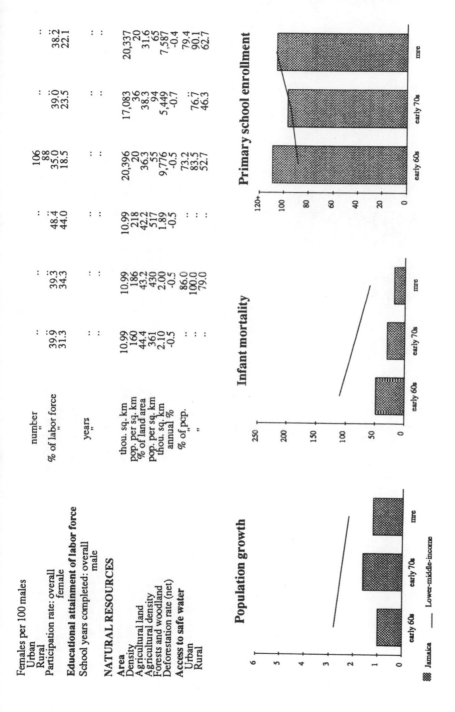

Population growth

Infant mortality

Primary school enrollment

Jamaica · Lower-middle-income

Jamaica

	Unit of measure	25-30 years ago	15-20 years ago	Most recent estimate (mre)	Same region / income group — Latin America, Caribbean	Lower-middle-income	Next higher income group
INCOME AND POVERTY							
Income							
GNP per capita (mre = 1988)	US$	550	1,240	1,080	1,940	1,270	2,940
Total household income	% of income						
Share to top 10% of households	"	..	..	..	..	..	..
Share to top 20% of households	"	..	..	..	..	..	..
Share to bottom 40% of households	"	..	..	..	..	..	..
Share to bottom 20% of households	"	..	..	..	..	..	..
Poverty							
Absolute poverty income: urban	US$ per person	..	..	..	..	..	..
rural	"	..	..	..	..	..	..
Pop. in absolute poverty: urban	% of pop.	..	..	..	..	..	..
rural	"	..	..	..	..	..	..
Prevalence of malnutrition (under 5)	% of age group	..	..	8.0	..	..	..
EXPENDITURE							
Food	% of GDP		22.4	26.7	..	..	..
Staples	"		9.8				
Meat, fish, milk, cheese, eggs	"		7.6				
Cereal imports	thou. metric tonnes	200	343	412	17,643	36,712	35,596
Food aid in cereals	"	..	6	208	..	7,851	..
Food production per capita	1979-81=100	113.7	97.9	100.1	100.7	97.0	104.3
Share of agriculture in GDP	% of GDP	9.9	7.4	6.1	11.7	16.0	12.3
Daily calorie supply	calories per person	2,231	2,678	2,590	2,704	2,767	2,980
Daily protein supply	grams per person	58	70	58	69	70	80
Housing	% of GDP		7.9	10.9	..	..	..
Average household size	persons per household	..	4	..	..	..	..
Urban	"	..	..	..	..	..	..
Fixed investment: housing	% of GDP	..	7.0	..	..	..	..

Indicator	Unit						
Fuel and power	% of GDP	..	1.9	4.9	..	..	..
Energy consumption per capita	kg of oil equivalent	703.0	1,378.2	852.5	974.1	886.3	1,427.7
Households with electricity	% of households						
Urban	"	..	..	..	..	..	..
Rural		..	..	..	..	..	..
Transport and communication	% of GDP	..	8.5	11.8	..	..	..
Population per passenger car	persons	38	22	..	16	27	14
Fixed investment: transport equipment	% of GDP	..	3.7	4.8	..	..	..
Total road length	km	..	..	17,700	..	..	..
Population per telephone	persons	..	20	..	11	16	9
INVESTMENT IN HUMAN CAPITAL							
Medical care	% of GDP	4.1	..	..	..	..	..
Population per: physician	persons	1,993	536	2,065	933	1,547	1,021
nurse	"	342	203	492	875	..	602
hospital bed		..	..	303	..	..	..
Access to health care	% of pop.	..	..	..	..	..	..
Immunized (under 12 months): measles	% of age group	..	..	62.0	52.7	62.6	..
DPT		..	..	81.0	62.4	64.7	..
Oral Rehydration Therapy use (under 5)	% of cases	..	..	6.2	33.6	28.2	..
Education	% of GDP	5.9	..	..	..	..	..
Gross enrollment ratios							
Primary: total	% of school-age group	109.0	97.0	106.0	108.1	106.8	103.5
female	"	106.0	98.0	107.0	105.2	101.3	99.4
Secondary: total	"	51.0	58.0	58.0	48.8	52.0	57.8
female	"	50.0	63.0	60.0	52.7	51.8	56.7
Tertiary: science/engineering	% of tertiary students	25.9	24.2	19.7	..	..	..
Pupil-teacher ratio: primary	pupils per teacher	24	32	36	26	28	27
secondary		..	34	29	..	18	..
Pupils reaching grade 4	% of cohort	..	..	98.6	66.3	81.0	76.8
Repeater rate: primary	% of total enrollment	..	3.6	3.9	17.9	8.0	18.1
Illiteracy rate: overall	% of pop. (age 15+)	..	..	..	16.7	26.2	21.8
female	% of females (age 15+)	..	..	..	19.0	32.5	25.6
Newspaper circulation	per thou. pop.	69.3	64.1	46.9	81.2	79.3	86.5

Source: World Bank International Economics Department, September 1989.

Lesotho

HUMAN RESOURCES

	Unit of measure	25-30 years ago	15-20 years ago	Most recent estimate (mre)	Same region / income group		Next higher income group
					Sub-Saharan Africa	Low-income	
Size, growth, structure of population							
Total population (mre = 1988)	millions	0.96	1.19	1.67	466	2,881	629
14 and under	% of pop.	40.7	41.7	43.0	46.8	35.4	38.3
15-64	"	55.6	54.7	53.5	50.4	60.2	57.4
Age dependency ratio	unit	0.80	0.83	0.87	0.98	0.66	0.74
Percentage in urban areas	% of pop.	6.0	10.8	18.5	31.7	34.2	56.1
Females per 100 males							
Urban	number	:	117	:	:	:	:
Rural	"	:	100	:	:	:	:
Population growth rate	annual %	1.9	2.4	2.7	3.1	2.0	2.2
Urban	"	11.0	6.5	7.7	6.1	3.7	3.5
Urban/rural growth differential	difference	9.6	4.6	6.1	4.1	2.2	2.5
Projected population: 2000	millions	:	:	2.26	673	3,625	805
Stationary population	"	:	:	5.73	:	:	:
Determinants of population growth							
Fertility							
Crude birth rate	per thou. pop.	42.4	42.4	41.0	47.2	30.4	31.5
Total fertility rate	births per woman	5.80	5.80	5.80	6.56	3.89	4.08
Contraceptive prevalence	% of women 15-49	:	:	:	:	57.4	:
Child (0-4) / woman (15-49) ratios							
Urban	per 100 women	:	50	:	:	:	:
Rural	"	:	65	:	:	:	:
Mortality							
Crude death rate	per thou. pop.	17.5	16.3	13.3	15.8	10.0	8.6
Infant mortality rate	per thou. live births	142.0	125.8	100.0	113.6	72.6	59.1
Under 5 mortality rate	"	:	:	144.0	173.4	174.8	96.5
Life expectancy at birth: overall	years	48.4	50.4	55.6	50.6	61.4	63.8
female	"	49.9	52.0	57.4	52.3	62.3	66.1
Labor force (15-64)							
Total labor force	millions	0.51	0.60	0.78	189	1,343	232
Agriculture	% of labor force	91.6	88.0	:	:	:	:
Industry	"	2.6	3.6	:	:	:	:
Female	"	47.5	46.9	43.8	38.0	36.0	31.2

Females per 100 males							
Urban	number	..	128	..	..	..	..
Rural	"	..	100	..	..	..	..
Participation rate: overall	% of labor force	52.8	50.3	47.2	41.6	49.2	39.0
female	"	47.7	45.2	40.1	30.8	34.9	23.5
Educational attainment of labor force							
School years completed: overall	years	..	..	..	..	..	..
male	"	..	..	..	..	..	..
NATURAL RESOURCES							
Area	thou. sq. km	30	30	30	22,242	36,997	17,083
Density	pop. per sq. km	32	39	54	20	76	36
Agricultural land	% of land area	84.8	78.2	76.4	32.7	36.1	38.3
Agricultural density	pop. per sq. km	37	50	70	62	211	94
Forests and woodland	thou. sq. km	..	..	..	6,634	9,154	5,449
Deforestation rate (net)	annual %	..	..	..	-0.5	-0.3	-0.7
Access to safe water	% of pop.	..	17.0	35.0	36.5	..	..
Urban	"	..	65.0	65.0	75.5	73.4	76.7
Rural	"	..	14.0	30.0	24.2	..	46.3

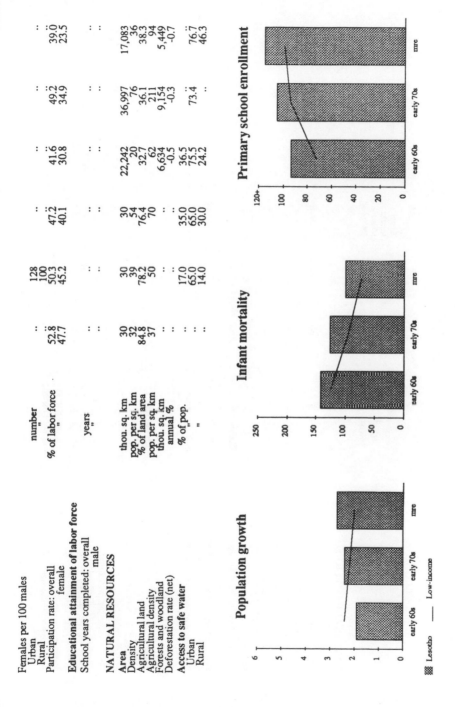

Population growth

Infant mortality

Primary school enrollment

▨ Lesotho   — Low-income

Lesotho

	Unit of measure	25-30 years ago	15-20 years ago	Most recent estimate (mre)	Same region / income group		Next higher income group
					Sub-Saharan Africa	Low-income	
INCOME AND POVERTY							
Income							
GNP per capita (mre = 1988)	US$	60	230	410	320	310	1,270
Total household income							
Share to top 10% of households	% of income	..	..	..			..
Share to top 20% of households	"	..	..	..			..
Share to bottom 40% of households	"	..	..	..			..
Share to bottom 20% of households	"	..	..	..			..
Poverty							
Absolute poverty income: urban	US$ per person	..	..	..			..
rural	"	..	..	..			..
Pop. in absolute poverty: urban	% of pop.	..	..	..			..
rural	"	..	..	..			..
Prevalence of malnutrition (under 5)	% of age group	..	..	27.0			
EXPENDITURE							
Food							
Staples	% of GDP	..	..	..			..
Meat, fish, milk, cheese, eggs	"	..	..	..			..
Cereal imports	thou. metric tonnes	24	56	94	8,252	27,738	36,712
Food aid in cereals	"	..	18	55	3,786	7,122	7,851
Food production per capita	1979-81=100	115.7	103.3	79.6	94.4	116.4	97.0
Share of agriculture in GDP	% of GDP	65.2	32.5	20.7	35.1	33.0	16.0
Daily calorie supply	calories per person	2,065	2,044	2,303	2,095	2,392	2,767
Daily protein supply	grams per person	63	62	66	52	57	70
Housing							
Average household size	persons per household	..	..	5			
Urban	"	..	..	..			..
Fixed investment: housing	% of GDP	..	2.5	..			..

Indicator	Unit						
Fuel and power	% of GDP						
Energy consumption per capita	kg of oil equivalent	..	..	..	103.7	323.7	886.3
Households with electricity	% of households	..	..	..	..	..	..
Urban	"	..	..	..	..	..	..
Rural	"	..	..	..	..	..	..
Transport and communication	% of GDP						
Population per passenger car	persons	332	341	246	..	..	27
Fixed investment: transport equipment	% of GDP	..	3.9	..	..	..	..
Total road length	km	..	..	4,000	..	..	..
Population per telephone	persons	..	..	108	..	..	16
INVESTMENT IN HUMAN CAPITAL							
Medical care	% of GDP						
Population per: physician	persons	20,063	30,400	18,614	..	1,462	1,547
nurse	"	4,698	3,870	..	..	1,746	..
hospital bed	"	..	600	..	..	756	..
Access to health care	% of pop.	..	..	50.0	..	..	..
Immunized (under 12 months): measles	% of age group	..	..	79.0	52.9	43.4	62.6
DPT	"	..	..	77.0	45.7	41.3	64.7
Oral Rehydration Therapy use (under 5)	% of cases	..	..	68.0	18.4	21.6	28.2
Education	% of GDP						
Gross enrollment ratios							
Primary: total	% of school-age group	94.0	105.0	115.0	78.0	99.3	106.8
female	"	114.0	123.0	127.0	67.6	87.8	101.3
Secondary: total	"	4.0	13.0	22.0	22.0	33.4	52.0
female	"	4.0	14.0	26.0	12.3	26.1	51.8
Tertiary: science/engineering	% of tertiary students	29.1	21.5	8.8	..	..	..
Pupil-teacher ratio: primary	pupils per teacher	57	53	53	40	10	28
secondary	"	20	26	21	35	19	18
Pupils reaching grade 4	% of cohort	..	79.3	73.1	..	..	81.0
Repeater rate: primary	% of total enrollment	..	6.0	22.6	..	..	8.0
Illiteracy rate: overall	% of pop. (age 15+)	..	..	26.4	53.4	43.3	26.2
female	% of females (age 15+)	..	..	15.5	64.0	56.5	32.5
Newspaper circulation	per thou. pop.	..	0.8	31.8	5.2	20.4	79.3

Source: World Bank International Economics Department, September 1989.

Malawi

<table>
<tr><td rowspan="3"></td><td rowspan="3">Unit of measure</td><td rowspan="3">25-30 years ago</td><td rowspan="3">15-20 years ago</td><td rowspan="3">Most recent estimate (mre)</td><td colspan="3">Same region / income group</td></tr>
<tr><td>Sub-Saharan Africa</td><td>Low-income</td><td>Next higher income group</td></tr>
<tr><td colspan="3"></td></tr>
<tr><td colspan="8">HUMAN RESOURCES</td></tr>
<tr><td colspan="8">Size, growth, structure of population</td></tr>
<tr><td>Total population (mre = 1988)</td><td>millions</td><td>3.98</td><td>5.24</td><td>8.16</td><td>466</td><td>2,881</td><td>629</td></tr>
<tr><td>14 and under</td><td>% of pop.</td><td>45.8</td><td>47.2</td><td>46.0</td><td>46.8</td><td>35.4</td><td>38.3</td></tr>
<tr><td>15-64</td><td>"</td><td>51.8</td><td>50.6</td><td>51.3</td><td>50.4</td><td>60.2</td><td>57.4</td></tr>
<tr><td>Age dependency ratio</td><td>unit</td><td>0.93</td><td>0.98</td><td>0.95</td><td>0.98</td><td>0.66</td><td>0.74</td></tr>
<tr><td>Percentage in urban areas</td><td>% of pop.</td><td>5.2</td><td>7.7</td><td>13.4</td><td>31.7</td><td>34.2</td><td>56.1</td></tr>
<tr><td>Females per 100 males</td><td></td><td></td><td></td><td></td><td></td><td></td><td></td></tr>
<tr><td>Urban</td><td>number</td><td>:</td><td>:</td><td>:</td><td>:</td><td>:</td><td>:</td></tr>
<tr><td>Rural</td><td>"</td><td>:</td><td>:</td><td>:</td><td>:</td><td>:</td><td>:</td></tr>
<tr><td>Population growth rate</td><td></td><td></td><td></td><td></td><td></td><td></td><td></td></tr>
<tr><td>Urban</td><td>annual %</td><td>2.3</td><td>2.9</td><td>3.1</td><td>3.1</td><td>2.0</td><td>2.2</td></tr>
<tr><td>Rural</td><td>"</td><td>5.5</td><td>7.5</td><td>8.6</td><td>6.1</td><td>3.7</td><td>3.5</td></tr>
<tr><td>Urban/rural growth differential</td><td>difference</td><td>3.3</td><td>4.9</td><td>6.1</td><td>4.1</td><td>2.2</td><td>2.5</td></tr>
<tr><td>Projected population: 2000</td><td>millions</td><td>:</td><td>:</td><td>12.28</td><td>673</td><td>3,625</td><td>805</td></tr>
<tr><td>Stationary population</td><td>"</td><td>:</td><td>:</td><td>96.47</td><td>:</td><td>:</td><td>:</td></tr>
<tr><td colspan="8">Determinants of population growth</td></tr>
<tr><td>Fertility</td><td></td><td></td><td></td><td></td><td></td><td></td><td></td></tr>
<tr><td>Crude birth rate</td><td>per thou. pop.</td><td>56.0</td><td>55.6</td><td>53.1</td><td>47.2</td><td>30.4</td><td>31.5</td></tr>
<tr><td>Total fertility rate</td><td>births per woman</td><td>7.75</td><td>7.66</td><td>7.60</td><td>6.56</td><td>3.89</td><td>4.08</td></tr>
<tr><td>Contraceptive prevalence</td><td>% of women 15-49</td><td>:</td><td>:</td><td>:</td><td>:</td><td>57.4</td><td>:</td></tr>
<tr><td>Child (0-4) / woman (15-49) ratios</td><td></td><td></td><td></td><td></td><td></td><td></td><td></td></tr>
<tr><td>Urban</td><td>per 100 women</td><td>:</td><td>:</td><td>:</td><td>:</td><td>:</td><td>:</td></tr>
<tr><td>Rural</td><td>"</td><td>:</td><td>:</td><td>:</td><td>:</td><td>:</td><td>:</td></tr>
<tr><td>Mortality</td><td></td><td></td><td></td><td></td><td></td><td></td><td></td></tr>
<tr><td>Crude death rate</td><td>per thou. pop.</td><td>26.3</td><td>23.3</td><td>19.6</td><td>15.8</td><td>10.0</td><td>8.6</td></tr>
<tr><td>Infant mortality rate</td><td>per thou. live births</td><td>199.8</td><td>182.6</td><td>150.0</td><td>113.6</td><td>72.6</td><td>59.1</td></tr>
<tr><td>Under 5 mortality rate</td><td>"</td><td></td><td></td><td>224.0</td><td>173.4</td><td>174.8</td><td>96.5</td></tr>
<tr><td>Life expectancy at birth: overall</td><td>years</td><td>39.1</td><td>42.0</td><td>46.0</td><td>50.6</td><td>61.4</td><td>63.8</td></tr>
<tr><td>female</td><td>"</td><td>39.8</td><td>42.9</td><td>47.7</td><td>52.3</td><td>62.3</td><td>66.1</td></tr>
<tr><td colspan="8">Labor force (15-64)</td></tr>
<tr><td>Total labor force</td><td>millions</td><td>1.94</td><td>2.38</td><td>3.33</td><td>189</td><td>1,343</td><td>232</td></tr>
<tr><td>Agriculture</td><td>% of labor force</td><td>92.0</td><td>87.0</td><td>:</td><td>:</td><td>:</td><td>:</td></tr>
<tr><td>Industry</td><td>"</td><td>3.2</td><td>5.6</td><td>:</td><td>:</td><td>:</td><td>:</td></tr>
<tr><td>Female</td><td>"</td><td>45.5</td><td>44.7</td><td>41.7</td><td>38.0</td><td>36.0</td><td>31.2</td></tr>
</table>

Females per 100 males							
Urban	number	:	:	:	:	:	39.0
Rural	"	:	:	:	:	:	23.5
Participation rate: overall	% of labor force	48.9	46.1	43.3	:	41.6	49.2
female	"	42.8	39.8	35.6	:	30.8	34.9
Educational attainment of labor force							
School years completed: overall	years	:	:	:	:	:	:
male	"	:	:	:	:	:	:
NATURAL RESOURCES							
Area	thou. sq. km	118	118	118	22,242	36,997	17,083
Density	pop. per sq. km	34	44	67	20	76	36
Agricultural land	% of land area	32.3	34.8	35.6	32.7	36.1	38.3
Agricultural density	pop. per sq. km	104	127	187	62	211	94
Forests and woodland	thou. sq. km	51	51	44	6,634	9,154	5,449
Deforestation rate (net)	annual %	0.0	0.0	-2.4	-0.5	-0.3	-0.7
Access to safe water	% of pop.	:	:	55.0	36.5	73.4	76.7
Urban	"	:	:	97.0	75.5	..	..
Rural	"	:	:	50.0	24.2	..	46.3

Population growth

x-axis: early 60s, early 70s, mre
y-axis: 0, 1, 2, 3, 4, 5, 6

Infant mortality

x-axis: early 60s, early 70s, mre
y-axis: 0, 50, 100, 150, 200, 250

Primary school enrollment

x-axis: early 60s, early 70s, mre
y-axis: 0, 20, 40, 60, 80, 100, 120+

Legend: ▓ Malawi   — Low-income

Malawi

| | Unit of measure | 25-30 years ago | 15-20 years ago | Most recent estimate (mre) | Same region / income group | | Next higher income group |
					Sub-Saharan Africa	Low-income	
INCOME AND POVERTY							
Income							
GNP per capita (mre = 1988)	US$	60	120	160	320	310	1,270
Total household income	% of income						
Share to top 10% of households	"	..	..	..	..	..	..
Share to top 20% of households	"	..	..	..	..	..	..
Share to bottom 40% of households	"	..	..	..	..	..	..
Share to bottom 20% of households	"	..	..	..	..	..	..
Poverty							
Absolute poverty income: urban	US$ per person	..	..	..	..	..	..
rural		..	..	..	..	..	..
Pop. in absolute poverty: urban	% of pop.	..	..	..	..	..	..
rural		..	..	..	..	..	..
Prevalence of malnutrition (under 5)	% of age group	..	..	22.6	..	..	..
EXPENDITURE							
Food	% of GDP	..	42.2	22.9	..	..	..
Staples	"	..	20.1	..	..	..	..
Meat, fish, milk, cheese, eggs	"	..	6.8	8.5	..	..	..
Cereal imports	thou. metric tonnes	19	41	11	8,252	27,738	36,712
Food aid in cereals	"		0	109	3,786	7,122	7,851
Food production per capita	1979-81=100	82.2	95.8	82.9	94.4	116.4	97.0
Share of agriculture in GDP	% of GDP	49.9	39.2	37.2	35.1	33.0	16.0
Daily calorie supply	calories per person	2,244	2,473	2,310	2,095	2,392	2,767
Daily protein supply	grams per person	66	72	65	52	57	70
Housing	% of GDP	..	4.9	6.8	..	..	..
Average household size	persons per household	..	3	..	..	..	..
Urban	"	..	4	..	..	..	..
Fixed investment: housing	% of GDP	..	3.6	1.1	..	..	..

Fuel and power

Indicator	Unit						
Energy consumption per capita	kg of oil equivalent	..	46.4	40.5	103.7	323.7	886.3
Households with electricity	% of households	..	..	..	..	..	..
Urban	"	..	..	..	..	..	..
Rural		25.3	2.1	3.6	..	..	..

Transport and communication

Indicator	Unit						
	% of GDP	..	6.0	7.8	..	..	..
Population per passenger car	persons	621	477	542	..	..	27
Fixed investment: transport equipment	% of GDP	..	6.7	2.2	..	..	..
Total road length	km	..	..	13,280	..	..	..
Population per telephone	persons	..	262	164	..	..	16

INVESTMENT IN HUMAN CAPITAL

Medical care

Indicator	Unit						
	% of GDP	..	1.5	2.1	..	..	..
Population per: physician	persons	47,321	5,333	11,564	..	1,462	1,547
nurse	"	40,979	..	3,135	..	1,746	..
hospital bed	"	5,333	..	..	..	756	..
Access to health care	% of pop.	..	..	54.0	..	..	..
Immunized (under 12 months): measles	% of age group	..	..	53.0	52.9	43.4	62.6
DPT		..	..	55.0	45.7	41.3	64.7
Oral Rehydration Therapy use (under 5)	% of cases	..	..	42.0	18.4	21.6	28.2

Education

Indicator	Unit						
	% of GDP	..	3.1	8.2	..	..	..
Gross enrollment ratios Primary: total	% of school-age group	44.0	44.0	64.0	78.0	99.3	106.8
female	"	32.0	32.0	55.0	67.6	87.8	101.3
Secondary: total	"	2.0	2.0	4.0	22.0	33.4	52.0
female	"	1.0	1.0	3.0	12.3	26.1	51.8
Tertiary: science/engineering	% of tertiary students	20	6.4	10.6	..	10	..
Pupil-teacher ratio: primary	pupils per teacher	..	61	63	40	19	28
secondary	"	..	19	21	35	..	18
Pupils reaching grade 4	% of cohort	..	66.5	60.3	..	..	81.0
Repeater rate: primary	% of total enrollment	..	16.5	20.5	..	..	8.0
Illiteracy rate: overall	% of pop. (age 15+)	..	..	58.8	53.4	43.3	26.2
female	% of females (age 15+)	..	..	69.2	64.0	56.5	32.5
Newspaper circulation	per thou. pop.	..	..	5.2	5.2	20.4	79.3

Source: World Bank International Economics Department, September 1989.

Mexico

	Unit of measure	25-30 years ago	15-20 years ago	Most recent estimate (mre)	Same region / income group		
					Latin America, Caribbean	Lower-middle-income	Next higher income group
HUMAN RESOURCES							
Size, growth, structure of population							
Total population (mre = 1988)	thousands	44,752	61,918	83,593	416,138	629,214	424,306
14 and under	% of pop.	46.7	46.5	38.7	36.9	38.3	34.1
15-64	"	49.9	50.1	57.8	58.6	57.4	60.2
Age dependency ratio	unit	1.00	1.00	0.73	0.71	0.74	0.65
Percentage in urban areas	% of pop.	54.9	62.8	71.1	72.6	56.1	68.8
Females per 100 males							
Urban	number	::	101	::	104	::	::
Rural	"	::	94	::			
Population growth rate	annual %	3.2	3.0	2.1	2.0	2.2	1.8
Urban	"	4.7	4.2	3.1	3.2	3.5	3.1
Urban/rural growth differential	difference	3.3	3.2	3.6	3.7	2.5	3.8
Projected population: 2000	thousands	::	::	104,840	516,308	805,063	521,035
Stationary population	"	::	::	170,243	::	::	::
Determinants of population growth							
Fertility							
Crude birth rate	per thou. pop.	44.9	37.7	28.7	28.7	31.5	26.4
Total fertility rate	births per woman	6.72	5.48	3.58	3.59	4.08	3.39
Contraceptive prevalence	% of women 15-49	::	::	53.0	::	::	::
Child (0-4) / woman (15-49) ratios							
Urban	per 100 women	::	75	::	::	::	::
Rural	"	::	100	::	::	::	::
Mortality							
Crude death rate	per thou. pop.	10.6	7.9	5.8	7.5	8.6	8.3
Infant mortality rate	per thou. live births	81.8	63.6	47.0	54.2	59.1	46.9
Under 5 mortality rate				55.0	65.0	96.5	58.4
Life expectancy at birth: overall	years	59.6	64.3	68.6	66.4	63.8	67.2
female	"	61.4	66.9	72.1	69.2	66.1	69.8
Labor force (15-64)							
Total labor force	thousands	12,571	17,928	28,724	146,446	232,336	156,018
Agriculture	% of labor force	49.6	40.3	::	::	::	::
Industry	"	21.9	26.6				
Female	"	16.5	22.6	27.1	26.6	31.2	29.5

Females per 100 males

	unit	Mexico early 60s	Mexico early 70s	Mexico mre	Lower-middle-income early 60s	Lower-middle-income early 70s	Lower-middle-income mre
Urban	number	..	103	..	106	..	..
Rural	"	..	92	..	88	..	..
Participation rate: overall	% of labor force	28.9	29.8	33.8	35.0	39.0	38.2
female	"	9.5	13.5	18.3	18.5	23.5	22.1

Educational attainment of labor force

	unit	Mexico early 60s	Mexico early 70s	Mexico mre	Lower-middle-income early 60s	Lower-middle-income early 70s	Lower-middle-income mre
School years completed: overall	years	..	..	..	..	..	..
male	"	..	..	..	..	..	..

NATURAL RESOURCES

	unit	Mexico early 60s	Mexico early 70s	Mexico mre	Lower-middle-income early 60s	Lower-middle-income early 70s	Lower-middle-income mre
Area	thou. sq. km	1,958	1,958	1,958	20,396	17,083	20,337
Density	pop. per sc. km	23	32	42	20	36	20
Agricultural land	% of land area	50.0	50.2	50.7	36.3	38.3	31.6
Agricultural density	pop. per sc. km	46	63	83	55	94	65
Forests and woodland	thou. sq. km	565	512	446	9,776	5,449	7,587
Deforestation rate (net)	annual %	-0.9	-1.0	-1.2	-0.5	-0.7	-0.4
Access to safe water	% of pop.	..	62.0	70.0	73.2	76.7	79.4
Urban	"	..	70.0	79.0	83.5	..	90.1
Rural	"	..	49.0	51.0	52.7	46.3	62.7

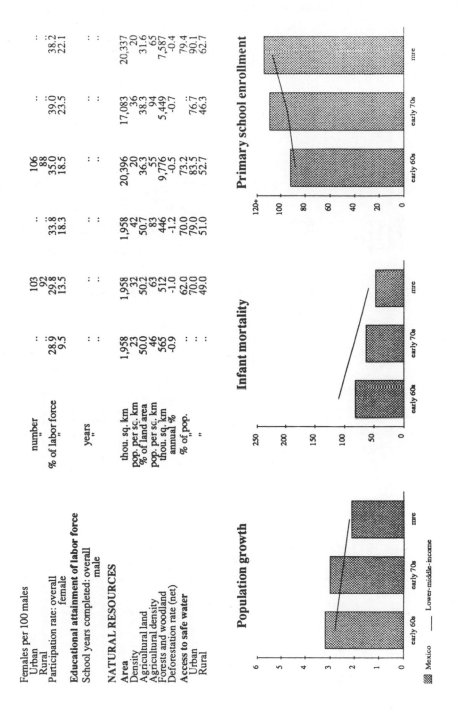

Population growth

Infant mortality

Primary school enrollment

Mexico   —— Lower-middle-income

Mexico

	Unit of measure	25-30 years ago	15-20 years ago	Most recent estimate (mre)	Same region / income group		
					Latin America, Caribbean	Lower-middle-income	Next higher income group
INCOME AND POVERTY							
Income							
GNP per capita (mre = 1988)	US$	470	1,360	1,820	1,940	1,270	2,940
Total household income	% of income						
Share to top 10% of households	"	61	61	..	..	..	..
Share to top 20% of households	"			..	..	..	..
Share to bottom 40% of households	"	10		..	..	..	..
Share to bottom 20% of households		3		..	..	..	..
Poverty							
Absolute poverty income: urban	US$ per person	..	..	..	..	..	..
rural	"	..	..	..	..	..	..
Pop. in absolute poverty: urban	% of pop.	..	..	..	..	..	..
rural	"	..	..	..	..	..	..
Prevalence of malnutrition (under 5)	% of age group	..	..	..	..	..	..
EXPENDITURE							
Food							
Staples	% of GDP	..	29.0	22.0	..	..	..
Meat, fish, milk, cheese, eggs	"	..	6.8	..	..	..	..
Cereal imports	thou. metric tonnes	175	3,720	4,797	17,643	36,712	35,596
Food aid in cereals	"	..	12.7	32	..	7,851	..
Food production per capita	1979-81=100	89.9	92.7	92.5	100.7	97.0	104.3
Share of agriculture in GDP	% of GDP	13.9	10.8	10.4	11.7	16.0	12.3
Daily calorie supply	calories per person	2,644	2,861	3,132	2,704	2,767	2,980
Daily protein supply	grams per person	67	72	81	69	70	80
Housing							
Average household size	persons per household	..	6.4	5.1	..	..	..
Urban	"	..	6	..	..	..	..
Fixed investment: housing	% of GDP	..	6.3	4.4	..	..	..

Fuel and power	% of GDP						
Energy consumption per capita	kg of oil equivalent	604.7	869.8	1,299.4	974.1	886.3	1,427.7
Households with electricity	% of households	..	..	..	..	..	..
Urban	"	..	..	..	..	..	..
Rural		..	..	..	..	..	..
Transport and communication	% of GDP	..	6.0	7.7	..	..	..
Population per passenger car	persons	59	26	16	16	27	14
Fixed investment: transport equipment	% of GDP	..	2.2	3.0	..	..	..
Total road length	km	..	..	212,626	..	..	..
Population per telephone	persons	21	21	10	11	16	9
INVESTMENT IN HUMAN CAPITAL							
Medical care	% of GDP	..	2.9	3.5	..	..	..
Population per: physician	persons	2,078	1,499	1,242	933	1,547	1,021
nurse	"	977	1,444	880	875	..	602
hospital bed		..	800	..	..	..	..
Access to health care	% of pop.	..	..	..	..	..	..
Immunized (under 12 months): measles	% of age group	..	..	54.0	52.7	62.6	..
DPT		..	..	62.0	62.4	64.7	..
Oral Rehydration Therapy use (under 5)	% of cases	..	..	72.3	33.6	28.2	..
Education	% of GDP	..	2.7	3.5	..	..	..
Gross enrollment ratios							
Primary: total	% of school-age group	92.0	109.0	114.0	108.1	106.8	103.5
female	"	90.0	106.0	113.0	105.2	101.3	99.4
Secondary: total	"	17.0	34.0	55.0	48.8	52.0	57.8
female	"	13.0	28.0	54.0	52.7	51.8	56.7
Tertiary: science/engineering	% of tertiary students	29.0	30.5	26.1	..	..	27
Pupil-teacher ratio: primary	pupils per teacher	47	45	32	26	28	28
secondary	"	14	18	18	..	18	18
Pupils reaching grade 4	% of cohort	..	59.3	74.2	66.3	81.0	76.8
Repeater rate: primary	% of total enrollment	14.7	11.0	9.5	17.9	8.0	18.1
Illiteracy rate: overall	% of pop. (age 15+)	..	..	9.7	16.7	26.2	21.8
female	% of females (age 15+)	..	..	11.7	19.0	32.5	25.6
Newspaper circulation	per thou. pop.	106.4	..	132.9	81.2	79.3	86.5

Source: World Bank International Economics Department, September 1989.

Nigeria

	Unit of measure	25-30 years ago	15-20 years ago	Most recent estimate (mre)	Same region / income group		Next higher income group
					Sub-Saharan Africa	Low-income	
HUMAN RESOURCES							
Size, growth, structure of population							
Total population (mre = 1988)	millions	58	75	110	466	2,881	629
14 and under	% of pop.	45.9	47.6	48.3	46.8	35.4	38.3
15-64	"	51.7	50.0	49.1	50.4	60.2	57.4
Age dependency ratio	unit	0.93	1.00	1.03	0.98	0.66	0.74
Percentage in urban areas	% of pop.	17.0	23.4	33.1	31.7	34.2	56.1
Females per 100 males							
Urban	number	:	:	:	:	:	:
Rural	"	:	:	:	:	:	:
Population growth rate	annual %	2.5	2.4	3.2	3.1	2.0	2.2
Urban	"	7.2	5.3	6.6	6.1	3.7	3.5
Urban/rural growth differential	difference	5.6	3.8	4.8	4.1	2.2	2.5
Projected population: 2000	millions	:	:	157	673	3,625	805
Stationary population	"	:	:	500	:	:	:
Determinants of population growth							
Fertility							
Crude birth rate	per thou. pop.	51.3	50.2	46.6	47.2	30.4	31.5
Total fertility rate	births per woman	6.89	6.90	6.50	6.56	3.89	4.08
Contraceptive prevalence	% of women 15-49	:	:	5.0	:	57.4	:
Child (0-4) / woman (15-49) ratios							
Urban	per 100 women	:	:	:	:	:	:
Rural	"	:	:	:	:	:	:
Mortality							
Crude death rate	per thou. pop.	22.6	19.2	15.0	15.8	10.0	8.6
Infant mortality rate	per thou. live births	177.2	133.6	105.0	113.6	72.6	59.1
Under 5 mortality rate				173.0	173.4	174.8	96.5
Life expectancy at birth: overall	years	41.7	45.7	51.1	50.6	61.4	63.8
female	"	43.3	47.3	52.9	52.3	62.3	66.1
Labor force (15-64)							
Total labor force	millions	21	27	40	189	1,343	232
Agriculture	% of labor force	72.1	69.6	:	:	:	:
Industry	"	10.2	11.1	:	:	:	:
Female	"	37.3	36.9	35.1	38.0	36.0	31.2

Females per 100 males							
Urban	number	:	:	:	:	:	:
Rural	"	:	:	:	:	:	:
Participation rate: overall	% of labor force	42.3	40.5	37.5	41.6	49.2	39.0
female	"	31.1	29.5	26.1	30.8	34.9	23.5
Educational attainment of labor force							
School years completed: overall	years	0.5	:	:	:	:	:
male	"	:	:	:	:	:	:
NATURAL RESOURCES							
Area	thou. sq. km	924	924	924	22,242	36,997	17,083
Density	pop. per sq. km	63	81	115	20	76	36
Agricultural land	% of land area	52.5	54.9	56.6	32.7	36.1	38.3
Agricultural density	pop. per sq. km	121	148	204	62	211	94
Forests and woodland	thou. sq. km	209	179	146	6,634	9,154	5,449
Deforestation rate (net)	annual %	-1.4	-1.6	-2.0	-0.5	-0.3	-0.7
Access to safe water	% of pop.	:	:	41.0	36.5	73.4	76.7
Urban	"	:	:	100.0	75.5	:	46.3
Rural	"	:	:	20.0	24.2		

Population growth

6
5
4
3
2
1
0

early 60s   early 70s   nrc

Infant mortality

250
200
150
100
50
0

early 60s   early 70s   nrc

Primary school enrollment

120+
100
80
60
40
20
0

early 60s   early 70s   nrc

Nigeria   —— Low-income

Nigeria

				Most recent estimate (mre)	Same region / income group		Next higher income group
	Unit of measure	25-30 years ago	15-20 years ago		Sub-Saharan Africa	Low-income	
INCOME AND POVERTY							
Income							
GNP per capita (mre = 1988)	US$	100	430	290	320	310	1,270
Total household income							
Share to top 10% of households	% of income	..	..	..	..	..	..
Share to top 20% of households	"	..	..	..	..	..	..
Share to bottom 40% of households	"	..	..	..	..	..	..
Share to bottom 20% of households	"	..	..	..	..	..	..
Poverty							
Absolute poverty income: urban	US$ per person	..	..	696	..	..	..
rural	"	..	..	341	..	..	..
Pop. in absolute poverty: urban	% of pop.	..	..	10.9	..	..	..
rural	"	..	..	..	..	..	..
Prevalence of malnutrition (under 5)	% of age group	..	..	..	..	..	..
EXPENDITURE							
Food							
Staples	% of GDP	..	..	31.9	..	..	..
Meat, fish, milk, cheese, eggs	"	..	..	11.3	..	..	..
Cereal imports	thou. metric tonnes	98	447	677	8,252	27,738	36,712
Food aid in cereals	"	..	2	0	3,786	7,122	7,851
Food production per capita	1979-81=100	127.8	105.5	100.9	94.4	116.4	97.0
Share of agriculture in GDP	% of GDP	53.6	30.5	34.6	35.1	33.0	16.0
Daily calorie supply	calories per person	2,185	2,075	2,146	2,095	2,392	2,767
Daily protein supply	grams per person	50	47	48	52	57	70
Housing							
Average household size	persons per household	..	..	2.5	..	..	..
Urban		..	5	..	..	..	..
Fixed investment: housing	% of GDP	2.2	2.2	0.9	..	..	..

Fuel and power	% of GDP	..	..	1.0	..	..	..
Energy consumption per capita	kg of oil equivalent	34.5	57.6	132.9	103.7	323.7	886.3
Households with electricity							
Urban	% of households	..	..	..	..	..	..
Rural	"	..	..	..	..	..	..
Transport and communication	% of GDP	..	..	2.2	..	..	..
Population per passenger car	persons	1,008	476	..	..	..	27
Fixed investment: transport equipment	% of GDP	..	2.8	1.0	..	..	..
Total road length	km	..	..	108,000	..	..	..
Population per telephone	persons	..	..	370	..	..	16
INVESTMENT IN HUMAN CAPITAL							
Medical care	% of GDP	..	..	7.8	..	..	..
Population per: physician	persons	29,525	24,700	7,978	..	1,462	1,547
nurse	"	6,156	5,235	1,018	..	1,746	..
hospital bed	"	..	2,200	..	..	756	..
Access to health care	% of pop.	..	..	..	..	..	..
Immunized (under 12 months): measles	% of age group	..	..	31.0	52.9	43.4	62.6
DPT	"	..	..	20.0	45.7	41.3	64.7
Oral Rehydration Therapy use (under 5)	% of cases	..	..	20.0	18.4	21.6	28.2
Education	% of GDP	..	..	..	..	..	..
Gross enrollment ratios							
Primary: total	% of school-age group	32.0	51.0	92.0	78.0	99.3	106.8
female	"	24.0	..	81.0	67.6	87.8	101.3
Secondary: total	"	5.0	8.0	29.0	22.0	33.4	52.0
female	"	3.0	..	14.0	12.3	26.1	51.8
Tertiary: science/engineering	% of tertiary students	20.7	24.3	12.5	..	..	..
Pupil-teacher ratio: primary	pupils per teacher	33	34	40	40	10	28
secondary	"	18	84	38	35	19	18
Pupils reaching grade 4	% of cohort	..	65.3	..	..	..	81.0
Repeater rate: primary	% of total enrollment	..	..	..	..	..	8.0
Illiteracy rate: overall	% of pop. (age 15+)	..	..	57.6	53.4	43.3	26.2
female	% of females (age 15+)	..	..	68.5	64.0	56.5	32.5
Newspaper circulation	per thou. pop.	6.7	8.2	5.3	5.2	20.4	79.3

Source: World Bank International Economics Department, September 1989.

Pakistan

	Unit of measure	25-30 years ago	15-20 years ago	Most recent estimate (mre)	Same region / income group		Next higher income group
					Europe, Middle East, North Africa	Low-income	
HUMAN RESOURCES							
Size, growth, structure of population							
Total population (mre = 1988)	millions	53	71	106	503	2,881	629
14 and under	% of pop.	46.3	45.5	45.5	38.3	35.4	38.3
15-64	"	50.1	51.6	52.2	56.8	60.2	57.4
Age dependency ratio	unit	0.99	0.94	0.92	0.75	0.66	0.74
Percentage in urban areas	% of pop.	23.5	26.4	30.9	49.7	34.2	56.1
Females per 100 males							
Urban	number	..	84	87	..	..	..
Rural	"	..	89	92	..	..	..
Population growth rate	annual %	2.8	3.1	3.1	2.0	2.0	2.2
Urban	"	4.0	4.2	4.9	3.4	3.7	3.5
Urban/rural growth differential	difference	1.5	1.5	2.6	2.2	2.2	2.5
Projected population: 2000	millions	..	..	156	662	3,625	805
Stationary population	"	..	..	513	..	..	..
Determinants of population growth							
Fertility							
Crude birth rate	per thou. pop.	48.0	47.4	47.0	33.5	30.4	31.5
Total fertility rate	births per woman	7.00	7.00	6.70	4.58	3.89	4.08
Contraceptive prevalence	% of women 15-49	..	11.0	11.0	..	57.4	..
Child (0-4) / woman (15-49) ratios							
Urban	per 100 women	..	69	71	..	..	..
Rural	"	..	76	76	..	..	..
Mortality							
Crude death rate	per thou. pop.	20.9	16.9	12.4	10.6	10.0	8.6
Infant mortality rate	per thou. live births	149.0	134.0	109.0	70.9	72.6	59.1
Under 5 mortality rate		..	..	142.0	100.2	174.8	96.5
Life expectancy at birth: overall	years	45.8	50.5	56.5	62.7	61.4	63.8
female	"	44.5	49.8	56.5	64.5	62.3	66.1
Labor force (15-64)							
Total labor force	millions	17	22	32	173	1,343	232
Agriculture	% of labor force	59.8	56.8	..	..	..	..
Industry	"	18.3	17.2	..	..	..	..
Female	"	8.6	9.8	12.1	25.6	36.0	31.2

Indicator	Unit	Pakistan early 60s	Pakistan early 70s	Pakistan mre	Low-income early 60s	Low-income early 70s	Low-income mre
Females per 100 males							
Urban	number	..	79	83	..	..	..
Rural	"	..	89	92	..	..	..
Participation rate: overall	% of labor force	30.2	29.4	29.9	37.7	49.2	39.0
female	"	5.4	6.0	7.5	19.0	34.9	23.5
Educational attainment of labor force							
School years completed: overall	years	..	1.2	2.5	..	..	..
male	"	..	..	..	..	..	..
NATURAL RESOURCES							
Area	thou. sq. km	796	796	796	12,216	36,997	17,083
Density	pop. per sq. km	66	89	129	40	76	36
Agricultural land	% of land area	30.5	31.2	32.4	29.7	36.1	38.3
Agricultural density	pop. per sq. km	217	286	398	135	211	94
Forests and woodland	thou. sq. km	21	28	33	926	9,154	5,449
Deforestation rate (net)	annual %	5.5	1.4	4.4	0.2	-0.3	-0.7
Access to safe water	% of pop.	..	25.0	43.0	62.0	73.4	76.7
Urban	"	..	75.0	83.0	88.4	..	..
Rural	"	..	5.0	27.0	44.2	..	46.3

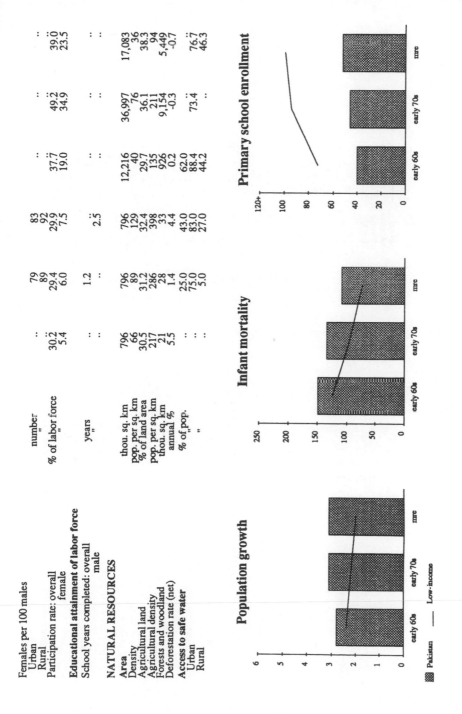

Population growth

Infant mortality

Primary school enrollment

Legend: Pakistan (shaded) — Low-income (line)

Chart axes: early 60s, early 70s, mre

Pakistan

| | Unit of measure | 25-30 years ago | 15-20 years ago | Most recent estimate (mre) | Same region / income group | | Next higher income group |
					Europe, Middle East, North Africa	Low-income	
INCOME AND POVERTY							
Income							
GNP per capita (mre = 1988)	US$	110	140	350	1,660	310	1,270
Total household income							
Share to top 10% of households	% of income	30	27	..	..	..	..
Share to top 20% of households	"	45	42	..	..	..	..
Share to bottom 40% of households	"	18	21	..	..	..	..
Share to bottom 20% of households	"	6	8	..	..	..	..
Poverty							
Absolute poverty income: urban	US$ per person	..	68	176	..	..	..
rural	"	..	47	122	..	..	..
Pop. in absolute poverty: urban	% of pop.	..	42.0	32.0	..	..	..
rural	"	..	43.0	29.0	..	..	..
Prevalence of malnutrition (under 5)	% of age group	..	..	57.1	..	..	..
EXPENDITURE							
Food	% of GDP	..	46.1	31.9	..	..	..
Staples	"	..	16.0		..	..	..
Meat, fish, milk, cheese, eggs	"	..	14.0		..	..	..
Cereal imports	thou. metric tonnes	1,591	1,349	378	40,185	27,738	36,712
Food aid in cereals	"		789	657		7,122	7,851
Food production per capita	1979-81=100	86.2	94.5	107.0	103.7	116.4	97.0
Share of agriculture in GDP	% of GDP	40.2	32.0	26.2	15.4	33.0	16.0
Daily calorie supply	calories per person	1,761	2,106	2,315	3,014	2,392	2,767
Daily protein supply	grams per person	50	58	61	83	57	70
Housing	% of GDP	..	9.4	14.1	..	..	..
Average household size	persons per household	..	6	7	..	..	..
Urban	"	..	6	7	..	..	..
Fixed investment: housing	% of GDP	..	2.0	1.9	..	..	..

Indicator	Unit						
Fuel and power	% of GDP	..	3.8	4.2	..	..	..
Energy consumption per capita	kg of oil equivalent	135.3	136.5	207.3	1,157.7	323.7	886.3
Households with electricity	% of households	..	..	..	..	..	..
Urban	"	..	..	..	..	..	..
Rural	"	..	..	..	..	..	..
Transport and communication	% of GDP	..	1.6	11.4	..	..	..
Population per passenger car	persons	428	349	213	29	..	27
Fixed investment: transport equipment	% of GDP	..	1.6	..	..	..	..
Total road length	km	..	..	107,673	..	..	..
Population per telephone	persons	..	296	154	16	..	16
INVESTMENT IN HUMAN CAPITAL							
Medical care	% of GDP	..	3.8	0.8	..	..	..
Population per: physician	persons	9,909	4,300	2,941	1,009	1,462	1,547
nurse	"	..	6,607	5,050	798	1,746	..
hospital bed	"	..	1,900	1,703	446	756	..
Access to health care	% of pop.	..	..	64.0	69.7	43.4	62.6
Immunized (under 12 months): measles	% of age group	..	..	53.0	68.7	41.3	64.7
DPT	% of age group	..	..	62.0	30.1	21.6	28.2
Oral Rehydration Therapy use (under 5)	% of cases	..	..	41.5	..	..	..
Education	% of GDP	..	1.6	0.8	..	..	..
Gross enrollment ratios							
Primary: total	% of school-age group	40.0	46.0	52.1	87.4	99.3	106.8
female	"	20.0	28.0	35.1	78.4	87.8	101.3
Secondary: total	"	12.0	15.0	23.5	47.5	33.4	52.0
female	"	5.0	7.0	13.7	38.7	26.1	51.8
Tertiary: science/engineering	% of tertiary students	..	25.1	28.7	..	..	..
Pupil-teacher ratio: primary	pupils per teacher	42	40	41	31	10	28
secondary	"	20	18	18	18	19	18
Pupils reaching grade 4	% of cohort	..	56.8	48.3	77.5	..	81.0
Repeater rate: primary	% of total enrollment	84.6	79.3	..	7.4	43.3	8.0
Illiteracy rate: overall	% of pop. (age 15+)	..	..	70.4	49.5	..	26.2
female	% of females (age 15+)	..	..	81.4	56.8	56.5	32.5
Newspaper circulation	per thou. pop.	35.0	5.0	18.3	68.1	20.4	79.3

Source: World Bank International Economics Department, September 1989.

Philippines

	Unit of measure	25-30 years ago	15-20 years ago	Most recent estimate (mre)	Same region / income group		
					Asia	Lower-middle-income	Next higher income group
HUMAN RESOURCES							
Size, growth, structure of population							
Total population (mre = 1988)	millions	32	43	60	2,516	629	424
14 and under	% of pop.	45.0	42.8	40.4	33.2	38.3	34.1
15-64	"	52.1	54.5	56.1	62.1	57.4	60.2
Age dependency ratio	unit	0.92	0.83	0.78	0.61	0.74	0.65
Percentage in urban areas	% of pop.	31.6	35.6	41.0	36.8	56.1	68.8
Females per 100 males							
Urban	number	..	103	..	..	..	..
Rural	"	..	95	..	..	..	..
Population growth rate							
Urban	annual %	3.5	2.7	2.1	1.8	2.2	1.8
Rural	"	4.3	4.1	4.0	3.2	3.5	3.1
Urban/rural growth differential	difference	1.2	2.3	2.9	1.9	2.5	3.8
Projected population: 2000	millions	..	..	74	3,055	805	521
Stationary population	"	..	..	127	..	..	..
Determinants of population growth							
Fertility							
Crude birth rate	per thou. pop.	41.6	36.6	30.0	26.8	31.5	26.4
Total fertility rate	births per woman	6.80	5.46	3.94	3.34	4.08	3.39
Contraceptive prevalence	% of women 15-49	..	..	44.0	57.8	..	..
Child (0-4) / woman (15-49) ratios							
Urban	per 100 women	..	52	..	..	..	..
Rural	"	..	74	..	..	..	..
Mortality							
Crude death rate	per thou. pop.	11.7	9.7	7.6	8.8	8.6	8.3
Infant mortality rate	per thou. live births	72.4	58.0	45.0	61.5	59.1	46.9
Under 5 mortality rate		..	..	58.0	101.7	96.5	58.4
Life expectancy at birth: overall	years	55.5	59.1	63.4	63.7	63.8	67.2
female	"	57.2	60.7	65.4	64.6	66.1	69.8
Labor force (15-64)							
Total labor force	millions	12	16	21	1,212	232	156
Agriculture	% of labor force	58.0	53.3	..	..	..	..
Industry	"	15.8	16.1	..	..	..	..
Female	"	33.7	32.8	31.6	36.6	31.2	29.5

		Philippines early 60s	early 70s	mre	Lower-middle-income early 60s	early 70s	mre
Females per 100 males							
Urban	number	: :	108	: :	: :	: :	: :
Rural	"	: :	96	: :	: :	: :	: :
Participation rate: overall	% of labor force	37.1	37.2	36.7	50.5	39.0	38.2
female	"	25.1	24.6	23.3	36.6	23.5	22.1
Educational attainment of labor force							
School years completed: overall	years	: :	: :	: :	: :	: :	: :
male	"	: :	: :	: :	: :	: :	: :
NATURAL RESOURCES							
Area	thou. sq. km	300	300	300	18,343	17,083	20,337
Density	pop. per sq. km	106	144	195	135	36	20
Agricultural land	% of land area	25.8	27.3	30.4	38.5	38.3	31.6
Agricultural density	pop. per sq. km	410	526	640	350	94	65
Forests and woodland	thou. sq. km	170	135	112	4,803	5,449	7,587
Deforestation rate (net)	annual %	-0.3	-1.6	-1.8	-0.2	-0.7	-0.4
Access to safe water	% of pop.	: :	: :	52.0	72.5	76.7	79.4
Urban	"	50.0	50.0	49.0	: :	46.3	90.1
Rural	"	: :	: :	54.0	: :	: :	62.7

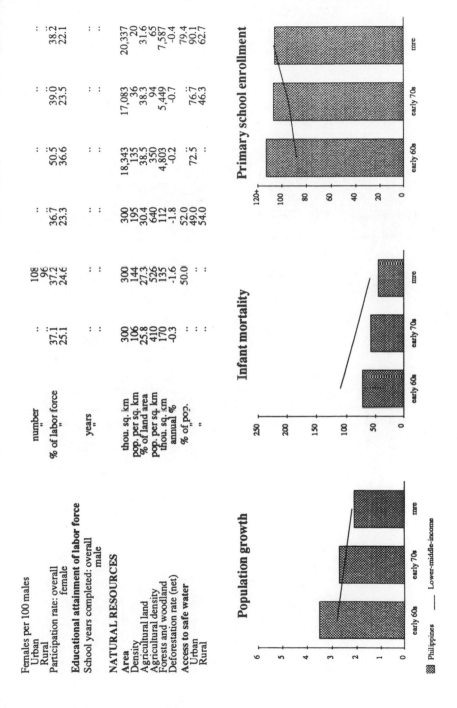

Population growth

Infant mortality

Primary school enrollment

early 60s   early 70s   mre

Philippines ▧   Lower-middle-income ——

Philippines

	Unit of measure	25-30 years ago	15-20 years ago	Most recent estimate (mre)	Same region / income group — Asia	Lower-middle-income	Next higher income group
INCOME AND POVERTY							
Income							
GNP per capita (mre = 1988)	US$	180	360	630	410	1,270	2,940
Total household income							
Share to top 10% of households	% of income	40	39	37	..	..	..
Share to top 20% of households	"	56	56	53	..	..	..
Share to bottom 40% of households	"	12	14	14	..	..	..
Share to bottom 20% of households	"	4	5	5	..	..	..
Poverty							
Absolute poverty income: urban	US$ per person	..	..	..	..	..	..
rural	"	..	..	..	..	..	..
Pop. in absolute poverty: urban	% of pop.	..	..	..	..	..	..
rural	"	..	..	..	..	..	..
Prevalence of malnutrition (under 5)	% of age group	..	..	19.0	..	..	..
EXPENDITURE							
Food							
Staples	% of GDP	..	37.5	48.2	..	..	..
Meat, fish, milk, cheese, eggs	"	..	14.1	..	..	..	..
Cereal imports	thou. metric tonnes	1,070	824	910	33,549	36,712	35,596
Food aid in cereals	"	..	62	471	3,461	7,851	..
Food production per capita	1979-81=100	81.8	93.5	87.1	118.7	97.0	104.3
Share of agriculture in GDP	% of GDP	25.9	28.9	23.0	27.5	16.0	12.3
Daily calorie supply	calories per person	1,924	2,086	2,372	2,452	2,767	2,980
Daily protein supply	grams per person	44	51	54	58	70	80
Housing							
Average household size	persons per household	..	6.2	18.1	..	..	..
Urban	"	..	6	..	..	..	..
Fixed investment: housing	% of GDP	..	3.5	2.5	..	..	..

Fuel and power	% of GDP	..	1.6	5.0	..	..	..
Energy consumption per capita	kg of oil equivalent	159.5	257.1	241.3	386.8	886.3	1,427.7
Households with electricity	% of households	..	..	..	..	..	..
Urban	"	..	..	..	..	..	..
Rural	"	..	..	..	..	..	..
Transport and communication	% of GDP	..	1.5	3.7	..	..	..
Population per passenger car	persons	232	112	155	..	27	14
Fixed investment: transport equipment	% of GDP	..	4.1	0.6	..	..	..
Total road length	km	..	..	155,669	..	..	..
Population per telephone	persons	..	96	66	..	16	9
INVESTMENT IN HUMAN CAPITAL							
Medical care	% of GDP	..	2.3	2.1	..	..	..
Population per: physician	persons	1,130	9,100	6,700	1,422	1,547	1,021
nurse	"	..	2,687	2,741	1,674	..	602
hospital bed	"	..	600	600	733	..	..
Access to health care	% of pop.	..	..	68.0	41.0	62.6	..
Immunized (under 12 months): measles	% of age group	..	..	73.0	48.6	64.7	..
DPT		..	..	..	..	..	..
Oral Rehydration Therapy use (under 5)	% of cases	..	..	23.5	27.9	28.2	..
Education	% of GDP	..	3.8	3.3	..	..	..
Gross enrollment ratios							
Primary: total	% of school-age group	113.0	107.0	106.0	105.3	106.8	103.5
female	"	111.0	..	106.0	94.4	101.3	99.4
Secondary: total	"	41.0	54.0	68.0	37.5	52.0	57.8
female	"	40.0	..	69.0	30.5	51.8	56.7
Tertiary: science/engineering	% of tertiary students	9.8	16.3	37.8	..	..	27
Pupil-teacher ratio: primary	pupils per teacher	31	29	32	10	28	..
secondary	"	33	..	..	19	18	..
Pupils reaching grade 4	% of cohort	..	78.4	76.2	..	81.0	76.8
Repeater rate: primary	% of total enrollment	..	..	1.8	..	8.0	18.1
Illiteracy rate: overall	% of pop. (age 15+)	..	..	14.3	39.5	26.2	21.8
female	% of females (age 15+)	..	..	14.6	52.3	32.5	25.6
Newspaper circulation	per thou. pop.	17.8	15.9	36.9	26.6	79.3	86.5

Source: World Bank International Economics Department, September 1989.

Turkey

	Unit of measure	25-30 years ago	15-20 years ago	Most recent estimate (mre)	Same region / income group		
					Europe, Middle East, North Africa	Lower-middle-income	Next higher income group
HUMAN RESOURCES							
Size, growth, structure of population							
Total population (mre = 1988)	thousands	31,151	40,025	53,772	502,676	629,214	424,306
14 and under	% of pop.	42.0	40.1	35.1	38.3	38.3	34.1
15-64	"	53.8	55.4	60.6	56.8	57.4	60.2
Age dependency ratio	unit	0.86	0.81	0.65	0.75	0.74	0.65
Percentage in urban areas	% of pop.	34.1	41.6	47.2	49.7	56.1	68.8
Females per 100 males							
Urban	number	..	..	..	..	..	..
Rural	"	..	..	..	..	..	..
Population growth rate							
Urban	annual %	2.5	2.4	2.2	2.0	2.2	1.8
	"	5.1	4.0	3.6	3.4	3.5	3.1
Urban/rural growth differential	difference	3.9	2.6	2.5	2.2	2.5	3.8
Projected population: 2000	thousands	..	..	67,454	661,662	805,063	521,035
Stationary population	"	..	..	111,446			:
Determinants of population growth							
Fertility							
Crude birth rate	per thou. pop.	40.6	33.0	30.1	33.5	31.5	26.4
Total fertility rate	births per woman	5.82	4.60	3.80	4.58	4.08	3.39
Contraceptive prevalence	% of women 15-49	..	38.0	50.0			:
Child (0-4) / woman (15-49) ratios							
Urban	per 100 women	..	..	..	..	..	..
Rural	"	..	..	..	..	..	..
Mortality							
Crude death rate	per thou. pop.	14.7	10.8	8.5	10.6	8.6	8.3
Infant mortality rate	per thou. live births	162.2	127.2	76.0	70.9	59.1	46.9
Under 5 mortality rate	"			95.0	100.2	96.5	58.4
Life expectancy at birth: overall	years	53.8	59.3	64.1	62.7	63.8	67.2
female	"	55.4	61.5	65.8	64.5	66.1	69.8
Labor force (15-64)							
Total labor force	thousands	14,856	17,640	22,772	173,176	232,336	156,018
Agriculture	% of labor force	74.7	64.8	..	..	..	..
Industry	"	11.2	14.3	..	..	..	..
Female	"	39.3	36.5	33.8	25.6	31.2	29.5

Indicator	Unit	Turkey early 60s	Turkey early 70s	Turkey mre	Lower-middle-income early 60s	Lower-middle-income early 70s	Lower-middle-income mre
Females per 100 males							
Urban	number	::	::	::	—	::	::
Rural	"	47.7	44.1	43.4	37.7	39.0	38.2
Participation rate: overall	% of labor force	47.7	44.1	43.4	37.7	39.0	38.2
female	"	38.2	32.7	30.2	19.0	23.5	22.1
Educational attainment of labor force							
School years completed: overall	years	::	::	::	::	::	::
male	"	::	::	::	::	::	::
NATURAL RESOURCES							
Area	thou. sq. km	779	779	779	12,216	17,083	20,337
Density	pop. per sq. km	40	51	68	40	36	20
Agricultural land	% of land area	47.8	48.7	47.0	29.7	38.3	31.6
Agricultural density	pop. per sq. km	84	105	144	135	94	65
Forests and woodland	thou. sq. km	202	202	202	926	5,449	7,587
Deforestation rate (net)	annual %	0.0	0.0	0.0	0.2	-0.7	-0.4
Access to safe water	% of pop.	68.0	::	62.0	::	76.7	79.4
Urban	"	74.0	::	88.4	::	::	90.1
Rural	"	64.0	::	44.2	::	46.3	62.7

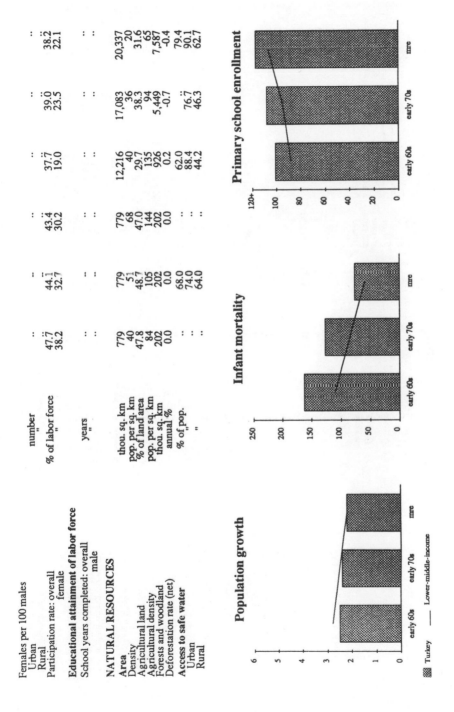

Population growth

Infant mortality

Primary school enrollment

Turkey —— Lower-middle-income

Turkey

	Unit of measure	25-30 years ago	15-20 years ago	Most recent estimate (mre)	Same region / income group — Europe, Middle East, North Africa	Lower-middle-income	Next higher income group
INCOME AND POVERTY							
Income							
GNP per capita (mre = 1988)	US$	270	830	1,280	1,660	1,270	2,940
Total household income							
Share to top 10% of households	% of income	..	..	..	..	..	..
Share to top 20% of households	"	61	57	..	..	..	..
Share to bottom 40% of households	"	11	12	..	..	..	..
Share to bottom 20% of households	"	4	4	..	..	..	..
Poverty							
Absolute poverty income: urban	US$ per person	..	..	..	..	..	..
rural	"	..	..	..	..	..	..
Pop. in absolute poverty: urban	% of pop.	..	..	..	..	..	..
rural	"	..	..	..	..	..	..
Prevalence of malnutrition (under 5)	% of age group	..	..	..	..	..	..
EXPENDITURE							
Food							
Staples	% of GDP	..	..	30.2	..	..	..
Meat, fish, milk, cheese, eggs	"	..	..	6.1	..	..	..
Cereal imports	thou. metric tonnes	360	560	624	40,185	36,712	35,596
Food aid in cereals	"	..	4	1	..	..	..
Food production per capita	1979-81=100	88.3	98.1	93.7	103.7	97.0	104.3
Share of agriculture in GDP	% of GDP	34.3	29.1	17.3	15.4	16.0	12.3
Daily calorie supply	calories per person	2,659	2,976	3,229	3,014	2,767	2,980
Daily protein supply	grams per person	81	86	91	83	70	80
Housing							
Average household size	persons per household	6	6	9.4	..	..	..
Urban	"	5	7	..	..	..	..
Fixed investment: housing	% of GDP	..	2.6	3.2	..	..	..

Indicator	Unit						
	% of GDP	..	..	5.0	..	..	..
Fuel and power							
Energy consumption per capita	kg of oil equivalent	257.5	507.0	762.9	1,157.7	886.3	1,427.7
Households with electricity	% of households						
Urban		..	..	..	..	..	..
Rural		..	..	..	..	..	..
Transport and communication							
Population per passenger car	persons	356	104	51	29	27	14
Fixed investment: transport equipment	% of GDP	..	..	2.3	..	..	..
Total road length	km	..	..	329,793	..	..	..
Population per telephone	persons	..	40	12	16	16	9
INVESTMENT IN HUMAN CAPITAL							
Medical care							
Population per: physician	persons	2,900	2,197	1,381	1,009	1,547	1,021
nurse	"	..	1,003	1,030	798	..	602
hospital bed	"	..	499	469	446	..	..
Access to health care	% of pop.	..	..	..	..	..	..
Immunized (under 12 months): measles	% of age group	..	..	50.0	69.7	62.6	..
DPT		..	..	71.0	68.7	64.7	..
Oral Rehydration Therapy use (under 5)	% of cases	..	..	26.0	30.1	28.2	..
Education	% of GDP	..	..	1.0	..	..	..
Gross enrollment ratios							
Primary: total	% of school-age group	101.0	108.0	117.0	87.4	106.8	103.5
female	"	83.0	..	113.0	78.4	101.3	99.4
Secondary: total	"	16.0	29.0	44.0	47.5	52.0	57.8
female	"	9.0	19.0	33.0	38.7	51.8	56.7
Tertiary: science/engineering	% of tertiary students	19.3	20.9	23.3	..	..	..
Pupil-teacher ratio: primary	pupils per teacher	46	34	31	31	28	27
secondary		25	31	26	18	18	..
Pupils reaching grade 4	% of cohort	..	79.7	..	77.5	81.0	76.8
Repeater rate: primary	% of total enrollment	79.7	..	7.5	7.4	8.0	18.1
Illiteracy rate: overall	% of pop. (age 15+)	54.0	39.7	25.8	49.5	26.2	21.8
female	% of females (age 15+)	..	..	37.5	56.8	32.5	25.6
Newspaper circulation	per thou. pop.	46.0	36.8	..	68.1	79.3	86.5

Source: World Bank International Economics Department, September 1989.

References

Abadan-Unat, Nermin. (1986). "Turkish Migration to Europe and the Middle East: Its Impact on the Social Structure and Social Legislation." In L. Michalak and J. Salacuse (Eds.), *Social Legislation in the Contemporary Middle East.* Berkeley: Institute of International Studies. Pp. 325–69.

―――― (Ed.). (1976). *Turkish Workers in Europe; 1960–75.* E. J. Brill.

Abella, Manolo I. (1984). "Labor Migration from South and South-East Asia: Some Policy Issues." *International Labour Review,* 123(4): 491–506.

Addo, N. O. (1972). "Population Movements in West Africa." In *West African Regional Seminar on Population Studies.* University of Ghana, Legon.

Adegbola, O. (1976). "The Migrant as a Factor in Regional Development: The Case of Ghana Returnees in Western Nigeria." *Jimlar Muntane,* 1(1).

Adepoju, A. (1983a). "Linkages between Internal and International Migration: The African Situation." Paper presented at the Unesco symposium on "Issues and New Trends in Migration: Population Movements within and across National Boundaries." Paris, October.

―――― (1983b). "Undocumented Migration in Africa: Trends and Policies." *International Migration,* 21(2).

―――― (1984a). *International Migration in Africa South of the Sahara, Project Report to Population Division.* Paris: Unesco.

―――― (1984b). "Linkages between Internal and International Migration: The African Situation." *International Social Science Journal,* 101(3).

―――― (1985). *Intra-regional Migration and the Employment of Nationals of Economic Community of West African States (ECOWAS) Project Report to Population Division.* Paris: Unesco.

Adler, S. (1980). "Swallows' Children: Emigration and Development in Algeria." Geneva: International Labour Office, International Migration for Employment Branch. WEP-2-25/WP-46.

―――― (1985). "Emigration and Development in Algeria: Doubts and Dilemmas." In R. Rogers (Ed.), *Guests Come to Stay.* Boulder: Westview Press. Pp. 263–84.

Ahmad, Atigque. (1978). "Fears about Immigrant Workers in Saudi Arabia: A Special Report." *The Times,* October 30.

Ahmad, Mansoor. (1982). *Emigration of Scarce Skills in Pakistan.* Geneva: International Labor Office (International Migration for Employment Working Paper 5).

Ahmed, Akbar S. (1977). *Social and Economic Changes in the Tribal Areas.* Karachi: Oxford University Press. Pp. 11–23.

Alba, Francisco. (1978). "Mexico's International Migration as a Manifestation of Development Pattern." *International Migration Review,* 12:502–13.

Alegre, L. (1974). "Migration and the Development of Bolivia." *ICMC Migration News,* 23:12–38.

Alexandris, T. (1985). "Analysis of Investments of Greeks from Abroad in the Context of Public Law 1262/1982" (in Greek). Athens: General Secretariat of Greeks Abroad. Mimeo.

Ali, Syed Ashraf, et al. (1981). *Labor Migration from Bangladesh to the Middle East.* Washington, D.C.: World Bank (World Bank Staff Working Paper 454).

Anarfi, J. K. (1984). "International Labor Migration in West Africa: A Case Study of the Ghanaian Migrants in Lagos, Nigeria." M.Sc. thesis, Regional Institute of Population Studies, University of Ghana.

Anderson, P. (1985). "Migration and Development in Jamaica." In R. A. Pastor (Ed.), *Migration and Development in the Caribbean.* Boulder: Westview Press. Pp. 117–39.

————. (1987). "Manpower Losses and Employment Adequacy among Skilled Workers in Jamaica, 1976–1985." In P. Pessar (Ed.), *When Borders Don't Divide: Labor Migration and Refugee Movements in the Americas.* New York: Center for Migration Studies of New York.

Andrus, J. Russell, and Azizali F. Mohammad. (1958). *The Economy of Pakistan.* Stanford, California: Stanford University Press. P. 464.

Appleyard, R. (1987). "The Impact of International Migration on Developing Countries." OECD: Migration and Development. Seminar organized jointly by the OECD Development Center, Intergovernmental Commission for Migration (ICM), and CICRED. February.

Arbelaez, C. (1977). "El Exodo de Colombianos en el Periodo 1963–1973." *Boletin Mensual de Estadistica,* 310:7–43.

Arizpe, L. (1981). "The Rural Exodus in Mexico and Mexican Migration to the United States." *International Migration Review,* 15:626–49.

————. (1983). "The Rural Exodus in Mexico and the Mexican Migration to the United States." In P. G. Brown and H. Schue (Eds.), *The Border That Joins Mexican Migrants and U.S. Responsibility.* Totowa, N.J.: Rowman and Littlefield. Pp. 162–83.

Arnold, Fred, and Nasra Shah. (1986). *Asian Labor Migration: Pipeline to the Middle East.* Boulder: Westview Press.

Auldt, D. E., and G. L. Rutman (1985). "The Rural African and Gold Mining in Southern Africa 1976–1980." *South African Journal of Economics,* March.

Bach, Robert L. (1978). "Mexican Immigration and the American State." *International Migration Review,* 12:536–58.

Balan, J. (1985). "International Migration in the Southern Cone." Occasional Paper Series, Hemispheric Migration Project, Center for Immigration Policy and Refugee Assistance, Georgetown University, Washington, D.C.

Baletic, Z. (1982). "International Migration in Modern Economic Development: With Special Reference to Yugoslavia." *International Migration Review,* 16: 736–56.

Bank of Greece Report of Governor. Annual Statistical Bulletin. Athens: Bank of Greece.

Barrera, C. (1986). "La Migracion Illegal de Mano de Obra Colombian a Venezuela, periodo 1973–1985: El Caso de Los Trabajadores Deportados." Mimeo, Universidad de los Andes, Bogota, Colombia, prepared at the request of the Center for Immigration Policy and Refugee Assistance, Georgetown University, Washington, D.C.

Baucic, I. (1974). "Some Economic Consequences of Yugoslav External Migrations." Paper presented at the Colloque sur les Travailleurs Immigres en Europe Occidentale, Paris, June 5–7.

Baxevanis, G. G. (1972). *Economy and Population Movements in the Peloponnesos of Greece.* Athens: National Centre of Social Research.

Bennell, P. S., and M. Godfrey. (1983). "The Professions in Africa: Some Interactions Between Local and International Markets." *Development and Change,* 14(3).

Berger, S., and M. Piore. (1980). *Dualism and Discontinuities in Industrial Societies.* Cambridge: Cambridge University Press.

Bleier, Ungar E. (1986). "Impacto de La Crisis Recesiva Venezolana Sobre La Migracion de Retorno a Colombia: El Caso de Los Principales Contextos Urbanos Expulsores." Universidad de los Andes, Bogota, Colombia. Prepared at the request of the Center for Immigration Policy and Refugee Assistance, Georgetown University, Washington, D.C.

Bogan, M. (1985) "Los Impactos Socioeconomicos de La Migracion Internacional en Costa Rica." San Jose, Costa Rica: Octavo Seminario Nacional de Demografia. Pp. 213–23.

Böhning, Roger. (1972). *The Migration of Workers in the United Kingdom and the European Community.* Oxford: Oxford University Press for the Institute of Race Relations.

Böhning, W. (1975). "Some Thoughts on Emigration from the Mediterranean Basin." *International Labour Review,* 3:251–77.

———. (1976a). "Return Migrants' Contribution to the Development Process—The Issues Involved." Geneva: International Labour Office, International Migration for Employment Branch. WEP-2-26/WP/2.

———. (1976b). "The ILO and Contemporary International Economic Migration." *International Migration Review,* 10:147–56.

———. (1977). "The Migration of Workers from Poor to Rich Countries: Facts, Problems, Policies." International Population Conference, Mexico, Vol. 1. Liège: I.U.S.S.P.

Böhning, W. R. (Ed.). (1981). *Black Migration to South Africa.* Geneva: International Labour Organization.

———. (1984). *Studies in International Labor Migration.* London: Macmillan.

Bor, Wout van den. (1981). "Island Adrift: The Social Organization of a Small Caribbean Community, The Case of St. Eustatius." Leiden, Netherlands: Linguistics and Anthropology.

Bosch, Juan. (1978). *Composicion Social Dominicana.* Santo Domingo: Editoral Alfa y Omega.

Bouvier, Leon, and David Simcox. (1986). *Many Hands, Few Jobs: Population, Unemployment and Emigration in Mexico and the Caribbean.* Washington, D.C.: CIS.

Bovenkerk, Frank. (1981). "Why Returnees Generally Do Not Turn Out to be 'Agents of Change': The Case of Surinam." In W. Stinner, K. de Albuquerque, and R. Bryce-Laporte (Eds.), *Return Migration and Remittances: Developing a Caribbean Perspective.* Washington, D.C.: Research Institute on Immigration and Ethnic Studies, Smithsonian Institution.

Brana-Shute, Rosemary, and Gary Brana-Shute. (1982). "The Magnitude and Impact of Remittances in the Eastern Caribbean: A Research Note." In W. Stinner, K. de Albuquerque, and R. Bryce-Laporte (Eds.), *Return Migration and Remittances: Developing a Caribbean Perspective.* Washington, D.C.: Research Institute on Immigration and Ethnic Studies, Smithsonian Institution.

Bray, David. (1984a). "Economic Development, the Middle Class and International Migration in the Dominican Republic." *International Migration Review,* 18(2):217–36.

———. (1984b). "Strategies of Industrialization and International Labor Migration: A Comparison of Puerto Rico, Jamaica and the Dominican Republic 1945–1975." Paper presented at the Ninth Annual Meeting of the Caribbean Studies Association, St. Kitts.

Briggs, Vernon M., Jr. (1975). "Mexican Workers in the United States Labor Market: A Contemporary Dilemma." *International Labour Review,* 112:351–68.

Briquets, S. (1983). *International Migration within Latin America and the Caribbean: A Review of Available Evidence.* New York: Center for Migration Studies.

———. (1985). "Impact of Alternative Development Strategies on Migration: A Comparative Analysis." In R. A. Pastor (Ed.), *Migration and Development.* Boulder: Westview Press. Pp. 41–62.

Brydon, L. (1985). "Ghanaian Responses to the Nigerian Expulsions of 1983." *African Affairs,* 84:337.

Bundesanstalt für Arbeit (various). Presse Information. Nuernberg.

Burke, B. N. (1981). *The Outlook for Labor Growth and Employment in Lesotho, 1980–2000.* Maseru: World Bank/UNDP Team Report.

Burki, Shahid Javed. (1979). *Pakistan under Bhutto, 1971–1977.* New York: St. Martin's Press.

———. (1980). "What Migration to the Middle East May Do to Pakistan." *Journal of South Asian and Middle Eastern Studies,* 3(3):47-66.

———. (1984). "Urban Boom; Will it Burst?" *The Muslim,* August 14.

———. (1984–85). "Pakistanis in the Middle East." *The Muslim,* December 19 and 27, January 4.

Burki, Shahid Javed, and Norman Hicks. (1977). "Meeting Basic Needs in Pakistan." Washington, D.C.: World Bank. Mimeo.

Bustamante, Jorge A. (1977). "Undocumented Immigration from Mexico: Research Report." *International Migration Review,* 11:149–77.

Byerlee, D. (1974). "Rural-Urban Migration in Africa: Theory, Policy and Research Implications." *International Migration Review,* 7:543–66.

Caldwell, J. (1969). *African Rural-Urban Migration.* Canberra: Australian National University Press.

Calvaruso, C. (1984). "Return Migration to Italy and the Reintegration of Returnees." In Kubat (Ed.), *The Politics of Return.* New York: Center for Migration Studies. Pp. 123–28.

Caporaso, J. (1978a). "Introduction." *International Organization,* 32:1–12.

―――. (1978b). "Dependence, Dependency, and Power in the Global System: A Structural and Behavioral Analysis." *International Organization,* 32:13–43.

Cardoso, F., and E. Faleto. (1979). *Dependency and Development in Latin America.* Berkeley: University of California Press.

Carnegie, Charles. (1982). "Strategic Flexibility in the West Indies: A Social Psychology of Caribbean Migration." *Caribbean Review,* 11(1): 10–13.

Castells, M. (1975). "Immigrant Workers and Class Struggles in Advanced Capitalism: The Western European Experience." *Politics and Society,* 5:33–66.

Castles, S., and G. Kosack. (1973). *Immigrant Workers and Class Structure in Western Europe.* Oxford: Oxford University Press.

Cerase, F. P. (1974). "Expectations and Reality: A Case Study of Return Migration from the U.S. to Southern Italy." *International Migration Review,* 8:245–62.

Chaney, Else. (1985). "Migration from the Caribbean Region: Determinants and Effects of Current Movements." Hemispheric Migration project, Occasional Paper Series. Washington, D.C.: Georgetown University and the Intergovernmental Committee for Migration.

Chilivumbo, Alifeyo. (1985). "Malawi's Labour Migration to the South: An Historical Review." In *United Nation Economic Commission for Africa.* New York.

Christenson, R. (1984). "The Pattern of Internal Migration in Response to Structural Change in the Economy of Malawi 1966–69." *Development and Change,* 15(1).

Chukwura, A. O. (1984). "Obstacles to Labor Migration and Residence." In A. B. Akinyemi, S. B. Falegan, and I. A. Aluko (Eds.), *Readings and Documents on ECOWAS.* Lagos: Nigerian Institute of International Affairs.

Cobbe, J. (1982a). "Emigration and Development in Southern Africa, With Special Reference to Lesotho." *International Migration Review,* 16(4): 837–68.

Cobbe, J. (1986). "Labour Migration and Agricultural Development in Lesotho." In F. de Vletter (Ed.), *Labour Migration and Agricultural Development in Southern Africa.* Rome: FAO.

Colclough, C. (1980). "Some Aspects of Labour Use in Southern Africa: Problems and Policies." *Bulletin of the Institute of Development Studies,* 11(4).

Cole, Robert. (n.d.) "On the Problems of the Reverse Transfer of Technology (Brain Drain) and Human Resources in Grenada." Mimeo.

Collaros, T. A., and L. M. Moussourou. (1978). *The Return Home: Socioeconomic Aspects of Re-integration of Greek Migrant Workers Returning from Germany.* Athens: Re-integration Center for Returning Migrants.

Conde, J. (1979). "Migration in West Africa: Some Considerations." Paris: OECD. Mimeo.

―――. (1987). "Measures to Encourage Return Migration and Reintegration of Returned Migrants in Their Home Country." OECD: Migration and Development. Seminar organized jointly by the OECD Development Center, Intergovernmental Commission for Migration (ICM), and CICRED. February.

Corbett, John G. (1979). "Mexico-United States and West European Labor Migration: A Comparative Analysis." In R. E. Krane (Ed.), *International Labor Migration in Europe*. New York: Praeger. Pp. 223–44.

Cornelius, Wayne A. (1978). *Mexican Migration to the United States: Causes, Consequences, and U.S. Response*. Cambridge, Mass.: Migration and Development Study Group, Center for International Studies, Massachusetts Institute of Technology.

———. (1990). "Labor Migration to the United States: Development Outcomes and Alternatives in Mexican Sending Communities." *Working Papers of the Commission for the Study of International Migration and Cooperative Economic Development*, no. 38 (May).

Corwin, Arthur F. (Ed.). (1978). *Immigrants—and Immigrants: Perspectives on Mexican Labor Migration to the United States*. Westport, Conn.: Greenwood Press.

Cross, H. E., and J. A. Sandos. (1981). *Across the Border Rural Development in Mexico and Recent Migration to the United States*. Berkeley: Institute of Governmental Studies, University of California.

Davies, Rob J. (1985). "The Migrant Labour System and Patterns of Accumulation, Investment and Development in Southern Africa." In United Nations Economic Commission for Africa (Ed.), *Migration in Southern Africa*. New York.

de Janvry, A., and C. Garramon. (1982 [1977]). "Laws of Motion of Capital. In F. de Vletter (Ed.), *Labour Migration and Agricultural Development in Southern Africa*. Rome: FAO.

de Vletter, F. (Ed.). (1982). *Labour Migration and Agricultural Development in Southern Africa*. Rome: FAO.

Diaz, L. (1987). "The Impact of the Economic Crisis on Rural Migration from Colombia to Venezuela." OECD: Migration and Development. Seminar organized jointly by the OECD Development Center, Intergovernmental Commission For Migration (ICM), and CICRED. February.

Diaz-Briquets, S. (1982). *International Migration within Latin America and the Caribbean: An Overview*. Occasional Papers and Documentation, Center for Migration Studies, Staten Island, New York.

Dimitras, E. (1971). *Sociological Surveys on Greek Emigrants*. Athens: National Center for Social Research.

Duarte, Is, and Andre Corten. (n.d.) "Procesos de Proletarization de Mujeres: Las Trabajadores de Industrial de Ensemblaje en La Republic Dominicana." Universidad Autonoma de Santo Domingo: Departamento de Sociological. Mimeo.

Duvall, R. (1978). "Dependence and Dependencia Theory: Notes toward Precision of Concept and Argument." *International Organization*, 32:51–78.

Ebiri, K. (1985). "Impact of Labor Migration on the Turkish Economy." In R. Rogers (Ed.), *Guests Come to Stay*. Boulder: Westview Press. Pp. 207–30.

Economic Commission for Africa (E.C.A.). (1966). "Measures to Facilitate the Return and Reintegration of Highly Skilled Migrants into African Countries." *International Migration*, 24(1).

———. (1986). *International Migration, Population Trends and Their Implications for Africa*. African Population Studies Series No. 4, Addis Ababa.

Elkan, W. (1980). "Labour Migration from Botswana, Lesotho and Swaziland." *Economic Development and Cultural Change*, 28(3).

Emke-Poulopoulos, I. (1986). *Problems of Emigration and Return* (in Greek). Athens: IMEO.

Entzinger, H. (1978). "Return Migration from West European to Mediterranean Countries." Geneva: International Labour Office, International Migration for Employment Branch. WEP-2-26/WP-23.

Ethier, Wilfred. (1985). "International Trade and Labor Migration." *American Economic Review,* 75(4): 69–77.

Evangelinides, M. (1975). "Regional Development: Core-Periphery Relations in Greece." *Greek Review of Social Research,* 24(B): 230–55.

Everitt, J. C. (1984). "The Recent Migration of Belize, Central America." *International Migration Review,* 18:319–25.

Fakiolas, R. (1984) "Return Migration to Greece and Its Structural and Sociopolitical Effects." In D. Kubat (Ed.), *The Politics of Return.* New York: Center for Migration Studies. Pp. 37–44.

Farag, A. M. (1976). "Migration between Arab Countries." In International Labor Office (Ed.), *Manpower and Employment in Arab Countries: Some Critical Issues.* Geneva: ILO. Pp. 84–109.

Farraq, A. (1987). "International and Regional Movements of Egyptian Population and Labour." OECD: Migration and Development. Seminar organized jointly by the OECD Development Center, Intergovernmental Commission For Migration (ICM) and CICRED. February.

Fashoyin, T. (1985). *Public Policy and Labour Markets in the ECOWAS: A Case Study of the Alien Expulsion Order by Nigeria* 1983. Working Paper Series No. 2, Department of Industrial Relations and Personnel Management, University of Lagos, Lagos.

Felix, David. (1977). "Latin American Power: Takeoff or Plus C'est La Meme Chose?" *Studies in Comparative International Development,* 12(1): 59–85.

Fergany, N. (1982). "The Impact of Emigration on National Development in the Arab Region: The Case of the Yemen Arab." *International Migration Review,* 16:757–80.

———. (1983). "Intra-Arab Migration and Development." Mimeo.

Filgueira, C. H., D. Veiga, and J. L. Petruccelli. (1978). "Models of Population Displacement in Uruguay." Montevideo: Centro de Informaciones y Estudios del Uruguay. Mimeo.

Filias, V. (1967a). "Emigration—Its Causes and Effects." In *Essays on Greek Emigration.* Athens: Social Sciences Research Center. Pp. 11–39.

———. (1967b). "Emigration of Greek Workers to Western Germany and Its Consequences." In *Essays on Greek Emigration.* Athens: Social Sciences Research Center. Pp. 127–39.

———. (1975). "Some Aspects of the Greek Migration Problems." In A. Kudat and Y. Ozkan (Eds.), *Workshops on the Comparative Study of Reintegration Policy.* Berlin: IICSS. Pp. 120–69.

Finkle, Jason L., and C. Alison McIntosh. (1982). *The Consequences of International Migration for Sending Countries in the Third World.* Washington, D.C.: Bureau of Program and Policy Coordination, U.S. Agency for International Development (USAID).

Fogel, Walter A. (1978). *Mexican Illegal Alien Workers in the United States.* Los Angeles: Institute of Industrial Relations Monograph 20, University of California.

Fong, P. E., and L. Lim. (1982). "Foreign Labor and Economic Development in Singapore." *International Migration Review,* 16:757–80.

Fox, Robert. (1982). "Issues Paper." Presented at PAHO-IDB Seminar on Health Problems in Urban Areas in Latin America, Washington, D.C.

Fragos, D. M. (1975). "Internal Migration: 1966-71." *Greek Review of Social Research,* 23(A): 118–33.

Frank, A. (1969). *Latin America Underdevelopment or Revolution: Essays on the Development of Underdevelopment and the Immediate Enemy.* New York: Monthly Review Press.

Frisbie, Parker. (1975). "Illegal Migration from Mexico to the United States: A Longitudinal Analysis." *International Migration Review,* 9:3–13.

Frucht, Richard. (1968). "Emigration, Remittances, and Social Change: Aspects of the Social Field of Nevis, West Indies." *Anthropological,* 10(2): 193-208.

Galbraith, John K. (1957). *The Affluent Society.* Boston: Houghton Mifflin.

———. (1979). *The Nature of Mass Poverty.* Cambridge: Harvard University Press.

———. (1981). *A Life in Our Times.* Boston: Houghton Mifflin.

Garganas, N. (1967). "Regional Unemployment and Underemployment in Greek Agriculture" (in Greek). Athens: Agricultural Bank of Greece.

Gendt, Rien van. (1977). *Return Migration and Reintegration Services.* Paris: OECD.

George, A. (1979). "Case-Studies and Theory Development: The Method of Structured, Focused Comparison." In P. G. Lauren (Ed.), *Diplomacy: New Approaches in History, Theory, Policy.* New York: Free Press. Pp. 43–68.

Gilani, Ijaz. (1983a). "Overseas Pakistanis: An Overview about the Volume of Migration and Its Socio-economic Impact on the Home Communities." Paper prepared for the Conference on Asian Labor Migration to the Middle East, East-West Population Institute, Honolulu, 19–23 September.

———. (1983b). "Effects of Emigration and Return on Sending Societies." Paper presented at the Unesco Symposium on "Issues and New Trends in Migration: Population Movements within and across National Boundaries." Paris, October.

Gilani, Ijaz, M. Fahim Khan, and Munawar Iqbal. (1981). *Labor Migration from Pakistan to the Middle East and Its Impact on the Domestic Economy: Final Report in Three Parts.* Islamabad: Pakistan Institute of Development Economics (Research Report Series 126, 127, 128).

Gillespie, F., and H. Y. Browning (1979). "The Effect of Emigration upon Socioeconomic Structure: The Case of Paraguay." *International Migration Review,* 13:502–18.

Gitmez, Ali. (1984). "Geographical and Occupational Reintegration of Returning Turkish Workers." In D. Kubat (Ed.), *The Politics of Return.* New York: Center for Migration Studies.

———. (1989). "Turkish Experience of Work Emigration: Economic Development or Individual Well-Being?" In *Yapi Kred Economic Review,* 3(4):3–27.

Glubb, Faris. (1978). "Saudi Arabia: The Hajj." *Financial Times,* March 20.

Go, Stella P., Leticia T. Postrado, and Pilar R. Jimenez. (1983). *Effects of International Contract Labor Philippines,* vol. 1. Manila: Integrated Research Center, De La Salle University.

Gökdere, A. Y. (1978). *Yabanci Ülkelere Isgücü Akimi ve Türk Ekonomisi Uzerine Etkileri.* Anakara: Tükiye Is Bankasi.

Goldring, Luin. (1990). "Development and Migration: A Comparative Analysis of Two Mexican Migrant Circuits." *Working Papers of the Commission for the Study of International Migration and Cooperative Economic Development,* no. 37 (May).

Gomez Jimenez, A., and Diaz Mesa, L. M. (1983). "La Moderna Esclavitud: Los Indocumentados en Venezuela, Fines." Bogota: Editorial La Oveja Negra.

Goodwin-Gill, Guy S. (1989). "International Law and Human Rights: Trends Concerning International Migrants and Refugees." *International Migration Review,* 23(3): 526–46.

Gordon, E. (1981). "Analysis of the Impact of Labour Migration on the Lives of Women in Lesotho." *Journal of Development Studies,* 17(3).

Gould, W. T. S. (1985). "International Migration of Skilled Labour within Africa: A Bibliographical Review." *International Migration,* 23(1).

Goutos, M. (1967). "The Need for a Social Policy of Emigration." In *Essays on Greek Emigration.* Athens: Social Sciences Research Center. Pp. 55–60.

Government of Pakistan, Ministry of Finance and Economic Affairs.

Grasmuck, Sherri. (1982). "The Impact of Migration and National Development: Three Sending Communities in the Dominican Republic." New York: Center for Latin American and Caribbean Studies, New York University. Occasional Papers No. 33.

———. (1984). "The Consequences of Dominican Urban-Outmigration for National Development: The Case of Santiago." In S. Sanderson (Ed.), *The Americas in the New International Division of Labor.* New York: Holmes Meier.

Gravil, R. (1983). "The Nigerian Aliens Expulsion Order of 1900." *African Affairs,* 84:337.

Greenwood, Michael. (1983). "Leading Issues of Fact and Theory." *American Economic Review,* May.

Gregory, D. (1978). *La Odisea Andaluza Una Emigracion Intereuropea.* Madrid: Tecnos.

Gregory, D., and J. Perez. (1985). "Intra-European Migration and Regional Development: Spain and Portugal." In R. Rogers (Ed.), *Guests Come to Stay.* Boulder: Westview Press. Pp. 231–62.

Griffin, Keith. (1976). "On the Emigration of the Peasantry." *World Development,* 4(5).

Griffith, David. (1983). "International Labour Migration and Rural Development: Patterns of Expenditure among Jamaicans Working Seasonably in the United States." *Stanford Journal of International Law,* 19(2):341–57.

Guisinger, Stephan, and Norman L. Hicks. (1978). "Long-term Trends in Income Distribution in Pakistan." *World Development,* 6:1272.

Haberl, O. (1978). *Die Abwanderung von Arbeitskräften aus Jugoslawien.* Munich: Oldenbourg.

Hadjipanayotis, I. (1981–85). "Greek Employment in Numbers" (in Greek). Athens: Department of Labor. Mimeo.

Haris, K. (1980). "The Greek Experience in Educating Second Generation Greeks in West Germany" (in Greek). Athens. Mimeo.

Harris, J. (1978). "Economic Causes and Consequences of Migrations within the Context of Underdevelopment in West Africa." Working Paper Number 6, African Studies Center, Boston University.

Harris, John R., and Michael P. Todaro. (1970). "Migration, Unemployment and Development: A Two Sector Analysis." *American Economic Review,* 60(1): 126–42.

Hendricks, Glenn. (1974). *The Dominican Diaspora From the Dominican Republic to New York City—Villagers in Transition.* New York: Columbia University Teachers College Press.

Hiemenz, U., and K. W. Schatz. (1979). *Trade in Place of Migration: An Employment-Oriented Study with Special References to the Federal Republic of Germany, Spain, and Turkey.* Geneva: International Labour Office.

Hirschman, A. (1957). *The Strategy of Economic Development.* New Haven: Yale University Press.

Hobson, J. (1971). *Imperialism.* Ann Arbor: University of Michigan Press.

Hoepfner, K. H., and M. Huber. (1978). "Regulating International Migration in the Interest of the Developing Countries: With Particular Reference to Mediterranean Countries." Geneva: International Labour Office, International Migration for Employment Branch. WEP2-26/WP-21.

Hönekopp, E., and H. Ullman. (1982). "The Status of Immigrant Workers in the Federal Republic of Germany." In E. J. Thomas (Ed.), *Immigrant Workers in Europe and the Question of Their Legal Status.* Unesco.

Ignatius, David. (1981). "Sri Lankan Buys Rice Mill . . . after Saving Four Years." *Wall Street Journal,* March 20, p. 1.

Ijaz, Gilani, M. Fahim Khan, and Munawan Iqbal. (1981). *Labor Migration from Pakistan to the Middle East and Its Impact on the Domestic Economy.* Islamabad: Pakistan Institute of Development Economics.

ILO. (1973). *Migration of Workers as an Element in Employment Policy.* Geneva.

———. (1974). *Some Growing Employment Problems in Europe.* Geneva.

———. (1978). International Labour Conference, 63rd Session, *Record of Proceedings.* Address by Crown Prince Hassanbin Talal of Jordan. Geneva. Pp. 279–83.

———. (1979). *Implementation of the International Labour Organization Program of Action on New International Standards Concerning Migrant Workers.* New York: United Nations. Document E/CN.5/572.

Immigration and Naturalization Service. (1989). *Statistical Yearbook of the INS.* Washington, D.C.

———. (1990). "Provisional Legalization Application Statistics." Washington, D.C.

Institute of Labor and Manpower Studies (ILMS). (1983). *Socio-Economic Consequences of Contract Labor Migration in the Philippines,* vols. 1 and 2. Manila Ministry of Labor and Employment.

Interamerican Development Bank. (1987). *Economic and Social Progress in Latin America: 1986 Report.* Washington, D.C.

Intergovernmental Committee for European Migration. (1974). "Spontaneous Migration, Assisted Migration and International Cooperation." In *International Migration.* Proceedings of a Seminar on Demographic Research in Relation to International Migration. Paris: CICRED.

Intergovernmental Committee for Migration (ICM). (1985). "Economic and Social Aspects of Voluntary Return Migration: Report of the Seminar." Geneva: Seventh Seminar on Adaptation and Integration of Migrants.

Izzard, W. (1984). "Migrants and Mothers: Case Studies from Botswana." *Journal of Southern African Studies*, 2(2).

Journal of International Affairs. (1979). *Politics of Labor Migration*, 33(2).

Kasimatis, K. (1984). "Current Status of Studies on Return of Second Generation Greek Migrants." In K. Kasimatis (Ed.), *Emigration and Return Problems of Second Generation*. Athens: National Center of Social Research.

Katsanevas, T. (1983). "Greek Employment and Unemployment" (in Greek). *Oikonomikos Tachydromos*, 17:1512.

Kearney, M. (1986). "From the Invisible Hand to the Visible Feet: Anthropological Studies of Migration of Development." *Annual Review of Anthropology*, 15(3): 31–61.

Keely, Charles. (1980). *Asian Worker Migration to the Middle East*. New York: The Population Council, CPS Paper 52.

Keyder, Caglar, and Aksu-Koc, Ahyan. (1988). *External Labour Migration from Turkey and Its Impact: An Evaluation of the Literature*. IDRC Manuscript Report 185e, April.

Kim, Sooyong. (1982). *Contract Migration in the Republic of Korea*. Geneva: International Labor Office (International Migration for Employment Working Paper 4).

Kindelberger, Charles P. (1967). *Europe's Postwar Growth: The Role of Labor Supply*. Cambridge, Mass.: Harvard University Press.

King, R., J. Mortimer, and A. Strachan. (1984). "Return Migration and the Development of the Italian Mezzogiorno: A Research Report." In D. Kubat (Ed.), *The Politics of Return*. Pp. 79–86.

Kiray, M. (1976). "The Family of the Immigrant Worker." In N. Abadan-Unat (Ed.), *Turkish Workers in Europe*. Leiden: E. J. Brill.

Kirwan, F. X. (1981). "The Impact of Labor Migration on the Jordanian Economy." *International Migration Review*, 15:671–95.

Kiss, Judith. (1984). "Rural-Urban Migration in Africa: Causes, Consequences and Remedies." *Development and Peace*, 5, no. 2 (Fall).

Knowles, J. C., and R. Ankar. (1981). "An Analysis of Income Transfers in a Developing Country: The Case of Kenya." *Journal of Development Economics*, 8(2).

Korale, R. B. M. (1984). "Middle East Migration: The Sri Lankan Experience." Paper presented at the ESCAP-PCF (Economic and Social Commission for Asia and the Pacific-Population Center Foundation) Expert Group Meeting on International Migration in Asia and the Pacific, Manila, 6–12 November.

Krane, Ronald E. (1975). *Manpower Mobility across Cultural Boundaries: Social, Economic, and Legal Aspects: The Case of Turkey and West Germany*. Leiden: Brill.

———. (Ed.). (1979). *International Migration in Europe*. New York: Praeger.

Kudat, Daniel. (Ed.). (1979). *The Politics of Migration Policies*. New York: Center for Migration Studies.

———. (Ed.). (1984). *The Politics of Return: International Return Migration in Europe*. Rome: Centro Studi Emigrazione.

Kudat, A. (Ed.). (1975). Workshop on the Comparative Study of the Reintegration Policy of Five European Labor Exporting Countries. Berlin: IICSS.

Kudat, A., and H. Kallweit. (1976). *Rückwanderung ausländischer Arbeiter Zwangsweise oder freiwillig?* Berlin: Wissenschaftszentrum.

Laquian, A., and A. Simmons. (1975). "Public Policy and Migratory Behavior in Selected Developing Countries." Ottawa, Ontario. Mimeo.

Lazo, Lucita S., Virginia A. Teodosio, and Patricia A. Santo Tomas. (1982). *Contract Migration Policies in the Philippines*. Geneva: International Labor Office (International Migration for Employment Working Paper 3).

Lee, E. (1966). "A Theory of Migration." *Demography*, 3:47–57.

Legassick, Martin, and Francine de Clerq. (1984). "Capitalism and Migrant Labour in Southern Africa." In Marks et al. (Eds.), *International Labour Studies: Historical Perspectives*. Middlesex: Maurice Temple Smith.

Lenin, V. (1939). *Imperialism, The Highest Stage of Capitalism*. International Publishers.

Lewis, W. Arthur. (1954). "Economic Development with Unlimited Supplying Labour." *Manchester School of Economics and Social Studies*, 22(2):139–91.

Lianos, T. P. (1974). "Flows of Greek Out-Migration and Return Migration." *International Migration*, 13(3):119–33.

———. (1975a). "The Structure of Greek Industry and Labor Supply." *Greek Review of Social Research*, 23(A):160–66.

———. (1975b). "Industrial Structure and Potential Labor Supply." *Greek Review of Social Research*, 24(B):356–61.

———. (1977). "Movement of Greek Labor to Germany and Return." Unpublished manuscript.

Lijphart, A. (1971). "Comparative Politics and the Comparative Method." *American Political Science Review*, 65:892–911.

Lohrmann, R. (1987). "Irregular Migration: A Rising Issue in Developing Countries." OECD: Migration and Development. Seminar organized jointly by the OECD Development Center, Intergovernmental Commission for Migration (ICM), and CICRED. February.

Lopez, Jose Roberto, and Mitchell Seligson. (1990). "Small Business Development in El Salvador: The Impact of Remittances." *Working Papers of the Commission for the Study of International Migration and Cooperative Economic Development*, no. 44 (June).

Lowenthal, David. (1972). *West Indian Societies*. New York: Oxford University Press.

Lucas, Robert E. B. (1983). "Emigration Employment and Accumulation: The Miners of Southern Africa." Migration and Development Program, Discussion Paper #4. Cambridge: Harvard University.

Lutz, Vera. (1963). "Foreign Workers and Domestic Wage Levels with an Illustration from the Swiss Case." *Banca Nazionale del Lauoro Quarterly Review*, 16:64–67.

Mabogunje, A. C. (1972). *Regional Mobility and Resource Development in West Africa*. McGill: Queens University Press.

Mahmud, W., and S. R. Osmani. (1980). "Impact of Emigrant Workers' Remittance on the Bangladesh Economy." *Bangladesh Development*, 8(3). (Publication of Bangladesh Institute of Development Studies, Dhaka.)

Mahu, J. E. A. (1983). "Performances of the Economy in the 70s: Country Perspective—Ghana." In R. E. Ubogo, G. M. Adamu, and T. A. Gogue (Eds.), *Development Planning in the Economic Community of West African States—Priorities and Strategies*. Lagos: Heinmann Education Books (Nig.) Ltd.

Marks, Shula, and Peter Richardson. (Eds.). (1984). *International Labour Migration: Perspectives*. Middlesex: Maurice Temple Smith Limited.

Marshall, A. (1981). "Structural Trends in International Labor Migration: The Southern

Cone of Latin America." In M. M. Kritz, C. B. Keely, and S. M. Tomasi (Eds.), *Global Trends in Migration: Theory and Research on International Population Movement*. Staten Island, N.Y.: Center for Migration Studies. Pp. 234–58.

Marshall, Dawn. (1985). "Migration and Development in the Eastern Caribbean." In R. Pastor (Ed.), *Migration and Development in the Caribbean*. Boulder: Westview Press.

Martin, Philip L. (1980). *Guestworker Programs: Lessons from Europe*. Washington, D.C.: DOL, ILAB.

———. (1990). *The Unfinished Story: Turkish Labor Migration to the Federal Republic of Germany*. Geneva: International Labor Office.

Martin, Philip, and Alan Richards. (1977). "Issues in the Evaluation of European Labor Flows." *Social Science Quarterly*, 58:255–69.

———. (1980). "International Migration of Labor: Boon or Bane?" *Monthly Labor Review*, October. Pp. 4–9.

Marx, K. (1853). "Forced Emigration." In K. Marx and F. Engels (Eds.), *Ireland and the Irish Question: A Collection of Writings*. International Publishers.

Massey, D., R. Alarcon, J. Durand, and H. Gonzalez. (1987). *Return to Aztlan The Social Process of International Migration from Western Mexico*. Berkeley: University of California Press.

Mathew, E. T., and Gopinath Nair. (1978). "Socio-Economic Characteristics of Emigrants and Emigrants' Households—A Case of Two Villages in Kerala." *Economic and Political Weekly* (Bombay), 13(28): 1141–53.

Matzouranis, G. (1974). *Greek Workers in Germany* (in Greek). Athens: Gutenberg.

Mehrländer, U., R. Hofmann, P. Konig, and H. Krause. (1981). *Situation der Ausländischen Arbeitnehmer und Ihrer Familien. Angehörigen in der Bundesrepublik Deutschland Repräsentative Untersuchung '80*. Bonn: Der Bundesminister für Arbeit und Sozialordnung.

Meillassoux, C. (1981). *Maidens, Meal and Money*. Cambridge: Cambridge University Press.

Mendez, J., and O. Moro. (1976). "The Relation between Migration Policy and Economic Development." *International Migration*, 14(1/2): 134–61.

Merlopoulos, P. (1967). "Emigration in Greece in the Post-War Years." In *Essays on Greek Emigration*. Athens: Social Sciences Research Center. Pp. 39–54.

Michel, Aloys A. (1967). *The Indus Rivers: A Study of the Effects of Partition*. New Haven, Conn.: Yale University Press.

Mill, G. E., and Paul Robertson. (1974). "The Attitudes and Behavior of the Senior Civil Service in Jamaica." *Social and Economic Studies*, 23(2).

Miller, M., and D. Papademetriou. (1983). "Immigration Reform: The U.S. and Western Europe Compared." In D. Papademetriou and M. Miller (Eds.), *The Unavoidable Issue*. Philadelphia: Institute for the Study of Human Issues. Pp. 271–98.

Mills, Frank. (1987). "Determinants and Consequences of the Migration Culture of St. Kitts-Nevis." In P. Pessar (Ed.), *When Borders Don't Divide Labor Migration and Refugee Movements in the Americas*. New York: Center for Migration Studies of New York, Inc.

Mines, Richard. (1982). *The Evolution of Mexican Migration to the U.S.: A Case Study*. Berkeley: Giannini Foundation.

Mines, R., and D. S. Massey. (1985). "Patterns of Migration to the United States from Two Mexican Communities." *Latin American Research Review*, 20:104–23.

Ministry of National Economy. (1986). "Microcensus of Greek Returning Immigrants" (in Greek). Athens: Mimeo.

Mintz, Sidney. (1974). *Caribbean Transformations*. Chicago: Aldine.

Mlay, W. (1983). *Migration: An Analysis of the 1978 Census*. Dar-es-Salaam. Mimeo.

———. (1985). "Decision-Making Process in Migration: The African Case." Paper presented at IUSSP Seminar on Emerging Issues in International Migration. Bellagio, Italy. April.

Morokvasic, M., and R. Rogers. (1982). "Return Migration to Yugoslavia: Policies, the Innovative Return Migrant, and Prospects for Economic Development." Report submitted to the Rockfeller-Ford Research Program on Population and Development Policy.

Morrison, Thomas. (1982). "The Relationship of U.S. Aid, Trade, and Investment to Migration Pressures in Major Sending Countries." *International Migration Review*, 16(1): 4–26.

Morrison, T., and R. Sinkin. (1982). "International Migration in the Dominican Republic: Implications for Development Planning." *International Migration Review*, 16(4): 819–36.

Muhammed, Amir. (1979). "National Wheat Perspective—Analysis of the Production Strategy for Last Wheat Crop and Priorities for Future." Keynote address delivered at the Second National Seminar on Wheat Research and Production, Islamabad, Pakistan, August 6-9.

Murillo Castano, G. (1984). "Effects of Emigration and Return on Sending Countries: The Case of Colombia." *International Social Science Journal*, 36:453–67.

Murray, C. (1980). "From Granary to Labor Reserve: An Economic History of Lesotho." *South African Labor Bulletin*, 6(4).

Myers, Robert. (1976). "I Love My Home Bad, But . . . The Historical and Contemporary Context of Migration on Dominica, West Indies." Ph.D. diss., University of North Carolina.

NACLA. (1985). "Dominican Republic—The Launching of Democracy." 16 (6): 1–35.

Naseem, S. M. (1977). "Rural Poverty and Landlessness in Pakistan." In *International Labor Office, Poverty and Landlessness in Rural Asia*. Geneva: ILO.

National Council on Employment Policy. (1976). *Illegal Aliens: An Assessment of the Issues; A Policy Statement and Conference Report with Background Papers*. Washington, D.C.

National Statistical Service of Greece. (Annual). *Greek Statistical Yearbook*. Athens: National Statistical Service.

Nikolinakos, M. (1971). "Zur Frage der Auswanderungseffekte in dem Emigrationsländern." *Das Argument*, 13:782–99.

———. (1973). *Politische Ökonomie der Gastarbeiterfrage Migration und Kapitalismus*. Rowohlt.

North, David S., and Marion Houstoun. (1976). *The Characteristics and Role of Illegal Aliens in the U.S. Labor Market: An Exploratory Study*. Washington, D.C.: Linton.

OAED (Greek Office of Manpower Planning). (1981-84). *Employment and Unemployment in Greece* (in Greek). Athens.

Obasi, N. K. (1983). "Factors Influencing the Brain Drain of Ghanaians to Nigeria." Unpublished M.Sc. thesis, Department of Demography and Social Statistics, University of Ife, Ife, Nigeria.

Oberai, A. S. (1983). "An Overview of Migration-Influencing Policies and Programmes." In S. Oberai (Ed.), *State Policies and Internal Migration Studies in Market and Planned Economies.* London and Canberra: Croom Helm.

Oberai, A. S., and H. K. M. Singh. (1980). "Migration, Remittances and Rural Development: Findings of a Case Study in the Indian Punjab." *International Labor Review,* 119(2): 229–42.

OECD. (1975). *The OECD and International Migration.* Paris.

———. (1978a). *Migration, Growth and Development.* Paris.

———. (1978b). *The Migratory Chain.* Paris.

———. (1987). *The Future of Migration.* Paris.

OECD, SOPEMI (Systeme d'Observation Permanente des Migrations). (Various years). Directorate for Social Affairs, Manpower and Education. Paris.

Ohadike, P. O., and H. Tesfaghiorhes. (1975). *The Population of Zambia.* Paris: CICRED.

Onwuka, R. I. (1982). *Development and Integration in West Africa: The Case of Economic Community of West African States.* Ife, Nigeria: University of Ife Press.

Ostle, Robin. (1978). "The Islamic Community." *Financial Times,* March 20.

Paine, S. (1974). *Exporting Workers: The Turkish Case.* London: Cambridge University Press.

Pakistan Institute of Public Opinion. (1983). *Left Behind or Left Out: A Study of the Left-Behind Families of Overseas Pakistanis.* Islamabad: Pakistan Institute of Public Opinion.

Papademetriou, D. (1976). "The Social and Political Implications of Labor Migration in Europe: A Re-Appraisal and Some Policy Recommendations." Ph.D. dissertation. College Park: University of Maryland.

———. (1978). "European Labor Migration: Consequences for the Countries of Worker Origin." *International Studies Quarterly,* 22(3): 377–408.

———. (1979). "Assessing Labor Emigration: The Greek Case." In R. E. Krane (Ed.), *International Labor Migration in Europe.* New York: Praeger. Pp. 187–201.

———. (1982). "The Impact of International Labor Migration on the Development of the Countries of Worker Origin: The Case of Greece." Report prepared for the Ford Foundation, New York.

———. (1983a). *International Migration in Western Europe and North America: Trends and Consequences.* Report prepared for the Population Division of Unesco.

———. (1983b). "Rethinking International Migration: A Review and Critique." *Comparative Political Studies,* 15:469–98.

———. (1983c). "A Retrospective Look at Mediterranean Labor Migration to Europe." In C. G. Pinkele and A. Pollis (Eds.), *The Contemporary Mediterranean World.* New York: Praeger. Pp. 237–56.

———. (1984a). "Dilemmas in International Migration: A Global Perspective." *Environment and Planning C: Government and Policy,* 2:383–98.

———. (1984b). "International Migration in a Changing World." *International Social Science Journal: Migration,* 36(3).

———. (1985a). "Emigration and Return in the Mediterranean Littoral." *Comparative Politics*, 18:21–39.

———. (1985b). "Illusions and Reality in International Migration: Migration and Development in Post–World War II Greece." *International Migration*, 23(2): 211–25.

———. (1985c). "Illegal Caribbean Migration to the U.S. and Caribbean Development." In R. A. Pastor (Ed.), *Migration and Development*. Boulder: Westview Press. Pp. 207–36.

———. (1987). "International Migration in North America and Western Europe." In R. Appleyard (Ed.), *International Migration Trends and Consequences*. Paris: Unesco. Pp. 123–209.

Papademetriou, D., and N. DiMarzio. (1986). *Undocumented Aliens in the New York Metropolitan Area: An Exporation into Their Social and Labor Market Incorporation*. New York: Center for Migration Studies.

Papademetriou, D., and G. Hopple. (1982). "Causal Modelling in International Migration Research: A Methodological Prolegomenon." *Quality and Quantity*, 16:369–402.

Papademetriou, D., and M. Miller. (1983). "U.S. Immigration Policy: International Context, Theoretical Parameters, and Research Priorities." In D. Papademetriou and M. Miller (Eds.), *The Unavoidable Issue*. Institute for the Study of Human Issues. Pp. 1–41.

Papademetriou, D., P. Martin, and M. Miller. (1983). "U.S. Immigration Policy: The Guestworker Option Revisited." *International Migration*, 21:39–55.

Papageorgiou, K. (1975). "The Role of Agriculture in the Development of the Periphery." *Greek Review of Social Research*, 23(A):166–71.

Papantoniou, A. (1985). "Gastarbeiter Policies and Return Migration: The Example of Greece." Athens: Reintegration Center for Returning Migrants.

Papantoniou-Frangoulis, M. (1983). "Activities Report for the Year 1981-1983." Athens and Salonica: Reintegration Center for Returning Migrants.

Pastor, R. A. (Ed.). (1985a). *Migration and Development in the Caribbean: The Unexplored Connection*. Boulder: Westview Press.

Pastor, R. A. (1985b). "Relating Migration and Development Policies." In R. Pastor (Ed.), *Migration and Development*. Pp. 409–29.

Pear, R. (1987). "Reagan Rejects Salvadoran Plea on Illegal Aliens." *New York Times*, May 15.

Pellegrino, Adela. (n.d.). *Migracion Internacional de Latinoamericanos en las Americas*. Caracas, Venezuela: Universidad Catolica Andres Bello.

Penninx, R. (1982). "A Critical Review of Theory and Practice: The Case of Turkey." *International Migration Review*, 16:781–816.

Penninx, R., and L. Van Velzen. (1976). "Evaluation of Migrants' Investment and Their Effects on Development in Bogazliyan District." In N. Abadan-Unat (Ed.), *Migration and Development*. Ankara: Ajams Türk Press.

Pennisi, G. (1981). *Development, Manpower and Migration in the Red Sea Region*. Hamburg: Deutsches Orient Institut. Research Report 15.

Pepelasis, A. (1975). *Employment in Greek Agriculture*, 1963–1973 (in Greek). Athens: Agricultural Bank of Greece.

Perwaiz, Shahid. (1979). *Pakistan Home Remittances*. Islamabad: U.S. Agency for International Development.

Pessar, Patricia. (1982). "The Role of Households in International Migration and the Case of U.S.-Bound Migration from the Dominican Republic." *International Migration Review,* 16(2): 342–64.

Peterson, L.S. (1986). *Central American Migration: Past and Present, Center for International Research.* CIR Staff Paper, No. 25, Washington, D.C.: U.S. Bureau of the Census.

Petras, Elizabeth. (1980). "The Role of National Boundaries in a Cross-National Labor Market." *International Journal of Urban and Regional Research,* 4(2): 157–95.

————. (1981). "Black Labor and White Capital: The Formation of Jamaica as a Global Labor Reserve, 1930–1980." Ph.D. dissertation, State University of New York at Binghamton.

Petras-McLean, E., and M. Kousis. (1988). "Immigrant Worker Characteristics and Labor Market Demand in Greece." *International Migration Review,* 22(4): 586–608.

Petropoulos, N. (1985). "The Distribution of Returning Greeks in Different Nomos in Greece" (in Greek). *Apodemos* (November): 30–31.

————. (1988). "The Returning Greek Migrants: Dynamics of Socioeconomic Reintegration." OECD, Directorate for Social Affairs, Manpower and Education.

Petruccelli, J. L. (1979). "Consequences of Uruguayan Emigration: Research Note." *International Migration Review,* 13:519–26.

Philpott, Stuart. (1973). "West Indian Migration: The Montserrat Case." London: London School of Economics Monographs of Social Anthropology.

Piore, Michael J. (1979). *Birds of Passage Migrant Labor and Industrial Societies.* Cambridge: Cambridge University Press.

Pitayanond, Sumalee, and Watana S. Chancharoen. (1982). *Thai Contract Labor Migration and Its Economic Impact on Families and Communities: A Case Study in Northeastern Villages.* Bangkok: Economics Department, Chulalongkorn University (in Thai).

Polyzos, N. J. (1970). "Consequences des Retours en Grece des Emigrants." OECD, Direction de la Main-d' Oeuvre et des Affaires Sociales, MS/M/404/365.

Portes, A., and L. Benton. (1984). "Industrial Development and Labor Absorption: A Reinterpretation." *Population and Development Review,* 10:589-611.

Portes, Alejandro, and Luis E. Guarnizo. (1990). "Tropical Capitalists: U.S.-Bound Immigration and Small-Enterprise Development in the Dominican Republic." *Working Papers of the Commission for the Study of International Migration and Cooperative Economic Development,* no. 57 (July).

Portes, A., and J. Walton. (1981). *Labor, Class and the International System.* New York: Academic Press.

Power, J. (1979). *Migrant Workers in Western Europe and the United States.* London: Pergamon.

Prakash, B. A. (1978). "Impact of Foreign Remittance: A Case Study of Chavakkad Village in Kerala." *Economic and Political Weekly* (Bombay), 1(27): 1107–11.

Price, C. (1987). "Long-Term Immigration and Emigration: Its Contribution to the Developing World." OECD: Migration and Development. Seminar organized jointly by the OECD Development Center, Intergovernmental Commission for Migration (ICM), and CICRED. February.

Prompunthum, Vichitra. (1983). "Overseas Employment Policy in Thailand." Paper presented at the Conference on Asian Labor Migration to the Middle East, East-West Population Institute, Honolulu, 19–23 September.

Ranney, S., and S. Kossoudji. (1983). "Profiles of Temporary Mexican Labor Migrants to the United States." *Population and Development Review,* 9:475–93.

Reichert, J. S. (1983). "Profiles of Temporary Mexican Labor Migrants to the United States." *Population and Development Review,* 2:195–219.

Repräsentative Untersuchung Beschäftigung Ausländischer Arbeitsnehmer. (1973). Stuttgart: Bundesministerium für Arbeit und Sozialordnung.

Reubens, Edwin P. (1978). "Illegal Immigration and the Mexican Economy." *Challenge,* 21:13–19.

Reynolds, Clark W. (1979). "Labor Market Projections for the United States and Mexico and Their Relevance to Current Migration Controversies." Palo Alto: Stanford University, Food Research Institute.

Richards, Alan, and Philip Martin. (1983a). *Migration, Mechanization, and Agricultural Labor Markets in Egypt.* Boulder: Westview Press.

———. (1983b). "The Laissez-Faire Approach to International Labor Migration." *Economic Development and Cultural Change,* 31:455–74.

Richardson, Bonham. (1974). "Labor Migrants from the Island of Carricou: Workers on the Margins of the Developed World." Proceedings of the Association of American Geographers. 6:149–52.

———. (1984). *Caribbean Migrants: Environment and Human Survival on St. Kitts and Nevis.* Knoxville: University of Tennessee Press.

Rivera-Batiz, F. (1980). "A Demand-Pull Model of Labor Migration." Bloomington: Indiana University, Department of Economics. Discussion Paper 80-2.

Roberts, George. (1974). "Working Force of the Commonwealth Caribbean at 1970—A Provisional Assessment." Mona, Jamaica: Department of Sociology, University of the West Indies.

Roberts, K. D. (1982). "Agrarian Structure and Labor Mobility in Rural Mexico." *Population and Development Review,* 8:299–322.

Rogers, R. (Ed.). (1985). *Guests Come to Stay: The Effects of European Labor Migration on Sending and Receiving Countries.* Boulder: Westview.

Roongshivin, Peerathep, and Suchai Piyaphan. (1982). *Thai Gold Diggers in the Desert: Thai Labor in the Middle East.* Bangkok: National Economic and Social Development Board (in Thai).

Ross, Stanley R. (Ed.). (1978). *Views across the Border: The United States and Mexico.* Albuquerque: University of New Mexico Press.

Rubenstein, Hymie. (1976). "Black Adaptive Strategies: Coping with Poverty in an Eastern Caribbean Village." Ph.D. dissertation, University of Toronto.

———. (1983). "Remittances and Rural Underdevelopment in the English-Speaking Caribbean." *Human Organization* 42(4): 295–306.

Rugege, Sam. (1985). "International Labour Agreement in Southern Africa." In United Nations Economic Commission for Africa (Ed.), *Migration in Southern Africa.* New York.

Salt, John. (1981). "International Labor Migration in Western Europe: A Geographical Review." In Mary Kritz et al. (Eds.). *Global Trends in Migration.* New York: CMS. Pp. 133–57.

Sandis, J. E. (1973). *Refugees and Economic Migrants in Greater Athens.* Athens: National Centre of Social Research.

Sassen-Koob, S. (1984). "Direct Foreign Investment: A Migration Push-Factor?" *Environment and Planning C; Government and Policy,* 2:399–416.

Schechtman, J. B. (1963). *The Refugees in the World.* New York: Barnes.

Schiller, B. (1976). "Mutual Perspectives of Development and Underdevelopment in Europe." In N. Abadan-Unat (Ed.), *Turkish Workers in Europe: 1960–75.* Leiden: E. J. Brill. Pp. 151–80.

Seccombe, I. (1985). "International Labor Migration in the Middle East: A Review of Literature and Research, 1974-1984." *International Migration Review,* 19: 335–52.

Sheikh, Aslam. (1985). "Upsurge in Remittances: Adding New Debt Burden." *The Muslim,* November 30.

Sherbiny, N. A. (1984). "Expatriate Labour Flows to the Arab Oil-producing Countries in the 1980's." *Middle East Journal,* 38(4): 643–67.

Siampos, G. S. (1967). "The Trend of Urbanization in Greece: Demographic Aspect." In *Essays on Greek Emigration.* Athens: Social Sciences Research Center. Pp. 164–73.

———. (1976). "Emigration from Greece to Industrialized Europe." In Franco Angeli (Ed.), *L'Emigrazione dal Bacino Mediterraneo Verso L'Europa Industrializzata.* Cure del'Instituto di Demografia dell'Universita di Roma.

———. (1985). "Thirty Years of Demographic Developments in Greece." In *The Demographic Crisis.* Athens: EDEM.

Siddiqui, A.M.A.H. (1983). *Rural Vocational Training Needs—A Case Study of Bangladesh.* Dhaka: Bangladesh Manpower Planning Center, Ministry of Labor and Manpower. (Mimeo).

Singhanetra-renard, Anchalee. (1983). " 'Going Abroad': Thai Labor Movement to the Middle East from the Village Standpoint." Paper presented at the Conference on Asian Labor Migration to the Middle East, East-West Population Institute, Honolulu, 19–23 September.

Sjaastad, L. (1962). "The Costs and Returns of Human Migration." *Journal of Political Economy,* 70: 80–92.

Skocpol, T. (1977). "Wallerstein's World Capitalist System: A Theoretical and Historical Critique." *American Journal of Sociology,* 82:1075–90.

Smart, J. E. (1984). Worker Circulation between Asia and the Middle East: The Structural Intersection of Labour Markets. Paper presented at the IUSSP Workshop on the Consequences of International Migration, Canberra.

Soulis, S. (1985). "Emigration from and Immigration to Greece" (in Greek). Athens: Special Studies, OOSA. Mimeo.

Stahl, C. W. (1981). "Migrant Labour Supplies, Past, Present and Future; With Special Reference to the Gold Mining Industry." In W. R. Böhning (Ed.), *Black Migration to South Africa.* Geneva: ILO.

———. (1984). International Labour Migration and the ASEAN Economies. Geneva, ILO, International Migration for Employment Project. (Working paper, 13).

Stahl, G. (1982). "Labor Emigration and Economic Development." *International Migration Review,* 16:869–99.

Standing, Guy. (1981). "Migrations and Modes of Exploitation: Social Origins of Immobility and Mobility." *Journal of Peasant Studies*, 8(2): 173–211.

Stark, Oded, and Robert Lucas. (1988). "Migration, Remittances, and the Family." *Economic Development and Cultural Change*, 36(3): 465–82.

Strachan, A. J. (1983). "Return Migration to Guyana." *Social and Economic Studies*, 32:121–42.

Straubhaar, Thomas. (1988). *On the Economics of International Labor Migration*. Bern: Paul Haupt.

Swamy, Gurushi. (1985). *Population and International Migration*. Washington, D.C.: World Bank Staff Working Paper, No. 689.

Tabbarah, R. (1984). *Consequences of International Migration*. Organiser's Statement, Seminar on Social and Economic Consequences of International Migration. IUSSP Committee on Social and Economic Aspects of International Migration, Canberra.

Tandon, A. K. (1983). "Policies and Programmes Concerning Labor Migration from India to the Middle East." Paper prepared for the Conference on Asian Labor Migration to the Middle East, East-West Population Institute, Honolulu, 19–23 September.

Tapela, H. M. (1979). "Labour Migration in Southern Africa and the Origins of Underdevelopment." *Journal of Southern African Affairs*. College Park: University of Maryland.

Tapinos, G. (1982) "The Economic Effects of Intra-Regional Migration. In ECWA (Ed.), *International Migration in the Arab World*." Beirut: ECWA.

Teitelbaum, Michael. (1985). *Latin Migration North*. New York: Council on Foreign Relations.

Temporary Worker Programs: Background and Issues. (1980). Prepared by the Congressional Research Service for the Senate Committee on the Judiciary, February, CP 987.

Thomas, Doina. (1978). "Development at a Peak." *Financial Times*, June 26.

Thomas-Hope, Elizabeth. (1978). "The Establishment of a Migration Tradition." In A. Marks and H. Vessuri (Eds.), *White Collar Migrants in the Americas and the Caribbean*. Leiden, Netherlands: Department of Caribbean Studies, Royal Institute of Linguistics and Anthropology.

————. (1985). "Return Migration and Its Implications for Caribbean Development." In R. Pastor (Ed.), *Migration and Development in the Caribbean*. Boulder: Westview Press. Pp 157–77.

Tingay, Michael. (1978). "Labor: Growing Force in United Arab Emirates." *Financial Times*, June 26.

Todaro, M. (1976). *International Migration in Developing Countries: A Review of Theory, Evidence, Methodology and Research Priorities*. Geneva: International Labor Office.

————. (1981). *Economic Development in the Third World*. London: Longman.

Torrado, S. (1980). "El Exodo Intelectual Latinoamericano Hacia Los Estados Unidos Durante El Periodo 1961–1975." *Migraciones Internacionales en las Americas*, 1:19–39.

Trebous, M. (1970). *Migration and Development The Case of Algeria*. OECD.

Tuna, O. (1967). "Yurda Dönen Iscilerin Intibak Sorunlari." Ankara: DPT. Mimeo.

Tzeugas, J., and G. Tziafetas. (1988). "The Impact of International Migration on Fertility: An Econometric Population Model." *International Migration*, 27(4): 581–94.

Tziafetas, G., and J. Tzougas. (1986). "Prospects of Greek Population with the New Data on Natural Growth" (in Greek). Athens. Mimeo.

Unger, K. (1981). "Greek Emigration and Return from West Germany." *Ekistiks*, 48:369–74.

United Nations. (1983). *National Account Statistics: Main Aggregate and Detailed Tables, 1983*. New York.

United Nations Economic Commission for Africa. (1985). *Migrant Labour in Southern Africa*.

United Nations International Migration Policies and Programmes: A World Survey (1982). New York: United Nations.

Urzua, R. (1981). *Population Redistribution Mechanisms as Related to Various Forms of Development in Population Redistribution Policies in Development Planning*. New York: United Nations.

U.S. Committee for Refugees. (1986). *World Refugee Survey: 1986 in Review.* Washington, D.C.

U.S. Congress. Joint Economic Committee. Subcommittee on Inter-American Economic Relationships. (1977). *Recent Developments in Mexico and Their Economic Implications for the United States*. Hearings, 95th congress, 1st session. January 17 and 24. Washington, D.C.: U.S. Government Printing Office.

Van Arsdol, M. (1987). "The Impact of International Migration on Third World Development: Sociological and Related Issues." OECD: Migration and Development. Seminar organized jointly by the OECD Development Center, Intergovernmental Commission for Migration (ICM), and CICRED. February.

Van der Horst, Sheila T. (1942). *Native Labour in Southern Africa*. London: O.U.P.

Van Gendt, R. (1977). *Return Migration and Reintegration Services*. Paris: OECD.

Vlachos, E. (1974). "Worker Migration to Western Europe: The Ramifications of Population Outflow for the Demographic Future of Greece." International Studies Association, Comparative Interdisciplinary Studies Section, Migration Internet, Working Paper 22, July.

Wallerstein, I. (1974). *The Modern World System: Capitalist Agriculture and the Origin of the European World Economy in the Sixteenth Century.* New York: Academic Press.

Ware, H. (1978). *Population and Development in Africa South of the Sahara: A Review of Literature 1970–78*. Mexico City: IRG, El Colegio de Mexico.

Washington Post. (1985). December 9.

Weiner, M. (1982). "International Migration and Development: Indians in the Persian Gulf." *Population and Development Review*, 8:1–36.

Weintraub, Sidney. (1980). "North American Free Trade." *Challenge*, 23(4): 48–51.

Wilson, Francis. (1972). "Migrant Labour." Johannesburg: South African Council of Churches. SPRO-CA8.

———. (1973). *Labour in the South African Gold Mines 1911–1969*. Cambridge: Cambridge University Press.

Wilson, Monica, and Leonard Thompson (Eds.). (1969–71). *The Oxford History of South Africa*. Vols. 1–2, Oxford: Clarendon Press.

Wilson, Rodney. (1978). "Building Gets Green Light for 1980s." In *Saudi Arabia: A Special Report. The Times*, October 30.

Wogugu, M. O., and J. K. Anarfi. (1985). "International Labor Migration and the Expulsion of Illegal Immigrants in West Africa: Emerging Trends, Issues and Implications." Paper prepared for the Symposium on Population and Development, Cairo Demographic Centre, Cairo.

Wood, C. (1982). "Equilibrium and Historical-Structural Perspectives on Migration." *International Migration Review*, 16:298–319.

World Bank. (1978). *World Development Report.* New York: Oxford University Press.

———. (1981). *Accelerated Development in Sub-Saharan Africa: An Agenda for Action.* Washington, D.C.

———. (1985). *Mozambique: An Introductory Economic Survey.* Washington, D.C.

———. (1986a). *Population and Policies in Sub-Saharan Africa.* Washington, D.C.

———. (1986b). *Zimbabwe Land Subsector Study.* Washington, D.C.

———. (1987). *World Bank Atlas.* Washington, D.C.

Wright, Theodore, Jr. (1974). "Indian Muslim Refugees in the Politics of Pakistan." *Journal of Comparative and Commonwealth Politics*, 12:189–205.

Yarbrough, Beth, and Robert Yarbrough. (1988). *The World Economy.* New York: Dryden Press.

Yesufu, T. M. (1978). "The Loss of Trained Personnel by Migration from Nigeria." In U. G. Damachi and V. P. Diejomaoh (Eds.), *Human Resources and African Development.* New York: Praeger.

Zachariah, K. C. and J. Conde. (1981). *Migration in West Africa: Demographic Aspects; A Joint World Bank–OECD Study.* London: Oxford University Press.

Zolberg, Aristide R. (1989). "The Next Waves: Migration Theory for a Changing World." *International Migration Review*, 23(3): 526–46.

Zolotas, X. (1966). *International Labor Migration and Economic Development.* Athens: Bank of Greece.

Index

Abadan-Unat, Nermin, 30, 32–33
Adegbola, O., 60
Africa: arbitrary borders of, 3–4, 45–46; brain drain problem in, 63; causes of emigration in, 50–53; major migratory flows in, 46–50; manpower and skill losses in, 15; policy challenges in, 61–63; remittances in, 58–60; return migration in, 60–61; sending countries in, 49, 53–63; sub-Saharan, 45–63. *See also* Southern Africa
Afrikaners, 70
Ahmad, M., 167
Amnesty programs, 184
Anarfi, J. K., 56
Andean Pact, 198
Anderson, Patricia, 206–7
Asia, 176–78; employment in, 164–68; labor exporting policies of, 163–64; remittances in, 170–76; return migration to, 178; and skill formation, 168–70
Asymmetric development, 31–34, 107–8

Balanced growth, 29–31
Balance of payments, 155–56
Bleier, Ungar, 191–92
Böhning, Roger, 33, 59
Border development, 240

"Border effect," 192
Bovenkerk, Frank, 209
Brain drain, 6; in Africa, 63
Briquets, S., 6
British South Africa Company (BSAC), 71
Browning, H. Y., 189–90

Caporaso, J., 10
Caribbean, 201–10; emancipation and, 201–3; middle class, 203–4; migration and agriculture in, 207–9; population growth in, 204–5; remittances and return migration in, 209; unemployment and skill depletion in, 205–7
Caribbean Basin Initiative (CBI), 226–27
CARICOM, 227
Case studies, 12
Central American Common Market, 198, 227
Cerase, F. P., 125
Chaney, Else, 207
Classical economics models, 8–9
Colombia, 191–92
Colonial rule, 46, 71–77
Comparative advantage, 34
Conde, J., 47, 51, 67
Conflict theory, 9–11
Construction, 19
Co-production, 230–31
Cornelius, W. A., 193

Cross, H. E., 188
Cyclical migration, 48–49

Dependency, 10
Development: asymmetric, 31–34; border, 240. *See also* Migration and development

Economic Community of West African States (ECOWAS), 46–48
Education, 236–37
El Salvador, 190
Emancipation, 201–3
Emigration, significant countries of, 3–4
Employment, 53–57
Ethier, Wilfred, 36
Evangelinides, M., 93

Factor-price-equalization theorem, 34
Farag, A. M., 150
Felix, David, 203
Feminization of agriculture, 207
Fergany, Nadir, 5
Final demand linkages, 9
Forced repatriation, 49
Foreign aid, 238
Free trade, 225–26
Fruct, Richard, 208

Galbraith, John K., 27–28, 39
General Agreements on Tariffs and Trade (GATT), 218
George, A., 12
Ghana, 51–52
Gilani, Ijaz, 167
Gillespie, F., 189–90
Global interdependence, 67–68
Glubb, Faris, 143
Goldring, Luin, 194
Grasmuck, Sherri, 205, 208
Greece, 91–111; characteristics of emigrants, 95–98; emigration in, 92–107; industrial investments in, 108–9; occupational upgrading, 101–2; remittances and capital transfers, 102–7; return migration to, 94–95, 109–10; social demography of, 98–99; unemployment in, 99–101

Greenwood, M., 30
Griffin, Keith, 116
Growth, balanced, 29–31
Gulf states, 147

Harris, J., 9, 66–67
Harris-Todaro model, 66–67
Historical-structural models, 9–11
Homo economicus, 8
Housing, 111
Human resources, 235–37

ILO (International Labor Organization), 27–28, 33; Migration for Employment Recommendation of, 30
Immigration control, 4; in Africa, 61–63
Immigration Reform and Control Act (IRCA), 222
India, migration from, 140–41
Indirect consequences of migration, 154–55
Industrial investment programs, 108–9
Inflation, and remittances, 19
Informal sector, 193

Kallweit, H., 125
Keyder, C., 116
Kirwan, F. X., 19
Korea, remittances to, 68
Kudat, A., 125

Labor reserve, 11
Labor senders, frustrations of, 5
Latin America, 183–99
Lesotho, 51; as labor reserve, 54; remittances to, 58
Lewis, Arthur, 66, 201
Lewis two-sector model, 66

Marshall, Dawn, 205, 210
Marx, Karl, 9
Marxism, 10–11, 67
Massey, D., 17, 20, 193–97
Mexico: free trade with, 226; local effects of emigration in, 193–96; migration within, 27; and recruitment networks, 38; symbiosis with U.S., 3, 241

Middle East, 141–60

Migration: in Africa, 46–63; and agriculture, 57, 207–9; classical economics models of, 8–9; cooperative approaches to, 218, 239; cyclical, 48–49; and development, 3–23; and the domestic economy, 149–57; emancipation and, 201–3; employment consequences of, 164–68; and families or households, 213–14; in Greece, 91–111; historical and contextual variations in, 11–13; historical-structural models of, 9–11; human aspect of, 130–32; from India, 140–41; indirect consequences of, 154–55; in Latin America, 183–99; local consequences of, 192–96; middle-class, 203–4; national consequences of, 185–91; nationalist reaction against, 63; nonselective, 121; and occupational upgrading, 101–2; oscillatory, 50; overview of, 29–34; from Pakistan, 139–60; policy responses to, 6–7; political status of, 4, 189; receiving country–sending country nexus, 13–23; regional consequences of, 191–92; and skill formation, 168–70; temporary and irregular, 7; theories of, 7–13; tradition of, 27; Turkish, 115–33; types of, 5–6; women's roles in, 12. *See also* Return migrants; Southern Africa

Migration and development, 213–20; agency for, 240–41; Commission for the Study of International Migration and Cooperative Economic Development, 221–41; in Latin America, 196–99; reality of, 37–40; research agenda, 40–42; theory of, 34–37

Migration selectivity, 14–16

Mills, Frank, 210

Mines, R., 40, 194

Mining: in South Africa, 71–79; in Zambia and Zaire, 79

Mobility migrants, 5–6

Models: CGE, 174; classical economics, 8–9; historical-structural, 9–11; neoclassical, 66–67

Modernization, migration-induced, 16–17

Morrison, Thomas, 34, 205

Nationalist reaction, 63

Natural resources and the environment, 237–38

Nigeria, 52–53

Nomads, 47, 49

OECD (Organization for Economic Cooperation and Development), 29, 31; reassessment by, 33

Oscillatory migration, 50

Pakistan, 139–60; balance of payments of, 155–56; domestic economy of, 149–57; exports of, 157; geographic origin of migrants from, 143–47; return migrants, 157–60; skill loss in, 167

Paraguay, 189–90

Pass regulations, 73

Petrucelli, J. L., 190

Plantation system, 10

Polyzos, N., 92

Poor households, 150

Receiving countries, 13–14, 217; as de facto immigration nations, 20–21

Recruitment, 28; in Africa, 49–50; in colonial South Africa, 72–74; and development, 37–38; of employed workers, 32; internal, 78–79; stop to, 30–31

Refugees, 7, 49–50; from India, 140–41

Reichert, J. S., 194–95

Reintegration, 126–28

Remittances, 18–20; in Africa, 58–60; in Asia, 170–76; and balance of payments, 155–56; via Bank of Korea, 68; in the Caribbean, 209; to Costa Rica, 188; and development, 39–40; economic impact of, 173–74; to Greece, 102–7; "nonproductive" use of, 32–33; output and employment consequences of, 174–76; in Pakistan, 151–54; and public intervention, 22

Return migrants: in Africa, 60–61; am-

biguous policies toward, 38; to Asia, 178; in the Caribbean, 209; and development, 40; geography and political economy of, 16–17; in Greece, 104–7, 109–10; to Pakistan, 157–60; skills and remittances of, 17–20; Turkish, 123–28
Rhodes, Cecil, 71
Rogers, R., 131

Sandos, J. A., 188
Saudi Arabia, labor demands of, 142–43
"Secondary socialization," 132
Sending countries, 14–20, 214–16; benefits to, 21; effects of emigration on, 53–63; investment in, 22; and southern Africa, 80–85; in sub-Saharan Africa, 49, 53–63; targeted for growth, 232
Servicing debt, 235
Settler immigration, 14, 122
Siddiqui, A.M.A.H., 168
Sinkin, R., 205
Skills: formation of, 168–70; losses of, 15–16, 96, 167, 188–89, 205–7; relative flow of, 55–56; of return migrants, 17–18, 60
Smart, J. E., 170
"Smugglers," 56
South Africa: Aliens Control Act (1963), 50; Chinese miners in, 73; colonial period, 71–77; dominance of, 69–70; postcolonial, 78–80; precolonial, 70–71; separate ethnic homelands in, 83
Southern Africa, 65–87; benefits and costs of migration to, 80–85; population of, 69
Southern African Development Coordinating Council (SADCC), 69, 85–86
Stahl, G., 70, 73

Statistical-correlative approach, 12
Stroessner, A., 189
Survival migrants, 5
Swamy, Gurushi, 68

Tapela, H. M., 76
Tapinos, G., 53
Temporary and irregular migration, 7
Theories: of development, 34–37; global interdependence, 67–68; Marxist, 67; of migration, 7–13
Thomas, E., 147
Thomas-Hope, E., 209
Todaro, M., 9, 66–67
Torrado, S., 188–89
"Tourist workers," 122
Trade and investment, 224–27
Turkey, 115–33; emigration of workers, 117–23; expectations of, 117; remittances to, 129–30; return migration to, 123–28; and the world economy, 129

Unemployment, 99–101
Unger, K., 104
Urzua, R., 5, 59

Venezuela, 191–92
Village and area studies, 32

Weintraub, Stanley, 218
Wilson, Francis, 70
Women: and the "feminization of agriculture," 207; as heads of households, 57; opportunities for, 131; roles in migration of, 12
Worker rights, 231

Zachariah, K. C., 47, 51, 67
Zolberg, Aristide R., 219

Contributors

ADERANTI ADEPOJU, United Nations Development Program, Mbabane, Swaziland.

DIEGO C. ASENCIO, Commission for the Study of International Migration and Cooperative Economic Development.

SHAHID JAVED BURKI, Director, International Relations Department, World Bank, Washington, D.C.

SERGIO DIAZ BRIQUETS, Research Director, Institute for World Concerns, Duquesne University, Pittsburgh, Pennsylvania.

IRA EMKE-POULOPOULOS, Institute for the Study of the Greek Economy, Athens, Greece.

ALI S. GITMEZ, Middle East Technical University (METU), Ankara, Turkey.

ANSANUL HABIB, University of New Castle, New South Wales, Australia.

PHILIP L. MARTIN, Professor, Department of Agricultural Economics, University of California, Davis.

DEMETRIOS G. PAPADEMETRIOU, Director, Immigration Policy and Research, Bureau of International Affairs, U.S. Department of Labor, Washington, D.C.

PATRICIA R. PESSAR, Research Director, Center for Immigration Policy and Refugee Assistance (CIPRA), Georgetown University, Washington, D.C.

CHARLES STAHL, Senior Lecturer, Department of Economics, University of New Castle, New South Wales, Australia.

TIMOTHY T. THAHANE, Vice President and Secretary, The World Bank, Washington, D.C.